LETTERS OF A TRAVELING ARCHITECT

LETTERS OF A TRAVELING ARCHITECT

KRISTEN ALGER

To Levi and Chloe,
I pray I did your story justice.

LEGEND

PROLOGUE

PROLOGUE

The SS Leviathan departed New York City on October 24, 1925. It was the second year that one of the largest ships in the world connected the Big Apple to Southampton, England via Cherbourg, France. Three friends, all Notre Dame University graduates, set sail that day. One from that trio, Levi Geniesse, wrote in his travel journal that it was the beginning of a great adventure as he watched New York recede as a *scene on a movie screen*.

This traveling trio consisted of Levi Geniesse, Vince Engels, and John Connell. Levi and Vince were childhood friends who remained close through high school and college. Their homes were only one street apart on Green Bay's east side in Wisconsin. Levi and John met and grew their friendship in the Architectural Engineering Department at Notre Dame, while Vince's focus was on Journalism.

The three travelers bid New York City goodbye without a planned return date, other than a potential target of June 13, 1926, to attend Notre Dame's next commencement ceremony in South Bend, Indiana. Their little brothers, Os Geniesse and Norbert Engels, were slated to move their tassels on the campus with the Golden Dome.

During their travels, Levi wrote letters, took hundreds of photos, and reflected on their exploits in his personal travel journal. Now, one hundred years later, pounds of ephemera intertwine to reveal the story. Merriam-Webster defined ephemera as "something of no lasting significance, paper items that were originally meant to be discarded after use." Every acquired piece is significant, but the ability to treasure them is lost if they are only viewed individually.

I cherish every ounce of paper and embrace my unexpected title, "Keeper of the Family History." As the daughter of a photographer, genealogist, photo archivist, and restorer, I attribute any success found in relating this story to a magnificent woman, my mother, Juanita (Hill-Hawkins) Martínez. If it were not for the abilities passed on to me by my mother, I would be buried under a pile of apparently unrelated clutter. The love for research and discovery that she passed along energizes me.

Critical to this story is my husband, Paul, and his family. When we met in 1992, he had already lost his mother, father, and grandfather. His grandfather was the young architect who set sail aboard the Leviathan in 1925, Levi Geniesse.

Over our thirty-plus years of marriage, I have gathered letters, photographs, journals, Bibles, and scrapbooks, so I could become acquainted with my husband's parents and grandfather in some way. Through my research, this story about three young men and one grand adventure emerged.

It was 1925, and international travel was rare. The President of Trans International Airlines was quoted in a 1968 article as saying,

"Only six out of every 100 Americans had ever been abroad," and that was more than forty years after our trio set out for the Old Country ("Charter Airlines Push for Tours" 92).

Before we begin, a small disclaimer; all letters are conveyed exactly as written, including misspellings and grammatical errors. Some words reflect the time, such as to-nite and o'clock, or are terms we no longer use, as in union suits and mouthorgans. Grammatical structure follows the rules used by a past generation. Sections from letters, journals, or articles are italicized to avoid endless use of quotation marks. Added details are provided in brackets or parentheses and are not italicized since they are not part of the original document. Many letters are not included in their entirety, but selections are provided where needed, contributing to the overall storyline. Every effort has been made for accuracy in the research provided. The photographs were taken by Levi Geniesse unless otherwise noted.

Without further ado, the hands of time turn back a little farther, to eight months before their sail date. It was February 1925, and one small choice was about to change history. A spark started this wheel in motion, a blind date.

Green Bay &
Door County, WI
Albany, NY
NYC
Aboard the
Leviathan
D.C.
Champ, VA

UNITED STATES
February 1925 - October 1925

CHAPTER 1
THE BLIND DATE

In February 1925, in Washington, D.C., Calvin Coolidge had just been elected President in November. He was set to start his first elected term on March 4, a post he had held since President Harding's untimely death in August of 1923. Coolidge defeated John W. Davis by a landslide.

Levi Geniesse was twenty-five. He had lived and worked in Washington, D.C. since graduating from the University of Notre Dame in 1924. There were fewer prospects in his hometown of Green Bay, Wisconsin. Opportunities for a new architect were better in the city.

An old neighborhood friend from the Bay, Clayton Van Thullenar, lived in D.C. He took classes at George Washington University. These two had been friends for years, having grown up on opposite sides of South Clay Street. The families of two boys from the Bay were Catholic, neighbors, and their children attended the same schools. With so much in common, they were perfect roommates.

Levi was a building inspector for the District of Columbia. In his scrapbook, the photo on the left was captioned, "Where I put in my time." The District Building, known today as the John A. Wilson Building, is prestigiously located at 1350 Pennsylvania Avenue.

Where Levi focused on architecture and buildings, Clayton's interests were in meteorology. His workdays were spent in "The Weather Factory," at least that was Levi's name for the building. Officially, it was the Weather Bureau on M Street. All remnants of the building below are long gone, replaced by an apartment complex with a Starbucks on the ground floor.

Levi and Clayton roomed together in a boarding house on I Street that was managed by Mrs. Johnson and Mrs. Kreigen. They looked out for the young men and treated them like sons. As was the case with the Weather Bureau Building, the boarding house is long gone, engulfed by progress.

The two watchful "mothers" and a few of their "sons" were captured on the front steps, shown above. Levi is in the center, with Clayton on his right, the one without a hat.

One thing was true about people from Green Bay: they stayed in contact. Another friend from the old neighborhood, Gertrude Flanagan, lived in the Government Hotels by Union Station, closer to the Capitol. Back in Green Bay, she lived in a house on Webster Avenue with her aunt and uncle. The only thing that separated her backyard from Clayton's was a jumpable fence.

Gertrude and Clayton spent hours together in their youth and were giving a relationship a try now that they were older and out on their own. Gertrude was a stenographer, a common profession for the girls living in the Government Hotels. Like the boarding house, a chaperone was responsible for overseeing the safety and welfare of all the young ladies who lived there.

As Clayton and Gertrude got closer to forming some sort of relationship, Levi quickly became a third wheel. To remedy this, Levi, Clayton, and Gertrude made plans for a double date one Sunday evening in February 1925. Gertrude invited Chloe Wells, a sweet girl from Virginia who lived just down the hall.

Chloe was a seventh-grade teacher at Wheatley School. Shown here are her photos of the school and students. She taught in a few rural locations before moving to D.C. and enjoyed her time there, but longed for experiences that could only be found in the big city. Chloe accepted Gertrude's invitation, and the partial blind date was set for Sunday, February 8. The only one who was completely "blind" in this situation was Chloe, since the other three were well acquainted. Levi would no longer be a "third wheel," but Chloe might end up being the "odd man out."

Chloe was an interesting choice for a blind date with a Northern Catholic, given that she was a lifelong Presbyterian from a little southern town, known then as Champ, Virginia. The only Catholic Chloe met before Gertrude was Mary Woodville Ferguson, a classmate at Harrisonburg Normal Teachers College. Mary, or "Maynie" as they called her, was well-known on campus. She backed the suffrage movement and was the envy of all the girls with her auburn curls.

As the blind date approached, final plans were made; attending a dance or taking in a show were not options. Chloe did not participate in those events on the Lord's Day. However, the Washington Rapid Transit Company had recently added ten double-decker buses to its fleet. Chloe said that they were all the rage. On that chilly February evening, the two couples headed down to the National Mall and rode for hours in the moonlight from the Lincoln Memorial to the Capitol and back again. Levi tried to impress them all with his architectural knowledge while Clayton was at a loss. Discussing the weather on a cold night on an open-air bus would not have been a desirable conversation.

After meeting the two boys from Green Bay, Chloe was thankful. She found Levi to be the more handsome of the two, and Clayton would have been a tall match for Chloe's shorter stature. According to Chloe, everything about Levi was pleasing, if you could exclude his name, religion, and birthplace.

Finding herself not partial to the name Levi, Chloe simply called him Lee. It was not important that Levi was a Northern Catholic, since he was leaving in July for Europe to study church architecture. He would make a fine date for a few months, but was not to be considered a true suitor. This was a definite benefit of living miles away from her small Virginia hometown of Champ, where everyone knew anyone's everything. In the city, Chloe could have her fun without her mother needing to know or finding out.

The date ended without fireworks or fanfare. The four parted by gender and headed home, the boys to their boarding house and the girls to the Government Hotels. The first date was a success. Chloe wrote about it in her autobiography.

> *Levi G. asked for more dates! I thought he was fun. As he was going to Europe in July nothing serious could develop. I'd never see him again!*

Levi recorded his memories of that night in a letter to Chloe a few months later.

> *I was thinking of the night we met, how you looked. How I first liked a pretty face, a smile and the Southern speech; thinking how I broke my first rule by asking for a second date. Do you remember how I called up to make a change of dates, you were "peeved" and ordinarily I would have been "sore." After I had known you about a month I was surprised one day to find myself adding you to that small list of those of whom we think while saying our daily prayers.*

CHAPTER 2
A 1925 SITUATIONSHIP

From February to June, Levi and Chloe spent time together, but little was written about these first few months. Levi worked as a building inspector while Chloe taught and attended classes at George Washington University.

Washington, D.C., was the perfect place for an architect in 1925. The National Cathedral, a beautiful example of Gothic Revival, was in the midst of construction. Below is a photo Levi took during one of his many visits to the site, along with his sketch of the place.

The Lincoln Memorial was new, completed, and dedicated in 1922. In the first photo of the memorial, Levi's camera pointed northwest, from an area that now honors those who fought in the Korean War. Independence Avenue, which defines the south side of the National Mall, lies just past the Korean War Veterans Memorial.

The photograph to the right was taken while facing the northeast corner of the Lincoln Memorial. The Vietnam Veterans Memorial is now located just behind the camera's position. Constitution Avenue, the northern boundary of the National Mall, is not far away.

The Reflecting Pool was not completed in time for the monument's 1922 dedication. Before the end of 1923, visitors could take in this iconic view while standing in front of the memorial to the sixteenth president of the United States.

The above photo was taken from the west end of the Lincoln Memorial Reflecting Pool. In the distance is the Rainbow Fountain, which has since been incorporated into the World War II Memorial. Levi stood there, camera case in hand, while Chloe captured the moment during one of their walks through the National Mall.

Many details of their dates would have been lost if it were not for the autobiography Chloe's family shared.

> *Six of us girls at the Gov't Hotels decided to move into a flat and do our own housekeeping – 229B St., N.E. was the first. Virginia Weirich, 1st grade teacher at Wheatley School, Grace Fleming from IL and her friend, Gertrude Flanagan from Green Bay, WI, Ruth Graves from Wilmington, DE and Chloe Wells, 7th grade teacher at Wheatley from Champ, VA. Virginia W. said Chloe was the needed chaperone. Levi G. asked for more dates! The Roman Catholic faith was a problem. We invited friends for dinner, sometimes Lee was my guest. Our private conversation ended in religious discussions. Why do Christians differ? Same creed, same scriptures! Interpretation?*

It was the middle of March when the girls moved from the Government Hotels to their first flat together in a row house on B Street N.E. Chloe had been the Secretary-Treasurer of the Music Club there, a position she had to relinquish. The first concert of the season took place on February 19 with a dance afterwards. Every lady in attendance lived at the Government Hotels, paying $0.50 admission to attend. Their Mardi Gras ball took place on Tuesday, February 24 that year. Gentlemen had to pay $1.00 to attend. You could save a quarter if you attended as a couple. Levi and Chloe enjoyed the ball, their first together.

Though the Government Hotels events were no longer an option, there was plenty to do about town. During the week of March 30, they enjoyed the Saint Patrick Players' Production of "The Holy City," a benefit for the Archdiocesan Community House for the Catholic Daughters of America, located in New York. The Saint Patrick's Players were a drama group from St. Patrick's church, Levi's parish, located a mile east of his boarding house. This is the oldest parish in

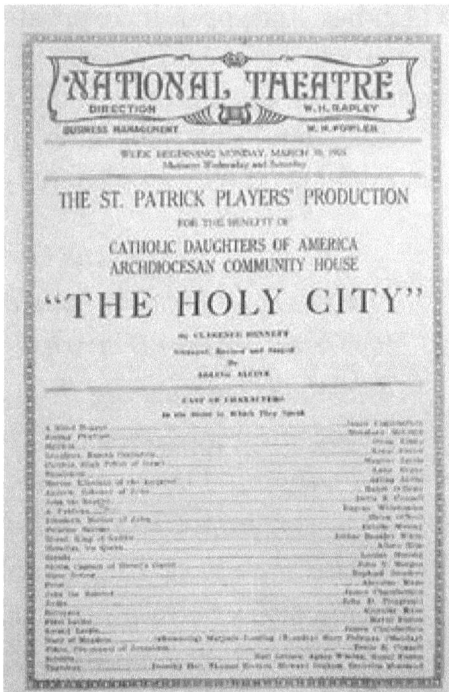

the city, established in 1794.

They enjoyed the power and beauty of the Potomac during the months when it was not warm enough to splash in the water. The trolley ran to Great Falls Park, which made this a favorite outing.

As the temperatures warmed, the two met at the Potomac Boat Club and took a canoe out. It is still located where the Potomac River bends just south of Georgetown University.

Many hours were spent on the river. He read poetry to her, and they would paddle, float, and swim. Chloe's handmade pillows made the ride more comfortable.

Dates were scheduled and rescheduled. At times, they were even certified in writing.

*This is to certify that I have a date to go to the circus
Friday, May 15, 1925 at seven o'clock or thereabouts.*

Signed Sincerely, Chloe E. Wells.

This situationship was soon to end. There was no need to redefine whatever this was between them. Levi's plan was to head to Europe in June, and he planned to be off to a new job in Baltimore when he returned. Chloe would complete her school year and head home to Champ, Virginia, for the summer. Her autobiography continued.

Lee didn't go to Europe in June!

We had said good-bye. The teachers stayed 2 days longer to complete records! I looked up from my desk amid stacks of books, etc. to find him sitting in the back of my classroom! Miss Austin, my principal, was suspicious!! When I said he was a Catholic, she agreed that I shouldn't marry him. She too was a Sou. Presbyterian and said that Priests and Nuns lived like roosters and hens! — and echoed Virginia Weirich's stories about a tunnel under the Capital which was filled with gunpowder, ready to be exploded and bring the Pope to live in the U.S.! Instead of going to my art teacher's fancy wedding that evening, I stayed home and cried on Lee's shoulder! Sept, 1925 was the next date he set to depart.

They were together again. Though Levi did not leave for Europe in June, Chloe was set to head home to Champ, Virginia, on June 19. Her ticket was purchased, and Mom awaited her arrival.

He took me to the R.R. station with a parting gift, The Imitation of Christ by T. A. Kempis, from your preacher Lee! (Mother didn't like it!) He put me on a Pullman instead of a day coach to McKenney! The conductor looked at my ticket, then said "A young man put you on this car? Umph! Umph!" and showed me to the day coach. Lee sent letters ahead of my train! Who is he! The news spread! Everyone was shocked. The minister, Mr. Herzer, at Concord talked against me from the pulpit! I went down to 118 lb. "TB?", Watson Bishop said.

Watson Bishop was Chloe's first cousin. His mother, Nettie, and Chloe's mom were sisters. Watson was five years older than Chloe, and at the age of thirty in 1925, he was aware that tuberculosis was a leading cause of death in Virginia.

Watson and Chloe were close; they grew up together. Watson was only a toddler when his father died. That was when he and his mother moved onto her parents' farm. The Sturts were also Chloe's grandparents, and their farm was just down the road.

When Levi left Chloe at the train station, tears flowed, time stood still, and they were almost a couple, for a moment.

CHAPTER 3
YOU'VE GOT MAIL

Friday Night
June 19, 1925

Dear Chloe,

You have been gone two hours – dentist chair hours to me – you are even now on a train speeding away and I am thinking of the time I shall see you again; thinking of the night we met, how you looked. How I first liked a pretty face, a smile and the Southern speech; thinking how I broke my first rule by asking for a second date. Do you remember how I called up to make a change of dates, you were "peeved" and ordinarily I would have been "sore." After I had known you about a month I was surprised one day to find myself adding you to that small list of those of whome we think while saying our daily prayers.

As the day passed I found that prayer becoming a petition, a request to God for help. I could not tell just what I wanted but it concerned you. – I was trying to make you like me and when I realized that (for some reason that is beyond my understanding) you might, I was all hope. - Then I started to plan and you know how far I got. Stone walls are hard to break but they have been broken and (yes, I am conceited) will be again.

Virginia gave me credit for acting like fifteen years, I'm less than that. You think I'm crying for the moon. Yes and praying for it. It may not be good for me, I may not get it but to have tried and failed is infinitely better than not to have tried at all.

Sincerely yours, Levi - When I say "sincerely" it means that and much more.

Champ, Virginia
June 20, 1925

Dear Lee,

Don't you know my train did not leave until ten minutes of seven — so our rush was unnecessary. If we hadn't been on time the train would have been, wouldn't it? This is question first and last! It isn't so easy to break a habit, but I am still trying.

My sister and cousin met me at the station and we spent the night at McKenney and Watson brought us home this morning, he is helping Collier cut wheat to-day.

I went to McKenney to see about my trunk this afternoon and it hadn't come. The agent said that it would be there in the morning.

Mama was planning to go to Albany, Tuesday, but I think we'll go the next Tuesday. I haven't had enough sleep yet and I also have some more shopping to do. — Aren't you glad you don't have to chase around with me this time?

I hope you'll like your Baltimore job. Have a good time "and everything"!

Again, let me tell you I appreciate your coming with me to the station and your helping me to get ready.

I haven't slept any to-day and I got up this morning about six o'clock

— so goodnight! Chloe

Chloe incorrectly addressed the letter to *L. A. Geneisse*, instead of Geniesse. She began the letter with *Dear Lee*, her preferred name for him. Chloe called him Levi when he was first mentioned in her autobiography, but within the paragraph, she switched his name to Lee and clarified, *I didn't like the name Levi.*

Sunday Night
June 21, 1925

Dear Chloe,

Sunday night — I don't remember ever spending a day like this before. Got up and went to early Mass then sat in Lafayette Square until noon with the birds, squirrels and nuts. — I wonder what class my fellow park loungers put me in.

In the afternoon I went out to the Catholic University to see how the cathedral was progressing. Then while wandering around I came to a negro Catholic church and entering I said a prayer for a special intention concerning a Southern girl.

Still trying to find peace of mind and being only the more disturbed by the row houses along the way. I finally arrived at the Memorial Church of the Holy Land. Here scenes from the Holy Land and the Catacombs are reproduced.

Wandered around the church and grounds and was all set to join the Franciscans but thought I'd wait until I heard from you. (Hand brushed thru hair).

Back to our "attic" again (as Van calls it) and the land-lady brings me up some magazines to read because she says, "You look homesick or something."

Never "occurred" to me to go to a movie tonight. Guess I've contracted a bad habit of staying away from shows on Sunday from someone.

Also I've petitioned the commissioner to have double deck busses removed from the streets. They might be the cause of someone losing his head.

If you go to New York by train the phone was Franklin 3577 or the District Bldg.

Sincerely yours, Levi

The cathedral Levi visited at the Catholic University is actually the Basilica of the National Shrine of the Immaculate Conception. The foundation stone was laid in 1920, and even the crypt was still incomplete in 1925. Today, this is the largest Catholic church building in North America.

In the 1920 printing of the *Rand McNally Washington Guide to Places of Interest in the City and Environs*, Saint Augustine and Saint Cyprian are the only two churches listed as Catholic in the "Colored" section (203). Saint Augustine was on 15 Street, near M Street NW, not far from Levi's boarding house, so he must have offered up his prayer there. Saint Augustine is a well-established church community that dates to 1858, though they have relocated over the years. Their present church is not where it was in 1925.

The row houses had to be the most disturbing for Levi, given the sheer quantity of them. Each was a reminder of the flat on B Street, shown on the previous page, that Chloe left behind for the summer.

A few candid shots captured evening life in the "attic." What else was there to do in an unairconditioned space in the middle of summer than recline in front of an open window, in full-length pajamas?

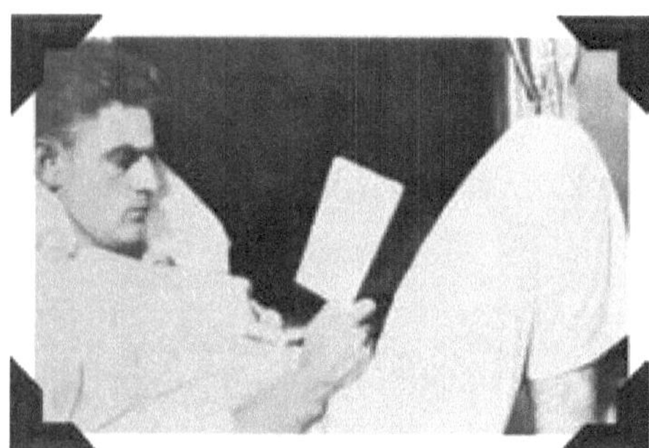 

Tuesday Night
June 23, 1925

Dear Chloe,

That I was glad to find your letter waiting my return from work hardly expresses it. It didn't wait any longer than I could help, for I started out from the District building at a walk and like a movie comedy I soon had quickened my step so that I made the last block in nothing flat. I didn't dare expect it but there it was – "sure enough".

You thank me for seeing you to the station. That hurts. Would you thank your father or sister?

Your train did not leave on time and I paced up and down that concourse for a long time after I thought you were gone – "gone" I kept saying until it is a wonder that I wasn't taken to St. Elizabeth's. – Van's words were "I'm warned and I'm thru with girls from now on".

Which is Watson and Collier? And what do you mean by

telling me they are cutting wheat at this time of the year? Don't worry about the trunk. I usually get things all balled up anyway.

Heard from my friend Londo yesterday. After telling me he thought I was crazy he says, "If she feels the same way about mixed marriages she must be a damn sensible kid so go to it and win her over". – Why does every one insult you by calling you sensible. It's a shame and I'll have to bawl him out. – He ends his letter by saying, "Now for the love of Mike don't do anything rash over that girl until you at least let me know".

I'll have to tell him that I would have done something very rash but – .

Haven't heard from Baltimore but don't be surprised if I stick it out in Washington. Our rooming house is the gloomiest place on earth. I believe they must be prohibitionists. The guest of the happy medium is still on.

Please write to, Lee.

Tucked in the envelope with Levi's letter was an article. The source and date are unknown. The clipping is trimmed perfectly from left to right, top to bottom, revealing only the article itself. No other identification as to the journalist, editor, or newspaper survives.

If ever Our Lord had to be plain in His words it was on this momentous occasion when He gave to mankind His greatest gift. We have no right to correct His words. He made use of His sovereign power as God and changed bread and wine into His flesh and blood. It is a mystery; we cannot comprehend it. There is no religion without mystery. It is enough to know that Christ has taught it; He cannot deceive nor be deceived.

Saturday Afternoon
June 27, 1925

Dear Chloe,

 I want to hear from you. You seem to have decided that it is best that I do not. All I can say is, 'you promised'.

 You find enclosed a bunch of clippings. If I can't show them to you I'll have to send them. "Pussyfoot" Johnson you'll remember was the leading speaker for prohibition a few years ago. (I shouldn't mention prohibition but now that Bob La Follete is dead someone whilll have to champion the cause of the people.)

 Mr. Anderson was head of the Temperance league and after getting out of jail feels that he can go the organizers of the K.K.K. one better.

 I enclose the article about David Van Wallace because you would not find that in any other university paper.

 Van met Virginia the other day and from what he told me I guess I lost my "drag" by keeping you away from her home that evening. It was worth it.

 I intend to call up 229 B − N.E. some time and get Gertrude's address and phone number but if you have them please send them along. I want to "bawl" her out for getting me into a lot of trouble. What's that one about, "Sweet are the causes of adversity"?

 Yesterday, Father Londo, the brother of my pal up in Pennsylvania stopped over and I had to show him the town. If anyone was ever glad to see a face from home it was "me". Took him to the National to see another roaring comedy. He left for New York at midnight and I came back to our "attic" feeling better than for some time.

 They have offered me a job in Baltimore but I have such a good chance of getting my old classification here that I'm sticking. My mother has written that she wants me to take a vacation and Baltimore means none so –.

You will write to, Lee.

Newspaper Clipping #1 – No Source Given

MAN HAS A RIGHT TO TAKE HIS DRINK, 'PUSSYFOOT' ADMITS

KANSAS CITY, Mo. – A reformed William E. ("Pussyfoot") Johnson, bringing with him ne tenets of individualism, drifted into Kansas City yesterday and deposed to gaping newspaper men that a man has as much right to drink liquor as he has to cat-food which might be distasteful to others. Jonson said that after all his years of battling for this and that, he had decided that men and women will, after all is said and done, do about as they please, and he admitted that this was as it should be. "Let them do it," he said magnanimously. "They are living their own lives, not mine."

Newspaper Clipping #2 – No Source Given

Heads New Organization Founded By Himself
William H. Anderson

NEW ORDER STARTED BY W. H. ANDERSON
Launching of American Protestant Patriotic Protective Association Announced

NATIONAL MOVEMENT

Former Head Of New York Anti-Saloon League To Be Secretary Of Organization

New York, June 24 (Special). – William H. Anderson, former superintendent of the Anti-Saloon League of New York, announced today "a national movement of allied Protestant Americans," of which he is founder and secretary. No other names are listed. The organization is called "The American Prohibition Protestant Patriotic Protective Alliance" and its announced purpose, among others, to "protect future generations of Americans who may dare to oppose a wet alien anti-protestantism dominant in the larger American cities." The announcement does not refer by name to the A. P. A., the avowed purpose of which closely paralleled those of the more alliterative A. P. P. P. P. A., nor to the Ku Klux Klan.

Covert Allusions at K. K. K.

It contains, however, what are taken to be covert allusions to both, together with assurances that the A. P. P. P. P. A., will skillfully avoid the tactical and other blunders that destroyed the A. P. A. and crudities which have changed the K. K. K. into a commission-basis membership-selling proposition. "While working openly in some respects," the announcement says, "in others, it will be more secret than any incorporated organization can be."

Touches On His Prosecution.

Further, Mr Anderson hints, his prosecution, conviction and imprisonment for third-degree forgery in connection with the finances of the Anti-Saloon League now will become a boomerang; "By driving me out of a position with an agency limited to the liquor question, the enemy has forced me to consider other phases of anti-Americanism and anti-Protestantism."

The last article that Levi included was lengthy. Robert G. Hennes wrote the story of a classmate at the University of Notre Dame who entered the School of Engineering in the Fall of 1923. While home on summer vacation, he had a diving accident that left him paralyzed from the neck down. The article went into detail concerning his difficulties, near-death experiences, and recoveries. Levi underlined a portion of the article near the end. This was the paragraph that drew his attention the most, and he underlined the part he did not want Chloe to miss.

Newspaper Clipping #3 – The Notre Dame Scholastic (716)

DAVID VAN WALLACE

Notre Dame was a joy to Van, and now his great ambition is to return in the Fall. In his present plight, nothing pleases him more than a letter from a Notre Dame man, and nothing helps him more than the <u>prayers of a Notre Dame man</u>. The gratitude he feels for such offerings is comprehensible to us only when we imagine ourselves in his place and as alive as he is with the love of life and of Notre Dame.

Champ, Virginia
June 28, 1925

Dear Lee,

Your three letters last week surprised me. This doesn't look like you are trying to forget – at least you aren't letting me forget. I can't say that I was sorry to hear from you – I was pleased and pained too – a queer feeling? Well, I have that experience quite often.

My trunk came Tuesday, so don't worry about it. Are you insulted because I mispelled your name? I'll get it right from now on.

What have I done during this past week? – (it seems ages long) – served, packed my trunk, went to see some of my relatives, entertained some of them here – taken care of the babies, and helped keep house in general – I forgot – slept, of course – Now I am ready to leave for Albany, Tuesday morning. I have a number of relatives in and around Albany and we shall first visit an Aunt of mine in Mechanicsville, N.Y. – If you care to write to me there address my letter in care of Mrs. Jennie Vandecar.

As for my being "sensible" – I think I'm far from it – you can tell Londo I say this. If anyone calls me sensible after this I think that person had better refer to Mr. Webster.

The letter you wrote on Sunday night was sarcastic! I was peeved when I read it and should have been more so if you hadn't warned me before I left.

Yes, this is wheat cutting and threshing time for us – Collier is my brother-in-law and Watson is one of my kid cousins – Satisfied?

What do you mean by leaving one of your sentences unfinished? – "I would do something very rash but – " Don't you forget what you promised me.

How are the pillows and canoe? I hope you are enjoying them – have a good time –

Sincerely, Chloe

P.S. We are going to New York by boat.

Tuesday Night
June 30, 1925

Dear Chloe,

You "bawl" me out for writing three letters. My next bet was to send a telegram if the letters did not bring results. You will not make that necessary, will you?

Started to work this morning with my usual "grouch" and met the mailman at the door with your letter. My first impulse was to declare the 30th of June a holiday but then decided to go to the office and let the boys see what I looked like when feeling well. They just couldn't make me sore today; t'was no use.

Your letter came near causing me to be "dispersed" all over the Avenue pavement for I found myself reading it out in the middle of the car track with the Black and White dusting off my coat sleeves.

The enclosed clipping describes the way I felt at the Government Hotels. I suppose you are saying, "Would that he had never come back". – I am glad you were not sensible then or later and I hope you never do get any – well I sure got myself in a fine mess with that sentence.

Van just came back from work. He was announcing weather reports over the radio. He'll be a second 'Roxy' soon. I see him every night at bedtime. He eats over at a regular boarding house but I would rather take my chance on being poisoned in a restaurant. I was out in the canoe tonite all alone. – You read of men finding companionship in a dog and pipe. – Mine is a mouthorgan and four radiantly beautiful pillows. As I slowly floated down to Key Bridge tonite alone with memories – memories that are summoned back only to hurt us.

We learn to like things that cause us worry and pain else – how explain a mother's love. Do you remember what someone said of mother's love. That it was given us that we might have a bare glimpse of the love of Christ for us.

– I start with the idea of sending a "cheerie" letter and it ends up in a sermon. Anyway you don't have to read mine just send me yours.

I'll say a prayer tonite for a certain girl who may be very sea sick by now.

Sincerely, Lee

P.S. – It never rains but what it pours. – I was notified today that I was back to my old rating and salary.

Levi's letter was mailed the same day Chloe departed for New York, Tuesday, June 30. He addressed the envelope to Miss Chloe Wells, c/o Mrs. Jennie Vandecar, Mechanicville, N.Y., as instructed. Though more than 7,500 people lived in Mechanicville in 1925, this address was enough. As with the letters to Champ, a name, town, and state were all that was required for proper delivery.

CHAPTER 4
START SPREADING THE NEWS

June 30, 1925
Old Dominion Steamship Co. Letterhead

Dear Lee,

We have started on our trip at last. – Our boat is the George Washington – we are traveling 'de luxe' I suppose. When we came aboard I heard a porter say that the same stateroom had been assigned to a lady and then to a gentleman – I immediately thought of the comedy we saw at the National Theater just before I left Washington.

Mama is seasick! She couldn't eat any dinner and cannot even sit up. I am sorry this part of her trip is spoiled – I can't get sick too – that would never do – probably this thought helps me to remain well. Our ship docks in New York to-morrow morning at 9 o'clock. We left Norfolk at four o'clock this afternoon so you see we'll make very good time. I think we'll spend the day and to-morrow night in New York City before leaving for Albany – maybe Mama will enjoy the ride up the Hudson better if we do this.

Your letter came last night – so you feel better – that's good. Father Londo's visit helped – did it? Didn't he say that I'm right in my decision?

I have to promenade the deck alone to-night – – rather lonely – – I'd enjoy the trip more if I had someone to talk and walk with me.

Your sincere friend, Chloe E. W.

P.S. If you are going to fuss with Gertrude I'm not sending you her address. This affair isn't her fault. The blame is on both of us.

P.P.S. If this letter is "scratchy" – blame it on the rocking of the boat. C.E.W.

Chloe's envelope was postmarked July 1, 1925, 2:30 pm, New York, N.Y. Levi responded the next day, from Washington.

Thursday Night
July 2, 1925

Dear Chloe,

I wish I could have been promenading the deck with you on the George Washington – but then I probably would have been sea sick and love sick both. Speaking from experience a person affected with both is in need of more than sympathy.

Last night upon leaving the Library of Congress I suddenly found myself walking towards the battle ground where in a momentous struggle the fate and destiny of two people hung balanced (and still does). – Upstairs I found Grace entertaining "Mac". Everytime I see her I think of the old song, "I Wonder Who's Kissing Her Now".

Ruth was home and thin as ever. I've offered to play

tennis with her so that she can work up an appetite.

Your umbrella – it caused Ruth and I a headache trying to figure how to send it. I hope the pieces arrive safely. – I now have Gertrude's address and you can imagine all the terrible things I'm going to say to her.

I didn't ask Father Londo's advice. He probably knows of my woes (poetry) from the grin he gave me but like the rest he has faith in my 'common sense'. That's the one thing I'm going to bury, "common sense". "And cleansed of wisdom let us see our Lady Follys face again".

Notice all the corrections – Ever so often I recall that it's a school marme that will be reading this.

The other package – I just couldn't keep from enclosing those pamphlets. I'm not going to have you believe we worship statues, buy "sin permits", worship the Pope or countless other things which we hold as ridiculous as you do.

May go down to Richmond over the weekend. Would like to see how Southerners celebrate the Fourth.

If I live thru it I'll have to write a special article for the Green Bay Press Gazette.

Yours, Lee

Mechanicville, New York
c/o Mrs. Jennie Vandecar
July 13, 1925

Dear Lee,

My umbrella and trunk rod came last Monday night. Will you be insulted if I thank you? I appreciate your trouble. I know it was an unwieldy package to wrap. It came in good shape – due to your skillful packing? I think so.

I intended to write in the first of my letter my impression of New York City – I've seen so much since my recollection is somewhat vague – Rush! is the one word that best describes it to me. We were only there from 10:30 a.m. Wednesday to 9 a.m. Thursday, so you see I did not have time to see very much. Mama was tired so we rested at our hotel a couple of hours — then she had to go to the publishing house of the Christian Herald (her favorite magazine) and see some of the editors. — Mrs. Margaret E. Sangster, especially — After this we took a double deck bus up Fifth Avenue, around by Central Park, East Riverside drive, Grant's Tomb, Cathedral of St. John the Divine, St. Patrick's and we saw Columbia University in the distance — This took about two hours — Mama was tired and wouldn't go with me to a show that night — I was disappointed — we only crossed Broadway — and I didn't even ride on a subway.

I took a snapshot of the Statue of Liberty as we came by and it is very good, in spite of the fog.

The trip to New York was predominantly for Chloe's mother, Emma Sophia (Sturt) Wells. She was born there. At the age of five, her family moved from Roseboom, New York, to a farm near McKenney, Virginia, about 1871. Only one sibling stayed behind in New York, Ruth, the eldest of six at that time. Ruth was the aunt Chloe mentioned visiting, and Jennie Vandecar was one of Ruth's fifteen children.

Chloe's July 13 letter to Levi recalled the trip from New York City to Albany, and finally, Mechanicville, and the surrounding areas.

The scenery along the Hudson is so pretty I can't describe it — even prettier than the pictures and the description you've heard people give. — I think the Palisades were most beautiful.

My cousin lives right on the Hudson River and we see the canal boats very often — I haven't seen a lock open yet — I've been to Albany several times. It is quite pretty — but I don't think any of the cities are as pretty as Washington — New York is ugly! — (I didn't see Long Island).

Those were the heydays of travel by boat from New York City to Albany, NY. Though the photo on the next page may not depict the vessel they embarked on that day, it could be one of the seven steamers used in 1925.

As they traveled, the Bear Mountain Bridge came into view, though it is almost lost in the fog in the center photo.

West Point's military academy looked like a fortress on the hill. The photo on the right captured the view from the Hudson River, port side, as they approached.

Chloe's July 13 letter to Levi continued.

*Last Tuesday morning a cousin of mine took Mama
and me to see some friends in Hyndsville – which is about 80
miles from here. We stayed until Friday and they brought us
home through the Catskill Mts. – we camped over night in a
little town right in the Catskill Reservation. A thunderstorm
came up during the night so we heard Hendrick Hudson's
crew rolling ten pins. During our travels, we took the Rip
Van Winkle Trail to the town of Catskill on the Hudson.
The scenery is beautiful! We returned through Cooperstown
– where J. Fenimore Cooper lived (needless to tell you) but
did not stop. Taking this trip makes me want to read
Irving's Sketch Book and Cooper's Leatherstocking Tales
over again.*

Chloe's reference to having heard *Hendrick Hudson's crew rolling
ten pins* goes back to a legend from the Catskills. Washington Irving
wrote the story of Rip Van Winkle in 1819, a story in the *Sketch
Book* that Chloe referenced. In that tale, Rip escaped his nagging wife
and walked off into the mountains. He came across the ghost of
Henry Hudson, an English explorer who worked for the Dutch West
India Company in the 1600s and claimed territory in the area for
the Dutch. There were many "short, square-built old fellows," (72)
Irving wrote, and they were playing ninepins, a precursor to the ten

pins used today in bowling. Irving stated that "nothing interrupted the stillness of the scene, but the noise of the balls, which, whenever they were rolled, echoed along the mountains like rumbling peals of thunder" (75). This explains why Henry Hudson, Hendrick in Dutch, was the cause of the sounds of thunder, as Chloe remarked.

Henry Hudson endured a mutiny on his ship during his last adventure to explore and claim new lands for the Dutch. Along with his teenage son and several loyal members of his crew, Hudson was set adrift and never seen again. This river and a Canadian bay carry his name, marking his accomplishments in this area.

Also mentioned in Chloe's letter was James Fenimore Cooper. He was a prized author during his time for his work, *Leatherstocking Tales*, a series of five novels set in the 1700s. It was a time when central New York State was being developed out of a predominantly Iroquois area. To date, Cooper's most famous tale is *The Last of the Mohicans*. All five volumes were published in the early to mid-1800s.

In less than a month, Chloe ventured from D.C. to Champ, Virginia. The SS George Washington took her to New York City, and a steamer chugged up the Hudson River, delivering her to Albany. Along with her mother, she visited Mechanicville and had just returned from a camping trip in the Catskill Mountains. This was quite an experience for a young maiden in 1925, not to mention her mother, a recent widow, in her early sixties. They never shied away from adventure.

The visit to Hyndsville included an additional jaunt further west to Roseboom, the place of Emma Sophia's birth. She found their old homestead. Though much of the farm on Hoose Road was gone, Emma Sophia drank from the old spring and rejoiced in the revived memories.

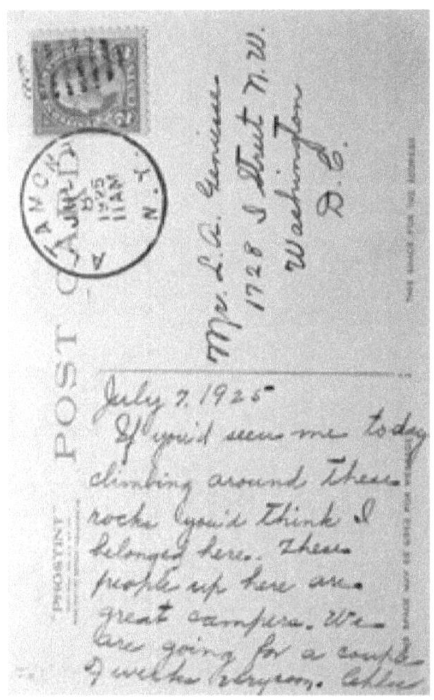

The above postmark reads, "Altamont, NY – July 8, 1925, 11 AM"

July 7, 1925

If you'd seen me to-day climbing around these rocks you'd think I belonged here. These people up here are great campers. We are going for a couple of weeks very soon.

Chloe

CHAPTER 5
MONKEY BUSINESS IN TENNESSEE

Chloe and Levi deliberated religion often. The topic of secular versus religious-based education was an important point for debate in 1925. Current events infiltrated their discussions, and the hottest debate in American religious circles during the 1920s played out in Dayton, Tennessee, between July 10 and July 21, 1925. Levi and Chloe's conversation on the topic plodded along. Pertinent snippets gather here, cohesively.

The Scopes Trial, officially known as the State of Tennessee versus John Thomas Scopes, and unofficially as the "Monkey Trial," overtook life in small-town Tennessee. The Butler Act had just become state law in March. Prohibited was the teaching of "any theory that denies the story of the Divine Creation of man as taught in the Bible, and to teach instead that man has descended from a lower order of animals" (1). The Scopes Trial was the first challenge to the new law.

Lead counsel for the State's prosecution was Mr. William Jennings Bryan, who previously ran on three occasions to become president of the United States. When the Democratic Party finally took the presidency, Mr. Bryan served as Woodrow Wilson's Secretary of State beginning in 1912.

Clarence Darrow was the lead defender, representing John T.

Scopes. Darrow was an agnostic and a prominent attorney at the time. He was a leading member of the recently founded American Civil Liberties Union (ACLU). Bryan and Darrow had faced off many times over the topic of prohibition, with Bryan supporting the 18th Amendment and Darrow opposing.

The trial held the attention of many within and beyond the borders of the United States. According to the Public Broadcasting System's documentary, "American Experience," WGN Radio out of Chicago spent $1,000 a day for host Quinn Ryan to broadcast the trial. The station, which was only a year old at the time, was the first in American history to broadcast a live courtroom trial. "The World's Most Famous Court Trial" compiled a word-for-word report of the proceedings.

It may surprise many today that the trial began with a prayer, some 603 words strung together by Rev. Lemuel M. Cartwright. Day two opened similarly, with a prayer from Rev. Moffit. Though he did not reflect on creation itself, he did not let this opportunity pass him by. He began, "Oh, God, our Father, Thou Who are the creator of the heaven and the earth and the sea and all that is in them" (45). The defense objected to starting the proceedings in this manner on days two and three. The judge overruled the objection both days. By day four, the prayer was down to 83 words, as offered by Dr. Allen, a Church of Christ pastor, but it still included sentiments such as, "We pray Thy blessings upon the deliberations of this court, to the end that Thy Word may be vindicated, and that Thy truth may be spread in the earth" (95).

Levi did not mention the Scopes trial until Wednesday night, July 15, 1925. In Monkey Trial terms, that was the end of day four of the proceedings.

> *In the office they have noticed a marked improvement*
> *in my work. A veritable machine that starts and stops with*
> *the clock. A Charles Dickens character, a man whose soul is*
> *engrossed in one thing, whose god is mathematics, whose*
> *only diversion is reading about the monkey festival down in*
> *Tennessee. If you were only here I could keep you*
> *listening sleepy eyed to my opinion of the surprising number*

*of "dumbbells" to be found south of the Potomac. At times
I'm tempted to cheer for Darrow. A man who I firmly
believe is in this trial for the sole purpose of discrediting
Christianity. Bryan and the other sincere but mistaken
Fundamentalists are playing into Darrow's hands and
Protestantism is the loser. I might here ask what has become
of private interpretation in Tennessee. (The advantage of
reading a letter, like a phonograph, is that you can stop at
any time you do not like it) but read on please.*

What happened in the trial to give Levi his negative opinion? On the first day of the proceedings, Jim Riley, a potential juror, was questioned by lead defense counsel, Clarence Darrow (13).

"Do you know anything about evolution?"
"No, not particularly."
"Have you any opinion about it – prejudice?"
"No, I have no prejudice."
"Have you any feeling that it is a wrong teaching at this time?"
"Well, I haven't studied very much about it."
"Ever talk to anybody about it?"
"None to amount to anything; no, sir."
"Ever hear Mr. Bryan speak about it?"
"No, sir."
"Ever read anything he said about it?"
"No, sir; I can't read."
"Well, you are fortunate. You can be a perfectly fair juror, can you?"
"Yes, sir."

Mr. Riley was asked to sit, and that line of questioning concluded. Shortly afterwards, following questions concerning peremptory challenges, Mr. Darrow continued questioning Mr. Riley (14).

"You said you couldn't read. Is that due to your eyes?"
"No, I am uneducated."

"That is because of your eyes?"

"I say I am uneducated."

"Have your eyes bothered you?"

"No, I am uneducated."

The "dumbbell" here seemed to be the defense attorney rather than the uneducated potential juror. The transcripts, historic video presentations, and recordings made the trial seem staged, more akin to a comedy than a live trial.

From Chloe's letter, written July 20 in Mechanicville, she had this to offer.

> *So you are keeping up with the Scopes' case – I thought you would. I read about it once in a while. I think after 'all is said and done' we'll not know any more than we did before the 'festival' as you call it. I have to disagree with you when you call the folks south of the Potomac "dumbbells" – you want to start an argument don't you? Well, I can't argue on paper very well. - I can't see how the Scopes' case is weakening Protestantism any more than Catholicism. It does seem to be a blow at Christianity.*

Tuesday evening, Levi's July 21 letter had this to say concerning the Scopes trial and the state of religion.

> *Can you imagine me reading Newman's "Apologia Pro Vita Sua"? No, it is not written in Latin. It is a history of John Henry Newman's religious convictions in which he defends himself for leaving the Anglican church. I have come to enjoy religious controversy. It is a sad state of affairs and something of which you should be truly sorry. Yes – I'm blaming you.*

> *By tonite's paper I see that Scopes is guilty. It ends here as every one expected. Do you know that I can't help believing that Bryan is a bit doubtful as to the security of his doctrines?*

> *Protestantism is harmed because scientists can prove that the Bible can not be interpreted literally. Fundamentalism is the choice of the South and those among you who begin to doubt certain parts of your Bible are confronted with – 'A little knowledge is a dangerous thing.' Catholicism is not harmed because the question of the interpretation of the Bible along with choosing the books of the Bible was settled in the fourth century. More than a thousand years ago the Church discussed and settled the problem of Evolution. The Sunday supplement paper is responsible for the question arising again, outside of scientific circles.*

Could Protestantism be harmed when it came to the theory of evolution, while leaving Catholicism unharmed? It could be, especially in 1925.

In 1924, the position of the Presbyterian Church in the United States on evolution was affirmed, "Adam's body was directly fashioned by Almighty God, without any animal parentage of any kind, out of matter previously created from nothing" (Bringe). William Jennings Bryan was an elder in the Presbyterian church who led the fundamentalist opposition to evolution, supporting the idea that Holy Scripture was to be taken literally. This did not align with the teaching of the Catholic church and is no longer the belief among most Presbyterian denominations.

When Levi wrote, "the question of the interpretation of the Bible, along with choosing the books of the Bible, was settled in the fourth century," he was referring back to Saint Augustine, concerning interpretation, and Saint Athanasius, for the determination of the books of the Bible.

Levi's statement that *more than a thousand years ago the Church discussed and settled the problem of Evolution* is potentially pointed to Saint Thomas Aquinas, from the thirteenth century. He found harmony between science and faith. In 1879, Pope Leo XIII expounded on the Saint's writings in his encyclical *Aeterni Patris* (Of the Eternal Father), stating that true faith could not be opposed to good science since both sought to find truth.

At the time of Levi's letter, a difference between Catholicism and Protestantism dealt with the Holy Scriptures and whether they were to be taken literally. Since Catholicism is based on the Holy Spirit guiding the Church, belief is in the literary meaning of Scripture. This was not the case among Presbyterians and other Protestant denominations in 1925, who interpreted Scripture literally.

The Scopes Trial seemed to put God and Christianity on the stand, but in actuality, it tested the constitutional validity of the Butler Act. Scopes was a teacher, but he did not recall ever teaching evolution. He was recruited to bring this case and the attention that came with it to Dayton. In the end, Scopes was fined, and the Butler Act stood. Evolution was not taught in the Tennessee classroom until after the act was repealed in 1967.

Chloe responded to Levi's explanation in her letter from Mechanicville. This is the section that pertained to her impression of his remarks.

> *My! But you must be reading deep literature – It's above my head – Lee, if you don't stop studying so many religious books you'll become a fanatic. You know I told you that I believe if you spent so much time on the intellectual you'd lose the spiritual part in religion – This is the end of the lecture (No. I).*
>
> *(No. II) Lee, you make me angry when you insinuate that the folks down South are so ignorant. If we like what we believe isn't it all right? You have a right to your own opinion. We may be just as correct in our belief as you are in yours – So there – ! Finis –*
>
> *Let's talk about something a little more pleasant – Forget the fuss –*

Chloe wrote that on July 27, six days after the trial ended. For Levi and Chloe, the Scopes trial opened up new investigations into their own religious beliefs. Was the Bible to be taken literally or literarily? Levi, being Catholic, followed the more liberal interpretation of Scripture, while Chloe aligned with the Presbyterian beliefs of the era. Differences like this caused both families to question the potential of a fruitful relationship between these two. As far as the Scopes Trial was concerned, as Chloe said, it was time to *forget the fuss*. The newspaper headline the next day would shock the nation, *William Jennings Bryan Dies in His Sleep at Dayton on Eve of Crusade Against Modernism* (1). Levi wrote again on July 28.

> *Possibly you think I should not continue the fight since Bryan is dead. You will wonder when I tell you that I'm sincerely sorry that Bryan is dead. Also it is better for him that he is. The last sounds uncharitable but 'tis true. The argument when finally settled will show that Bryan was wrong and if he were alive when the religious belief was shattered it would hurt more than death. Bryan was sincere in all that he did, he was a fighter and I liked him for that.*
>
> *I was tickled to get that lecture from you on the study of religion. Not that I thought it funny but rather it was like my mother would say. Chloe, I feel that faith based on reason is the only safe basis for religion. Blind faith is as good as educated faith in the eyes of God but my parents sent me to Notre Dame and I can't help remembering the words, "To him whom much is given much will be expected."*
>
> *When I say anything of the South it is to arouse that fighting blood. You say, "If we like what we believe, isn't it all right?" – It is right only when what you believe is right. Thinking a thing is true does not make it so nor does it excuse one from searching for the truth.*
>
> *I ought to tear this up and start over but I'm hoping that you will again consider it necessary to lecture,*
>
> *Lee*

On Saturday, August 1, William Jennings Bryan was laid to rest in Arlington Cemetery. *The Washington Daily News* reported, "Bryan Goes to His Rest." They estimated that, "at least 500 people braved the downpour to be present when the body of the great fundamentalist was lowered beneath the earth" (3). Immediately following this report, the next headline was printed, "Crosses Burned for Bryan." From Columbus, Ohio, the news read, "Fiery crosses with burning words of eulogy, were lighted last night in Toledo, Dayton and Columbus for William Jennings Bryan. The inscription said: 'In memory of the greatest klansman'"(3).

Levi sent another clipping, but it was separated from its envelope. Chloe addresses it in her August 3 letter.

> *I read the other clipping you sent — so you were neutral in the Scopes case — Well, it ended as I expected and of course I'm sorry Mr. Bryan is dead. Did you hear the funeral service? — Foolish question? — Mama heard them over the radio.*

Though impossible to verify whether this was the missing article or not, this potential candidate was worth including. The following appeared in *The Washington Post* on Monday, July 13, 1925.

EVOLUTION TOPIC OF SERMONS IN 3 CAPITAL PULPITS

Evolution was the subject in three Washington pulpits yesterday. Father Shehan at St. Patrick's took occasion at morning mass to state the Catholic attitude towards the theory. The Catholic does not have to forsake the Bible, he said, to believe in evolution. It is for the members of this church to take it or reject it as they saw fit, so long as they adhered to the belief that God was the power behind it all and that He made a separate creation of the soul.

Father Shehan said he was speaking in the absence of any statement of the church's attitude in the present controversy. His church, he said, does not believe in the literal interpretation of the Bible. St. Augustine pointed out in the fourth century, he said, that the Bible was not supposed to be an accurate chronology of events

but was so written in order that its message and purpose would be understood.

Attacks "Atheistic Science."

At First Congregational church Dr. George Rutledge Stuart took issue with the "atheistic scientist." He divided scientists into four classes. Atheistic, theistic, agnostic and infidel.

In the first place, he said, a student becomes a scientist when he definitely establishes the truth by searching. He should know every vital point in nature, Dr. Stuart said, yet he doesn't. They teach, he related, that animal life first existed in a conglomerate, a handful of jelly for instance. In this are forms all of which are sentient. When they come together they become conscious and organized. This organization is the first process of development.

"We ask," Dr. Stuart continued, "where the atoms got their sentient nature, where they got their power to organize?" The atheistic scientist says he doesn't know.

"When they start out with their organization," he asked, "who decides whether they are to be elephants or goats, monkeys or ants?"

"All of this development is too artistic, too well planned, too marvelously executed for chance," he declared.

Furthermore, the scientist does not know the reason for the two great exceptions in nature, Dr. Stuart said. "Explaining that the law of nature is that heat expands all bodies and cold contracts," he points out, "that clay contracts with heat and water expands with cold. Were the two exceptions not true there would be no earthenware, china ware or the like, he said, and every Northern

lake would so freeze in the winter that no summer sun could thaw it out.

The Rev. John E. Briggs, pastor of the First Baptist church, said he feared no good would come "of the Dayton, Tenn., trial. People will never get anywhere by "splitting hairs" as they are doing there, he said. Evolution is all right as a theory but not as a fact," he declared (2).

The trial started on a Friday. At the time of these sermons, deliberation had not begun. The only accomplishments made in the courtroom were the jury selection and the reading of the First Chapter of Genesis.

Though the trial was over, Levi's had mentioned the Scopes Trial in his last letter from July 28. A response was in order. In Chloe's last letter sent from Mechanicville, she offered this paragraph on the topic.

> *You returned the lectures I sent, didn't you? Maybe I deserved them as I shouldn't argue in letters — I told you that I didn't know how. — but you've heard the saying — 'Convince a man against his will and he's of the same opinion still' — I think I've quoted this correctly.*

With the trial over, and Chloe and Levi's deliberation having lasted longer than Bryan and Darrow's combined, all discussion of Mr. Scopes, the trial's effect on religion, and the classification of those south of the Potomac as *dumbbells*, the rumination could rest, like Bryan.

CHAPTER 6
WRITING LINES TO READ BETWEEN

Wednesday Night
July 15, 1925

Dear Chloe,

When I received your card postmarked 'Altamont' and Van reported that he couldn't find that place on the map I just tore great gobs of hair from my head as I madly paced the floor crying "Where will I write now?"

His sympathetic, "On a table you darn fool," came near breaking the family tie.

I'm glad you are having an enjoyable time and find the North a "not so half bad place". If you think New York is ugly I wonder at your impression of Chicago or some other industrial city. On my first visit to Chicago I felt that there was plenty of material for a hell a la Dante or Milton.

Gertrude, Ruth, Van and I went canoeing about a week ago. That has been my only experience with femininity. I'll have to do something to break the armor of indifference which I find I have been building around me since you left.

After a short interlude to cover Levi's opinion on the Scopes's Trial, he continued abruptly without a title or any introduction with the following.

Beside the little mountain lough
I told you all and you
Spoke not but raised your eyes to me,
Your sweet sad eyes of blue.
And then you gazed across the lake
And sighed as though your heart would break.

The perfume of the heather sweet
Comes back to me to-day,
The vision of the misty hills,
The gorse o'er glen and brae.
You spoke no word, you shed no tear.
I loved you for your silence, Dear.

It's not original but must have been written for
— Lee

P.S. – A clipping is enclosed. – Anything to make a letter so
that in return I may read a letter from Chloe.

The poem was written by Nora Ni Chathain and titled "Revelation" (498). Though Levi's replication of the poem ended with the second stanza, the original did not. Nora Ni Chathain continued:

"The wee brown lough is still the same,
Though I am far away.
I wonder do you ever go
Up there to dream – to pray
For one who seemed to love you not,
For one who never has forgot.

Levi's postscript mentioned a clipping. Unfortunately, none remains with the letter. Future correspondences allude to the Government Hotels having been the topic of the pieces sent.

The only mention of the Government Hotels in Washington, D.C. papers around this time was under the heading "30 Days' Annual Leave" (7). *The Washington Daily News* ran a piece that would have assured a response from Chloe.

A fictional character named Swelterin' Sam went on a date with a girl from the Government Hotels, his fourth option after making several calls around town that night. Swelterin' Sam disapproved of the rules and regulations at the Government Hotels. He did not want to sit far apart under the watchful eyes of the lady at the desk. Leaving by 11 was not his idea of a fun evening, and the front steps outside could not even provide him a place where he could "get in some necking." The Hotel cop had that area covered. Sam said the evening with Edyth felt like it lasted a week.

Under the heading, "Mail Bag: Marjie's Peeved," a nonfictional young lady who lived at the Government Hotels had these words to say, among many others.

> **Swelterin' Sam, the guests of the Government Hotels are happy and contented in the pursuit of single blessedness, and most decidedly are not on the trail of any stray biped of the male species that may appear in sight and which often has the aspect of "something the cat brought in." It is suggested that you spend the remainder of your Annual Leave at the Public Library in an effort to supplement your education and enlighten your ignorance (6).**

If these pieces were the ones Levi cut out and sent along, they would not have made good conversation starters with family members in New York. Their disappearance may have been intentional.

Mechanicville, N.Y.
c/o Mrs. Jennie Vandecar
July 20, 1925

Dear Lee,

When I returned Saturday night I found your letter awaiting me. I had been to Lake Champlain for several days. I saw a little of Lake George on this trip too. It was beautiful even in the rain.

Mama has gone on a camping trip with two cousins. Isn't she a sport? We are planning to join them this week. They are camping near Friend's Lake in the Adirondacks.

The next two paragraphs dealt with the Scopes Trial. Chloe responded to Levi's commentary on the south of the Potomac *dumbells* and the weakening of Protestantism, while Catholicism was left unaffected. She retorted, *You want to start an argument, don't you? Well, I can't argue on paper very well.* From there, her letter continued.

Why don't you go over to the Gov't Hotels and see some of those inmates – I can imagine what you are thinking when you read this. I thought you were going to play tennis with Ruth – For my sake go to see someone, don't sit around doing nothing in the evenings, but reading – This is a suggestion as to how to break that, 'Once is enough never again' feeling you said you had.

When I first read the little poem at the end of your letter I thought it was original and that you were on the verge of changing your profession. The clipping you enclosed is clever – also true – Don't you think so?

Sincerely, Chloe

Day – District Bldg. Inspector of Building Office
Night – Franklin 3577
Tuesday Evening
July 21, 1925

Dear Chloe,

I am writing this perched on top of a trunk so just omit what you can not decipher. Just had to move again so this morning Van and I took our extra shirts and climbed up to the third floor. The room is a stone's throw from the Powhatan Hotel and its roof garden. I can now join (in spirit) not (with spirit) the revelry each night while alone I read "high brow stuff". Can you imagine me reading Newman's "Apologia Pro Vita Sua"? No its not written in Latin. It is a history of John Henry Newman's religious convictions in which he defends himself for leaving the Anglican church. I have come to enjoy religious controversy. It's a sad state of affairs and something of which you should be truly sorry. Yes – I'm blaming you.

Gertrude, Va, Ruth and I played tennis last Saturday afternoon. We had a circus with Gertrude. She started with all the enthusiasm possible and at the end of an hour and a half of futile effort to drive the ball over the net she de-clared, "never again". Sunday Ruth and I went swimming and tonight the four of us were to have gone up the river for a marshmellow roast but its raining 'to beat the cars' so that's postponed. Out of my shell for a while. Am planning on a three weeks vacation home beginning Aug 12, which may help. When do you expect to visit Washington? There must be no conflict (of vacations) if I can help it.

Levi's letter transitioned here to the Scopes Trial. This is where he explained how Protestantism was harmed by the trial, but Catholicism was not. Since that portion was already included in the last chapter, little remained of his letter to Chloe.

I try to picture you camping. A sort of 'Camp Fire Girl' dress but where are the braided tresses of the sun burned maiden who skips across the brook? Gone, gone, gone (I'm crying now).

Chloe, is this tiresome to you? Do you write from charity alone? I have never wanted to write an interesting letter more and it all results in this.

From, Lee

The above postmark reads, "Chestertown, NY – July 22, 1925, 3PM"

July 22, 1925

We are camping here for a few days – maybe a week – We went boat riding yesterday afternoon and it rained last night!

Chloe

Mechanicville, N.Y.
July 27, 1925

Dear Lee,

You and Clayton have a dreadful time with your boarding houses. You can now listen to the wild revelry of the night – Why not join in? – but not with spirits.

She followed with a few lines about the Scopes Trial, where she said they should forget the fuss. Then this letter continued.

I had a letter from Gertrude last week. She said that you and Clayton were going home for a few weeks but didn't say whether she was going or not. She wrote that she gave the lecture to you – so you didn't have a chance (to deliver yours) did you?

We came back from our camping trip Saturday after-noon – (earlier than we expected) I enjoyed it thoroughly. We were asked by some visitors if we were Camp Fire Girls! (I used to be one – but our organization fell through before we had our first camping trip.) Maybe the braids are gone – but I surely have the sunburn and mosquito bites. We had lots of fun hiking, fishing, sitting around the camp fire toasting marshmallows and weenies, telling stories and playing the 'uke'. I did the playing – Aren't you sorry for my audience? I actually went fishing – baited my hook and took three of the five fish I caught off the hook. Don't you think I'm learning?

Did my letter last week sound "charitable"? Several people were talking around me when I was writing so maybe that's the reason.

I don't know yet when we are going home – We expect to stay longer than Aug. 1. I'll let you know. Hope you'll enjoy your trip home. Don't worry about your letters I am glad to hear from you.

Chloe

Tuesday Evening
July 28, 1925

Dear Chloe,

Van and Gertrude are going canoeing tonite, "To experiment with the romance of moonlight" as he expresses it. I could tell him a whole lot; I know I ought to warn him and yet I let him go like the unwary fly. It's too late when your in the web but misery loves company.

*When I read of your fishing experience I shudder. What
kind of a girl have you become that squirming worms and
wriggling fish do not bother you. That coupled with playing
a "uke" (I don't know how to spell it) shows that you have
become a "Hard hearted Hannah." Tell me it isn't so. —*

His letter drifted off to articles no longer enclosed with the letter. The remainder of Levi's letter pertained to the Scopes Trial.
Chloe's trip to Mechanicville, New York, was drawing to a close.

Mechanicville, N.Y.
August 3, 1925

Dear Lee,

*Let me first comment on the enclosure from your last
letter — I'm glad the Gov't Hotels aren't so bad after all as I
may live there again. I don't know whether Ruth and Grace
have any other girls with them or not. They didn't when I
last heard from them.*

An almost required paragraph or two on Scopes followed, and
this correspondence ended this way.

*We planned to come home last Friday but one of our
cousins insisted that we stay as he had several trips planned
for us to take and as Mama was feeling better (She had a
terrible headache and was afraid of getting sick away from
home) we stayed.*

*We are thinking of coming home Friday of this week
as last week's letter from my married sister stated that she
wasn't very well. We may stop in Washington, if we do, I'll
send you a card.*

Sincerely, Chloe

The above postmark reads, "Mechanicville, NY – Aug. 5, 1925, 1:30 PM"

August 5, 1925

We are planning to arrive in Washington Friday evening about eight o'clock (Standard Time). I am writing Ruth by this same mail.

Sincerely, Chloe

Tuesday Night
August 4, 1925

Dear Chloe,

Van just invited me over to the Circle. I refused, telling him that I had more important things to do than watch movies. How's that for faithfulness? Tonite – I'm feeling exceptionally well. Every time I hear from you I feel like going out to celebrate. It is tough that the thought that produces the joy also prevents me from following it to its logical conclusion. – Of course not, – I wouldn't think of arguing Prohibition, but – – – – – – – (far into the night).

I stopped to listen to a band concert in Washington Circle a few nights ago. I, a few policemen and many of our colored brethren were there. The band played "Marchin' Thru Georgia", the crowd cheered and I groaned at the thought that we Northerners were responsible for the arrogant Washington negro. – It will be only a few centuries when the blacks will be a majority in this country then what chance will our hunchbacked, bespectacled government clerks have against the brawny negroes who now do all the manual labor in Washington. Yes – I'm worried.

The Klan is coming Saturday. I have already covered the line of march and spotted every loose cobble stone. You are also coming. That will be great because I had been worried as to how I was to distinguish your friends and neighbors amongst our "night gowned" countrymen. And if we lose, you could like Pocahontas plead that I be spared a coat of feathers.

"Convince a man against his will and he's of the same opinion still." This is true but is it right that it should be?

If the flower be lovely,
Perfect to the eye,
And the fragrance wanting,
Can it satisfy?

Since the Lady's face is fair
And her grace refined,
Doth her beauty, then, suffice,
If she be not kind?

Just an engineer off on a tangent again. – I have a lot of crazy ideas I'm just 'aching' to tell you and a lot of scandal about "Major Hoople". You will stop off at Washington or –––––––––.

Now that's a threat from, Lee

Major Hoople was a character in a popular newspaper comic strip titled "Our Boarding House." In D.C., *The Washington Daily News* printed the cartoon. One single-lined black box was filled with a sample of lodgers involved in the happenings of that day. Mrs. Hoople ran the place, but Major Hoople stole the show. Fans returned daily to follow the story.

Levi mentioned the Klan was coming, coinciding with Chloe's arrival. He had firsthand knowledge of the Klan's hatred towards Catholics. In the 1920s, many feared that Black Americans would gain power in society. The Great War, what modern historians refer to as World War I, caused a need for workers to fill the places vacated by those serving in the military. Hundreds of thousands left the Jim Crow Law-strangled South to fill the labor needs in the industrial North and Midwest.

The Klan capitalized on those fears and extended their hatred to include anyone who threatened their image of what traditional American culture was and what the "fabric" of America should be. Anti-Catholicism, antisemitism, and a hatred for immigrants combined with their well-established abhorrence of the African American at the height of their power in the 1920s.

CHAPTER 7
KU KU IN 1925

Many associate the Ku Klux Klan (KKK) with the Reconstruction Era, those years after the American Civil War, when six Confederate veterans banded together to form a group to try to combat the freedom obtained through the ratification of the 13th Amendment. Thanks to federal intervention, the group disbanded in the 1870s. The 1920s saw a resurgence of the hate group, brought on by the massive migration of Southern Blacks to the large cities of the North and Midwest.

The largest gathering of the Ku Klux Klan, regardless of the era, was in Washington, D.C., on August 8, 1925. Some articles stated that 30,000 members were present for the parade, while others increased those figures to 50,000.

This was not Levi's first exposure to the hate group. In May of 1924, while completing his senior year and preparing for finals, Levi was on campus at Notre Dame University in South Bend, Indiana. A recorded 2,000 Klansmen descended on the town to target the largest Catholic

University in Indiana. Local officials denied the Klan a permit to gather in a large group, but they still came.

Twenty-five percent of the all-male student body jogged two miles into town and confronted the Klansmen. A skirmish ensued, and Father Matthew Walsh, President of Notre Dame, rushed to the scene and pulled many of his students from the brawl. He was a veteran of the Great War and no stranger to conflict. Once gathered, Father Walsh led them back to campus, singing hymns and praying. Whether Levi participated or not is unknown, but his meticulous records offer clues.

Over 53 ledger pages accounted for every penny he spent from his first day on campus, September 8, 1920, until graduation day, June 15, 1924. The following entries were made during the days the Klan descended on South Bend.

May 17	*Drawing paper*	*0.45*
May 17	*Plaster Paris, oil, eraser*	*1.15*
May 18	*Church collection*	*0.10*
May 19	*Carfare, drinks, pretzels*	*1.00*
May 20	*Newspaper, telephone*	*0.10*

The last paper Levi bought before May 20 was over a month earlier, on April 3, 1924.

Missing the skirmish in 1924 may have prompted Levi to venture out along the parade route in D.C. on Saturday, August 8, 1925. His

feelings toward the Klan were clearest in the captions found in his scrapbook. Beneath the photo where Levi appears to have jumped into a historical moment, he wrote, "trying to steal a tablecloth."

The photo on the right captured the marchers as they rested, with their faces revealed. It was July in The District. Levi captioned the image perfectly, *100% Ku Ku.*

While Levi was confronting the Klan in Washington, D.C., Chloe had returned from her trip to New York State the night before. On the way back to Champ, Virginia, Emma Sophia insisted they stop in Washington. Levi was invited to Chloe's flat for dinner on Sunday night.

CHAPTER 8
TWO TRAINS THAT CANNOT PASS

Champ, Virginia
August 12, 1925

Dear Lee,

No one knew how late it was when you left Sunday night – Mama awoke soon after I was in bed. I pretended to be asleep, of course, and shuddered to think of what might have been said if I'd only been ten minutes later. She still hadn't said anymore about you until this morning when she was putting hot applications to her head and I inquired whose remedy she was trying now and she said yours. Was the engineer off at a tangent again?

We arrived in McKenney about two o'clock to the great surprise of my relatives there. I spent the night with one Aunt and Mama stayed with the other – (so no partiality was shown).

Lee, I'm afraid your people will not understand when this letter arrives before you. If they say anything about it you'll explain, won't you?

I was glad to see my sisters again and the little children are just as cute as ever – although I'm leaving again in a day or two to visit cousins in McKenney. I don't expect to be home very long at a time from now on. You know it won't be long before school starts.

You left for home this morning so you are now speeding away to the 'west' – Good luck to you! I'm still believing you'll keep your promise – about what? Prohibition.

I'm not living a very exciting life now – Emma Ruth has just called me and asked if I'd help her with dinner so I'm going to cook the "cobs" of corn. Would you like one?

She said that I could have two – this is about all the dinner I want – Don't you think it's enough? –

I hope you had a very pleasant trip – no wrecks, etc. –

Sincerely, Chloe

Chloe returned home to Champ, to the house her father, David Frances Wells, built. He served four years in the Civil War, and Champ was the place he wanted to call home. He was taken prisoner just a few miles from here during the Battle of Five Forks.

This two-room log cabin has a narrow staircase inside, hidden behind a door that seems to conceal only a closet. The wooden steps lead to an upstairs room. This was the girls' bedroom throughout their formative years. Emma Sophia had lived here since she and David married in 1898.

In the above photo, an upstairs window is visible beside the chimney of the log cabin. It is one of two that illuminated the upstairs bedroom, with a matching window on the opposite end.

By 1925, a larger structure was built. A covered back porch joined the two structures together.

Chloe's sister Lucinda and her husband Collier lived in the big house with their three small children.

Levi started a letter to Chloe in Champ that same day.

Aboard the Capitol Limited
Somewhere in Pennsylvania
August 12, 1925
6:15 P.M.

Dear Chloe,

How is your hayfever? I've been asking everyone I see for remedys for your illness but they tell me there is no cure. While searching for something that would help you a man told me this story, "Once upon a time there was a man and a maid. The man loved the maid (sad but true) and met her one evening after a long time in which he had not seen her, being torn with doubt and despair all this while. He rushed to meet her. There were tears in her eyes; her voice was hoarse with emotion. Ah! She loves me he thought and rejoiced but alas! His joy was short lived for she said, 'I have

*a bad cold and my eyes water so; I believe it's hayfever.'" For
the life o' me I couldn't see anything funny in the story but
was courteous enough to laugh anyway. I must eat now. Will
see you later.*

This first section of Levi's letter was written a little over three
hours into his trip to Chicago. He departed Washington, D.C. at 3:00
in the afternoon and arrived in Chicago at 9:00 the next morning.

The use of the term hayfever for Chloe's illness was a sign of the
times. Though this was a common term used in the twenties, today
those who suffer from this malady say they have "allergies."

A few hours later, Levi's letter continued.

8:30 P.M.
Still Moving

*Will say with Uncle Josh, "Train riding is all right for
those as likes it." This infernal click-a-clack is getting on
my nerves. It makes one feel like in a dentists chair. I'll swear
that there are more curves on the Baltimore and Ohio than
on the merry-go-round at Glen Echo.*

*I share a whole Pullman car with four other sufferers.
One of them is a girl whom ordinarily I would consider
pretty. She is an experienced traveler and returns my smallest
suggestion of a smile with a cold stare. I suppose I do look
like a villain or upon second thought it's probably because I
do not know that she ignores me. ——*

*We are passing some lighted coke ovens along the track.
They send out a cheery glow which relieves the feeling of
rushing headlong thru space. As you notice its getting worst.*

*Do you know that I lived next to a Kluxer and never
knew it. When I left the rooming house today the landlady
told me that the woman who roomed next to us was a
Klanswoman and had marched in the parade. When I think
of the fun I missed I could cry. — A funny thing, a remarkable coincidence that this same landlady should just when I*

was leaving engage me in a conversation which led to mixed marriages. I was in a hurry to get away but lingered to hear her give advice and recite her experiences. It was the same old story and the result is a bunch of children who believe in doing right because it is respectable.

Morality then becomes subject to the whims of the "Four Hundred". This is getting close to a religious argument and I intend to steer clear tonight so ———.

The porter has just hung a sign saying 'Quiet'. The irony of it, if I only had my mouthorgan here now I'd defy the law.

Please excuse me for a while. I must see why this train has stopped.

This evening section of the letter began with thoughts of Uncle Josh. Levi was not referring to a blood relative, but rather, a fictional character created in the mind of Cal Stewart. His full name was Josh Weathersby. Uncle Josh appeared in silent films, and his voice was among the earliest captured sound recordings. He was a country character from Punkin Centre, a fictitious farming community, who had a thick southern drawl and an unforgettable chuckle.

At this point in the letter, Levi was five hours into his ride to Chicago and less than a third of the way there. Most thoughts centered around the inescapable topic of trains. He likened the B&O Railroad to the merry-go-round at Glen Echo Amusement Park, but not everyone was familiar with this place in 1925.

The Glen Echo Amusement Park was in Maryland, a scenic trolley ride north of the city. It is more of an Arts and Cultural center now. The park closed in 1968 after a fifty-seven-year run. It was here, on the carousel, that Howard University students organized a sit-in. They rode the carousel until they were arrested. The unlawful action of the officers prompted the passing of the Civil Rights Act of 1964, which prohibited segregation in public places. Though the park no longer looks like it did in its heyday, the 1921, fifty-animal menagerie continues to run in circles.

The final term in this section of writing that harkens back to the twenties was Levi's reference to the *Four Hundred*, New York City's high society during the Gilded Age. They were the Astors, Vanderbilts, and Rockefellers, to name a few, a group whose members gained entry by invitation only. Levi alluded to their rules of morality and made this a religious topic, which he promptly dropped. The members of this elite group were predominantly Protestant, and resolution of any moral dilemma defaulted to *doing right because it is respectable.* Mixed marriages were to be avoided at all costs. This topic was better left alone.

> *August 13, 1925*
> *5:30 A.M.*
> *(by my watch)*
> *Somewhere in the U.S.A.*

*All my experience (I forgot to say **Good Morning**) with street car noise at Kreigans has availed me little for I slept nary a wink all night. Am lying in bed looking out at a flat country. We are passing fields of grain in shock. Oats I believe. The corn looks about two feet higher than that in Maryland last night. I have to notice all this because some uncle of mine will surely want to know how the crops are "out your way".*

"And when the Sun his beacon red" – We are speeding away from the East at sixty miles an hour but the crimson sky is gaining on us. It reminds me of the lines:

> *"Roads of adventure! wandering on,*
> *Over the hills to the sea*
> *(Pale in the night mist; ruddy at dawn),*
> *What will you promise to me?"*
> (Hennes, 725)

Joyce Kilmer didn't get his idea of train rides from a stage coach. That poem of his expresses just how I would like to describe it.

From now on farms, houses, silos, and people will look about the same. The great Middle West from Ohio to Nebraska represents the wealth and strength of the Nation. You could cut this section away from the rest of the country and find that it is self sustaining with its mineral, agricultural and manufacturing resources. We are stopping at a place called 'Garrett'. Guess I'll dress and see what it's all about.

Adventure, trains, and the poetry they inspire were the focus of Levi's letter at 5:30 that morning. He had three-and-a-half hours left in his train ride to Chicago. The poem he quoted appeared in the Notre Dame Scholastic. The author, Robert Hennes, was the same person who wrote the article on David Van Wallace.

Though Levi only made reference to Joyce Kilmer's poem and did not include it in the letter, this was how Kilmer described train riding. Levi agreed with his description, wholeheartedly.

THE TWELVE-FORTY-FIVE
(For Edward J. Wheeler)

"WITHIN the Jersey City shed
The engine coughs and shakes its head,
The smoke, a plume of red and white,
Waves madly in the face of night.
And now the grave incurious stars
Gleam on the groaning hurrying cars.
Against the kind and awful reign
Of darkness, this our angry train,
A noisy little rebel, pouts
Its brief defiance, flames and shouts –
And passes on, and leaves no trace.
For darkness holds its ancient place,
Serene and absolute, the king
Unchanged, of every living thing.
The houses lie obscure and still
In Rutherford and Carlton Hill.

Our lamps intensify the dark
Of slumbering Passaic Park.
And quiet holds the weary feet
That daily tramp through Prospect Street.
What though we clang and clank and roar
Through all Passaic's streets? No door
Will open, not an eye will see
Who this loud vagabond may be.
Upon my crimson cushioned seat,
In manufactured light and heat,
I feel unnatural and mean.
Outside the towns are cool and clean;
Curtained awhile from sound and sight
They take God's gracious gift of night.
The stars are watchful over them.
On Clifton as on Bethlehem
The angels, leaning down the sky,
Shed peace and gentle dreams. And I –
I ride, I blasphemously ride
Through all the silent countryside.
The engine's shriek, the headlight's glare,
Pollute the still nocturnal air.
The cottages of Lake View sigh
And sleeping, frown as we pass by.
Why, even strident Paterson
Rests quietly as any nun.
Her foolish warring children keep
The grateful armistice of sleep.
For what tremendous errand's sake
Are we so blatantly awake?
What precious secret is our freight?
What king must be abroad so late?
Perhaps Death roams the hills to-night
And we rush forth to give him fight.
Or else, perhaps, we speed his way
To come remote unthinking prey.
Perhaps a woman writhes in pain
And listens–listens for the train!

The train, that like an angel sings,
The train, with healing on its wings.
Now "Hawthorne!" the conductor cries.
My neighbor starts and rubs his eyes.
He hurries yawning through the car
And steps out where the houses are.
This is the reason of our quest!
Not wantonly we break the rest
Of town and village, nor do we
Lightly profane night's sanctity.
What Love commands the train fulfills,
And beautiful upon the hills
Are these our feet of burnished steel.
Subtly and certainly I feel
That Glen Rock welcomes us to her
And silent Ridgewood seems to stir
And smile, because she knows the train
Has brought her children back again.
We carry people home—and so
God speeds us, wheresoe'er we go.
Hohokus, Waldwick, Allendale
Lift sleepy heads to give us hail.
In Ramsey, Mahwah, Suffern stand
Houses that wistfully demand
A father—son—some human thing
That this, the midnight train, may bring.
The trains that travel in the day
They hurry folks to work or play.
The midnight train is slow and old
But of it let this thing be told,
To its high honor be it said
It carries people home to bed.
My cottage lamp shines white and clear.
God bless the train that brought me here."
(Kilmer 13-16)

When Kilmer was thirty, and a father of five, he set everything aside to support America in the Great War. He was a sergeant with the "Fighting Sixty-Ninth." A sniper's bullet killed him on July 30, 1918, at the Second Battle of the Mame. He was buried along with over 6,000 other American soldiers in the Oise-Aisne American Cemetery (Isleib).

8:30 A.M.

We are in the industrial region South of Chicago. Of this district I do not brag. I have been sitting in the rear of the observation car watching the gap widen between us. It seems an age since I left home. In that time many things have happened. My future plans are all wrecked. I don't know where I'm at and do not seem to care. As we rush thru the murky gloom of steel furnaces I see a church spire surmounted by a cross. It seems to say, 'Lest you forget'.

If God wills I will be home tonite to read your letter. Till then I will say 'au Revoir'.

Lee

The eight-page letter came to a close at 8:30 AM, half an hour outside of the City of Chicago. After seventeen hours, it was time to switch trains and embark on the final stretch home to Green Bay. Melancholy overtook his writing. The lone church spire sparked scriptural knowledge of Deuteronomy 8:19. "And it shall be, if thou do at all forget the Lord thy God, and walk after other gods, and serve them, and worship them, I testify against you this day that ye shall surely perish" (The Holy Bible 196).

Supper Time – Sunday
August 16, 1925

Dear Chloe,

The storm hangs threatening over my head. It makes me uneasy because I expected a flood of questions. Even my brother has made no "wise cracks". Neither my father nor mother has mentioned you so it's up to me to "twiddle" my thumbs and wait. My father did not move an eyelid when an aunt of mine asked the usual, "When are you going to get married?" My answer was that present prospects indicated — never.

I have just been interrupted by Gertrude's mother who came over to see me. I had been over to their house this noon but she was not in. I have made about half the rounds and told all my relatives they look thinner or fleshier as the opposite case may be. There's a question; are they lies since they hurt no one not even my conscience?

Coming home I did not stop in Chicago but delayed four hours in Milwaukee while I looked up a friend who came down to Green Bay yesterday. Towards the end of this week he (Kenneth Callahan) and I plan to drive up about a hundred miles to Washington Island and Death's Door along Lake Michigan where a legend tells us that the Norsemen who came over about the ninth century wandered down until they reached this point where they settled. If I don't find any "blonds" there I shall brand the story as false. We intend to take a good supply of cheese and crackers along and sleep under the open stars or cuss under the pouring rain as the battling Celts or fierce Belgae did in ages past.

Wisconsin is heaven at this time of the year. I don't believe I praised it enough, though you would say too much. Yesterday was the Feast of the Assumption of the Blessed Virgin. Our family made the annual pilgrimage to Robinsonville. There was a field Mass, Sermon and Procession of the Blessed Sacrament. The same statue you referred to was carried in the procession tho the money was not in evidence. The sermon delivered before this same statue was a defense of your accusation that we worship statues and images. One of his sentences is worth quoting, "Not one of you ten thousand people who will accompany this statue in procession believe you are worshiping it or attribute to it any supernatural powers and yet some writers will in the next few days refer to your action as idolatry".

I took a few pictures of the place and will bring them back with me. One picture is that of a baby whose father and mother carried it around in a clothes basket.

The wine, wiskey and beer still flows freely here. Aparently my townsmen do not realize that another people has decided "Thou shalt not". When I see that every relative and friend, ev-ery person I know in Green Bay are lawbreakers my respect for law decreases. The first day I was home I became one of them. Am this moment eligible for a penitentiary so you had better advise me to burn your correspondence before you become involved in unpleasant court notoriety. I bottled some cherry wine for my father Friday afternoon, Saturday I had five glasses (I counted them) of good beer, all from an aunt of mine. Last night I met some of the gang and refused wiskey (I think it was moon). There might be other reasons for the refusal but I thought it would please you. I'll remember and keep the promise.

Went over to see my God-children next door and for the first time they didn't start to cry upon seeing me. They are both girls (twins) about eighteen months old. About that age I manage to get along with girls. Starting tonite I am going to make a desperate attempt to fall in love with someone. I have three dates scheduled and am going to try to fan the old "flames" into a fire that would consume all my troubles.

——I sure would miss my troubles and I can't help but hope that my present attempt to drown things in a "social whirl" will fail.

I don't know whether I should send this letter by parcel post or not. You shall please answer this soon and please,

Lee

P.S. My mother said nothing about your letter arriving a few hours after I did but she evidently noticed that I expected it because I wore a hole in the rug going to look for the mail.

Levi enclosed a few clipped articles with this letter. The first offered reflections on the topic of evolution, from a well-known Catholic author at the time, Alfred McCann. William Jennings Bryan had invited McCann to Dayton, and the article was his lengthy reply as to why he would not be interested in attending.

The second article recorded a sermon by Rev. Arnold Pinchard, delivered at the Anglican church of Saint Silas the Martyr in Kentish Town, England. The topic was the Assumption of Mary. Rev. Pinchard felt that Mary's position of honor, her place in the Kingdom of God, was reasonably assured if you accepted the divinity of Christ.

The final piece was aged, tattered, and torn. It was an in-depth article on the celebration of Mary's Assumption and the history behind Robinsonville, Wisconsin, now called Champion. Taking up almost half a page, the journalist, Harold T. I. Shannon, talked about the only place in America to witness a Marian apparition.

CHAPTER 9
ROBINSONVILLE

August 15 is the Feast of the Assumption of the Blessed Virgin Mary. Every year, thousands make a pilgrimage to a little town called Champion, Wisconsin, formerly known as Robinsonville, or Aux Premiers Belgeans, and even Grez-Daems before that. It was here that Mary, Mother of Christ, appeared to Adele Brise in 1859. Adele was about twenty-six at the time, an immigrant from Belgium who came to America with her family four years earlier.

Levi and his family made the pilgrimage together in 1925 as they had every year. His father had been attending since 1889, when Sister Adele asked him to sing. This was the very person who had seen and spoken with Mary. By this time, she had joined the Third Order Franciscans, a lay group. Though she lived, dressed, and was addressed as a nun, she never took formal vows.

The *Green Bay Press-Gazette* ran a

half-page article in 1925 on Sister Adele and the shrine. This holy place was then called Our Lady of Good Help.

The journalist started the story at the beginning.

THOUSANDS WILL JOIN 60TH PILGRIMAGE TO ROBINSONVILLE SHRINE ON SATURDAY
By Harold T. I. Shannon

"Go on Mother Pauline, tell us more about Sister Adele and the Mother of God!" Innocent eyes bulged from chubby little faces and the group of cherubs gathered even closer to the kindly old woman who was regaling them, on this festival day, with the very story we wanted to hear from her. For Mother Pauline, superioress of the little convent community which sprung up on the site where Adele Brice is believed by many to have seen and heard the Mother of God, is well along life's highway, and has lived the three score years and ten which are alloted to men. She is the last to have known Adele personally and to have shared the privations of the cloister with her, and daily this saintly old person, always believing, always enjoying a holy envy of one who had seen and spoken with the Queen of the Heavens, implored the devout Adele to repeat, again and again, the story of the apparition.

Levi circled the words "Mother Pauline" on the first line and added a note for Chloe in the margin, *Mother Pauline is a cousin of Harold Londo's father.* The article continued.

Ten Families Arrived

In 1853, there arrived in the country from the commune of Grez-Doiceau province of Brabant, Belgium ten immigrant families. In their native land for more than a year they had held frequent and regular meetings in each other's homes to plan the ocean voyage and determine where in America the greatest asurance of prosperity was to be found. This question was not settled when they left Antwerp on May 18, in the three masted sailing craft "Quennebec". And the discussions continued for the 48 days spent upon the sea. Not until the little band had disembarked at New York did the persuasive language of a Wisconsin leaflet have definite effect. Without relatives or friends the Belgians continued west to Outagamie county where they made first payments upon tracts of land. A mere happenstance changed their plans entirely and located the first Belgian colony in the Kewaunee-Door peninsula.

Upon arriving at Kaukauna one of the children of the party, a favorite with all, died and the Belgians, yet practical in their religion, journeyed to Green Bay to the Catholic church of St. John the Evangelist for the burial. Here a Father Daems of Kewaunee county was visiting and met his fellow countrymen and persuaded them to forfeit their land payments in Outagamie county and settle the forlorn lands of the peninsula.

Just above, Levi circled the name, St. John the Evangelist. On the side, he added a note, *Our Parish Church.* The article continued on to the next section.

First Settlement

And thus began "Aux Premier Belges" or the first Belgian settlement. By 1854 and 1855 a steady stream of immigrants was pouring in from Belgium to Brown, Door and Kewaunee counties. Thiry Daems, La Riviere Rouge, and numerous other little communities were established.

Levi made one last mark for Chloe along the side of the article. After circling "La Riviere Rouge," Levi added a note, *my birthplace.* To the left of the four included photos, Harold Shannon's piece on Robinsonville continued.

Times were hard. Where there was not a heavy stand of timber, logged off and clear away only under the greatest difficulties, there was stone, great ledges of it making soil husbandry almost impossible. There was real suffering in the settlements. Many of the men abandoned farming and sought labor of any description that their families might keep body and soul together.

Among these settlers were the parents of Adele Brice, a simple and native country girl whose single ambition in life had been to enter the convent. When the little family joined the movement to America Adele implored her practical father to leave her behind that she might enter the cloister in her native land. But Joseph Brice, the father of four daughters and no sons, saw work for the girls to do in making the new home in the land of their adoption.

Secretly at Mieux, in Belgium, Adele and a few girl companions vowed to keep themselves unspotted by the world that when the opportunity came they might be prepared to take the veil of the sisterhood, and after her vow she sought the counsel of her pastor and confessor who told her that there were times when "obedience was greater than sacrifice."

Prayed and Waited

Here we asked the good superioress of Adele's little convent to tell us the story of the simple girl who obeyed and prayed and waited and whom thousands believed was honored by an apparition and direct conversation from the Blessed Virgin to whom she had been so devoted and through whose mediation she hoped for all things to be well.

"How often good little Sister Adele would tell me." The serene countenance of one who has given all she might win all and who is supremely confident that it will not be long before the reward for her labors will be felt, lighted as she recalled thrice happy moments in ectasy with the little sister who had spoken to the Mother of God.

"The Brices lived two miles east of Robinsonville. Adele walked ten miles to Bay Settlement to church following an old Indian trail, and almost as far to Dyckesville mill, bearing half bushels of wheat upon her head.

Feast of the Assumption

"On the 15th of August 1858, the feast of Our Lady's Assumption, Adele was on her way to church. As she passed through the woodland where the shrine now stands there appeared between two trees, one a maple and the other a hemlock which stood for years after, a blinding white light which paralyzed the poor girl with fear. She cowered before it and prayed rapidly and breathlessly as the light took definite form and between the trees stood a marvelously beautiful lady, clothed entirely in dazzling white garments, with no touch of color save a wide yellow sash or girdle. Her hair was auburn; her eyes deep and dark and she bore a radiant and kindly smile. Adele trembled with fear. The vision faded gradually away.

"The poor girl told her mother who informed her that it might have been a departed relative who wanted prayers. The following Sunday, Adele still fearful, was accompanied on the long journey to church by Mrs. Van der Niesen and Isabella Brice. As she came to the little mound between the two trees she was about to describe her apparition when suddenly she screamed and fell to her knees turning to the death pallor in her sudden fright. Again she beheld the vision, precisely as she had seen it on Assumption Day. Reaching the church she confessed to the missioner of the order of the Fathers of the Holy Cross and told of the apparitions.

Father Daems Believed

"Later the Bay Settlement pastor, Father Daems, seeing the earnestness of Adele and believing that the girl was in no wise misrepresenting what she had actually seen, counselled her to take courage and speak to the apparition if ever she saw it again and to say "In the name of God, who are you and what do you wish of me?"

"On October 9th the dear girl wandered through the woodland again with the same companions, Mrs. Vander Niessen and Isabella Brice. They saw her drop to her knees again, and they did likewise though they beheld nothing, as it was given only to Adele to hear the word of the Blessed Mother. Adele took heart and slowly repeated the words her paster had taught her. This her companions heard,

"Queen of the Heavens"

"Our Blessed Lady spoke. How well do I remember the words as Adele so many times told us. 'I am the queen of the heavens' she said in a soft and wonderful voice 'who prays for the conversion of sinners. Adele grasped every word eagerly, 'I want you to do the same' the soft voice continued. Adele's companions watched her as she stared and listened. The Blessed Virgin instructed Adele to pray for 9 days for the conversion of sinners and then withdraw from the world and labor for the souls of the settlers who were falling away from their religion in the new country and whose children were being raised without a Christian education or a knowledge of the mysteries of faith.

"Adele's companions saw that she was weeping and wanted to disturb her. Later she told of her great hurt when our Lady censured her and asked 'What are you doing, while your little companions toil in the vineyard of my son? Teach the children. If your people are not instructed they will not believe.' After a considerable pause Our Mother said softly to Adele 'Blessed are they who believe; yet do not see' and the apparition faded again away."

And Adele took the message literally, wherever she received it, and she went about from home to home, from village to village, teaching the children the elements of the faith and the simple prayers, preparing them for their first communion and exhorting their parents to return to the church lest spiritual calamity befall them. Early she was joined by others, among them the eighty year old narrator of the apparition, Mother Pauline. Together they prayed with the little ones, sang French hymns and were finally made postulants in the Third Order of St. Francis.

Came in Numbers

People came in large numbers to the "sacred spot" and to listen to Adele who had changed from a bashful country girl, unlettered and unimposing, to a fiery preacher and teacher whose perseverance and enthusiastic obedience to the voice heard only by her won her converts at every turn. For several years she met opposition from the clergy who declared her alleged apparition a myth. Adele persisted to tell of the vision, and the pilgrims to the mound between the trees increased in number. Finally repeating the fate of Saint Joan of Arc, Adele was refused the sacraments of the church and threatened with excommunication if she persisted in her stories.

But Adele's enthusiasm only increased. Mrs. Dionne, a neighbor, donated five acres of ground including the holy knoll and Joseph Brice, now reconciled to Adele's vocation built a little chapel shrine ten by twelve feet.

Adele prayed in her grief to the Blessed Lady of her vision to give external signs that the incredulous might know and believe. And the lame are said to have walked; the blind are said to have seen; and those troubled long with wasting disease have sought the help of the "Help of Christians" and claim to have been made whole at the little wayside sanctuary. Wheel chairs have been abandoned, and crutches and canes piled high in the chapel as mute testimony of alleged cures at Wisconsin's "Lourdes."

While the bishop has never officially recognized the story or the alleged miracles, yet pastoral sanction was given to the erection of the larger chapel, the convent, the orphanage and other buildings of the little community and a regular priest ministers to the village and has charge of the annual pilgrimage on August 15th.

Thousands of Pilgrims

Every year thousands of pilgrims from many states visit the shrine and participate in the devotions, tarrying too to visit the well kept grave of Sister Adele in the tiny white fenced churchyard. In 1924, despite a down pour of rain a crowd estimated at 15,000 made the pilgrimage from the open air altar in the community to the original shrine more than a mile away, and knelt in the field and lane and highway in fervent supplication.

Sister Adele died July 5, 1896. Mother Pauline was born in 1846 and will enter her eightieth year, and her sixtieth year in the nunnery this winter. Her family name is La Plant, and she is one of the eight daughters of one of the pioneer Belgian settlers.

Crowded on Aug. 15

So far as is known there has never been a year since 1864 when the first larger chapel was erected, that Robinsonville has not been crowded on Aug. 15 with pilgrims from near and from far seeking the aid of the Mother of God, whom they firmly believe appeared before the little Belgian girl and through her saved the tottering faith of the discouraged husbandmen who were concerned more with the physical necessities of existence than with the consolations of their religion. Accordingly the pilgrimage to Robinsonville on Saturday, August 15th will be the 60th journey to the place where the blinding light in the forest brought inspiration to Adele Brice and faith to her followers (12).

The *Green Bay Press-Gazette*, on August 14, 1944, focused on one man's dedication to the Mother of God. The story was fifty-five years in the making.

10   Monday Evening, August 14, 1944   THE GREEN BAY PRES:

70-Year Old Tenor Has Sung at Chapel Since '89

Ever since he was a boy of 16, as shown in the inset, 70-year-old Lewis Genesse has sung at Assumption day services in the Robinsonville chapel.

Oneida Club to Play
Host to Shorewood

OBITUARY

70-YEAR OLD TENOR HAS SUNG AT CHAPEL SINCE '89

When 70-year old Lewis J. Geniesse, 720 S. Clay street, sings at Assumption day services in the Robinsonville chapel Tuesday, he will continue a tradition he began 55 years ago as a youth of 16.

Starting to sing at the chapel, Geniesse had no idea his presence there would become a tradition broken only three times in 55 years.

He had been hauling brick for the convent at Robinsonville one summer when he met there Sister Adele Brisse, the Belgian peasant to whom the Blessed Virgin is said to have appeared Aug. 15, 1857 on the spot where the chapel now stands.

Sister Adele gave him a picture and asked him to sing at the Assumption day services, and so the following year, Aug. 15, 1889, he hitched up a horse and buggy at his home in the town of Union and came over to sing.

There was no organ, and the singers had to know their own parts without the aid of accompaniment, he recalls. However, he was used to that as he had been singing without organ assistance since he was 12 years old in St. Francois church, Marchand, now known as Duval. By the time he was 14 he could sing the Gregorian proper of the mass.

Hired Horse and Buggy

In 1901 he moved to Green Bay and for the next 14 years hired a horse and buggy to make the annual pilgrimage with his family.

"You had to reserve a horse and buggy at the livery stable a month in advance of the Assumption or else not get one," Mr. Geniesse recalls, "because so many wanted to go."

Several times he didn't make the reservations soon enough and got to Robinsonville only by getting a farm horse from one family and a buggy from another so he could make the trip.

"Not one third as many worshippers visited the Shrine in those early days," according to Mr. Geniesse, who said the pilgrimage was an all-day, family affair.

Many people from the Bohemian settlement in Kewaunee county used to walk to the shrine, he remembers. They started the night before with a basket of food and rested along the roadside during the night when they became too tired to walk further.

Even with their horse and buggy the Geniesse family had to start out at 4 o'clock in the morning to reach Robinsonville on time. However, in about 1915 the family had the thrill of owning a model-T Ford and the succession of cars that has followed it solved their transportation problems.

Recalls Associates

Most of those with whom Mr. Geniesse began singing are now dead and many of the names have slipped from his memory. However, two of those who used to sing with him are the late Judes Defnet, town of Lincoln and the late Gus Lefebvre, of St. Sauver.

Circumstances beyond his control prevented his singing the only three times he missed in 55 years. In 1910 he was sick in the hospital, another year Bishop Paul P. Rhode discouraged the observance because undue commercialism, since abolished, had crept in, and in 1938 he was

in Richmond, Va., where his daughter-in-law, Mrs. Levi Geniesse, was ill.

He has completed all arrangements for the 1944 pilgrimage and will take a carload of the St. Cecelia Singers, with whome he sings tenor, to Robinsonville Tuesday when the group will commemorate the Assumption of the Blessed Virgin by singing for the procession and 10 o'clock high mass (10).

In both articles, the journalists were careful to respect that the Catholic church had not authenticated the apparitions in Robinsonville. The 1925 article specified that "Adele Brice is believed by many to have seen and heard the Mother of God" (12). Near the end of that report, Shannon told of the clergy's opposition to the acceptance of the miracle and the lengths they went to quell the enthusiasm of Sister Adele.

At the first mention of Sister Adele in the 1944 article, she was defined as being "the Belgian peasant to whom the Blessed Virgin is said to have appeared" (10). There are requirements to be met in order for the church to stand behind something as significant as a Marian Apparition.

In 2009, the Bishop of the Diocese of Green Bay, Reverend David L. Ricken, opened an investigation to review 150 years of historical documents about the Virgin Mary's appearance to Adele Brise. An important time in history involved the Peshtigo fire of 1871.

Over one million acres burned. The dead were impossible to count. Estimates varied between 1,200 and 2,400 people. This was the worst fire in American history.

Sister Adele was at her chapel. Many joined her seeking refuge and the protection of the Virgin Mary. They prayed, lifted a statue of Mary, and processed around the sanctuary, singing hymns that honored both Mary and Jesus. Morning finally came. Father Peter Pernin, one of the few survivors in Peshtigo, described it best.

"After hours of horror and suspense, the heavens sent relief in the form of a downpour. The fervent prayers to the Mother of God were heard. The fire was extinguished, but dawn revealed the ravages wrought by the conflagration. Everything about them was destroyed; miles of desolation everywhere. But the convent, school, and chapel on the holy land consecrated to the Virgin Mary shone like an emerald isle in a sea of ashes. The raging fire licked the outside palings and left charred scars as mementos. Tongues of fire had reached the chapel fence and threatened destruction to all within its confines; the fire had not entered the Chapel grounds."

Many miracles have occurred at the place now known as Champion.

The final decree, authenticating the 1859 apparitions, was signed in 2010. Sister Adele's Marian apparitions were found worthy of belief, though not required. Today, this holy place has grown and greets pilgrims under the new title, National Shrine of Our Lady of Champion.

Levi captured a few moments during the procession. They still carry a statue of Mary, meant as a way to honor her and to recall her intercession, and to help all remember her request to teach the children and show them the way to Christ.

CHAPTER 10
DEATH'S DOOR
AND MORE

McKenney, Virginia
c/o Mrs. W. J. Sturt
August 19, 1925

Dear Lee,

Your letter came Monday afternoon. — I wonder whether mine arrived in Green Bay before you. — I thought that it was mailed in time.

You asked about my "hay fever". It's gone — I'm glad to say. I think it was a false alarm.

I'm spending a couple of weeks in McKenney with one of my 'kid cousins' — (she's fifteen). Her father is my beloved Uncle Watson who is now in Florida.

I haven't been doing anything exciting — going down town late in the afternoon for the mail — etc. Talking to some of my old friends who seem but acquaintances now as I haven't seen them in so long.

We've had revival services at our church for the past week and we've been attending regularly of course. — I've started reading the life of John Calvin – you're the cause of this. Now I'll blame something on you.

Lee, you make me feel terrible when you say your plans are all wrecked and you don't know where you are and don't care. Please don't blame this on me. Go on with your former plans and forget all about your ideas of changing them. You'll make me wish I'd never known you if you keep on saying such terrible things. I think I'd better end this lecture as Sabra (my cousin) talks to me now and then and I can't think clearly.

I've written this letter in installments too, but just didn't date it. Since I started I've had several interruptions, – stopped to eat some watermelon – an old school friend with her four children dropped in and I had to talk to her – then dinner was served and Sabra and I are now in our room for our afternoon siesta. Lazy? This is vacation time still, you know.

I can't write about the agricultural and mineral resources of our section of Virginia but you know the saying – "with all her faults I love her still". I think I've quoted this correctly – I've had another interruption – someone came in and asked me what I was doing.

'So long', Chloe

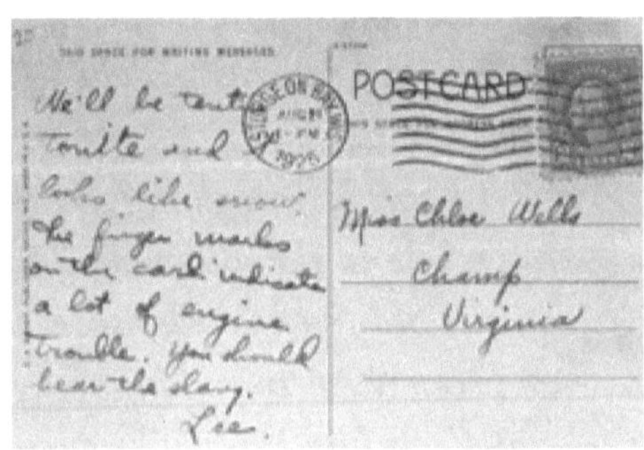

The postmark reads, "Sturgeon Bay, WIS – Aug 21, 1925, 1 PM

We'll be tentin' tonite and it looks like snow. The finger marks on the card indicate a lot of engine trouble. You should hear the slang.

Lee

While in Champ, Chloe received a letter from her roommate, Virginia Weirich.

Saturday
August 22, 1925

Chloe honey:

Are you angry cause I'm so lazy that without a thing to do I haven't written? Well I thought I'd surely write just as soon as I got your letter but as usual I put it off. Of course you know how crazy I am about baseball ----- when the team is in Washington I spend most of my spare time at the ball park and when they are out of town like friend Grace I spend my time parked by a radio, So now you know what I've been doing. Every afternoon this week I've been over at Theresa's listening to the ball reports. But I've made good use of the time for I've almost finished my luncheon set. I am putting on the edge now and will finish it the first part of the week as soon as I get some more floss but as I am broke if Warren doesn't get the floss for me I can't finish it. I have also finished the two small pieces to the linen buffet set that I showed you. Warren says he is real proud of me now isn't that nice?

I can't tell you how much I enjoyed your little visit and how much I would have liked having you longer. How is Lucinda and has the new arrival arrived yet? Has Emma Ruth found that time she was wondering whether she could ever find in which to think over all the things she saw this summer? I am so sorry that she was suffering so but I am mean enough to still be glad that she didn't know how far she had to come to get out here for she said that had she known it she wouldn't have come out and I did so want to meet her and of course no one could help but like her so very much.

My dear do you realize how close to school it is now and that I haven't even begun to start to Florida. I thought that I would surely start this week but Dad is selling some property in New Jersey and of all the legal red tape we have had to go through with. And until he gets that straightened up and gets in his money from that I won't go for my money has been gone this long while. Perhaps I'll really start this next week but even that is unsettled. Anyway write to me as soon as you get this so I will be sure to hear from you and I will write the day I start or the day before to let you know when and where I'll be in Florida. But if Dad doesn't get this settled until a few days before school starts I am thinking of starting teaching for the last of Sept. and then resign outright instead of asking for leave as I have planned doing. In that way I will get my Sept. check and also the money that was taken off last year that would give me a little to go on until I find something to do in Florida. I feel that it is sort of mean to work just for that Sept. check but I was told last year that a great many teachers do it and if I need the money I will too. And even though I would not be carried on the school roll here after resigning I am sure I could get back if I should ever have to and of course I could go on as a substitute until they called for me.

Last week Warren and I and my little kid cousin Ann K (Martha's little flapper sister) went out to the lake. While we were there a terrible storm came up. All the lights went out and it was pitch black. Warren was dancing with Ann K. and I was standing at one end of the pavilion waiting for them when all of a sudden out went the lights. Well they were at one end of the dance floor and talk about get to me quick. Warren was with me before I had a chance to realize what had happened. Honestly it was so dark that one couldn't see his own hand before him except when there was a flash of lightening. Warren said he knew I would be scared to death so he grabbed Anna by one hand and started running. They could tell where to go when ever there would be a flash of lightening. They would run while the floor was lighted then stop until the next flash. Warren said that he could see me standing there when ever there was a bit of lightening so he would head for me. But he sure got there in a hurry. The storm lasted for almost an hour but the orchestra played to keep down any excitement on the part of the people and every one danced or stood around in groups and talked or watched some fancy dancer show off. It really was lots of fun after the scare died down and of all the music ---- they played every thing from The Old Gray Mare Ain't What She Used to Be to Ain't We Got Fun. But as soon as the storm died down enough we headed for home. But thinking it over I don't think I have ever had such a good time at the Lake.

Has it been cold down there? It was dreadfully warm until Wednesday or Thursday then it started raining and has turned very cool. Last night I had a blanket and my winter coat on my bed and when I woke up this morning my legs ached as I was so cold so I got up put on my stockings and put on another coat (on the bed of course) and crawled in to try and get warm again. Dad is sick with a terrible cold and we had to put him to bed right after supper last night and doctor him up. But he won't take care of himself for he got up and started out selling real estate again this morning despite all our efforts to keep him in bed.

Really Chloe I am not a letter writer and you are the only person I have ever written such a long long letter to but it seems when I start talking to you I never known when to stop which I now see accounted for our wee hour sessions at the Hotels and also hindered our Saturday morning duties while at the apartment for as you know we would sit down and jabber in every room we started in to clean. I am going to start no I mean stop this just as soon as I deliver a few messages.

My folks all send love of course. Marion just got back from a trip to Canada and up where you spent some of your vacation and also the Falls and she stopped by here last night and I have instructions to send you her love.

Have you been writing to Muriel or did you call her up? For if you did this is old news but I have heard that no news is old news so I'll tell you anyway. Well Muriel has her hair bobbed. I saw Gertrude Lloyd --- Louis the fourteenth --- on the street car and she told me that Muriel bobbed it just before she went home. Aren't you glad? Also Tom and Doris are married and are spending their honeymoon and vacation at his home in Indianna. Darn I don't know how to spell that state but you know where his original home was so you know where I mean. I haven't called Gertrude or Ruth up yet isn't that mean? Guess I'll do it tomorrow sometime.

By by darlin' really I am going to stop. Please time yourself and let me know how long it took you to read this as I do believe it is a marathon letter don't you?

Lots of love, Virginia

PS. Regards to all and answer this at once even if it is only a card as I may be gone if you wait too long. Glad you and Lee fixed things on a friendly basis but can you keep it that way this winter if he comes back instead of going to Europe? Wouldn't you like to be present to hear the sessions he has with his folks? Of course I mean invisible listeners.

Darlin' please excuse mistakes and the fact that this is typed but such a long letter I couldn't never possibly write by hand or I'd get writer's cramps?

– Virginia

Virginia and Warren did marry on Thanksgiving Day in 1926, Chloe's twenty-sixth birthday. She was Virginia's only attendant. Virginia's parents did not come up from Florida to attend the nuptials at Foundry Methodist on 16th Street SW.

Chloe and Levi had "fixed things on a friendly basis," as Virginia put it in her letter. Of course, that information came straight from Chloe.

With Levi in Wisconsin and Chloe back home in Virginia, the letters between friends continued.

The Old Home Town
Monday Morning
August 24, 1925

Dear Chloe,

I'm going to be as cheerful as I can in this letter but with hayfever and a sunburned nose the odds are against it. One hates to be blamed for something of which he is innocent and it has been insinuated that my "nose blossom" does not look like sunburn.

Our camping trip up to Death's Door was a success; that is all except the cooking. I was cook at first and all things went well but for some unknown reason the other two members of the party decided to learn how and then I had cause to return their compliments.

Can you imagine a tiny camp fire along a rocky shore with four miles of pine woods to the nearest farm house; a mile of water stretching across to an island where it is believed the Norsemen had a settlement; a mile of water in which drowned hundreds of Indians who started to cross in canoes to give battle to a tribe on the mainland. There we could see the warning flash of red from a lighthouse which was accompanied by the tolling of a buoy. The lake steamers would feel their way thru a narrow passage their many lights the while viering with the sparkling stars of a clear northern sky. —— In this setting I argued for five hours with a friend who now is an Agnostic and thinks that Atheism is reasonable. He was a Congregationalist, (and still calls himself that) before spending four years at the U of Wisconsin and now he is —— well he's a big job for me. I had thought that possibly I misjudged our Northern Protestants in believing they were different from the hard-shelled Baptists of the South but I still believe there is a big difference which no one would notice more than you. As some one said they are a jump ahead in the "protesting" game.

Chloe, I'm sorry I spoke of "wrecked plans". I'm sorry I said anything that hurts you. I can never be sorry I met you and I hope that I shall never give cause that you would be sorry you knew me.

I still have a week at home to lose myself in a social whirl. I hope it doesn't turn out to be a whirlpool. I'm glad that you are reading the life of Calvin. Sometime I will tell you why. — My 'Ma' suggests that it's time to set the table. — Oh you ought to see me clean house. She says that the girl that gets me will be lucky but I can't convince the girl o' that.

Sincerely, Lee

P.S. — "The Mad Pursuit" is a study symbolizing man's desperate chase to pin down the affections of the flitting butterfly. The empty net is significant.

Eighty-seven miles separate Green Bay, Wisconsin from Death's Door. The three-man camping party consisted of Levi Geniesse, Kenneth "Cal" Callahan, and Leland Brown.

How all three and their camping gear fit into Cal's flivver is a mystery. With all three perched on the running board, the car looks big enough, but the next photo of Cal and his pal offers a different perspective.

Cal's vehicle was a 1917 Ford Model T Runabout, a two-seater. It could reach a maximum speed of 40-45 mph, though steering control was compromised. The maximum speed limit in the 1920s was 25 mph, keeping the driver well within a manageable speed.

There was one upholstered bench seat in the front, perched right over the gas tank. This provided enough space for the driver and one passenger. Both had to enter from the passenger side, since the driver's door was for looks only.

Levi captioned the photo on the left, *Cal and his Flivver*, a term not reserved for the Model T. A flivver was any car that seemed cheap or was in bad condition.

The trio met their challenges head-on and reached the planned destination. They camped near the shoreline at Death's Door, a shallow, rock-laden, traversable waterway, where Green Bay first joins Lake Michigan.

This is Door County, the peninsula known as the "thumb of Wisconsin." Several islands dot the end as seen in the photo below. The largest, Washington Island, is visible in the distance. A small island between Washington Island and the mainland is known as Plum and the waterway shown below is Death's Door, a ship graveyard.

Chloe continued her visit with family in McKenney, Virginia, while Levi's days in Green Bay dwindled. On a small folded page, with one silvery rough edge to the right of the fold, Chloe wrote above the heading, *Isn't this typical "country store" stationery?*

McKenney, Virginia
c/o Mrs. W. J. Sturt
August 25, 1925

Dear Lee,
Has the storm 'raged in all its fury'? Maybe you'll be
surprised — sometimes the 'unexpected happens' you know.
Advice is still being given freely to me. — enough to spare you
some.

My sister brought your letter to church with her Wednes-day night – It was so heavy my curiosity tempted me to read it during services – I resisted – but read it by an automobile light as soon as church was over.

You were home just in time for a special service in your church and I was home just in time for one in mine – 'the stone wall' between us is more forcibly in evidence. Isn't it?

I've finished reading the Life of John Cavin – it was dry and formal literature – but full of information. I'll have to read your book on the Reformation next.

Did you enjoy your trip along Lake Michigan? If it was as cold there as it was here Sun. night you'd have wished for extra blankets.

Wisconsin isn't alone in its boot legging. There is a plenty of it in McKenney. This doesn't decrease my respect for law – but makes me realize the need of law abiding citizens or our Constitution will be undermined. I'm glad you are remembering your promise – it's for your good – I'll always be interested in your welfare. I even home your 'social whirl' drowns all your troubles. Don't you think I'm generous?

The neighbors who 'run in' are very "gossipy" – all the while I've been writing this letter one has been downstairs loudly pouring maledictions on her landlord's head – as I know both parties I can't help being interested although I shut the door in order to dim the noise. If this letter seems disconnected

Please forgive, Chloe

As another month comes to a close, Levi finds himself in Chicago, mailing a postcard of his church back home. Chloe just left McKenney, so they will have to forward this one to Champ, Virginia.

The postmark on the following card reads, "Chicago, ILL. – Aug. 31, 1925, 5 PM"

The vacation ends tonite and Thursday will find me back at 1728 Eye N.W. I'm going to make the rounds of all my relatives now.

Lee

Champ, Virginia
September 1, 1925

Dear Lee,

Your last letter did not say exactly when you'd leave for Washington, but I concluded from it that your vacation ended Sept. 1.

I am home for a few days – Mama wasn't well so I came to help Emma Ruth care for the house and the children – I again have an opportunity to improve my 'culinary art' – Don't you hope the improvement can be noticed?

Your description of Death's Door was very vivid – It must be almost as pretty as some places in Virginia – I can imagine what you're thinking when you read this.

I finished your book on the Reformation – – Some of the references to John Calvin were similar to those given in the book on his life.

You have constant difficulty with your Protestant friends, don't you? Do you regard me as the 'hard-shelled Baptist, and your Congregationalist as the agnostic? You can't decide which is worse can you? As I've told you before

I think it is lamentable that our university products care so little for religion. Are there any Catholics who care so little? (I'm asking for information)

I had a letter from Ruth last night. She is expecting me to live with them this winter – even if we move into another apartment – Mrs. Tucker has been pestering them too much so she wrote.

Virginia hadn't gone to Florida last week but still expects to go any time. Her father is interested in his work with a real estate company in Washington and doesn't know when he'll go. I believe Virginia will be teaching in Washington, D.C. again this winter.

The picture you sent is very good. Where did you get the symbolical idea? So the engineer is a naturalist too – I'm learning something new about you each time you write.

I hope your hay fever and sun burn do you no more harm than mine did me –

Sincerely, Chloe

The last letter from Levi's vacation was mailed from Washington, D.C., on September 3, 1925. The envelope was from the *Pennsylvania Railroad System, Washington Broadway Limited.*

Somewhere in Ohio
September 3, 1925
5:30 P.M.

Dear Chloe,

Am in much the same mood as when I first left home for college. The difference is that in the last three weeks I have acquired the philosophy of the old men, "who sit by the fireside and wait". They wonder what is in store for them but the experience of years has taught them to be patient. It is easier to be patient when one has an eternity than when the problem has to be solved in a third of a lifetime.

The storm broke at last. Not the thunder and lightening of the hurricane but the slow steady rain that soaks to the skin.

My father said nothing. He just made me feel that he had confidence I would use my head. My mother's advice came while we were 'doing the dishes'. There was nothing new; your mother's talk would probably be identical, and get it "sunk in".

The "whirl" accomplished nothing but made me spend several weeks in 'nothing flat'.

We had a Notre Dame banquet (In Green Bay) last Saturday night and it seemed good to see some of the old gang again. In Joliet and Aurora I met a couple of fellows and girls with whom I had made the 'Prom' and 'Ball'. Was taken to one of Joliet's hidden dives where the pass-word must be given to get in. The 'doped' beer held no thrills for me and I was disappointed.

The friend whom I told you was tangled in the net of "love" has had a quarrel and is now trying to forget every-thing in the work of organizing a shingle manufacturing concern (no it has nothing to do with bobbed hair). I spent a day giving him advice and he said that if I stayed around another day he would be discouraged enough to sell out.

Guess I'll excuse myself and go and eat.

(In bed)
In Maryland
7 A.M. – Sept. 3, 1925

Good morning Chloe,

I am in fine spirits because I slept a little last night. It is the first time and I am encouraged. I sat looking out of my window for an hour this morning because I wanted to see Horshoe Curve. My watch was set for Central time and the schedule was Eastern time so I missed it. We learn by experience but missing a fast train in the morning (yesterday) because of daylight saving time is — or was 'cussed' experience.

I will be back on the job this noon and since Van stayed at the rooming house I remain there until —— (I know your mother —— and you? —— will be glad to hear this) I leave for France in October.

Guess I'll get up, Sincerely, Lee

CHAPTER 11
WHICH IS STRONGER, DISTANCE OR PARENTS?

1728 Eye St. N.W.
Saturday Evening
Sept. 5, 1925

Dear Chloe,

Your letter beat me here by half an hour and it was just like having someone welcome me at the door. I found myself glad to be back to Washington and can't account for it. When you compare it with Chicago it isn't a half bad place.

Wisconsins scenery is beautiful now which along with its good roads draws thousand of tourists there. I kept wishing you were along on several drives we took because then you could hardly keep from admitting that Virginia is not much nicer.

You have finished reading about the Reformation and now I hope you will read the "Faith of Our Fathers" so that I can ask you a bunch of examination questions. In reading this book it would be well to remember that the "Faith" which Cardinal Gibbons explains is the 'Faith' your fathers and mine believed.

You ask whether there are Catholics who care so little for religion. I do not like to answer this here. It requires a look of explanation but since you want an answer — they are many.

If all Catholics obeyed the teachings of the church they would by their good example have converted all peoples long ago. You do not find Catholics educated in Catholic schools with the philosophy — There is no God, there is no distinction between good and evil, the Bible is a fable, It's contrary to science, etc. Protestants have come to expect this of their university graduates; not that it should but it does. Half truths are dangerous — a little knowledge is a "dangerous thing" are words the truth of which is no more apparent than here.

There are Catholics who lead evil lives planning on death bed confessions. There are those who call themselves Catholics but who by their actions have been automatically excommunicated from the church. There are those who believe that God is too merciful to punish forgetting that God is also just. There are those whose attitude is, "We are saved; we should worry about others". I could go on all night like this but suffice it to say a real bad Catholic is the worst person there is, a very good one is a Saint.

Please send me your interpretations of the enclosed Biblical passage. Also I want to warn you that you will be expected to make that birthday cake I have coming. — Don't dare use two sheets of Van's paper so

— This is from, Lee

The enclosed Biblical passage that Levi referenced was clipped from *The Washington Herald.* The banner across the top of the editorial page, September 4, 1925, was from the pastor of Saint Patrick, Levi's church in Washington, D.C., "You shall receive the power of the Holy Ghost coming upon you, and you shall be witnesses of me in Jerusalem, and in all Judea and Samaria, and even to the uttermost part of the earth. Acts 1:8" (18).

An article from *Our Sunday Visitor*, a weekly Catholic newspaper out of Huntington, Indiana, was enclosed with this letter. Chloe's letter opener caught the fold and neatly tore the article into pieces. They were large enough to piece together and read a Catholic perspective on a Protestant topic.

A PROTESTANT "OECUMENICAL COUNCIL"

Catholic people would be the last people to discourage a real, conscientious, attempt to restore unity to Christendom. Indeed, their prayers, that Almighty God may speedily bring about the great desideratum, constantly ascend and especially during the Church Unity Octave of each year.

At the same time they recognize that Our Lord prayed, not only that His disciples might be united in Charity, but also in the Truth. The Christian Truth, upon which God may accept the union of Christians, cannot possibly be less than the whole deposit of Faith which was committed by the apostles of Christ to the Church of Christ, indwelt by the Holy Ghost. The Church is "the pillar and group of Truth." She is Christ's appointed custodian and interpreter of the Christian Truth.

Our separated brethren, in their desire for unity, seem to place all the emphasis on Charity. The Fundamentalists, who keep aloof from the "World Conference on Faith and Order," which is composed of the representatives of sixteen or more Protestant bodies, seem to emphasize Faith to the detriment of Charity. Over and over the Supreme Pontiffs of the Church have insisted that the true center of Christendom, which was forsaken at the Reformation, is the cathedra of both faith and charity.

Would that the promoters of the coming "Oecumenical Conference" of Protestants at Stockholm could see themselves in the light of that supernaturally unique Revelation and Foundation of God which calls them to the unity of all souls. They are groping, some of them. Others, inspired by a jealousy of the Catholic Church, and in anticipation of result which might come to pass during this Jubilee Year, seek to divert the attention of the multitudes from the way out of the maze in which Protestantism finds itself.

The projected Conference will discuss questions of dogma, strange to relate. It promises to be more than "sweetness and light." In looking over the pamphlet issued by the Conference, we notice a series of questions, number five of which is concerned with the Sacraments. This, in turn, is divided into two parts, the first devoted to questionings concerning "the two rites which all Christians call Sacraments," and the second to the "rites which many, but not all, Christians call Sacraments."

May we suggest that their efforts might really reach the mark, if, instead of looking for a "comprehensive catholicism" upon a least-common-denominator, they would look to the historical rock from which they were hewn and the pit from which they were dug! They are too ready to take the Reformation for granted. Their purpose seems to be to even further reduce the dogmatical fragments in size and substance. Instead of this, why do they not try to piece them together and find out what sort of a picture the whole will make? They have misplaced their emphasis. They should, instead of seeking for the least possible doctrinal residue, scent out the whole of which they possess fragments.

The Lutherans emphasize justification by faith – that is one fragment of the whole. The Calvinists emphasize the sovereignty of God – that is another fragment. The Methodists emphasize the warm love of God for the sinner, His ever-readiness to receive the prodigal – that is another.

The Episcopalians believe in an ordained ministry – that is another. The Finnish Apostolics practice confession and absolution – that is another. Protestant denominations emphasize good works more and more – that is another fragment. What part one Protestant denomination does not have, of the original Catholicism of our fathers, some other Protestant denomination has retained, nominally if not in substance. Seek out the whole! That is the real "comprehensive Catholicism" which Christendom needs.

The "World Conference" proposes to discuss this question: "Should the united Church insist that all persons must be baptized before they can become members of the Church of God?" The "Friends" are especially interested in eliciting a negative answer on this point. The scheme seems rather audacious to a Catholic, who believes that the Savior meant what he said when he stated: "Except anyone be born of water and of the Holy Ghost, he cannot enter into the kingdom of God." The "Conference" seems to be undecided about a great many other matters, which, up until now, Christians in general have regarded as essential to the retention of any Christianity at all (2).

Champ, Virginia
September 9, 1925

Dear Lee,

After reading your letter of Sept. 3, I was undecided as to whether it was best to write again. I thought maybe you'd feel better. Since your other letter came I think maybe it is all right for me to write.

I don't understand what you mean when in one letter you say you leave for Europe in October and in another you write that you are expecting me to bake your birthday cake. Do you have more than one birthday per year? – or how do you explain this?

I went to Petersburg yesterday and did some shopping — chiefly for Emma Ruth — and we are busy sewing this week. I am going to the dentist next week — ugh!

Mama went to see another doctor about her arm and shoulder. He advised an x-ray — so that ordeal was gone through — of course we do not know the results as yet — she has to go again the first of next week.

School starts out here to-morrow — It seems strange that no one from here will go (we are all grown up now). Emma Ruth goes to H.T.C. [Harrisonburg Teacher's College] on Sept. 21 and I leave for Washington Friday, Sept. 18 — I surely hope it will not be as warm then as it is now — the schoolroom will not be enticing if it is.

If you were around here sometimes when all three of Lucinda's children are crying — maybe you'd think that you were listening to a symphony orchestra. I told her that you'd call it music.

Just, Chloe

The date was set. Chloe would return to the city to prepare for the new school year on September 21. Levi was set to leave for Europe in October, but the exact day had not been finalized. As far as the birthday cake was concerned, Levi's birthday occurred on June 16, three days before Chloe left for the summer.

Thursday Night
September 10, 1925

Dear Chloe,

Of all the foolish things that have ever been done, yours, of making me feel better by not writing ranks on top. Van's remark about explains it, "You cuss all week because you didn't get a letter and now you cuss when you read it." —— You have a bawling out coming.

That remark about a birthday cake must have been a typographical error. I have but one birthday a year (strange).

It's past but the hope of getting a cake isn't. Do I have to take it to the courts?

Speaking o' courts reminds me that we still have to play some tennis. Also bring back your hiking shoes because I still must see what your temper is like at the end of a twenty mile hike. You might include your dancing shoes and roller skates.

Van and I went canoeing the other night. Had another swell meal of cheese and crackers with bologna for dessert.

It takes men to really prepare a good meal. — Played tennis against a couple strangers last night. They didn't beat us much. Haven't seen Ruth since you were here. Met Grace on the street and she almost nodded. Went up to see Gertrude when I returned. She seems to be right busy socially.

You mention children crying. You should be around when my cousin's babies see me. Two little girls and they both cry. Of course when they develop a sense of humor it will be different.

Your sister goes away to school, my brother returns to N.D. for his last try at a football letter and a sheepskin. You return to your school and I am planning on listening in at the University of Toulouse. – Life is one big school and in the past six months it has taught me much.

You are coming Friday. If you tell me when I will probably "inspect a building about that time."

And believing in the early bird saying — May I see you Sunday?

Lee

Champ, Virginia
September 16, 1925

Dear Lee,

So you have a bawling out for me. Wait until you hear my side first – I'll not try to explain in a letter – it won't be long until Friday. If you want to 'inspect a building' about nine o'clock Friday evening, you have my permission. If I'm able to take the through train that leaves here at three thirty I'll arrive about quarter of nine – if I have to take the local I'll change trains in Richmond and will not get in Washington until twelve o'clock. I surely hope I can take the three thirty train.

I went to Petersburg yesterday to do some more shopping for Emma Ruth and also to have some dental work done. I had only one cavity so it wasn't so bad. Next week this time I'll be at work – (my work) – I've been working the past two weeks.

I think I'm ready to say that I'll never marry a farmer. Maybe what my father said when I made this remark in his hearing will prove true.

Yes, "early bird" – you may see me Sunday night.

Sincerely, Chloe

With that, the letters stopped. Chloe returned to teaching, and Levi prepared to depart for Europe. They were both in Washington, so there was no cause for sending letters. The only letter that marked this time period was sent from the Government of the District of Columbia, Engineer Department. Mr. John W. Oehmann, Inspector of Buildings. He announced on October 15, 1925:

> *To Whom It May Concern:*
>
> *Mr. Levi A. Geniesse employed in the Engineering section of the Building Division as Civil Engineer and Computer since January 1925, is hereby recommended as thoroughly capable, energetic, and industrious in building construction and design.*
>
> *Mr. Geniesse is leaving this division to pursue studies in church architecture in Europe.*

With the beginning of a new school year keeping her busy, Chloe made some time for friendship; their "situationship" had finally been defined.

October 12, 1925
Monday 2 P.M.

Dear Levi,

 As I expect this is the last letter I am writing you for a while it makes me feel quite blue. Your socks did not come till today near noon. I hurried to wash them and as we had sunshine today they were dry after dinner. I hurried to mend them so Pa could take them back to mail them but he said you were liable not to get them in time and he wants to give them to Engels. I will leave a couple pairs out that are not worth mending. I did not know what union suits you meant so I sent the ones you wore last winter. I thought you would not have room in your grip for the real heavy ones. The trench mirror we did not find. Pa sent your overcoat and stuff this morning. Well my cold sent me to bed Friday and Saturday but I am feeling all right now and hope I keep able to go so that I can walk and work off my loneliness. It was awful those two days in bed with nothing to occupy my mind but the thought of your going. But Levi I know it is your wish and pleasure to go so I will forget myself and think only that it is for the best and do not starve yourself when you are over there for you know without health you can't enjoy anything and I hope you won't bring home a french girl for a wife. It would be too expensive for her to visit her people.

 Well Levi I had intended starting a novena of mass and communion last week but I think I will start tomorrow to ask God to take you safe across wherever you go. Levi my prayers will always be interceeding for your welfare and should we not meet again in life let us live in hopes of meeting in heaven. I must stop writing now so Pa can mail this so goodbye dearest son. May God bless and protect you and bring you home safe some day where a mother's love will always await you.

Mother

With an October 12 letter from Mom in hand, job resignation completed, bags packed, and a friendship secured with Chloe, Levi set out for New York City. The question remaining in Washington, D.C. was whether even a friendship could survive this trip. Which fighting force would win out, distance or parents?

An envelope arrived at 229 B Street N.E., Chloe's place near the Capitol. "Manger Hotels" was printed on the left third. "Hotel York: Absolutely Fireproof, Seventh Ave. Corner of 36th Street, one short block away from Broadway." It was postmarked October 19, 6:30 P.M. Levi was one block off Broadway, a place Chloe had wished to enjoy during her recent trip to New York.

The City of Noses
Monday Afternoon
October 19, 1925

Dear Chloe,

This is my first breathing spell since Londo met me. We have been trying to see all we can in nothing flat and I'm fairly 'dizzy' by now. [what's that remark?]

Friday's big events were: a visit to the Biltmore Country Club. My brother did not accompany the team and another fellow from the home town says he is thru football. At night we visited the Hippodrome Theatre but was disappointed in the show.

Saturday a "rubber neck" bus trip up 5th Ave. then a subway ride to the Yankee Stadium. The rushing smashing crowd trying to squeeze into the cars impressed me more than anything else. When I reached open air again after standing partly on my own and someone else's feet jammed against a mass of sweltering, sweaty, humanity while our train hurled itself thru the darkness I could not help but remark about our wonderful twentieth century. So terrific is our pace to get somewhere that we forget where.

[My new life's work, the decentralization of our

countries population. Laugh; just one more bug bit me.]

Of course you have not read that the Army beat N.D. 27-0. They were a much better team and deserved to win. The game was played before a crowd of 70,000 people which is the most I have ever seen assembled in one spot.

Saw Louis XIV, Saturday night and was disappointed again. Most big shows seem to have nothing but a name to justify their existence.

Sunday we went to mass at St. Patrick's. It is a wonderful church and is the most beautiful I have seen. How many times I will repeat the last sentence in the next few months I do not know but I hope it will be many.

The afternoon at the Metropolitan Museum and the evening at a movie. This morning a trip to the Woolworth Tower, a tour of Wall Street and the Stock Exchange, a boat ride to the Statue of Liberty where we studied New York's sky line.

I have seen it all so often in movies that nothing seems to impress me. – New York is a more beautiful city than Chicago but the industrial plants around Chicago would stun one by their "hellishness".

Am expecting Connell sometime this afternoon. Till then I am unsure as to our sailing time.

I wished I could send you an address. Till then I shall write the thought that a record of my wanderings is of interest.

Sincerely, Lee

P.S. – We have an agreement to tip our hats to every stub nosed girl we meet here. So far there has been no danger of catching cold.

P.S. – again – After a Hungarian dinner Sunday I decided that ham and cloves was not half bad. Will probably say that again.

Wednesday Night
October 21, 1925

Dear Chloe,

Haven't been sent over to Ellis Island yet for overstaying my leave in New York. We've made a thorough study of "Palestine" as the boys insist on calling it and here is the unanamous verdict. Chicago is more impressive, noisy, dirty. It has more traffic, murders than New York; all of which I claim favors New York. However the Irish policemen of this place are much less courteous than their brothers in Chi. and it hurts me to admit this but in a choice between Chicago and New York I wouldn't, I'd take Washington with its rowhouses and Government Hotels.

Spent Monday morning at the Cathedral of St. John the Divine. It is and will be beautiful and I was delighted and plunged into gloom at the same time. Sad because the building is not Catholic. It is up to us to make a more beautiful offering to God but I hope our work will never be inspired with the idea of simply producing a more beautiful building than our Protestant brothers. To merely enter a building competition with other religious

sects and forgetting the all important reason for building them would be a catastrophe both to you and us.

Connell's remark after talking with me was, "that girl has made you serious minded. Something will have to be done." I assured him that he would just have to put up with my seriousness because nothing could be done.

How are your new roommates? I suppose you are boss now. Don't forget Virginia's fate.

If you see Clay around tell him to concentrate on his work and forget about girls. Like my brother he always follows my advice.

We are sailing Saturday on the Leviathan. Landing at Cherbourg we shall probably spend a few days in Paris before heading South. — I will have my mail forwarded to the American Express in Paris. Give my best wishes to Grace and Ruth — and I had almost forgotten Mrs. Tucker. I expect a letter in Paris.

Don't disappoint, Lee

Friday Night
October 23, 1925

Dear Chloe,

I just have to get rid of all the clippings and besides look at the swell picture fresh from Metropolitan Art gallery. The original title "Who's Sorry Now" was removed accidentally so I'm calling it, "Auntie Chloe Goes A-picnicing".

The scraps of paper are mere packing but may be read in your spare moments. I can here you say how busy you are and that's as good an excuse as following fire departments any day.

I heard a foreigner, a Swede, sing "Carry Me Back to Old Virginia" last night so if they play the Washington and Lee swing in Spain I'll not be surprised.

There is an interesting article in the November – Forum called "The Disruption of Protestantism". It sounds a lot like my ravings. That's a good reason for avoiding it I suppose.

My next will be from La Belle France and there I'll try to write a real letter.

Till then, Levi

c/o American Express Company, 11 Rue Scribe, Paris, France

Levi's last letter sent stateside was signed, "Levi," and not "Lee." Something he had not done since his very first letter. A true sign of friendship, the end of pet names and considerations. Apparently, distance was not necessary. Parents had potentially won the battle.

Levi did not send along the article from *Forum Magazine*; it was quite lengthy. The discussion centered around the fundamentalist-modernist controversy, a conflict among Protestant denominations. Rollin Hartt started and ended strong. A lengthy nine-page article covered a variety of points on the topic. For any unfamiliar with the happenings within the Protestant religion, Hartt spelled it out this way.

Within the existing organization of the various Protestant sets, two religions coexist: Fundamentalism and Modernism or Liberalism. Between thee there is far greater chasm of differences than exists between the various sects, greater even than the difference between some form of Protestantism and Catholicism (678).

Hartt pointed out that the Fundamentalist and the Modernist were so different that both could not be true. For one to be correct, the other had to be wrong by default. The article continued to say that if these two factions had developed independently, there would be no thought about merging them. The differences between these two belief systems within Protestantism played out during the Scopes trial. Fundamentalists took the Bible literally and rejected any conflict science might impart on religious belief. The Modernists, also called Liberalists, had a more contextual understanding of the Bible; scientific advancements were embraced.

By the article's end, Hartt made the point that instead of having Catholicism and Protestantism, the divide among Protestants was so great that they truly were not unified under one umbrella. Hartt stated that the "three distinct temperaments would make more sense as three different churches.

The remaining articles Levi included were mostly humorous. "Meditations of a Wife," by Helen Roland, recited the different ways women are treated by their lover as they are by their husband, though the individual is the same. The source of the clipping is unknown.

Another small piece was a poem by Edgar A. Guest, titled "The Tragedy of a Bad Habit." Again, the source was lost since it is just a clipping. The bad habit of nail biting was revealed at the end.

Levi wrote diagonally across the final article. The small, trimmed piece of paper was covered, corner-to-corner, with the words, "Just my luck." The Klan was expanding in the Capital. They leased two floors of a recently renovated building at Seventeenth and I Streets, Northwest. The address of the boarding house he had hoped to return to was 1728 I Street, Northwest. It was too close for comfort.

With that final article, Levi's pockets were empty of packing material, his load lightened, his forwarding address recorded, and his adventure was about to begin. Chloe wrote to him the very next day, unsure of the amount of time the letter would take to arrive in Paris.

229 B Street N.E.
Washington, D.C.
October 24, 1925

Dear Lee,

You are probably out on the ocean and I'm at home listening to the drip, drip of the rain. Yes, it's raining and I haven't a date with you – so you see the clouds aren't weeping for us this time – On second thought, maybe you could call this a date – the silent kind – Letters really amount to this anyway – don't they?

I enjoyed your descriptions of New York – When I get there again I'll look for the things you mentioned.

We had a lot of fun teasing Ruth about "Onions – to keep the chap off my lips". It was appropriate I'll grant you that. I played the part of detective again – but I'm wondering whether "Gee, but I'm lonesome" was applicable to you or me – At least I'll admit it applies to me, whether meant for me or not.

There's been nothing unusual happening since you left – Alma called last Sat. and asked me to go with her to see "Artists and Models" – The show wasn't unusual – just about what you'd expect – I've seen musical comedies I liked better. – Sun. night Johnny took the whole bunch of us for a ride and we got cold in spite of winter coats –

We haven't had our expected test in Ed. 25 as yet – and I actually had courage to volunteer an answer to a question in History 30 – I still like this class but I'm not studying much – This is enough of college talk, isn't it?

Only one of our prospective roommates came. We haven't heard anymore from Miss Barnes. Miss Dieson is pleasant but we'd rather have a younger girl – We can't have everything we want, can we? So we have to make the best of what we get and smile.

You make me feel serious when you write me such things in regard to my influence on you. You'll change when gay Paris has you under her spell. Do you remember once I wrote you to be careful or you'd be a fanatic? I again repeat my warning.

I hope you had a very pleasant trip across the ocean — I even hope you did not suffer from the various kinds of sicknesses you talked about before leaving. We often talk of you — Ruth and Grace asked to be remembered to you. I haven't given Mrs. T. your message — but I'll not forget — There are lots of warnings I could give, about taking care of yourself, don't lose your temper, etc., but I'll leave all of these to your good judgement.

I saw Miss Christian on the car last night she talked of her experiences during the summer and did not forget to mention the Music Club — outside members are allowed this year so I'm invited (and expected) to return. If nothing else more interesting turns up I'll probably go but I'll not have the time to give to an official position. — If Va. could only hear me say that I'm going back to the Music Club wouldn't she rave?

We haven't had an answer to the community letter we wrote last week.

Thursday night I went to see "The Ten Commandments" — you saw this, didn't you? I liked it very much. — So many scenes were as my childish imagination had painted them. We had to wait in line about an hour and the crowd pushed more than the ones at the Columbia and Metropolitan.

I look for Clayton every night after college but haven't seen him yet, if I do I'll deliver your message. Don't you think I'm accommodating?

The gang downstairs is as noisy as ever — there was a party one night last week (Sat. I believe) — Grace saw empty bottles in the back hall. Aren't you sorry you weren't here? Now you'll be disappointed, she said they were grape juice and ginger ale bottles.

Ruth told me the names of your Notre Dame men but I've again forgotten them. I'll write them down next time and make the letter special delivery; shall I?

We haven't had baked ham since you left but I'm hungry enough to eat some now. It was too rainy to go out for lunch so I just ate left overs from breakfast and dinner last night.

Did you call Gertrude before you left? We were saying the other day that we wanted her over for dinner before long. I suppose it is my time to 'bawl' her out.

I had another homesick letter from my kid sister this week so I'm asking her to come to Washington for Thanksgiving. This may make her worse – but I hope it will not.

Write whenever you have time as I'm interested in your 'wanderings'.

I wish all three of you the best o'luck in your travels.

Just, Chloe

As Chloe finished her letter and put it into the evening post on October 24, both it and Levi began their trip across the Atlantic. It was left to be seen whether their letters would be "dates" or simply words between friends.

Soon, the Eiffel Tower would stand tall in the City of Love, and Levi would create memories to last a lifetime.

Cherbourg
Aboard the Leviathan
Lisieux
Caen
PARIS
Orleans
Vierzon
Bourges
Avignon
Nimes
Beaucaire / Tarascon
Arles
Italy
Aix-en-Provence
Toulouse
Montpellier
Nice
Carcassonne
Agde
Marseille
Narbonne

FRANCE
October 1925 – December 1925

CHAPTER 12
THE LEVIATHAN

October 24, 1925
⌈travel journal⌉

*This begins a series of notes of a great adventure. To plan
for years a study tour of Europe and at last to find myself
miles from shore bound for the "Old Country" of my grand-*

father's stories seems too true for me to realize at present.

On leaving the Statue of Liberty behind I tried to summon all the emotion I know a good American should feel on leaving the land of his birth but could only watch receding New York with the interest one has for the same scene on a movie screen.

I am hoping this trip is more than educational. I hope it results in my having two life long friends. I hope it helps me to find myself; to definitely decide in what manner the rest of my life is to be spent. To study church architecture is my main objective but to appreciate the spirit which resulted in noble monuments to God is my desire.

The other two members of our "three men in a boat" are John F. Connell of Denver, Colorado, and Vincent D. Engels of Green Bay. We are traveling with the proletariat on board the Leviathan. A deckhand tells me it is kicking up a storm outside. Yes I'm afraid of "Feeding the Fish."

The long-awaited adventure began as recorded on page one of Levi's travel journal. Everything that set this scene was monumental. The three Notre Dame boys were aboard the largest vessel in the world with a panoramic view of the world's largest city fading in the distance. Europe awaited on the other side of a six-day ocean voyage. First, they had to survive the week. Many were weary of cross-Atlantic travel, as the RMS Titanic carried many souls to a cold grave only 13 years earlier.

The name Leviathan was fitting, shared with a legendary monster of great size, a being that symbolized the forces of chaos and evil. According to Mike Thornton, Associate Curator of the *New York Historical Museum*, it was First Lady Edith Wilson who selected the name.

The grand vessel, then called the Vaterland, was in port in America when the Great War broke out. To avoid potential loss at sea, the German ship remained docked. Once America joined in, the Leviathan was seized as the spoils of war.

Cherbourg, France
Friday, Oct. 30, 1925

Dear Mother,

At last we are here and I feel just like the sentence sounds. Was I sick? Gloriously so. I ate five meals in six days aboard the ship. That is I kept five of them, the fish got the others. The food was good but the rolling and vibration of the engines got on my nerves. Enough of that, leave me describe the rest.

We met a couple fellows on the boat who told us the "ropes" and that helped a whole lot. The Leviathan usually carries about 4000 passengers and we had less than 800 this trip so you see things were pretty nice. The weather was rainy every day but the sea was not rough. It was no worse than I have seen on the Bay at home.

Here at Cherbourg this morning they took us off the big boat into a smaller one which carried us to the custom house. There our baggage was supposed to be examined (mine was not, all he did was question me as to whether I was bringing any tobacco into the country) and our passports stamped.

Everybody else went on to Paris on a Special train but Connell, Engels and myself are seeing this place today and tomorrow morning we are going to "Lisieux" which is the town that St. Theresa came from. From there we shall probably go to Paris. The railroad fares are about one half of what they cost at home.

The first bottle of rare white wine was good but had no "kick". The bottles come in 1/5 of a gallon and cost 20 francs which was 95¢. That is much more than they charge Frenchmen, but we shall soon get to be able to "Jew them down".

Our noon meal today consisted of a bottle of real—real—real good beer, bread without butter, codfish, potatoes, cheese and a pear. Tonight we shall see.

This is a very pretty place with all stone houses and stone roofs. The streets and people look just like in the movies. They have a small electric street car about half the size of those in Green Bay. They are run by women. The automobiles are little things not much longer than a motorcycle with funny squeaky horns. The people make a lot of noise on the cobbled, narrow streets with their wooden shoes. The older people seem to get the leather shoes but the kids have wood. And you should have seen the fish market this morning with the eels and snails piled up for sale. When I get good and hungry I shall try them but not now.

This town is the site of a big fort and was very important during the war. They have a naval airplane base here and it resembles Washington in that respect. The gendarmes wear bright uniforms and carry swords.

Levi was describing Fort d'Octeville. Allies dropped 1,000 tons of bombs on and around the city of Cherbourg during World War II. Much of the beauty Levi witnessed upon his arrival in Europe was destroyed after five days of fighting in 1944. The Germans prepared the town for a waterfront attack, which left them blind to an advance on land. Today, residential buildings stand where Fort d'Octeville once stood.

Levi's first look at Cherbourg was from the small vessel that took them to shore from the Leviathan. Though so much of the town was destroyed in World War II, the view of the porton the previous page is not very different from the views seen when disembarking today.

> *This morning we stopped in an old church built in 1450 in honor of the Blessed Virgin when the town was delivered from the English. A requiem mass was being said and the interior was decorated with many French flags. The place was filled and about half of them were French soldiers or men who had been in the army judging by the medals on display and the cripples among them. After mass three people in mourning stood out in front of the church and every one that came out bowed or shook hands with them.*

Levi's description from the morning of October 30, 1925, was a few days shy of seven years since Armistice Day and the end of World War I. The church was most likely the *Basilique Sainte-Trinite de Cherbourg* (Holy Trinity Basilica), though a nearby church *L'eglise Notre-Dame de la Delivrande* (Basilica of our Lady of Deliverance), also fits his description well. Levi's first letter home continued.

> *Our French, — that's another matter. John and I were pricing bicycles this morning and the conversation went something like this. I would say 'combien'; the man would give me a string of words which came too fast to understand then show me a price tag which usually ran about 450 to 500 francs. We are getting 23 francs for a dollar at the present rate of exchange with a franc in normal times worth 19¢ but we have not the advantage you would imagine because people just raise their prices accordingly.*
>
> *To go back to the bicycles, they have old fashioned tires with inner tubes and you can't find any with coaster brakes. They have a hand brake on the front rim which I had never seen before. I suppose we shall have to get use to the French style because they probably have a prohibitive duty on*

American goods. I saw some Colgate's shaving soap and some Palmolive soap so I know we can get some things Americaine over here.

I am going to try to mail this tonite. There is a boat out of here in the morning but I don't know if this will make it as I haven't seen any place to mail letters yet and besides the French don't seem to be in a hurry about anything. — Don't worry if you do not hear from me often because mail service on this side is very irregular. Remember no news is good news.

I'm going down to eat now and intend to ask for some "lait" instead of wine. They will probably try to throw me out but I'm as tough as any I've seen so far.

With love, Levi

P.S. — The address will still be c/o American Express Co., 11 Rue Scribe, Paris.

CHAPTER 13
CONQUERING CAEN

Levi wrote to his father once they arrived in Paris. The letter was dated November 3. He shared these reflections on their experiences.

From Cherbourg we took a hop of eighty miles to Caen where we spent two nights. Caen is a place of 300,000 people but you cannot realize it. Green Bay would seem much bigger by comparison. Went to mass in a very old church dating from the fifteenth century. I don't know if it was because of the Feast of All Saints but the church was crowded. Sunday afternoon we went thru the Church of St. Etienne which was built by the English King William the Conqueror in expiation for his sin of marrying his cousin (eleventh century) Queen Matilde. The church was built on the site of a still older crypt dating from 1026 A.D. – We went down in this old, dark basement and viewed the altar and remains of the original church. It was hard to realize that we were looking at an altar upon which the Sacrifice of the Mass was offered 999 years ago.

Levi was a bit confused about the population of Caen. Caen is the prefecture of the Calvados department of France. The population of the whole department was 300,000, not the city. Caen is about half the size of Green Bay, with a population of around 40,000 in 1925.

Levi's hometown had about 62,000 inhabitants then.

In Caen, two abbeys from the eleventh century were commissioned by William the Conqueror and his wife, Queen Matilda of Flanders, in reparation for their sin of marrying. Pope Leo IX had forbidden their marriage based on kinship; they were third cousins once removed. William married Matilda without the blessing of the church and tried to repair the damage by building two abbeys in Caen: *Abbaye-aux-Hommes* (Abbey for Men) and *Abbaye-aux-Dames* (Abbey for Women). The first is also known as *Saint Etienne* (Saint Stephen), and the latter is *La Trinité* (The Trinity).

Construction of both structures began about the time of the Battle of Hastings, 1066. William the Conqueror was buried inside Saint Etienne when he died a little more than twenty years later. History says a knight, Anselm Fitz-Arthur, stopped the services, declaring the king unfit to be buried there. The land had been stolen from the knight's father, and the king had no rightful ownership of it. The claim was verified, Anselm was compensated for the lands of his father's estate, and the funeral of William the Conqueror continued. As for Queen Matilda, she died almost four years before her husband and was buried at La Trinité.

Levi did not mention the burial spot of William the Conqueror in front of the high altar of Saint Etienne. Ransacked twice over the years, all that remains entombed there is a thigh bone. The letter to his father continued.

> *Of Caen I might tell this incident. We have been trying to teach Connell how to say some of the simple French phrases and getting up Sunday morning he greeted the hotel owner by saying, "Merci-beaucoup". We always have to watch that he doesn't get cheated because he can't count in French.*
>
> *You should see the variety of French coins. Aluminum, brass, bronze, copper, gunmetal. Most of them look like washers and we call them slugs.*
>
> *I had quite an argument with a taxi-driver last night upon arriving at our hotel. He wanted three francs extra*

for carrying our luggage and I wouldn't give it to him. He started raising a rumpus in French in front of our hotel and I was calling him names in English when an American lady stopped and asked me what the trouble was. — I found out I was wrong and had to pay it. They make a practice of cheating Americans so we have to watch them like "hawks".

CHAPTER 14
TO LISIEUX TO VISIT A SAINT

The village of Lisieux was filled with medieval buildings of half-timbered construction when Levi, Vince, and John visited. The above photo appears to be of John and Levi in the doorway, though it is hard to be certain. The medieval timbers were the focus of the image.

Portions of Levi's November 3 letter to his father described Lisieux, the town they visited after Caen.

On the way to Paris, we spent half a day in Lisieux and visited several churches as well as the church and convent from which St. Thérèse came. They have built a new church on the site of the old convent chapel and on the walls are carved the acknowledgements of different people who received favors.

There is a shrine of her on one side of the church around which are several hundred French medals for bravery during the world war. These medals were donated by the individuals who received them, in thanksgiving for coming out of the war safe.

On the same day, November 3, Levi told Chloe of his experiences following the footsteps of a saint.

We stopped at Lisieux before coming to Paris. This is the birthplace of the new Saint of France. St. Thérèse was canonized last Summer and has been dead but twenty-five years. A new church has been built on the site of the chapel in which she worshiped. There is a special shrine in her honor around which are carved hundreds of testimonials or words of thanksgiving for favors received thru her intercession. What struck me as very interesting was that about a thousand war medals of France as well as medals for bravery from other nations were placed around the shrine. The men who received these medals placed them around the shrine in thanksgiving for their safe deliverance thru battle. That this all happened at least seven years before her recognition by the Church is a thing that George Bernard Shaw might note.

Saint Thérèse was canonized less than six months before the trio's arrival. Making a pilgrimage to see the places where this saint lived and died was important to the three travelers. If Saint Thérèse had survived tuberculosis, she would have been twice their age when the three visited in November of 1925, but she was twenty-four when she died. That was an impactful age since Vince was twenty-three and both Levi and John were just settling into being twenty-five.

Saint Thérèse lived a quiet, simple life as a Carmelite nun. Were it not for the intercessions, apparitions, and miracles attributed to her, she would not have been known to these American travelers. Her recent canonization drew them to Lisieux.

One requirement in the process of becoming a saint is the verification of miracles attributed to the intercession of the person considered for sainthood. The two miracles utilized to meet these requirements involved the miraculous recovery of two women from serious medical ailments. One recovered from stomach ulcers and the other from tuberculosis. Medicine could not explain their miraculous recovery. These were in addition to the many soldiers who thanked Sister Thérèse for seeing them through the war.

The half-timbered buildings in Lisieux survived the First World War, but they were reduced to rubble in the Second. Reports estimated that 75% of the town was destroyed. The Advocate published an article in 1944, "Shrines Stand Intact Amid Lisieux Ruins," which reported that "11,000 of its 16,000 scattered people" were homeless (3). The basilica, the Carmelite convent, and the town cathedral stood intact among the ruins. This basilica did not exist in 1925. Construction did not begin on that site until 1929. It was a needed addition to the town of Lisieux to accommodate the large number of pilgrims visiting there.

Saint Désir was one of the two parish churches rendered to rubble during the Second World War. After the bombings in 1944, a tall crucifix stood unscathed among the ruins. Sergeant Wilkes of the No. 5 Army Film and Photographic Unit captured the moment British soldiers traversed Lisieux once the town was liberated. Saint Thérèse had celebrated her First Holy

Communion in this, her parish church, back in 1884.

Paris, France
November 10, 1925
[travel journal]

The quaint old town still gave evidence of the flock
of pilgrims that had visited the place during the summer
months. We visited the shrine in the new church built on the
spot where the old chapel in which she worshipped stood.
I especially noticed the number of war medals around the
shrine. I left my camera at the Hotel Moderne in Lisieux
and wrote for it when I reached Paris. It was returned in
good order and I feel indebted to St. Anthony for helping me.

The value of life does not depend
upon the place we occupy.
It depends upon the way
we occupy that place.

-Saint Thérèse de Lisieux

CHAPTER 15
PARIS - CITY OF LOVE

Paris, France
November 3, 1925

Dear Father,

*Paris at last and a mighty fine city it is. I can understand
how people sell their homesteads in America and come here
to live. We arrived here last night at 17 o'clock and although
we haven't had time to stop to see things yet we have decided
it's the nicest place we've been in.*

*We shall probably be here a week before buying our
bicycles and starting South. Connell and I have given up
the idea of going to school and we are going to try to be in
Rome for Christmas day for the ceremonies which close the
Holy Year.*

The remainder of Levi's letter to his father involved Caen and
Lisieux, since they had just arrived in Paris.

Paris, France
November 9, 1925

Dear Chloe, [Sec. of the Music Club by now]

*I am in a terrible way and am asking via mental
telepathy a question. The boys have bought semi-knickers for
our bicycle tour with golf socks and everything and there is*

nothing for me to do but follow 'suit'.

There I knew if I asked you that way you would allow me to 'right about face'.

The way John Connell bought his outfit is worth telling. He doesn't speak a word of French and equipped with a sketch pad and pencil he entered a department store covering three city blocks. He explained his wants to the clerk by drawing the picture of a man attired a la golf links. He received plenty of size for his money but intends to fill them out with a "Milwaukee front" just as soon as we hit the 'beer country'.

Our eating is quite a problem. One time we had to use the laying hens song of exultation to get us a couple eggs but this was one time that the end justified the means. It is surprising how few French people pronounce their language right. Either that or somehow my French teacher was wrong, very wrong.

We've been in Paris a week. The first day I saw it I thought it was wonderful. A week has gone by, a week in which we have hardly begun to see Paris and I still think it is great. You like Washington and you would like Paris because it is what Washington is trying hard to be, a beautiful city.

There are more than half a million foreigners here in the French capital and they give it a cosmopolitan touch that probably no other place on earth has. Paris and France are two distinct entities. France a sleepy, beautiful, quaint place where "time and tide" bother them not at all. Paris is a modern city; more efficient than the best we have in America. Paris seems to be a stage on which everyone is acting. The clerk and bellhop swagger down the street much as our college boys do at home. There are any number of uniformed footmen and keepers of the gate at the downtown offices and here and there on the streets we see our long-haired artists with their big hats.

French morals are the talk of our Sunday papers and as far as I can see French morals are not concerned in what goes on in Paris. The French of Paris see fit to allow we foreigners to conduct our lives as we see fit and Americans especially can't get used to being good without being forced to be so.

I must say this Chloe; you really are expecting it anyway; I haven't seen but one intoxicated man since landing in France. In New York we met possibly fifty while there. Everyone drinks intoxicating beverages here. Restaurants give you a choice of beer, wines or wiskeys at meals. At breakfast time we can get chocolate or coffee but most people drink a wine called "vin rouge". You already know my conclusions to the above.

While at the Louvre Sunday our party came across the famous picture, "The Wedding at Cana". One of the boys (I will not say which one) remarked, "It's lucky that didn't happen in America".

I couldn't get a thrill out of "Mona Lisa" although anyone could tell by the crowds around that it was the most advertised picture in the world. Murillo's, "The Immaculate Conception" was my favorite but I guess I was prejudiced before ever entering the galleries. The Louvre is a great gloomy place but contains so much that it would take weeks to cover it. We have spent two afternoons there and have walked thru less than one quarter of the floor area.

Am enclosing a note from Connell. The boys made several remarks about my undignified celebration in the American Express office this morning. I hope I have occasion to hear a lot more.

Give my regards to your "flat–mates" and tell Ruth that

they grow wonderful onions here.

The three of us have given up the school idea and are starting for Rome on Nov. 12. We hope to be there by Christmas.

Paris has helped but it will take much more than that.

From, Lee

P.S. – I want you to appreciate the sacrifice I am making in sending you the picture of the "Kitchen Mechanic" [It takes about a week to get a picture printed in France]. Mona Lisa hasn't a show when compared with her.

P.P.S. – Our mail will be forwarded to us. c/o American Express Co., 2 Rue du Congres, Nice, France

Middle of the first week in November I think
Paris

Dear Chloe,

You will no doubt think me rather rude to brake in in such haste but with a bit of explanation I am sure you will understand my situation.

Levi has been very grouchy and criticizes me very much but today after receiving your letter he was really pleasant so please have mercy on me and write to him very very often, and I am sure the good Lord will reward you for your kindness.

Thank you also for your kind words for our trip.

Yours truly, John

P.S. Blame Levi for any misspelled words for he would not tell me which was right.

One of the group's first outings in Paris was to the Louvre. From the portion of the Louvre that Levi covered in 1925, three paintings were noted: Leonardo da Vinci's *Mona Lisa* (1503), Paolo Veronese's *The Wedding Feast at Cana* (1563), and Bartolomé Esteban Murillo's *The Immaculate Conception of Los Venerables* (1678). The current size of the Louvre is 650,000 square feet. To put it in terms of a Washington D.C. landmark, the White House, with its ground floor, state floor, and two residence floors , is only 55,000 square feet. In 1925, all three masterpieces hung in the Salon de Carré, though none of them are on display in that room in the modern day.

Finding Salon Carré by utilizing old photographs and noting the paintings that once hung there can be a bit of a challenge. Knowing that it links the Galerie d'Apollon and the Grande Galerie offers some assistance. Arrival is confirmed by the ceiling. Blue panels are trimmed with gilded frames, which are further adorned by white figurines surrounding a central glass panel. Large white shields bearing the initials RF, for the French Republic, appear at every corner. The glass in the center of the ceiling was a brilliant 1789 design, the first to allow overhead lighting in a gallery. When Levi walked through these halls in 1925, he saw three of the most famous paintings in the world.

The *Mona Lisa*, known as *La Gioconda* in Italian, is a portrait of Lisa Gherardini, the wife of a Florentine silk merchant named Francesco del Giocondo. Only 14 years before Levi's visit, the painting was removed from the walls of the Salon de Carré by Vincenzo Peruggia, the worker who created the protective box that encased the masterpiece. He kept the stolen artwork in his apartment, only a few miles from the Louvre. Peruggia's goal was to return *La Gioconda* to Italy, since he assumed the painting had been stolen during Napoleon's escapades. However, France owned the painting outright; King François I purchased *La Gioconda* from Da Vinci in 1518 when he invited the painter to France. When Peruggia tried to sell the painting in Italy, the ruse was over. He was arrested, tried, and jailed for just under a year.

The Great War began within days of his release, which overshadowed any outcry that might have ensued over his short seven-month incarceration.

Within the first days of 1914, the lovely lady filled the empty spot in the Salon de Carré once again. In 1966, *La Gioconda* was escorted to the Salle Des Ètats, the largest room in the Louvre, where she resides today .

The Wedding Feast at Cana, the second masterpiece Levi mentioned, is the largest painting in the Louvre. Completed in 1563 for the monks of the Order of Saint Benedict in Venice, the commissioned work hung in the refectory of the monastery at San Giorgio Maggiore from 1563 until 1797. When Napoleon began his campaign for emperor, he ordered his soldiers to cut the canvas in half horizontally, with the plan of having the pieces reunited later in France. When reparations were made for looted artwork, the curator of the *Musée Napoléon* (La Louvre) falsely claimed that the painting was too fragile to move. Charles LeBrun's *Feast at the House of Simon* was sent instead. *The Wedding Feast at Cana* now hangs across from the *Mona Lisa*, consuming one wall of the Salle Des Ètats at the Louvre.

The third painting, *The Immaculate Conception of Los Venerables*, was also stolen in the same fashion as *The Wedding Feast at Cana*, as spoils of war. Originally commissioned for Justino de Neve, *The Immaculate Conception of Los Venerables* is one of approximately two dozen versions that Murillo painted, with this being the most famous version. The painting was later donated to the Hospital de los Venerables in Seville, Spain (1686).

One hundred and twenty-seven years later, the painting was removed from the frame and taken from Seville by Marshal Jean-de-Dieu Soult during the Peninsular War . The Louvre purchased the painting in 1852, paying more than had been paid for any other painting in existence until that time. An agreement has been made since then between the French and Spanish governments to return the painting to Spain, where the Virgin Mary adorns the walls of the Prado in Madrid. This painting held religious significance in its time, as the concept of the Immaculate Conception was not accepted by all but was promoted greatly throughout Spain and the Franciscan sects of Christianity. It was not until 1854 that Pope Pius IX declared the doctrine to be revealed by God. Belief in the Immaculate Conception became dogma with the release of the papal bull *Ineffabilis Deus* (Ineffable God).

As Levi stood in the Salon de Carré in 1925, he was in the very room where Napoleon married his second wife on April 2, 1810. Marie Louise, known fully as Maria Ludovica Leopoldina Franziska Therese Josepha Lucia, was an Austrian archduchess who became Empress of the French and Queen of Italy. For the celebration of his nuptials, Napoleon had the salon converted to appear as if it were a chapel. The director of the museum at the time of the wedding, Vivant Denon, opposed the removal of the largest paintings in this salon over concern for their well-being. Pierre Fontaine, the architect who designed a two-level tribune for those who attended the wedding, recorded the emperor's response to Denon's refusal to move the large paintings. Napoleon ordered "for the paintings to be removed, and as for any which could not be removed, they should be burned." The Salon Carré was promptly emptied of all masterpieces, the tribunes were built, and additional adornments, along with a crucifix and altar, were added in preparation for the grand celebration.

Walking through the room today does not bring up images of Napoleon's wedding. In fact, it seems too small for the many attendees. Artist Georges Rouget captured them beautifully in his painting, *The Wedding of Napoleon and Marie Louise* (1810), which hangs at Versailles.

It is difficult to imagine the Salons from the past and realize that the world-famous event took place here. Artwork filled every available space on the walls. In 1923, the *Fort Worth Record-Telegram* shared

an artist's rendering of the Paris Salon of 1783 ("Salon Carré of the Louvre 23). It is no wonder that this room captured Levi's interest.

The Salon Carré does not stand out as it once did. The present pieces are worth beholding, but these walls do not display artwork that rivals the fame of the *Mona Lisa*, the *Wedding Feast at Cana*, and the *Immaculate Conception*. The blank wall to artwork ratio today is at best two to one. The framed works are spaced apart from one another and hung only at eye level. As impressive as the Louvre is, no room exhibits the quantity of artwork once beheld within a single glimpse of the Salon Carré.

With his father and Chloe updated on the vistas of Paris, Levi made sure to get a letter off to his mom before venturing south, where letters were sure to take longer to reach home.

Paris, France
November 10, 1925

Dear Mother,

I had waited to see if there would be a letter from home before writing but it seems to take about sixteen days for a letter to cover the distance. We are starting South tomorrow morning. We take a train to Orleans which is about 90 miles from here. When we get to Orleans we are going to buy bicycles and start out. Engels, Connell and I are going together. We have given up the school idea and intend to be in Rome for the ceremonies which close the Holy Year at Christmas time.

We are leaving most of our luggage here in Paris at the American Express and are pushing ahead with knapsacks. I bought some riding breeches, golf socks and heavy shoes and feel completely equipped. Our packs are pretty heavy and no doubt we will discard things as we go along. I am enclosing a map showing our proposed route. We intend to see Lourdes on our way back.

We were over to the Basilica of the Sacred Heart the other day. This is the headquarters of the League of the Sacred Heart.

There are a lot of things we can buy at a bargain here, for instance good leather gloves both men's and women's cost about one dollar. But after you pay duty on them it isn't worth while. When we come home we are planning to come back loaded.

Paris is almost too great a task to describe. We have been here nine days and have hardly begun to see the sights.

Of course, we saw Notre Dame Cathedral; we went to High Mass there last Sunday. Pa should have heard the choir. I liked it but it would take him to really appreciate the music.

The Eiffel Tower impressed me more than anything. Connell and I rode to the top and enjoyed the panorama below us. The structure is about a

thousand feet high and is the highest ever constructed by man. The base spreads over an area about the size of a city block and it is only by drawing close that one appreciates its immensity.

Paris is probably the most beautiful city in the world. At least it is the nicest I have seen. France is very distinct from Paris. France is a quaint, slow place, where no one seems in a hurry. In Cherbourg the clatter of wooden shoes on the cobble stones kept us awake; here it is the automobile horns.

We have had so much bad weather [it has rained every day except one] that we have not had an opportunity to enjoy the parks and promenades of Paris. The Louvre Museum is an immense building, much larger than our buildings in America.

Have I told you about the big loaves of bread in France? They handle bread here like we do cordwood at home and both resemble each other in size. Tonite I ate a whole loaf of bread and six small cheeses and a pomegranate for sup-per (It's dinner here). The cheese we like is called "crème de gruyère" and it is served as a dessert. It costs about 32 cents a pound. I will surely bring some home when we pull up stakes from here.

Guess I'll close for a couple of days. Don't worry as we are all in fine health and no wheres near broke.

With love, Levi

John Connell posed at the side entrance of Sacre Coeur in the photo to the right. This arched doorway gave access to the basilica's dome. Even though the basilica is located at the top of Montmartre, the highest hill in Paris, the dome is surpassed in height by the Eiffel Tower.

It is not surprising that an architect would be impressed by the tallest structure in the world at the time. The Eiffel Tower held that honor when it surpassed the reigning Washington Monument in

1889. It would retain the title until 1930, when the Chrysler Building was completed in New York City.

Before Paris, the highest Levi had ever been was to the top of the Washington Monument back in his nation's capital city. The photo below was taken by Chloe Wells in either 1922 or 1923. The Lincoln Memorial was barely visible in the distance of this west-facing photo, with the Potomac River running just behind it. The Reflecting Pool was still under construction. As impressive as the Washington Monument had been for Levi, the Eiffel Tower rose 68% higher.

The similarities between Washington, D.C., and Paris are not accidental. City planner Pierre Charles L'Enfant, a Frenchman, was chosen by George Washington to draw up the plans for Washington,

D.C. He used the plans for Paris as inspiration. The streets cross in a grid-like pattern, albeit at perpendicular angles in the states, while the avenues cross on the diagonal.

All trains in France radiate out like the spokes from the hub of a bicycle, but they are not infinite. The trio found that other modes of transportation were required to reach places that were off the city-planned pathways.

The Travelers: John, Vince & Levi

CHAPTER 16
TRAVEL WOES

Toulouse, France
November 16, 1925

Dear Father,

Have just finished a good bottle of "biere" after having bargained all day in buying our bicycles. You should have heard me bargain in French, Belgian and English. The boys left the buying of the three bicycles to me. We started out this morning at 10:30 and tonight at 6:30 we had finished the transaction. The result of my telling them my name was Alphonse [Levi's middle name] along with the phrase "c'est trop" [it's too much] was that we received a ten percent "remise" or discount. The total cost of my bicycle equipped with a brake on either wheel, a bell, tools and a baggage carrier was $16.48. – We bought packs to carry our clothes on our backs but I had sore shoulders from carrying my pack about half an hour so I am planning to lash the pack on my bicycle carrier.

We have enquired about the weather at Lourdes and have decided to make that on our way back from Spain.

From Bourges we rode (third class) to Vierzon where we waited for the night train from Paris to Toulouse. Connell and I left the station about 9:30 P.M. in search of bread, cheese and wine for our all-night journey. Everyone on a French train seems to carry a lunch and we were going to try the same. We wandered to the edge of town without finding an open shop or any people about. — All of a sudden two men stopped us and just when I was set to start running, I noticed that they were gendarmes. They examined our passports and railroad tickets and wanted to know what we were doing prowling around the town. You can imagine me trying to tell them in French that we were innocent Americans searching for "fromage" (cheese). They finally let us go after directing us to a wine shop. Later when we boarded our train, I noticed that they had come to the station and were watching us.

In leaving Vierzon, Engels climbed into one coach and Connell and I got into the one ahead. French trains leave without warning and it's every man for himself. The ride of nine hours is something I shall not forget. Five other men, Connell and myself and one woman in a small compartment. The seats have straight backs without cushions. If you open the windows you freeze, if you close them the combination of cheeses and eight lunch boxes is enough to have you open them again. Morning and Toulouse arrived at last and as Connell muttered when we descended, "It is surprising what one can really endure."

When we reached Toulouse, we saw Engels' car was missing. It happens that he was awake which saved him from going all the way to Bordeaux before finding out that he was in the wrong car. They do not call stations or tell you when to change trains so that with us riding in French railroads it is all guesswork. He arrived a few hours later and you can imagine our choice adjectives describing the train service.

Travel in 1925 was anything but easy. The trains today can make the trip from Vierzon to Toulouse in less than five-and-a-half hours, as compared to nine hours in 1925, or eleven if your train gets switched at night. Ocean liners took a week to cross the Atlantic. Trans-Atlantic commercial flights did not exist until closer to the start of World War II.

The bicycles they purchased were single-gear, which made the ride through the mountains and rural areas of Europe challenging. Even walking has improved over the past hundred years; Levi and crew were still ten years away from experiencing rubber-soled sneakers.

Levi shared with his father on November 16 many of the same details he had with Chloe the day before. Of course, in the letter to Chloe, there was a little blank paper available to hold additional thoughts.

At the hotel every evening we meet an English and a French engineer. All of us get along well although the English man is as hard to understand as the Frenchman.

The boys are in despair. They are trying to buy me a mouth organ so I will stop singing, "The Prisoner's Song". They claim that I am thinking of you every time I start it, and in truth I am.

Every where I go and whenever we see anything interesting I think how you would enjoy it and how I would enjoy that. Your warning about fanatics came too late. I am one and the subject is a person, the identity of whom you might guess. — It will take more than Paris — more than Rome and I believe more than home.

I am tempted to tear this last page because it would be best so but you are my advisor and by now you'll guess that's no small job.

Sincerely, Lee

"The Prisoner's Song" was a big hit in 1925, a recent release from August of the previous year. The Bee, a newspaper out of Danville, Virginia, marketed the song in an advertisement for a local music store, "Big Hits on Columbia Grafonola at Benefield, Motley & Co.'s Music Dept., Corner Crahead and Main Streets" (15). The top release had the "John T. Scopes Trial" on the A-side and "The Santa Barbara Earthquake" on B, but "The Prisoner's Song" was listed next; an estimated seven million copies were sold nationwide. Though other favorites from 1925 easily come to mind, "Yes Sir, That's my Baby" and "Sweet Georgia Brown," even the singer of Levi's earworm, Vernon Dalhart, has been lost to time. The sound has the signature static that backed up every tune played on a Victrola. A male tenor voice with an artificial twang sings out as if he is trying to reach his love through the steel bars that hold him captive. The lyrics assured Levi's listeners that Chloe was the person he wished to call his own.

THE PRISONER'S SONG

Oh, I wish I had someone to love me,
Someone to call me their own.
Oh, I wish I had someone to live with
'Cause I'm tired of livin' alone.

Oh, please meet me tonight in the moonlight,
Please meet me tonight all alone,
For I have a sad story to tell you,
It's a story that's never been told.

I'll be carried to the new jail tomorrow,
Leaving my poor darling alone,
With the cold prison bars all around me
And my head on a pillow of stone.

Now I have a grand ship on the ocean,
All mounted with silver and gold,
And before my poor darlin' would suffer,
Oh, that ship would be anchored and sold.

Now if I had wings like an angel
Over these prison walls I would fly.
And I'd fly to the arms of my poor darlin',
And there I'd be willing to die.

By this time, Levi had only one letter from Chloe in his knapsack. Snail mail had been efficient and relatively quick back home, but sloth mail was quite bothersome. With the addition of an ocean voyage and Levi's continual change in location, it took a month or more for him to receive any news.

Saturday Morning
November 28, 1925

Dear Lee,

I had just sealed a letter to you when I went downstairs to look for the mail – There was another letter from you, so I'm enclosing the first and adding a note for the second.

It's quite lonely around here when the others are at work. I can stand it for one or two days but after that the empty house gets on my nerves. After a while I'm going down town and select my silver, (I belong to a silver club, and this month is my time to choose mine) then to the Pan-American building – to see the interior – and from there to the library. The library doesn't open until two o'clock and now it is about eleven.

Your letter was very interesting – The post cards were also – The French, I couldn't translate, of course – I am afraid to pronounce French names – even the cities.

You are having some exciting experiences – The Spaniards are more suspicious of foreigners than the French, aren't they? You may have more adventures ahead of you – Be careful!

I had an idea that the Germans were very fond of "smelly" cheeses – their next-door neighbors are too, are they? There was a German girl rooming on my hall at school and I well remember once when her mother sent her a big 'cake' of homemade cheese. She was so thrilled – and we? – well – imagine our feelings.

The pictures you took Sunday night before you left turned

out much better than I expected. I didn't think they would be even printed. You'll agree at last with me that Kodak pictures of me are not flattering – do you wonder that I dislike having them taken? Shall I feel complimented when you call me a "Kitchen Mechanic?" 'All my mind is clouded with a doubt'.

Lee, you have certainly placed a responsibility on me. What shall I say? I know how you feel – I have similar experiences – but we both know conditions could be worse and, in all probability, would be. As I've told you many times, I cannot forget what I've learned in the twenty-five years of my life – neither can you. I wouldn't be happy pretending I believed what I do not – neither would you. We just as well face the truth no matter how much it hurts. The only suggestion I can make is for you to find some girl of your own belief – You can do the pursuing you know. I wish you all the good luck and may you be always happy. Remember, I told you that I'd always like you no matter what you were or what you did. Let me be one of your best friends – Is it possible for us to have this kind of friendship and not rekindle the old flames from time to time? Sometimes I think maybe the happiness I've had a taste of isn't for me – At least it seems that way now. Only time will tell. What have I written? These questions I'm asking my-self and I'm wondering whether I should mail this or not – At least I hope you will understand

– Chloe

On the next page is a photo of the Pan-American building Chloe visited that Saturday afternoon in late November. It can still be seen in Washington, D.C., though hard to recognize from this 1920s design. Many additions have been made. The building faces 17th Street NW, just north of the Mall.

CHAPTER 17
LA PUCELLE d'ORLÉANS

Levi's letter to Chloe, dated November 15, from Toulouse, included a bit of information on their time spent on their way to Southern France, in Orleans.

We left Paris for Orleans and then examined the Cathedral and several lesser churches. There still remains parts of the wall Joan d'Arc stormed in defeating the Normans and English. Of course the city is full of reminders of the Saint who rescued the city. Most of the stained glass in the cathedral depicts scenes of her life and monuments everywhere seem to picture her as a Saint. These reminders of her are several hundred years old which shows that the French people were convinced that she was in Heaven long before the Church felt that the proof was absolute. (She was canonized three years ago) – What seems peculiar to me is the fact that the French regard St. Joan as their most famous personage and yet historians give her scant attention in their accounts of French history. Most towns give her a greater prominence in their statuary than even Napoleon.

At Orleans, also, is a statue and shrine called Notre Dame of Miracles. The history of the statue is over a

*thousand years old and as far as we have been able to
decipher from the French it is an Ebony statue of the Virgin
which is supposed to have miraculously moved to protect
those who carried it into a battle in 897 . – You possibly
wonder what I think of such stories. I admit its possibility
but since we are not required to believe these stories, I just
feel interested in them.*

Levi was off a little in his description of Orleans and what he discovered there. The images of Saint Joan of Arc are apparent throughout the town, as they should be, since this is the place where she began the liberation of France from England.

Joan of Arc, the Maid of Orléans, was a young, martyred saint who fought to restore the French monarchy. She cleared the way for the crowning of Charles VII, the Dauphin, at Reims Cathedral in 1429. The locals still recognize the 17-year-old girl who delivered the town from siege. To this day, one hundred years after Levi's visit and another World War later, sections of the medieval wall that existed when Saint Joan stormed the town are still visible.

As for the story of the Madonna, Ella Rozett, author of *Our Lady of Miracles*, provided the story in detail. The original Madonna was carved out of wood and came to Orleans with Syrian Christians in the fifth century. It was during the ninth century that the people of the town, then called Avenum, carried the Madonna to the protective gates and asked her to deliver them from a Norman invasion. The keeper of the gate shot arrows as he stood behind the Madonna. The invaders told him the only hope for survival was to surrender, come down, and open the gate. They shot an arrow in his direction, and the Madonna's leg moved to protect the gatekeeper. Seeing this miracle, the enemies proclaimed that the Mother of God was defending Avenum. They threw down their arms and asked for peace. The Madonna was returned to the chapel where she stood for many centuries with the arrow protruding from her knee.

In 1429, Joan of Arc used a private passageway to the chapel. She prayed there daily and had a special affinity for the Queen of Heaven. Over 100 years later, during the Wars of Religion, the Huguenot soldiers (French Protestants) burned the Black Madonna.

A new statue was commissioned and carved, but this time from stone. According to Rozett, an artist familiar with the original Madonna was commissioned to create the replacement. He worked hard to maintain the original facial features, but he made many changes to the body of the figure. Mary now stands, instead of sitting, and in remembrance of her blocking the Norman arrow, her right knee is bent. The carved folds of her garment fall to either side, making her bent knee a focal point. This feature is secondary only to the Christ child she is holding.

During the French Revolution, orders were given to destroy *Our Lady of Miracles.* An attempt was made by a man who was a trained metalworker, but his hammers did little damage to the stone, chipping away only parts of her left hand, Christ's toes, and a bit of Mary's garment.

The chapel was enlarged and embellished in 1805 and again in 1922. The stone Madonna standing in the chapel today is the same one Levi saw in 1925. The damage inflicted during the French Revolution is noticeable and was never repaired. Though the Second World War destroyed Saint Paul's church, the Madonna's chapel and the church's tower survived. It was an eerie sight at the close of the war to see the grand church and surrounding neighborhood turned to rubble while the chapel and tower stood in defiance, a miracle of sorts, easily attributed to Notre Dame des Miracles.

CHAPTER 18
TOULOUSE WITHOUT LAUTREC

Toulouse, France
November 14, 1925
[travel journal]

We sat along the banks of the Garonne River and sketched and ate cheese, bread and carrots for dessert. The sun was out and fairly warm and right here I might mention that it was the first time I had seen a clear day since leaving Washington.

Toulouse is one of the oldest French cities. It is a beautiful city of three hundred thousand and is the oldest center of civilization in France. The Romans had a city here and it appears that it has always been considered the centre of French culture. They have a cathedral of brick here with a tower that is gradually crumbling down. They have several old bridges, a wonderful museum of Roman antiquities, a very old cathedral, a university which dates back a thousand years and a Basilica of St. Sernin.

Imagine yourself in a crypt in which repose the bodies of the Apostles, St. Jude, St. Barnabas, St. Philip, St. Simon and St. James the Minor. Also, a great part of the body of St. James the Major who you remember was the brother of St. John the Evangelist. Here also lies the body of St. Thomas Aquinas who taught at the University of Toulouse. There are relics of many other Saints and martyrs in the crypt and you can imagine how I felt on suddenly finding this treasury of relics of the church. I never wished more that I could talk and understand French than when we were talking to the priest who is guardian of the church crypt. He explained that most of the relics had been given to Charlemagne who brought them to France to be distributed throughout the country at the pope's orders. Charlemagne in turn gave them to the Benedictines at Toulouse. During the French Revolution, when the Benedictines were driven from France and their property taken, these treasures were moved to the crypt of the church of St. Sernin where they remain until today.

Saint Raymond who is the patron Saint of Architects designed this church. In this church there is also a large piece of the True Cross which was discovered by St. Helena in the year 326 . – St. Helena was the mother of Emperor Constantine.

I could go on "spouting" church history all afternoon. We meet so many different characters and have so much of what I used to long for "adventure" that it all seems like a long movie of Pathé News.

At our hotel every evening we meet an English and a French engineer. All of us get along well although the Englishman is as hard to understand as the Frenchman.

We intend to buy our bicycles here and start for Rome next Tuesday. The weather is hardly warm enough but we shall have to get use to it.

Levi was enthralled with Saint Sernin Basilica. It is the largest of all Romanesque buildings in Europe. The basilica is located on Via Tolosana, along the "Arles Way," a French route pilgrims follow on the Camino de Compostella.

Construction of this cathedral began in the eleventh century and spanned two centuries. The lengthy duration of construction can be seen in the tower above the crossing. The base is Romanesque, like the basilica, but the top tiers are Gothic, reflecting later design trends. The spire was not added until the fifteenth century.

The basilica was named after the first bishop of Toulouse, who was martyred nearby. In 250 A.D., Pagan priests tied the bishop to a bull and sent it running through the streets of Toulouse. Saint Sernin was buried on the spot where his lifeless body came to rest. To accommodate the large number of pilgrims on the Camino who stopped to visit his tomb, this basilica was built nearby, and Saint Sernin's tomb was relocated. Saint Sernin's original burial place now lies beneath the edifice of *Notre-Dame du Taur* (Our Lady of the Bull) church, a fourteenth to sixteenth-century building.

The many relics that Levi visited in 1925 are still housed in the basilica. The bones of over 200 saints reside there. This grouping of relics is second in size only to those held at the Vatican.

Levi cast aside the cathedral of brick with a gradually crumbling tower as one might an insignificant pile of standing debris. In 1925, it was impossible to recognize the significance of this structure. This was the Church of the Jacobins, a term often used in France for the Dominican Order.

Saint Dominic formed the *Ordo Praedicatorum* (Order of Preachers) in 1216, and Toulouse was at the heart of the new order. Six years earlier, Saint Dominic established a convent nearby in Prouille, predating the formation of the Dominican friars.

Everyone within the Order of Preachers was forced to leave following the French Revolution of 1789, and this church was turned over to the city of Toulouse. In 1810, Napoleon took charge of the structure. He added a floor over the grand nave to serve as barracks for his troops. The ground level where the lay and religious attended and celebrated mass was turned into stables. All medieval wall art was whitewashed, and the stained-glass windows were removed.

The photo below, provided by the Municipal Archives of Toulouse, was taken by Eugène and Marie-Joseph Delon circa 1865. Napoleon's desecration of this House of God is unmistakable.

Renovations have taken place since Levi's visit, and the church is worthy of visitation today, though it is a deconsecrated Roman Catholic church, and services are no longer held there. The relics of Saint Thomas Aquinas returned here once the restoration work was completed in 1976. Housed in a golden box called a reliquary, the tomb of this revered philosopher lies below the altar, fittingly, in the Church of the Jacobins.

Had Levi been aware of the history behind these falling bricks or the importance of the Order of Preachers would have on his future, he would have spent more time here, reflecting. Two of Levi's children followed in the footsteps that Saint Dominic put into motion here, in Toulouse.

CHAPTER 19
CARCASSONNE,
A MEDIEVAL CITÉ

November 23, 1925
⌈travel journal⌉

*We arrived in Narbonne yesterday night after pedaling
54 kilometers from Carcassonne. The road wound thru the
foothills of the Pyrenees and it was a beautiful ride. We*

could see the snow-capped mountains in the distance and John kept telling us that it was just like Denver.

We spent three nights at Carcassonne which is a beautiful walled city dating from the time of the Romans. We read in history that the Roman Senate ordered built strongholds at Carcassonne and Narbonne to protect its communications with Spain. On the original Roman foundations at Carcassonne were built the medieval fortifications which figure so much in the history of Gaul.

They remain almost in perfect preservation and some parts have been repaired under the direction of Viollet le-Duc which I feel do not improve the walls at all.

The church of St. Nazaire inside the walls of the city has some very beautiful stained glass. Carcassonne is a fairy city and I shall remember for a long time our view of the place from a neighboring hill as twilight deepened into darkness and the twinkling lights appeared below us. On these same hills the Moors assembled to besiege the fortress and probably waited on the self-same hill where we stood and waited for the defenders to use their supply of food and then surrender.

A look into the 1888 publication of *La Cité de Carcassonne (Aude)* by Viollet le Duc revealed the extensive work undertaken to uncover the history of Carcassonne. Le Duc laid out his plan for the restoration of the walled town in his book. He was a renowned architect known for his work restoring medieval landmarks throughout France.

The tower roofs were missing when le Duc began reconstruction of the city. Several structures attached to the ramparts over the centuries were removed to restore

Carcassonne to medieval times. Apparently, not everyone embraced his mastery of architectural renovation.

Carcassonne, France
November 20, 1925

Dear Mother,

We are two days out of Toulouse on our bikes and we feel like standing up at meal time. Our first night we went to bed at seven o'clock. The ride has been wonderful. The weather is warm but rainy. As we rode along yesterday, we could see the snow-covered Pyrenees Mountains in the distance. This was my first view of real mountains and it was quite a thrill.

The many oxen plowing in the fields along the road remind me of the Paul Bunyan stories. This is a land where no one is in a hurry. Our arrival in a village is quite an event. The children scurry to shelter, the dogs bark while the pigs and chickens run to safety. If we get off of our wheels in the middle of the street the window shutters start opening and every woman in the block takes a good look at us – I suppose we are a treat to look at.

Today is Friday and as usual we have to start a row before we can get anything but meat to eat. They wouldn't give us eggs this noon but we sat tight and they finally gave in and hauled out some half-fried eggs. They load everything up with garlic and so far, we haven't managed to get used to it.

December 9 is Vinc Engels birthday and we are planning to have a big feed if we can find someone to cook us a Turkey.

Carcassonne is a beautiful walled town dating from the sixth century. The Romans had a fort here and part of the original walls remain. We climbed all around the walls this afternoon and watched a shepherd herd a flock of sheep and goats. It was the first time I had seen a sheep dog in action. We shall be in Marseilles in about two weeks and then to Nice.

With love, Levi

The name "Vinc," which appears in Levi's letter, is not a typo or a common nickname for anyone named Vince. Vince is the short form of Vincent, but Levi never referred to Vincent David Engels as Vincent or Vince; he was always Vinc, the son of Euphrasia and William Engels from Green Bay, Wisconsin. Levi always spells Marseille with an extra "s," Marseilles, but this is not correct in English or French.

Agde, France
November 24, 1925

Dear Chloe,

 Tomorrow, please tell the children entrusted in your care that the climate in Southern France along the Mediterranean is not warm in winter time. Tell them that geography books are fiction and warn them to take their overcoats and "heavies" to the Sunny climes.

 Our trio has shivered more in the last week down here than we would up in Wisconsin. (I just had to mention the dear old place).

 Many hotels have no heat whatever so when night comes, we put all our clothes on and drink 'vin rouge' to keep warm. If you could see me huddled up writing this with both of the boys wrapped up in bed clothes you would understand how hard it is to write a cheerful letter. Yes it would be very difficult were I not thinking of you.

 Engels just remarked, "Say, how many times are you going to read that letter?" It's the truth; I have one letter to read all the way to Rome and I shall probably read it many more times.

 We have stopped at many interesting little cities since leaving Toulouse but Carcassonne ranks first in interest. It still retains its medieval walls and turrets and its history is worth noting. Here goes:

Sometime B.C. Lucius Crassus of the Roman Senate established a military post at Carcassonne to protect communication with the Province in Spain. In 350 A.D. the Franks took the fort but it was recaptured by the Romans. Theodoric, King of the Visigoths was next to take possession in 436. Clovis tried to enter the town in 508 but failed. The Moors captured the city in 713 and for the next several centuries little is known of its history. In 1096 Pope Urban II came to Carcassonne to establish peace among its citizens and he laid the "corner stone" of the Cathedral of St. Nazaire which still stands. From then on it was one siege after another during the Middle Ages and today there remains traces of all the different fortifications.

We spent two days wandering around its walls and one evening we climbed a neighboring hill on which the Moors had encamped before taking the city.

The sun set and with darkness came the twinkling lights of the village folk while we sat and talked about the wars before the walls of Carcassonne.

Many historical layers combined to form this medieval city. The Basilica of Saints Nazarius and Celsus, referred to by Levi as the church of St. Nazaire, is a sandstone structure located within the medieval walls atop the hill overlooking the Aude River. The majority of the structures on the right side of the medieval city in Levi's panoramic photo belong to the Basilica.

Originally built in a Romanesque style, elements from the eleventh century are exemplified by rounded archways. Near the end of the thirteenth century, Gothic alterations were made, which were the prevailing style of that time period. Examples of Gothic design are evident with the addition of gargoyles and grotesques, pointed arches, and elongated windows, which illuminated the interior. This religious structure was once the Cathedral of Carcassonne, but in

1803, that title was given to Saint Michel, a church on the other side of the Aude River. Today, the seat of the Bishop of Carcassonne and Narbonne remains at the Cathédrale Saint-Michel de Carcassonne.

The trio rode due east from Carcassonne, in search of the waters of the Mediterranean. Since they traveled by bike, the route was foreseeable; the plan was to steer clear of the Pyrenees Mountains.

CHAPTER 20
MEANWHILE, BACK IN THE STATES

The Saturday before Thanksgiving was a perfect time of year for a football rivalry, especially in South Bend, Indiana. The trio would miss this one, of course, but a record of the win was found among Levi's letters. Maybe Levi's little brother, Os, short for Oswald, sent the update to delight the Notre Dame University graduates.

Os wore number 49 for the Fighting Irish. He was coached by Knute Rockne, who held the highest winning percentage of any coach in history for over eighty years. What Knute accomplished in 122 games took the new leader, Larry Kehres, 359 games to surpass. Rockne led the Fighting Irish to 105 wins, 12 losses, and five ties over 12 years. Knute Rockne was to football what God is to Christianity. He revolutionized the game by perfecting the forward pass.

Rockne was not the only notable part of the Fighting Irish's 1924 season. Four players from Notre Dame gained unforgettable fame with a fabulously coined nickname, the Four Horsemen of the Apocalypse. Grantland Rice, sportswriter for the *New York Herald Tribune*, described the scene from the Notre Dame versus Army game played at the Polo Grounds in New York that fall. *The South Bend Tribune* headline on Sunday read, "Notre Dame Bests Army." A full column was filled with Grantland Rice's recap, titled, "Cadets Prove No Match for Speedy Backs."

Outlined against a blue-gray October sky, the Four Horsemen rode again. In dramatic lore they are known as Famine, Pestilence, Destruction and Death. These are only aliases. Their real names are Stuhldreher, Miller, Crowley and Layden (1).

Jim Crowley, the halfback who laid claim to Pestilence, was from Green Bay. Jim and Os played on East High's football team. Their coach was none other than legendary Earl "Curly" Lambeau, founder and coach of the Green Bay Packers and namesake of their beloved stadium. In the 1920 issue of East High's yearbook, *The Aeroplane*, Jim Crowley was noted to have thrown "forward passes with deadly accuracy. It was through his marvelous passing that the 'Hilltoppers' were able to run up such large scores" (76). This was all attributed back to Knute Rockne, since Curly Lambeau learned from the best when he played for Notre Dame.

Returning to Levi's postcard from the Notre Dame versus Northwestern game, the photo captured their seventh meeting. Northwestern had defeated Notre Dame only once, back in 1901, with a score of 2-0. Both teams ended up with a scoreless tie in 1903. The

1925 game put another win into the books for Notre Dame, though Oswald was not on the field.

A month earlier, while Levi was in New York preparing to board the Leviathan, the Notre Dame football team attended a banquet in the Big Apple. Levi rushed over for a quick visit with his little brother before departing for Europe. In his October 19th letter to Chloe, from the *City of Noses*, Levi wrote:

> *Friday's big events were: a visit to the Baltimore Country Club to see the team. My brother did not accompany the team and another fellow from our home town says that he is thru football. At night we visited the Hippodrome Theatre but was disappointed in the show.*

The most likely reason for Os giving up on the team was a lack of playing time. He was the backup for one of the Four Horsemen, Jim Crowley. Regardless of the position, he would not see much ball time and, in fact, only played in one game during the 1924 season. But Blue and Gold ran through all their veins. Vince, the journalist of the traveling trio, worked as the sports correspondent for the South Bend News-Times alongside Frank Wallace, who went on to become a legendary sports journalist.

The season ended on New Year's Day of 1925. Notre Dame went up against Stanford in the 11th meeting of the Rose Bowl. That was the first postseason play for the Fighting Irish. Notre Dame's undefeated 1924 season ended with a 27-10 victory over Stanford. This win made Notre Dame the first National Champions in college football.

CHAPTER 21
BUTTRESSES TAKE FLIGHT

The trio spent two nights in Narbonne. Per Levi, it was *another Roman town with little that remains of interest outside the walls of the city museum.* He left no details concerning the city museum; perhaps it was the Musée d'Art et d'Histoire de Narbonne, a collection that began in 1833 and is housed in the Palace of the Archbishops.

Levi's travel journal offered a little more on the town of Narbonne.

> *The Church of St. Paul dates from the twelfth century and was never completed. Its construction is very heavy. The Cathedral of St. Just presents a problem for the student of architectural history. The chancel is completed and is wonderful as regards height and proportion. From the exterior the church is of interest only in the use of different flying buttresses which are arched from one to another. Several later attempts were made to complete the edifice but the indifference of the Reformation or the anarchism of the Revolution stopped what promised to be a Psalm of stone to Almighty God.*

Levi mentioned The Church of St. Paul and The Cathedral of St. Just, known today as *Basilique Saint-Paul* (Basilica of Saint Paul) and *Cathédrale Saint-Just-et-Saint-Pasteur* (Cathedral of Saint Just and Saint Pasteur). Of the two, the basilica is older, easily evident after a quick review of the exterior.

The construction of the basilica is very heavy, as Levi noted. It was the first Gothic church in Narbonne and is one of the oldest examples in Southern France. The evolution from Romanesque to Gothic architecture is visible throughout the cathedral's design. The windows are larger, and though the rounded Romanesque arches are evident, many come to a point in the center, which signifies a Gothic design. Though the windows have increased in size when compared to earlier structures, they do not compare to those of the designs to come.

Buttresses are another clear sign of Gothic design, and they are present at Saint Paul. These arched extremities offer support by extending from a high point on the wall to a separate structure some distance away. When viewed from above, these anchoring supports are akin to the legs of a crudely drawn caterpillar.

The addition of buttresses allowed the walls to climb higher, the windows to become larger, and the overall size of these buildings to in-

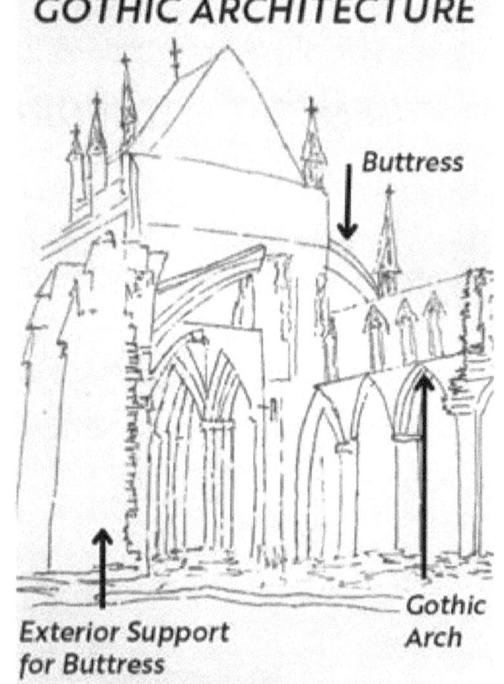

crease enough to serve the faithful. The buttresses at this basilica are heavy in structure, and the size of the windows does not compare to those that came later in the Gothic period.

The only confusion in Levi's recollection of Narbonne was the statement that Saint Paul was never completed. It was the Cathedral of Saint Just and Saint Pasteur that remained incomplete.

This cathedral, simply referred to as Narbonne Cathedral, is easily identified as High Gothic. The walls stretch toward the heavens, and light fills the interior, entering through massive windows. The buttresses of the Cathedral are delicate in design, offering more than simply support; they are pleasing to the eye and a wonder to behold.

Levi correctly noted that only the chancel was complete. In a cruciform church such as this, the chancel comprises the eastern end of the church where the priest, altar, and choir are located. A simplistic drawing of a generic cruciform church is shown below.

The crossing part of the church, called the transept, was never added to the Narbonne Cathedral. The nave, where the faithful would have been seated, is also missing. Though Levi hypothesized that either the Reformation or the Revolution was to blame for the Cathedral's lack of completion, most sources attribute it to a need for protection.

GENERAL CATHEDRAL FLOORPLAN

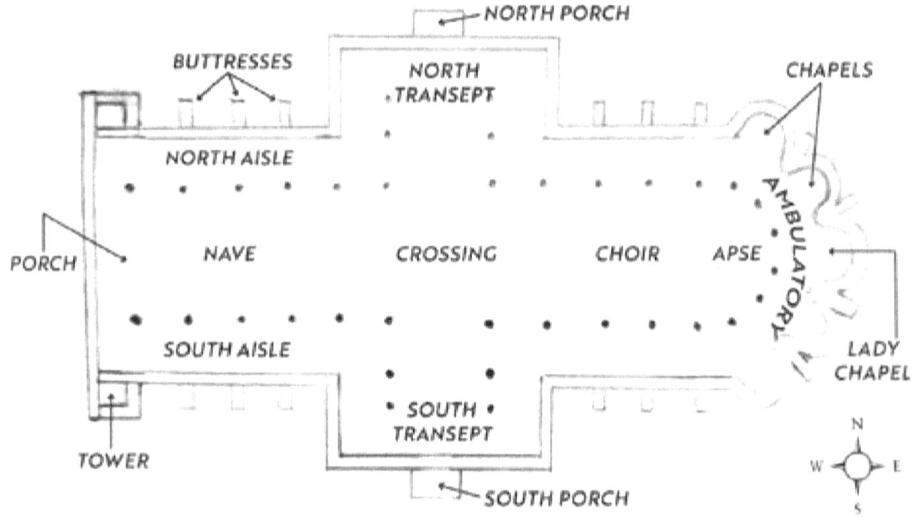

Town leaders chose to retain the city wall instead of demolishing sections to provide space for construction to continue.

Levi, John, and Vince continued by bicycle from Narbonne, following the arc of the coastline and riding just north of the Natural Regional Park. After 51 kilometers (31 miles), the cyclists reached the little fishing village of Agde, France. Levi shared the moment with Chloe.

Vinc and I took a walk along the quay and watched the

*fishing boats come in this evening and what appealed to me
was the sight of the fishermen's wives and children greeting
the small sail boats as they docked with their meagre catch
of various colored fish.*

*And speaking of fish, how do you open a can of sardines
without cutting your fingers? You can imagine me opening or rather smashing a box of sardines with a stone "a
la stone age style." We tear huge French breads apart and
devour the crunching crusts while at the breathing spells,
the gulps of red wine follow our favorite cheeses. Today we
bought large bunches of celery and munched that as we rode
along. As Engels said today, we are slowly reverting to our
original type of ancestors.*

*Am enclosing a card that is the picture of a miraculous
crucifix placed in a church here. I shall try to translate the
legend that appears in French on the card. There seems to
be a great number of such legends among the French people
and if we could only talk the language, we would probably
hear many interesting stories.*

This crucifix stands in the *Église Saint-Sever* (Church of Saint Sever), located among the winding, narrow, and predominantly pedestrian streets of Agde. The legend tells of a traveler who asked to be locked in a room and not bothered for a week. During that time, food was brought to the traveler's door. He remained isolated. At the end of a week, the visitor disappeared and left on the floor the beautiful Christ shown on this card. Many researchers believe this to be the work of Michelangelo, as the period

and style match other works attributed to the Renaissance master.

During the French Revolution, the Christ figure was thrown into the Hérault River but was later retrieved by a fisherman and hidden in his home. The river flows nearby as it approaches the Mediterranean Sea, separating the historic center of Agde from the farmlands west of town. Many miracles are attributed to the veneration of this crucifix.

This was a short stop in a small historic town after leaving Narbonne. If these well-travelled roads dropped the trio at the feet of a Michelangelo masterpiece, it was well worth the ride.

CHAPTER 22
OF YOU, LITTLE
IS WRITTEN

November 30, 1925
[travel journal]

Montpelier was next and it proved to be a surprise. We found it a clean and beautiful city. It has a fine museum and an old university. The arboretum of the school was well worth examining. Montpelier has a cathedral with a porch which is terrible for its design.

According to researcher Hilarie M. Hicks , the word Montpellier evokes an image of being in the mountains, existing in a space where one prolonged inhalation fills the lungs with healthy mountain air. This medieval French city was built on two hills with higher peaks visible in the distance. Though little was written in Levi's travel journal, Montpellier's fine museum, old university, school arboretum, and cathedral revealed a world like no other.

The museum Levi mentioned was undoubtedly Musée Fabre, the only museum listed on a mid-1920s map published by the Dufrénoy Printers. Located beside the library on Boulevard de l'Esplanade in 1925, the street name has since changed to Boulevard Bonne Nouvelle. Unfortunately, no attention was drawn to the artwork found in the museum.

The old university received a mention in Levi's journal, but the passiveness and brevity made the place seem insignificant. Montpellier is home to one of the oldest medical schools in the world , which traces its history back to 1137. The Jardin des Plantes, the place Levi referred to as the arboretum, was designed in 1593 by Pierre Richer de Belleval, the director of anatomy and botany at that time. This is the oldest botanical garden in France. The focus there is on the medicinal advantages of various cultivars.

The cloister from the monastery of *Saint-Benoît* (Saint Benedict) became part of the School of Medicine. The decorative faculty entrance is located just left of the porch of the *Cathédrale Saint Pierre* (Saint Peter Cathedral) . The cylindrical pillars and arched porch that Levi considered terrible for the design are the only remnants of the original medieval structure.

Catholics used this cathedral as a stronghold against the Protestants and referred to the structure as Fort Saint-Pierre during the War of Religion in the sixteenth century. Every religious building within the historic center of Montpellier was destroyed during that war. The cathedral was not restored until 1629, after Louis XIII returned Catholicism to Montpellier and the surviving medieval porch was retained in the redesign.

In the nineteenth century, attention turned to preservation. The Inspector of Historical Monuments, Prosper Mérimée, visited the site in 1835 and shared Levi's opinion towards the medieval pillars. Elsa Trani's paper on the cathedral revealed Mérimée's impressions of the grand porch. He, too, felt the massive columns detracted from the façade, that they hid the structure instead of adorning it as a porch should. Mérimée could not imagine a heavier or less graceful design. Regardless, given the historical importance of the porch, it remains.

As Levi focused on his own battles over religion while travelling through Southern France, he had no idea this terribly designed porch stood at the epicenter of a great conflict between Catholics and Protestants three hundred years earlier.

Photoglob Co., Publisher. Montpellier. *Cathédrale et Faculté de Médecine*
(Montpellier: Cathedral and Faculty of Medicine, 1906)

CHAPTER 23
PALM TREES AND CROCODILES

Levi wrote to his father when they stopped in Avignon, France, on November 30. A few lines touched on their visit to Nimes.

At Nimes we spent three days wandering around the old Roman ruins. There are remains of then public baths which make a better park system than anything we have in A merica. I am just beginning to realize that the things they told us in history classes were not fairy tales.

Les Jardins de la Fontaine (The Gardens of the Fountain) was one of the first public gardens in Europe. It is hard to realize when visiting here that the water features were once Roman baths. They make a perfect base for the park.

The gardens are vast. *The Tour Magne* (Great Tower), shown on the right, is located at the highest point of the park, farthest from the entrance. This Roman structure from the first century A.D. was built atop a 16-15 B.C. Gallic tower. A climb up an interior circular stone staircase leads to the panoramic view of Nimes from the highest point in the city.

This is the only remaining tower out of 80 from the wall that encircled Nimes by 16 A.D. Completed during a time of peace, the wall was built to represent the power of Rome and not as a means of defense.

A central theme appears in carvings and metal plaques throughout the city to this day. The crocodile chained to a palm tree symbolizes Nimes appearing first on a coin struck in Nemausus, the Gallic name for the ancient city. The crocodile represented Egypt, and the palm tree symbolized Rome's victory when Emperor Augustus defeated Marc Antony and Cleopatra. A few lines in Levi's December 2 letter to Chloe reflected their visit to Nimes.

Nimes was all that we had expected. It is here that the most perfect remains of Roman buildings are found. The amphitheatre is now used for bull fighting. We had hoped to see a performance but luck was not with us and we'll have to wait until we reach Spain.

The Roman amphitheater in Nimes is the best-preserved structure of this type, including the Colosseum in Rome. Inspired by and built just after the Colosseum in the first century A.D., this is an amphitheater. There is only one Colosseum.

Twenty-four thousand spectators were entertained in Nimes. The Colosseum in Rome could hold fifty thousand, as a conservative estimate. Some raise that number closer to ninety thousand. Attendees sat by rank with the highest-ranking individuals seated closest to the action. Historical reenactments, concerts, and bullfighting still take place in Nimes.

Levi stood at the highest point on the southeastern side of the amphitheater and faced northwest to take the above photo. Visible nearby is the steeple of Saint Paul with the Tour Magne in the distance, perched on a hill.

Before departing Nimes, they stopped at the *Monument Aux Morts* (War Memorial) for a moment of prayer. The walls were filled with the names of over twelve thousand local heroes who made the ultimate sacrifice, while the mosaic floor they surrounded listed out the many battles they fought in.

CHAPTER 24
FIFTY KILOMETERS TO NEMAUSUS

Avignon, France
November 30, 1925

Dear Father,

We pulled in here tonight after a tough climb in the mountains. Left Nimes this morning and reached an old Roman aqueduct by eleven o'clock where we camped and ate our cheese and bread. The bridge which is about 125 feet high and about 1,800 years old was built to carry water some forty or fifty miles away.

We crawled or rather walked into the tunnel which ran thru the ground under the hills. The tunnel was supposed to run for miles but 200 feet was enough for us before we turned back to daylight.

Vince's cheese and bread lunch came with a wonderful view of the Gardon River, a spot that was not truly accessible. He had to cross a waist-high stone wall to reach his perch.

According to Avignon-et-Provence, Pont du Gard was part of a fifty-kilometer-long Roman aqueduct system built to transport water from the small village of Uzès, across the Gardon River to Nemausus. The difference in elevation between start and finish was around forty feet. For gravity to power the flow of water, the aqueduct could not drop more than twenty-four centimeters every kilometer. That equates to fifteen-and-a-half inches for every mile, for approximately thirty-one miles. These calculations were made in 19 B.C., though some estimate construction to have taken place in the middle of the first century. The Pont du Gard aqueduct system served Nemausus, present-day Nimes, until the sixth century.

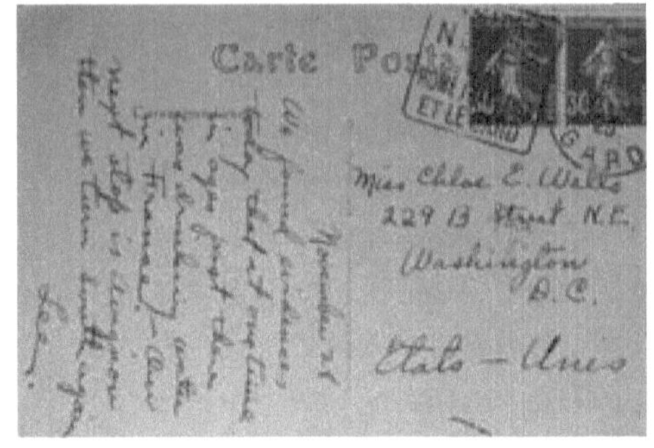

November 28

We found evidences today that at one time in ages past there was drinking water in France. – Our next stop is Avignon then we turn South again.

Lee

In Levi's December 2, 1925 letter to Chloe from Beaucaire, he added:

The famous aqueduct, a picture of which is seen in every history, is still in good condition. We spent an afternoon climbing around it and crawled thru an old Roman tunnel. We were afraid to investigate the old tunnel thru the hills and I don't believe anyone has gone to the end of it. We crawled about 200 feet from the entrance when one of us mentioned Floyd Collins and without a dissenting voice we turned back to daylight again.

In 1925, Floyd Collins was a household name. He tried to find a new entrance to the caves of Kentucky in a fight for the potential tourism dollars that could save his family's farm. In January, Floyd went into Sand Cave and was trapped. Once word got out, thousands gathered outside the mouth of the cave to witness the rescue efforts. Initially, a journalist from Louisville was able to reach Floyd and interview him while providing food and water for the trapped spelunker. For his efforts, Skeets Miller received a Pulitzer Prize. A second cave-in stopped their progress and cut off any access to Floyd. By day 18, a fifty-five-foot shaft reached Floyd, but he was not alive.

There was no mention of Floyd Collins in Levi's letter to his father. Some news can be used to amaze a potential girlfriend with your sense of adventure, but the same description when relayed to your parents provokes anxiety.

The aqueduct is no longer accessible to hillside penetrating exploration. It would not be permissible to have a picnic where Levi, Vince, and John enjoyed their bread and cheese, as the posted sign prohibits crossing the parapet.

The vantage point Levi used for the photo of the aqueduct on the previous page no longer exists. It seems, on inspection, that one of the hillsides crumbled over time. Today, gates and fencing prohibit tourists from contemplating a remake of the following photograph.

This image of Levi atop the aqueduct offers a sense of scale. The stones look more like a Roman road than the cap to a stone aqueduct. Their exhausting day in the mountains on the way to Avignon made it into the *Green Bay Press-Gazette* (15).

Former P.-G. Scribe Uses 'Bike' On Tour of France and Italy

VINCENT D. ENGELS

Engels, who is writing a series of articles for The Press-Gazette while touring Europe, was "snapped" by a companion as the trio of young men making the trip were about to embark on an intensive investigation of the rural communities of Southern France. The picture was taken at Avignon. At Genoa, snow interfered with the bicycles and the journey through Italy continued by train. Engels is a former member of The Press-Gazette editorial staff. He sailed for Europe last October.

FORMER P.-G. SCRIBE USES 'BIKE ON TOUR OF FRANCE AND ITALY
Vincent D. Engels

Engels, who is writing a series of articles for The Press-Gazette while touring Europe, was "snapped" by a companion as the trio of young men making the trip were about to embark on an intensive investigation of the rural communities of Southern France. The picture was taken at Avignon. At Genoa, snow interfered with the bicycles and the journey through Italy continued by train. Engels is a former member of The Press-Gazette editorial staff. He sailed for Europe last October.

CHAPTER 25
SUR LE PONT d'AVIGNON

Levi's November 30 letter to his father from Avignon continued.

Avignon is a place a little bit larger than Green Bay and is situated at the bottom of a bowl formed by mountains all around. We tested out our French brakes coming down the hills today and found that they work all right. The roads run about as good as the gravel roads in Wisconsin so that we bounce around quite a bit. Our hotel rooms cost us an average of 15 francs a night for the three of us or about 22¢ apiece. Proportionately however the meals are much higher. We live on a dollar a day but we expect to find it harder going in Italy. We expect to reach Rome a few days before Christmas and stay there at least ten days.

Avignon is the old town in which the popes lived for 77 years in the fourteenth century. We intend to go thru the old Papal palace tomorrow as well as see all the old churches and other places of interest.

Tonite I must darn my socks so I'll close.

With love, Levi

It is interesting to compare Levi's words to his father with those shared with Chloe. Two days after his letter from Avignon, Levi wrote to Chloe from Beaucaire, a two-hour ride away.

Beaucaire, France
December 2, 1925

Dear Chloe,

    I'm writing this in a wine shop so if you are terribly shocked you may stop reading now. The only places they have stoves in is the 'grog' shops and you couldn't read this if I wrote with mittens on in our room.

    Such rooms, we call them refrigerators in the States. Every night we eat our potage and then spend the evening until bed time in some wine shop and argue politics and religion. Every few minutes tonite we have been arguing as to our destination after leaving Rome. The gang has been talking about a trip to the Holy Land and Egypt. We have been trying to figure out some way of getting back after we do get there. It's a great life with our cheese and bread and arguing over half pennies as if they were dollars. Fighting over a widow's mite is more than a principle now. We see hard times coming next spring and Engels is writing desperate copy for the newspapers.

    Last night I must have had one beer too much because I attempted to write some poetry. Some time you shall laugh at my efforts but not today. Engels has written something real good and I'll send it along when he says it's ready for publi-cation.

Levi did not include his attempt at poetry in the letter to Chloe. Thankfully, a tattered notebook was found among his belongings. "Handy Notes" was printed across the cover. The only page still attached to the binding offers the missing poem, as provided on the following page.

Avignon [November 1925]

Avignon,
your glory a dusty memory of kings kneeling before thee.

What wilt thou now?

You have had all that mortar, stone and wood could envy.

It was not yours,
and pilgrims bared of head and foot no longer trod your
cobbled streets.

No longer do the shepherds of Christendom turn to thee.

Thy day is done and eternal Rome again guides the world.

Though Vince's poem never appeared in their letters, *The Commonweal* published the piece in 1927 (396).

Avignon

Gregory, mighty Pope, looks down
On the little twilit town,
Rosy town of Avignon;
Seeing rock and roof and spire
And the grey hill, rising higher,
Shutting out the sun;
Children playing, old men sleeping
By the white road-ribbon creeping
Where Rhone waters run.

Now the Provence moon is up,
Stars are jewels in night's cup,

God hath planned it fair.
Bells ring out the vesper hour,
Gregory, from his lofty tower,
Breathes a humble prayer
For the moon and stars that shine,
And earth, drinking of the wine
That skies gladly share.

Provence men in far-off Spain,
Flanders, Anjou, gay Touraine,
Dream them of their home ---
He, secure in Avignon,
Waits to see the morning sun
Striking through the gloam.
Ah, poor Lord of Christendom,
Listening, as for a drum
Beating, slow, in Rome.

Levi's early December letter to Chloe continued.

We spent two days at Avignon and enjoyed every bit of the time. We entered the town just as the sun set down the banks of the Rhone. An old fort soon outlined its dark form against the dusky sky as did the towers of the Papal palaces across the river.

Here seven popes lived and ruled for a period of seventy years. This almost forgotten city was the center of the Christian world from 1305 to 1377 and the removal of the popes from Rome during this period was the indirect cause of "the great schism." In 1791 the Papal properties were seized by the revolutionists and in 1797 a treaty was made with the pope in which France was given these buildings.

French troops were quartered there for about eighty years and practically all the art treasures and frescoes have been destroyed. The exterior resembles the other fortresses of the middle ages but the interior must have been wonderful if we judge by the few hints of greatness that remain.

Crossing the Rhone is a small bridge about a thousand years old which an old legend tells us was built by a shepherd boy twelve years of age. The story is given in the stained glass of a real old church which pictures an angel directing the boy who in turn showed the people how the bridge was to be built. There is a chapel on the bridge and the Saints bones are encased in its masonry. [you understand of course that legends such as this have nothing to do with the cannonization of a Saint].

Levi seems confused when it came to Saint Bénézet's bones, as they were never placed within the mortar of the Chapel of Saint Nicolas. Maybe the details were lost in translation. Saint Bénézet died before the bridge was completed. It was destroyed in 1226 by Louis VIII of France during the siege of Avignon.

A stone bridge replaced the original wooden bridge, and a chapel dedicated to Saint Nicholas, patron saint of the Rhone boatmen, was erected above the second pier. Several repairs were made over the years, but the flooding of the Rhone in the mid-1600s dealt the final blow. Only four of the original twenty-two arches remain.

To protect the remains of Saint Bénézet, they were removed from the chapel in the 1600s. His coffin was opened in the presence of the Grand Vicar, and the remains were found to be incorrupt, meaning that Saint Bénézet's body showed no signs of decomposition. He was initially placed in the Cathedral in Avignon and later moved to the Church of Saint Didier.

The Chapel of Saint Nicolas still stands above the second pier and has experienced substantial alteration over the years, though there are no significant differences when comparing Levi's photo from 1925 to how it looks today.

Though most research leaves a reader with the idea that Saint Bénézet's incorruptible body lies at rest in Avignon, there is more to the story. The saint's body had not changed for 700 years until his remains were desecrated during the French Revolution in 1791. What could be gathered in the aftermath was moved to the cathedral and now rests at Église Saint Didier. A Latin inscription marks the location, *Sancte Benedicte ora pro nobis* (Saint Benedict pray for us).

The location of the stained glass Levi mentioned remains a bit of a mystery. Though stained-glass windows exist in the Église Saint

Didier, none match Levi's description. The old church has not been identified.

On December 12, Levi added little to his travel journal concerning Avignon. He had just crossed into Italy and reflected on almost twelve days of travel.

> *At Avignon we saw the Palace of the Popes and then several other churches. There is also a small museum with a wonderful ivory crucifix. Crossing the Rhone at Avignon are the remains of a historic bridge which was built by a boy who was later canonized by the Church.*

The small museum Levi visited in Avignon was Musée Calvet. The ivory crucifix he appreciated seeing was commissioned by the *Pénitents Noirs de la Miséricorde* (Black Penitents of Mercy), a religious brotherhood formed in 1588. They dedicated themselves to Saint John the Baptist.

The Brotherhood served prisoners. In 1596, Pope Clément VIII granted them the privilege of saving the life of one condemned criminal annually, on the commemorated anniversary of Saint John the Baptist's beheading. Clément VIII was not an Avignon pope; the Papal court had returned to Rome some 200 years earlier.

A former museum curator, Joseph Girard, described the process of freeing a prisoner in his book, *Évocation du Vieil Avignon* (Evocation of Old Avignon). Once the vice-legate accepted a request for a condemned prisoner's release, the members of the Black Penitents returned to their chapel, dressed the former prisoner in a red robe with a garland of olive branches, and paraded together through the streets of the city, engulfed in song. Any procession made by the brotherhood was preceded by the Guillermin crucifix.

It was in 1659 that sculptor Jean-Baptiste Guillermin created the twenty-six-inch elephant-ivory crucifix. The brotherhood was abolished during the French Revolution in 1792, but its chapel remains. The façade still beautifully depicts two angels raising a platter holding the head of their patron saint.

The Christ figure was donated to the museum in 1862. It remains on exhibit today in the Saint-Priest Room.

CHAPTER 26
TRAVERSING PROVENCE

Nice, France
December 9, 1925

Dear Chloe,

I've reached the end of my yarn and there are still some socks to darn. Believe me I've "darned" them plenty. We reached here yesterday evening and today was "Saturday night" for us. A nice hotel with bath tubs and everything, a real heavenly or hell-ly warm radiator, these are comforts which we 'gentlemen of the road' consider real topics of conversation. I'll try to describe all we've seen since my last letter. After Avignon came Beaucaire, Tarascon and Arles.

Tarascon has the church of St. Martha, the sister of Mary, of whom is told the parable in the Bible. She came to Gaul in the year 36 A.D. and her body was discovered at Tarascon in the third century. A church was built on the spot and parts of the building dating from the seventh century still remain.

Arles of course is famous for its Roman remains and as at Nimes the amphitheatre is used for bull fighting.

At Aix-en-Provence I ate dinner with a French soldier who is studying to be a Methodist minister at Toulouse

University. As soon as he has put in his time in the army he is going to England and then to Ohio Wesleyan (University) in America. He told me that he preferred English speaking peoples to his own native French because he thinks them more religious. Yes, I told him he might be surprised.

"Without seeing Marseilles one has seen nothing." Whoever said that felt as we did on seeing the principal seaport of France. Here are gathered people from everywhere; one might even include hell along with the other countries.

Beachcombers, wharf rats, all manner of human wrecks eke out an existence however they may. The fishermen, the sailors and the women who live on the money some boy was saving to go home all make a scene which we had never seen before.

Above the city guarding the harbor, as does our own Statue of Liberty in New York, stands a church called Notre Dame de la Garde. A giant statue of Our Lady surmounts the church steeple. It is lighted after dark and looks down on a city from which one would say no good can come; --- and yet let me tell you a story.

Engels and I were sitting in a café looking dirty, unshaven and I suppose "hard up" when an Algerian sailor who had been three years in America stopped to buy us a cup of coffee and give us advice. He assumed that we were stranded there without even a bed for the night as was his case.

He told us how to "bum" someone for money, explained the technique of getting free meals and a place to sleep and offered to find us a job on some boat. He introduced us to two 'beachcomber' friends of his and while we were still with him, he gave another beggar the franc he had just collected saying, "He's worse off than I am and we're all in the same boat." That was an act of charity that I shall never forget.

After letting him believe we were broke we could not dis-illusion him to the fact that we still had several square meals ahead but I never wished anyone a more hearty "good luck" than he.

Nice seems to be what the Sunday papers tell us at home. A great part of the world's "society" spends their winters here and the hotels, shops, restaurants, and Casinos all give evidence that money comes to Nice every winter.

We are going to Monte Carlo tomorrow to buy a deck of cards and play "penny ante" just so we can tell the folks back home.

In another week I'll reach Rome and your letters.

Till then, Lee

There is some repetition between Levi's letter to Chloe and what he wrote three days later in his travel journal. A few details add to the description of their days in Provence, a southeastern region of France that runs from the Rhone to Italy.

Ventimiglia, Italy
December 12, 1925
⌈travel journal⌉

Before writing anything about Italy which we entered tonite I will briefly sketch the last few days in France.

We left Avignon and rode to Arles which has its amphi-theatre and other Roman ruins. The Church of St.

Trophime is the most interesting building in the city.

Beaucaire was our next stop where we viewed several old chateaus. Across the river is the town of Tarascon where in the Church of St. Martha lies the remains of St. Martha who was the sister of Mary of the biblical parable. Parts of the church crypt were built in the seventh century.

Aix-en-Provence was our next stop. This is a beautiful little city. Here I met a French soldier who was studying to be a Methodist minister. He said he liked English speaking peoples because they were more religious than his French.

Next to Paris I believe Marseilles to be our most interesting city in France. The big seaport with its population from all over the world presented to us a contrast of good and evil. The wharf rats, the beachcombers, the beggars, the fishermen and women and the "streetwalkers" all add to a scenic beauty which makes Marseilles the place of interest that it is. It was here that Vinc and I met our beachcomber friend who taught us a lesson of true charity. It is here that the beautiful Byzantine cathedral stands and over the harbor is the Church of Notre Dame de la Garde with its statue of the Virgin and Child lighted at night. I shall not forget the angelus bells ringing out over the city as darkness slowly draped itself over the sparkling lights. Some day I hope to go back to Marseille and again watch the battle of good and evil.

We took the train to Nice and had plenty of excitement when Vinc lost his wheel. We recovered the wheel from the taxi owner but Vinc was out a fountain pen and a belt when we found that someone had been thru my suitcase.

Nice is almost an American city and with Cannes, Monaco, Monte Carlo and Menton comprises the French Riviera, the playground of the rich. The place is beautiful, the casinos gorgeous, the Mediterranean with its deep blue color is an appropriate background for the gaily colored villas along the sea.

We did not have the trouble entering Italy that we had expected and tonite we find ourselves sleeping on Italian soil wondering how we are going to get along.

The boys headed southwest from Avignon, following the road that matched the bends of the Rhone River. They reached Beaucaire and took in the beauty of the castle that overlooked the Rhone, with Tarascon Castle visible on the east side of the river.

After exploring the two castles, an unexpected find awaited the travelers in Tarascon – a church dedicated to Saint Martha. Levi mentioned Martha, saying she was the sister of Mary, of whom the parable is told in the Bible. He was not referring to the mother of Christ, but rather, Mary of Bethany, the sister of Martha and Lazarus. Christ often visited the siblings in Bethany, called *al-Eiz-ariya* (Place of Lazarus) today. This Palestinian town is located only two-and-a-half miles from Jerusalem. This was the same Lazarus whom Christ raised from the dead. How did their remains come to be in Gaul, known today as France?

The legend holds that the siblings landed along with other disciples in Les-Saintes-Maries-de-la-Mar, a town in the Rhone River delta area of Provence, after crossing the sea in an oarless boat. They were fleeing persecution in Palestine and spreading the Gospel to new lands. The remains of Saint Martha were located during renovations made in the twelfth century. A third-century sarcophagus containing the relics of Saint Martha is in the crypt of the church.

Lazarus was reportedly the first Bishop of Marseille. His remains were transferred to Autun many years after his beheading. Saint Mary's relics are venerated in the town of Vézelay. Both Autun and Vézelay are located farther inland, closer to central France, a good distance north of Tarascon.

The church in Tarascon retains some of its Romanesque details, but the extensions made during the fourteenth, sixteenth, and seventeenth centuries are Gothic. This later style is evident in the pointed steeple, exterior buttresses, and the overall asymmetrical form of the building.

Though Levi did not mention the next locations to either Chloe or within the pages of his travel journal, an abbey and a chapel were notable stops that both Levi and John caught on film.

Abbaye de Montmajour (Montmajour Abbey), above, predates the Romanesque period and offers eight centuries of architectural style changes. The rough-hewn, Pre-Romanesque walls near the entrance give way to smoother-surfaced Romanesque rooms. Mason's marks fill the walls. They are the signatures of stonemasons from the Middle Ages. The Romanesque design of the cloister is shown above, visible in the arched openings.

The Gothic period appears in the monastery's chapel, *Notre Dame la Blanche* (Our Lady of the White), as well as throughout the defensive tower. Neoclassicism reigns over the most recent and highest sections of the site. This eighteenth-century addition conjures up images of Roman and Greek monuments.

As shown on the next page, John's camera captured a little chapel located a short distance away, *Chapelle de la Sainte Croix* (Chapel of the Holy Cross). The purpose of the chapel is revealed in the name. The monks acquired a fragment of the True Cross and built this chapel in the twelfth century to accommodate those making a pilgrimage to venerate the relic.

Their next stop was Arles, located a short distance from the abbey. John captured Levi and Vince on the Roman ruins in the center of the Roman Theater. The steeple of a Franciscan convent was visible just over the north wall. This steeple is as far from the North wall of the theater as it is from the Southwest wall of the amphitheater Levi mentioned in his letter to Chloe.

The boys spent one week traveling from Beaucaire to Nice. Where they stopped for the night or exactly how they spent their time investigating any location in detail is unknown, but the photos and letters provide some insight.

Riding from Arles to Aix-en-Provence and then on to Marseille could have been done in a day. Given Levi's conversation with a French soldier turning pastor, it is safe to assume they spent one night in Aix. The trip from Marseilles to Nice would have been a lengthy ride, which is why they chose to utilize the train for this section of their trip.

Near the Port of Marseille is the *Cathédrale La Major* (Major Cathedral). Whether they visited during this trip through Marseille

or during a later visit is unknown. Levi returned multiple times to the city and checked on the *beachcombers, wharf rats, and all manner of human wrecks that eke out an existence however they may.*

What he never discovered, or at least he left no record of visiting, involved Lazarus's connection to Marseille. Tradition says that Saint Lazarus was beheaded in the caves near the port. Though most of his relics are in Autun, his skull remains in Marseille and is venerated at this cathedral, La Major.

The above photograph of the cathedral was in Levi's scrapbook. Since the view was from the water, this photo was most likely taken during a later visit to Marseille when Levi and Vince sailed to Africa.

A rather arduous walk from the old port to Notre Dame de la Garde Basilica is worth the views of the city found there. The Old Port, the Mediterranean, the surrounding islands, and all that is Marseille can be seen from there. A gilded Mary and Christ Child look over the city from atop the tower at the main entrance.

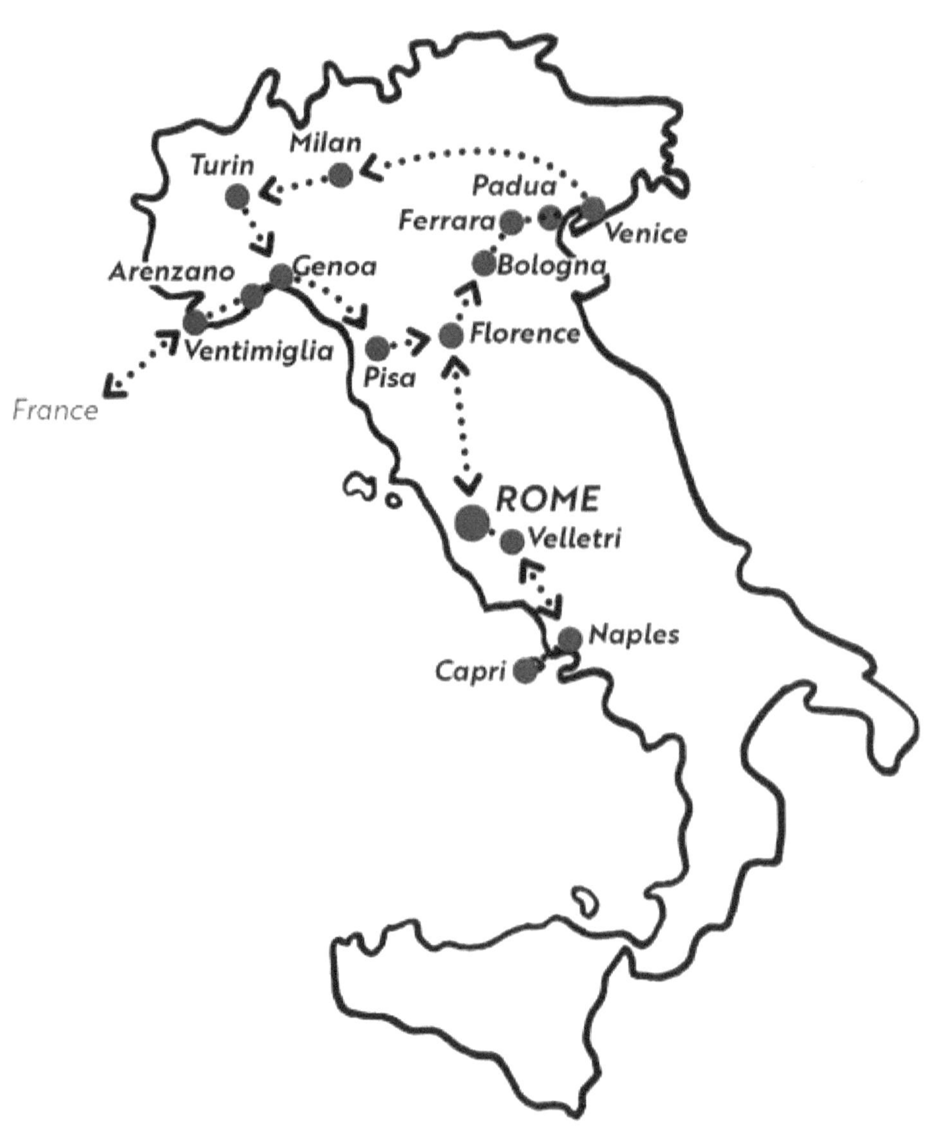
Milan
Turin
Padua
Ferrara
Venice
Arenzano
Genoa
Bologna
Ventimiglia
Florence
Pisa
France
ROME
Velletri
Naples
Capri

ITALY
December 1925 - February 1926

CHAPTER 27
CROSSING THE BORDER

They crossed into Italy near Ventimiglia and followed the Ligurian Sea. After an hour ride, Levi and John stopped to admire an unusual structure for the area, a Russian Orthodox church in Sanremo, shown below.

Since Levi's mom was the first to receive a letter from France, it was only fitting that his first letter from Italy be addressed to her.

Somewhere in Italy
December 13, 1925

Dear Mother,

We heard our first mass in Italy today and the attendance of the people gave me a better impression than that of the French. Of course, we didn't get one word of the sermon.

Tonite we are camped, Connell and I, in a hotel beside the sea. The waves of the Mediterranean roar about fifteen feet below our window and I suppose will lull us to sleep tonite.

We lost Engels down the road sometime this morning and probably will not meet him again until day after tomorrow at the American Express in Genoa.

Italian wine is terrible and we have been advised to drink it instead of water. I'll never complain about Pa's cherry wine again. In the big cities we shall be able to get German beer and that will taste much better. – Expensive wines here I suppose are all right but we'll have to drink with the natives.

We usually start the day with a bowl of chocolate and a couple queer shaped biscuits called cressons. The noon meal is eaten along the way and consists of bread, wine, cheese or sardines, a piece of chocolate and an apple or carrot.

At night we eat in a restaurant if we can find one with reasonable prices. If not, we have another picnic lunch. We do not gain weight on that but as long as we hold our own, we don't want to carry any fat up hill.

The scenery the last few days has been great. We ride along with mountains on the one side of us and the Mediterranean on the other.

The Italian roads are not so good especially where they have taken a notion to fix them. As John says, "I'm against these good road advocates. They spoil everything."

An Italian's idea of fixing a road is to spread a lot of crushed stone all over the road and wait until the wind will blow some fine dust to even things up a bit.

None of us have been able to learn any Italian yet so we try to pass as Frenchmen. Vinc and I can do that but Connell is always taken for a German.

Tonite I was talking to the Italian hotel keeper in French when an old Englishman or American heard our side conference in English and he said, "Where in hell are you boys going with that outfit." We had to explain the "why" of American talk and a French outfit.

He had passed thru Green Bay many years ago. Said the place had five thousand people when he was there. — Once in a while we meet some one like that and a few passing words makes one feel good.

We plan to be in Rome by the seventeenth so we can make the visits required for the pilgrimage before Christmas.

In another week if all goes well I shall see Father Geniesse provided he is still alive and kicking. I imagine we shall find Rome a crowded place but there ought to be enough eats to go around.

We haven't received any mail yet from home so the American Express Office will look like heaven to us. — I don't know how many of our letters get thru or if they arrive in bunches. I guess we have been mailing them in everything from fireboxes to garbage cans. The French do not mark their mail boxes so one guess is as good as another.

With love, Levi

Levi's mother, Louise Mary (Evrard) Geniesse, was born in July 1875 in Door County, Wisconsin. She was the daughter of Belgian immigrants who settled there.

In 1890, Louise's mother passed away unexpectedly, at roughly 40 years of age, after an illness of only a few days' duration. Louise was fifteen and the fourth of six children. Her sisters Emma and Mary were in their twenties and managed their own families. Victor was seventeen, and the two youngest, Juliette and Louis, were only ten and eight. Due to the family's needs, Louise took over the responsibility of housekeeping.

Louise married Lewis Geniesse nine years later, and they stayed in Door County for two additional years. In 1901, the couple relocated to Green Bay, where they remained for the rest of their lives.

Louise was worried about her son as he travelled through Europe.

Arenzano, Italy
Dec. 14, 1925
[travel journal]

Another tough day with a lot of rough road. The
repaired roads are terrible. Intended to ride on to Genoa
after dark but Connell discovered that he had a broken
handle bar post. Engels is still numbered among the missing.

After writing very little in his journal, Levi saved the majority of the evening in Arenzano for Chloe.

Arenzano, Italy
December 14, 1925

Dear Chloe,

Talk about babes in the wood, that's we. Today I ate a half a bar of laundry soap thinking it was a better brand of Italian cheese. When I discovered my mistake there was nothing to do but sing "I'm forever blowing bubbles."

We had no trouble passing the Italian border after stopping at four different customs posts along the road. The Touring Club of France, of which we are members, gave us much advice which we promptly disregarded. The Italian officers asked us many questions to which we shrugged our shoulders; that evidently was the right answer because they pointed up the winding road and we lost no time in leaving "La Belle France" behind.

For two days we have been riding a road cut for the most part out of solid rock. The waves of the Mediterranean roar below and to our left rises the Maritime Alps. The scenery is great but the nicer the scenery the harder the days work. We have stumbled up and down many a rocky hill in two days and find that their improved roads are the worse because an Italians idea of repairing a road is to dump a wagon load of stone in the center and leave the traveler smoothen it out.

Found a ride that equals Glen Echo for thrills. Last night Connell and I rode about fifteen kilometers thru the mountains after dark. It was a glorious adventure until I hit a pile of stone going down grade and you shouldn't have been around to hear what I had to say as I sorted my belongings out of the rocks. Today Connell and I were going to ride on to Genoa after dark when he discovered that his handle-bars (steering apparatus) were cracked and would surely have broken under any rough treatment. These are drops of several hundred feet along our route so we consider ourselves very lucky. We have lost Engels somewhere in the mountains and will hardly see him again until we reach Genoa or Rome.

All we can hope is that he doesn't collect any knives along the way. We are thinking of getting special jackets of boiler iron for this part of our travels because everyone warns us about being out after dark.

We rode along about fifty miles of railroad today and noticed soldiers on guard all the way. It seems that the Prince is going to pass over the line tomorrow so the army is called out to protect the right-of-way.

The Italian soldier looks much more neat and efficient than anything we have seen. I'm going to try to get one of their Alpine hats with a feather and everything.

Connell is in bed and complains that the light bothers him so to keep peace in the room I'll finish from Genoa.

Genova
December 15

We rode into this city at noon today and a few hours later it started to snow. It is cold and disagreeable outside and we three are lucky to have a roof overhead tonite. Yes, – Engels is back with us and tells of a wonderful meal he had yesterday. When we began this trip we talked about the wonderful scenery, beautiful paintings and architecture. Now we think first of "when do we eat".

We plan to store our wheels here and go to Pisa and Rome by train. When we leave Rome about New Years we shall try hiking to Naples and Sicily. If we can only buy a little grey donkey along the road there will be four of us. That's what we think most American tourists are, the American species of donkey.

I wish you could see some of the specimens that represent the United States over here. Americans with monocles, knickers, canes and acquired English mannerisms that make us itch to break something. Some Americans here are all right. This is how we recognize that one old grey haired man was a kindred spirit. As we dropped our packs to the hotel floor and tried to speak enough French to the Italian owner to convince him that we were not Americans the old man remarked, "Where in the h--- are you boys going with the outfit," and "What do you carry in those big bottles, - Ink?"

He had been in Green Bay many years ago and you can imagine how glad we were to talk to him.

Have you seen Van? Is Gertrude still in Washington? She told me she was going to leave in the early winter so I'm wondering if she's back in a real state. Oh — of course there is more than one good place, Virginia for instance.

I wished you and Ruth would start your tea room soon. I'll be bringing a hungry gang back that will be willing to split wood for a "handout". Might even consider a job as a waiter. I've had lot of experience waiting and Ruth can swear to that.

Jusque une autre temps, Lee

c/o American Express Co.
38 Piazza di Spagna
Rome, Italy

Two small pieces of paper, like a 1925 Post-it note, were folded in half and included with the letter Levi sent to Chloe. Judging from the handwriting, this piece was written by Vince.

Lee is of a rather cool, detached nature. Has much determination, strong will power and perseverance. He is one who shows talent and will succeed along one line. Belongs

*to a type that denotes a specialist. Is a little impulsive but
for most part, cautious and careful. Has a sense of humor.
A good substantial character. Is not much for frills. Conservative and not overly generous, except to a few. Is just and
fair. One whose industry, talent and perseverance will make
for great success. Thorough business character and planning
for future. Not a great deal of affection, but a bit romantic.
Will never give up if there is any giving up to be or is done,
that she will be the one to do it and if she wishes to break
off better stop right where they are. Stick-to-itness.*

This note described Lee, instead of Levi, which shows that the intended recipient was Chloe. Neither of Levi's friends addressed him as Lee.

CHAPTER 28
THE D.C. GIRLS

1800 K Street N.W.
Washington, D.C.
December 13, 1925

Dear Lee,

*I have exciting news to tell you this time! First —
Gertrude came for dinner Thursday night and told us that
she was going home for Christmas but was coming back the
first of January. Why? - Simply because she's engaged to
a Mr. Atchinson. All of this has taken place since August.
She hadn't planned to come back to Washington, but a few
days ago she changed her mind. Sudden? I was shocked and
thought she was only 'kidding' us at first. The wedding will
not take place for some time yet. She didn't seem so thrilled —
we were more excited than she. She plans to announce it soon
after she returns — rather informally I believe.*

*Second — We are moving to a real apartment house
Tuesday evening — to the Bradford — 1800 K St. N.W. It's
furnished, but not as nicely as this and at the same rates
— we only have two rooms, kitchenette, bath and reception
hall — we've talked about moving for some time but when
ten dollars of Ruth's disappeared last week, we decided we*

couldn't stand any more. This amounts to forty-five dollars that has mysteriously disappeared since September. We are paying dearly for this apartment — We have an idea who the thief is but no definite proof. Mrs. Tucker is unsympathetic and doesn't do anything to help. Aren't you glad to hear that I'm leaving the "slums"? I have to get up earlier and ride to school every morning but I'm nearer G. W. (George Washington University) and my church (Church of the Pilgrims) so this is an advantage. We haven't told Mrs. Tucker yet. Grace wanted the privilege and she hasn't come in.

Virginia is coming to Washington for Christmas. Warren's here. He didn't make good in Florida I suppose. She expects to arrive about the twenty-first. I leave for home the twenty-third. Emma Ruth writes that she is thrilled about going home. She has been so homesick and will be more so after the holidays. I'm judging from my own experience.

So, you haven't gotten but one letter from me — this is the fifth I've written. The cards you sent are very interesting and I enjoy reading about your experiences. I'm learning a lot from you — Geography, History, and _________?

Do you believe more firmly in evolution as you slowly revert to your ancestors? I believe in it to a certain extent. I believe that man was first a savage but had a soul from creation. This is too deep to discuss in a letter so I'll not attempt it.

Gertrude asked to be remembered to you. She wanted to know how you liked everything, etc. My mother also asked about you and then proceeded to lecture me — not to trifle with affections, etc. — true love is rare, etc.

This is from, Chloe

Gertrude and Virginia were Chloe's closest friends out of the group of six. Gertrude introduced her to Levi and was paired with Clayton back in February. In late July, Clayton was experimenting with the romance of moonlight while canoeing with Gertrude. Five months later, she announced her engagement to a previously unknown Mr. Atchinson. Just how bad did Clayton's experiment with romance go?

Virginia was now within a year of marrying Warren. As plans involving matrimony surrounded her, Chloe remained single, with no plans for marriage.

CHAPTER 29
ROUTE TO PISA

Rome
December 20, 1925
[travel journal]

We reached Genoa on the fifteenth and the snow and cold drove us to store our bicycles and take the train to Pisa.

In Pisa we saw the cathedral, the Leaning Campanile, the Baptistry and the Campo Santo. The cathedral seemed too much of an art museum but is very beautiful. The mosaic and inlaid marble in the Baptistry are the finest I have ever seen.

The Campo Santo with its fifty-three shiploads of ground from the Holy Land in which many notables are buried proved interesting.

I left Vinc and John in Pisa and spent eleven hours on the train with a bunch of Italian soldiers.

Anyone aware of the existence of Pisa's *campanile* (bell tower) knows that it leans. The Leaning Tower of Pisa began to sink in 1178, after only three of eight floors were completed. Construction halted due to a lengthy conflict with the rival coastal town of Genoa. In 1272, work continued, and five additional floors were added to the sinking three. Changes were made to the design to compensate for the incline.

Mussolini saw the tower as a black mark against Italian ingenuity. To correct this national embarrassment, he ordered the tower to be straightened in 1934. This was impossible since the adjusted design from 1272 compensated for the lean. If the lowest three levels were straightened, the tower would still bend in the same direction as its present tilt. Mussolini's attempt at straightening the tower caused it to lean farther.

Projections made in the late twentieth century anticipated a complete collapse between 2030 and 2040 if not stabilized. After the revisions were made, new calculations showed the tower would

survive 200 additional years without the need for further intervention.

Seven bells hang from the top of the tower, weighing approximately 23,000 pounds. Ropes were pulled to ring the bells in the past, but this threw off the equilibrium of the tower. Today, electromagnetic hammers ring the bells.

The cathedral is laid out in the usual fashion, with the entrance facing west. This places the altar at the east end, allowing the congregation to face Jerusalem. The Leaning Tower stands slightly east of the cathedral and does not extend past the length of the transept. Directly across from the entrance to the cathedral is the Baptistry.

Levi mentioned the beautiful Camposanto, located just north of the cathedral. It is similar in size to the outline of the cathedral, excluding the transepts. Laid out in the style of a Gothic cloister, this cemetery fails in comparison today to what Levi beheld in 1925.

Elena Franchi, in *Arte in Assetto di Guerra* (Art in Wartime), defined Pisa as one of the most damaged cities in Italy during World War II. On July 27, 1944, t he roof was struck by a bomb fragment, caught fire, and burned for days. Many frescoes were damaged or destroyed. Captain Albert Galloway Keller of the U.S. 5th Army in the Monuments, Fine Arts, and Archives program was among the first to enter Pisa once it was liberated from the Nazi party in early September. This member of the Monuments Men was so instrumental in the restoration of the Camposanto that a portion of his cremated remains was interred there by request.

The cathedral, bell tower, baptistry, and Camposanto are the tourist magnets of Pisa. The town has more to offer, but it is small and would be skipped by most visitors to Italy if it were not for the tower's lean.

The trains from Pisa to Rome pass through Florence today, just as they did in the past. Levi's trip with the soldiers from Pisa to Rome took eleven hours, which today could be completed in just under three.

The trio reunited the next day in Rome. They had plenty of time to meet the requirements for the pilgrimage before the end of the Holy Year on Christmas Eve.

CHAPTER 30
ALL ROADS LEAD TO ROME

Rome, Italy
December 18, 1925

Dear Father,

This is the letter I have been waiting to write and I know you have wanted to read. I reached here last night after riding for eleven hours ride with thirteen Italian soldiers in one compartment. An experience – at least that. When we reached Rome all the soldiers grabbed their packs and guns and ran for another train. Thinking it was a junction I did likewise but somehow decided that the station must be Roma. The natives game me a queer look when I asked them if this was Rome much as a New Yorker would if asked the same question about his city at the foot of the Woolworth building. Outside of the station I sat down on my packs and had a good laugh. It was freezing cold and my chuckles soon turned to chatters. The weather is anything but warm. They are having the coldest weather they have had here in years.

We stored our bicycles in Genoa and intend to do Southern Italy on foot and Northern Italy by the railroad.

Engels and Connell stayed in Pisa and will probably arrive here tonite. I wanted to get here in time to start the pilgrimage and again I find that I need not have hurried.

I had a little trouble finding a place to sleep last night. After being turned away from several large hotels I encountered a disreputable looking man who offered to guide me to a bed. I followed him really expecting that this was the night someone would try to borrow my few Italian lire. When I entered his little hotel, I was all primed for trouble. There was none. The 72¢ room wasn't so bad considering conditions here. The trap I arranged at my door to awaken me should any one try to enter was laughable and yet every-one I have talked to since says it was a sensible thing to do.

I found Don Gallagher this noon at the American College. He was our class president at Notre Dame and it is he who had his picture on the same book with mine in the "Dome."

DONALD S. GALLAGHER, Litt.B.

OGDENSBURG, N. Y.

President, Senior Class; S. A. C., 2; Vice-President Glee Club; K. of C.; New York Club.

Don was the logical man for the senior class presidency. Honors seem to fall naturally on his shoulders. We appreciate men like Don—men who give, and give generously that the greater good of the University and its men may be realized. Don is a leader, and we don't believe he had an enemy.

LEVI A. GENIESSE
Arch.E.

GREEN BAY, WIS.

Wisconsin Club; Engineers' Club; Palette Club; Knights of Columbus.

This man is in a class by himself, being the only senior in architectural engineering. His hobbies are swimming, boxing and wrestling. Needless to say, this combination of pressure and pleasure denotes a busy and competent man—which Levi is nothing else except. Lately society has entered the race for attention.

The American College has some two hundred American College graduates who are here studying for the priesthood. It seemed queer to find him in a cassock and a whole outfit but I soon found him to be the same old boy who taught me to play a mouth-organ. I am the first classmate he has seen since leaving the U.S.A. and we shall have much to say during the next two weeks. He lent me his topcoat and hat to wear around Rome and is going to try to get a special permission to accompany us around town Sunday. This is when one realizes all one has to go thru before becoming a priest.

In the afternoon after having my suit pressed and with Don's hat and coat, I started out to find Father Geniesse. He wasn't at the address I had but I found him at via 24 Maggio N.10 where he moved three years ago. I waited about three hours for him to come back but after spending a long time trying to understand what the Italian door keeper was saying to me an American priest came along and we talked football together. Father Geniesse is an old man 65 years of age. He is about my height and has a big "Milwaukee front." I liked him very much. In features he is typically Geniesse. I shall try to get a picture of him. He is bald completely. Had some kind of a disease which caused all his hair to drop out. We talked about our relatives and he says that there are two more cousins in Belgium.

Our cousin priest is a very learned man and holds the highest degrees it is possible to hold. He has written seven books in Latin for priests and taught theology both here and in America at Baltimore.

He has written a book on mixed marriages and I couldn't help but laugh when he showed it to me. His theory is to convert the non-Catholic party and so to avoid a mixed marriage. I told him it was all right in his book but that I found it didn't work. – He knows quite a bit about medicine and lectures at conventions of doctors. One of his books is written on the subject of death. If I could only read them, I have no doubt that they would be good reading because he doesn't seem to be afraid to say what he thinks.

I had supper with him tonite at a private boarding house where he eats and he has arranged to get us a room and we shall eat at the same place so I shall probably see him every day for the next two weeks.

Tomorrow, I go to confession and communion at St. Peters and start the visits required to make the pilgrimage.

We don't know just when we shall be in Naples but if you will address your next letter to: c/o American Express Co. 58 Piazza dei Martiri Naples, Italy

It ought to reach us when we take our hiking trip South. The weather is much colder than you would imagine and everyone dresses the same as at home.

Ma mentioned Christmas presents but I hope she didn't send anything because if it didn't get lost, we would have to pay duty on it.

As for money, I have enough that I don't have to worry about it for the next three months. We have no definite plans after leaving Rome except to try to avoid the cold weather as much as possible.

It is pretty cold in this room so I will warm up by going to bed. I shall write some more in a few days.

With love, Levi

The Dome that Levi referred to was the yearbook from Notre Dame University. Levi and Don Gallagher appeared side by side in their cap and gown, as shown on the previous page, since their surnames were closest in the alphabet among the two hundred and eighty graduates of 1924. The Pontifical North American College is where Don was studying for the priesthood in 1925.

The previous photo of Father John Baptiste Geniesse was taken just outside of his residence in Rome. Next door is a church dedicated to Saint Sylvester, La Chiesa San Silvestro al Quirinale. It dates to the ninth and tenth centuries and has a varied history, including use as a barracks. The beautiful dome and gilded wooden coffered ceiling are enough to turn heads towards the heavens.

Quirinal Hill is one of the Seven Hills of Rome. A short walk up from Father Geniesse's residence leads to the Quirinal Palace, passing the staircase to Villa Colonna, shown below.

At the crest of the hill lies the Quirinal Palace, which can be seen behind Father Geniesse in the photo to the right. The sentry no longer stands guard in the small capsule-shaped huts located on either side of the grand entrance facing the square. Being the official residence of the President of Italy, the entrance remains heavily guarded. These backdrops have remained virtually unchanged over the last hundred years.

Father Geniesse was Levi's first cousin once removed. A cousin "once removed" does not refer to a black sheep of the family who has been put out to pasture; instead, the term denotes that two first cousins are split by one generation.

Levi's father, Lewis, and Father John Baptiste Geniesse were first cousins, since their fathers were brothers. Lewis and John Baptiste shared the same grandparents. Since Levi is one generation off the line of being first cousins, he is Father Geniesse's first cousin once removed.

Levi's written descriptions of Father Geniesse continued the next day, in his letter to Chloe.

I found my cousin after taxiing all over town. The address I had was three years old but luckily he is well known among the clergy. This is his name as printed on his card – "Canonico Giovanni B. Dott. Geniesse." We call him Father John B. Geniesse. None of our family had ever seen him and I was ushered to his room with a queer feeling of what I might expect. The American priest I met at his door told me he could speak English and that I would find him a good fellow. He is. I found a man sixty-five years old, entirely bald and in appearance just like the pictures the movies give us of European priests. He sat in the midst of the greatest confusion of books, papers, clothing, etc. that I have ever seen. He reminded me of the pictures of Dante or of some great scientist searching for the missing link and in truth that is just about what he is doing.

This is the result of two days questioning on my part – He has been a missionary among the Indians and Mexicans in Arizona and taught Theology at Baltimore for two years. He possesses the highest possible degree from the universities here and is considered an authority on many subjects of morals and theology so much so he was called in as advisor to the late Pope Pius the X on several occasions. Most of his time is spent either writing or reviewing books on Theology etc. He has written seven books of his own in Latin which is a very good excuse for my not reading them!

The subject of his latest book is "mixed marriages" and I could not help but laugh when I heard it. His pet theory is to convert the non-Catholic party and so avoid the dangers of the mixed marriage. I told him his theory was all right but that it just didn't work in practice. My reasons followed and he listened to my tale of woe with interest. Chloe, you have been insulted again. I showed him a snapshot of you and he said that you looked like a good, intelligent --- and sensible girl. That almost caused a fight in the family but he apologized when I explained the seriousness of his mistake.

Many cousins up and down the family tree had similar names. Whether the name was Jean Baptiste in French, John Baptist in English, or Giovanni Battista in Italian, they all paid tribute to one person, Saint John the Baptist.

Levi's cousin was definitely a learned man. The abbreviation "Dott." on his business card was Italian for doctor, most likely a Doctor of Canon Law within the Roman Catholic Church. This knowledge allowed him to co-write *Efficax antidotum: ad matrimonia mixta praecavenda (An Effective Antidote: For Preventing Mixed Marriages)*, with fellow scholar M. V. Kelly. What a perfect book for a visiting first cousin, once removed.

Levi's letter to Chloe continued.

This noon I ate dinner with the wife of a Russian Count. I sure showed my lack of "polish" by forgetting all about kissing her hand when introduced. Her husband was a governor of a province in Russia until the advent of the Bolshevists. He is now in Switzerland negotiating the sale of a "Van Dyke" [Anthony van Dyck] picture which is the last of the family fortune. His father and my cousin were co-workers in research on the subject of "real and apparent death" and my cousin has been helping them here in Rome. The Count has just been appointed a Consul at Rome by the nation of Poland. The Countess is very likeable and while she does not speak English, [only French, Italian, German, Russian and Polish] we managed to follow the conversation in French. She could not understand why it was that I only knew one language. I was surprised when she said that Americans were considered more respectful and courteous toward womanhood than were Europeans. I should have told her that possibly it was because the women in America inspired that courtesy. I shall see her again and try to get a story of the "storm" which they experienced in Russia.

In her response letter, Chloe was intrigued by his tale of the countess.

The Countess must be interesting – Does she look the part? - I, too, would like to hear of her experiences in Bolshevik Russia.

Levi's cousin was the link to the countess. Father Geniesse was friends with the countess's father-in-law, Count Michel de Karnice-Karnicki. He had been the chamberlain to Russia's last czar, Nicholas II. It was his son, the countess's husband, who was trying to sell the family Van Dyck painting.

In 1896, Count Karnice-Karnicki patented a safety coffin to detect life and relieve Taphephobia, the fear of being buried alive. These two men, Father Geniesse and the count, contributed to a book that Father Geniesse translated from Spanish into French, Italian, and German, called "Death, Real and Apparent: In Relation to the Sacraments," by Rev. Juan Bautista Ferreres Boluda, S.J. The third appendix of the book explained the "Karnice," the count's safety coffin, from a medical and theological perspective.

Father Ferreres's main reason for being in Rome was to work on a two-volume series, *Compendium Theologiae Moralis (Compendium of Moral Theology)*. After his return home to Spain, a civil war broke out. Over 7,000 priests, monks, and nuns were killed in the first month. Father Ferreres was arrested but later released due to his old age. He struggled during captivity in San Miguel prison, was sentenced to death, and died of a stroke on December 29, 1936. Now he is known as Blessed among the faithful, one step below sainthood in the process of being canonized.

Levi received three letters from Chloe after he arrived in Rome. He planned to save them and read only one a day. His willpower was tested, and it failed; Levi read all three at one sitting.

The lengthy letter written from Rome on December 19 concluded.

To what you said in your last letter I have to agree, Chloe, even tho it hurts, but they call me a "bull headed Belgian" and something good is bound to come someday from that failing.

I have come to think of you as regular as my meals, my evening prayers. We Catholics are taught from earliest childhood to think of the Blessed Virgin as our inspiration in pleasing her Son. That explains the thousands of Madonnas in our churches and art galleries that were made to help men towards goodness and purity. If in my mind the image of a certain girl helps, it is but gratitude to add "for Chloe."

Sincerely, Lee

CHAPTER 31
CHRISTMAS IN ROME

The Eternal City
December 25, 1925

Dear Mother,

Christmas Day in Rome is a quiet affair and I was disappointed at the lack of interest displayed here. We went to midnight mass at St. Mary of the Angels, which is the church where the royal functions are held. I liked the services in St. John's in Green Bay better. This church is built in a part of the Baths of Constantine and dates from the third century. We are getting so used to antique things that they make no impression on us.

This afternoon we went thru a dungeon called the Mamertine Prison where history tells us St. Peter and St. Paul were placed before being killed. The legend is this - that when they placed St Peter there, he converted those in prison with him and he caused a spring to come forth from the rock to Baptize them. The spring still exists today.

Connell and I missed out on seeing the pope but Engels who got in St. Peters for the ceremony of closing the doors of the Holy Year said that we didn't miss much. There were 60,000 people in the place and you can imagine how much you can see if you're not in the front row. The pope has ceased giving audiences for the time being but we intend to try again to see him when we come back from Naples. When I tell you that 80,000 people have been crowded into St. Peters you get an idea of how large a place it is. When you get in it you can not appreciate it because it is so well proportioned that it seems much smaller than it really is.

In the center of the church lie the bones of St. Peter and all day long people pass by to venerate his relics. While we were making one of our required visits (for the pilgrimage) in St. Peters the other afternoon, the relic of Veronica's veil was displayed to the people as was a large piece of the True Cross. I was so far away that I could not see either of these two distinctly.

Yesterday afternoon Vinc and I went out to the church of St. Croce of Jerusalem. Here are many relics including these, a nail from the Cross of Christ, a large piece of the True Cross and a thorn from the Crown of Thorns. They also had the crossbeam of the cross of the Good Thief. We were allowed to touch the relics, many people bringing rosaries and medals there.

When we were coming home around the Colosseum last night, we met a procession of 200 German pilgrims marching along carrying lighted candles. We followed them inside of this amphitheatre where they had a lighted Christmas tree. They gathered around and sang several hymns and then we heard a priest get up and give a sermon in German. It was a scene I shall not forget to see these people. Some of them would kneel and kiss the ground where thousands of Christian martyrs died. The moon shone down on these Catholics who had come from Germany to make the pilgrimage and the prayers and devotion of these people impressed me more than any other religious ceremony I have seen.

We went out to a Trappist Monastery Wednesday, where a legend tells us that St. Paul was beheaded. According to this pious story he was killed on a hill and his head rolled to the bottom bouncing up three times. Three springs appeared and mark the spot to this day. We reached this spot at dusk and heard the monks chant their office. The chapel was dark, lighted only by the glow of the Sanctuary lamp. We were the only visitors and we sat entranced until their prayers were over. This was my first glimpse of monastic life and now I can understand how wealthy men, nobles and even kings have given up the world to have the privilege of joining in a prayer as beautiful as that. It made us appreciate one reason why they like their chosen vocation.

There are so many things I could tell you about that I feel helpless as to what I should choose each time I try to write. We intend to see the great museums and art galleries in the next few days, then about New Year's we are going South to Naples and then we may keep on going until we reach the toe of Italy and Sicily.

Before I forget it, Father Geniesse sends his affection, regards, and lot of other things I forgot, to the whole family. We are getting along fine. He introduced me to a Russian Count and last night the Count and I had a couple drinks together. You should hear me try to talk in French with him.

A Notre Dame fellow just came in to visit us, so I'll close and join in the conversation.

With love, Levi

Levi's travel journal offered a personal reflection on the relics mentioned in his letter to Mom.

The relics of St. Croce of Jerusalem did not excite the feeling or emotion in me that I had expected. The nail is supposed to have pierced the flesh of Christ. We were al-

*lowed to touch this nail and I did but I just could not feel
the reverence that this awful act should inspire. After all,
a Catholic who receives the Holy Eucharist should not feel
awed by relics or rather, the correct way to state that is that
one should be infinitely awed at the Holy Table and less so at
seeing holy relics.*

Levi began this letter with a description of the church where he attended midnight mass, at *Santa Maria degli Angeli e dei Martiri* (Basilica of Saint Mary of the Angels and Martyrs). As impressive as Levi's allusion attributing the baths to Emperor Constantine had been, a deeper story lies here.

Saint Mary of the Angels and Martyrs was Michelangelo's last architectural design. The ruins of a pagan bathhouse, the grandest of the ancient world, were engulfed and converted into a Catholic basilica. Emperor Maximian commissioned the building of these baths. He was a co-ruler of Rome with Emperor Diocletian and named them in Diocletian's honor. Constantine ruled shortly after these two and brought Christianity to the Roman Empire. He stopped the persecution of Christians ordered by Diocletian and his Caesar, Galerius. Unlike most Christian places of worship that are designed to honor Christian converts, this basilica memorializes a Christian persecutor.

In 1925, Levi made no mention of the wonders found within the basilica. Michelangelo was not mentioned in Levi's letters to those back home nor within the pages of his journal. Additionally, there was no mention of the meridian clock found inside.

Away from the main altar, tucked almost in a corner, a beam of light strikes a marble-encased bronze line in the floor at exactly noon. It passes through a well-placed hole in the wall. Where the light strikes the line determines the noon hour and also the time of year, following the Gregorian calendar. This meridian clock was commissioned by Pope Clement XI in 1702.

Levi also wrote to Chloe on Christmas Day. The parts that do not overlap with the letter to his mother are the following.

Christmas Day
In Rome

Dear Chloe,

Your Christmas greeting arrived yesterday. It made up for much that I've missed today. This is the first Christmas I have ever spent away from home and I'll admit it, I was "sort of" − "kind of" homesick.

I came over here to study church architecture; primarily cathedrals and other magnificent structures. Every day finds me liking the ornate, the gigantic less and favoring the plain places of worship. I believe that I always preferred the plain acts of worship to stately ceremonies but now I know that I do. [A little Calvinism from somewhere]

Met a Russian today who speaks a little English. He is traveling around Europe much as we are. He is a student of Diversity and aspires to become a Baptist minister in Russia. The most interesting thing I learned from him was that he had been to the ceremonies in St. Peter's and that he received his entrance ticket from a Protestant clergyman who receives a bunch of them to distribute among the non-Catholics. The services in St. Peters, of course, are always free but tickets are given out to avoid the confusion of too many people trying to enter the church at once.

The catacombs proved more interesting than we had expected. We really did not expect to see much and were surprised at their extent and preservation. There are approximately 200,000 Christians buried there and they discover new relics and tombs almost every day. Some were gruesome enough to cause one lady in our party to try to faint. We thought the epitaph on one tomb in which a wife describes her husband's life very humorous. She said, "He was good when he entered the world and good when he left it but during his life he was terrible." Another stone slab from the second century says, "He was a very good husband and we lived twenty two years together without quarreling." The last produced quite a laugh in our party.

As we were walking around the Coliseums night we met a procession of Germans carrying lighted candles and singing hymns. Naturally we followed and entered the arena with them where a lighted Christmas tree had been placed (A German custom you remember). A priest got up and gave a sermon in German and the people knelt and prayed, some kissing the ground. I wished I could do justice to the scene. A moon shining down on these people who had come to pay tribute to the thousands of Christian martyrs who had died on this spot. They sang their hymns and they echoed thru the empty arcades where once had sat the Roman populace who knew not mercy. — It is scenes like that that make our "bumming" worth while. Most tourists see nothing as interesting as that in a whole trip abroad.

Haven't mastered the art of eating (spag---ti?). Vinc says you do not spell it you wrap it around your fork. Mine is a distinct style. They call it inholing and laugh at me but yesterday I beat the bunch in an eating contest by about fifteen feet.

This is where the soup to nuts dinners originated. Invariably we start the meal with "zup" and end it with roasted chestnuts. Guess we get the same chestnuts back every day because we haven't acquired the habit.

It's no use. I can't think of a thing funny that will redeem this letter so I'll admit I wrote it and you can blame,

Lee

P.S. If the next boat doesn't sink you ought to receive several photographs of paintings that I liked. That's hardly a recommendation for them but they really appealed more than the famous ones. The Martyrdom of St. Allessandro which is modern had an appeal which some old masters did not have for me.

Levi mailed five large black-and-white photos he purchased at the Vatican Museums back to Chloe. It was a little something for Christmas. He saw these masterpieces in the Borgia Apartments, but in 1932, they were relocated to the Vatican Pinacoteca, commissioned by Pope Pius XI.

Martirio di S. Alessandro (The Martyrdom of Saint Alexander of Bergamo) by Loverini (1887). Saint Grata of Bergamo is holding the head of Saint Alexander, who was incarcerated multiple times and often escaped. Saint Alexander was beheaded in 303 A.D. for refusing to renounce his beliefs. Saint Grata was also martyred for recovering the body of Saint Alexander and ensuring that he received a Christian burial. In this painting, Saint Alexander is depicted as a soldier.

Incoronazione della Madonna (Coronation of the Virgin) by Raphael (1502-1504). Mary was assumed into heaven and crowned. This piece was commissioned to be an altarpiece for the Oddi chapel in the church of San Francesco al Prato in Perugia, Italy. In 1797, Napoleon took the piece to Paris, and it was not returned to Italy until 1815. The Raphael was then placed in the Vatican Pinacoteca rather than its original home in the Oddi Chapel. The church in Perugia experienced many structural problems over the years. It is now deconsecrated and used as an auditorium.

Santa Margherita da Cortona (Saint Margaret of Cortona) by Guercino (1646-1648). Saint Margaret wears the vestments of a Franciscan tertiary and kneels in prayer with her eyes turned to heaven. There are many miracles attributed to Margaret, who was canonized in 1728.

La Transfigurazione (The Transfiguration) by Raphael (1516–1520) was the last painting completed by the Italian High Renaissance master. While it was originally commissioned as an altar piece for the cathedral in Narbonne, France, it never hung there, though a copy does. The painting was left unfinished by Raphael, placed at the head of his deathbed, and carried at the front of his funeral procession to the Pantheon. Artists G. Romano and F. Penni completed the painting. A mosaic of this piece was completed in 1767 and is located in Saint Peter's Basilica.

Santo Giorgio uccide il Drago (Saint George Killing the Dragon), Bordone (1525). Saint George is shown here as he slew a dragon to save a princess and the town. Saint George was tortured and beheaded in 303 A.D. for his faith and refusal to denounce God. The painting was the high altarpiece in a Franciscan church, San Giorgio, in Noale, Italy.

CHAPTER 32
ANNO JVBILAE ROMAEI

Whether Catholic or not, the history behind the Jubilee of 1925 touched several historical high points: political intrigue, the communal aspect of religion, and finding inner peace.

The idea of holding a jubilee in the Catholic Church began with Pope Boniface VIII and the First Jubilee of 1300. With the fall of Acre, the last Christian stronghold in the Holy Land, pilgrimages to Jerusalem became perilous. Pope Boniface VIII prepared Rome to meet the needs of the faithful. This first celebration was attended by Dante Alighieri, who references his experience in his most infamous work, the *Divine Comedy*.

The celebration was based on Jewish traditions and originally observed every fifty years. The Jubilee was a time to cleanse and renew: crops were not planted and harvested during the year to allow the Earth to rest, slaves were liberated, and debts were forgiven. This reset was meant to shrink the difference between the wealthy and the poor and prepare the land for heartier harvests in the coming years.

Petrarch, one of the three crowns of Italian literature, made the pilgrimage to the second jubilee in 1350 and recorded his thoughts in this way.

> **"How well it is for the Christian soul to behold the city which is like heaven on earth, full of the sacred bones and relics of the martyrs, and bedewed with the precious blood of these witnesses for truth; to look upon the im-**

age of our Saviour, venerable to all the world;...to roam from tomb to tomb rich with memories of the saints, to wander at will through the Basilicas of the Apostles with no other company than good thoughts"(Chrystie).

The jubilee celebration evolved. The beginning date changed; the length between celebrations was altered, and some years had to be skipped altogether for a variety of reasons. The specific requirements for the pilgrimage are determined by the current pope.

In 1925, anyone following the requirements of the pilgrimage was offered a chance at reconciliation, called an indulgence, which provided forgiveness for committed sins. Pope Pius XI established the parameters of 1925's Jubilee in his papal bull, *Infinita Dei Misericordia* (Infinite Mercy). Delivered at St. Peter's on May 29, 1924, he set the jubilee year to begin at first vespers, an evening time of prayer, on Christmas Eve in 1924. It would last until that same service on Christmas Day, 1925. The pilgrimage requirements were to go to confession, receive communion, and walk through the holy doors of four major basilicas in Rome: Saint Peter, Saint Paul, Saint John Lateran, and Saint Mary Major. While visiting the basilicas, the pilgrim was to pray and include the special intentions of the Holy Father.

Pope Pius XI's focus was peace, an almost expected topic given the proximity to the Great War. It was not only the peace found through treaties, the Pope clarified, but the restoration of peace in the hearts of people. Two additional prayers in the interest of religion were to return "all non-Catholics to the true Church of Christ" and to reach a "definitive settlement and ordering of Palestine, as the sacrosanct rights of Catholicism demand."

Levi arrived in Rome on December 17, which gave him eight days to complete the requirements for the pilgrimage.

Rome, Italy
December 27, 1925
[travel journal]

John and I have not seen the Pope but Vinc was at the closing exercises. St. Peter's is becoming more impressive with each succeeding visit.

I completed the required visits for the pilgrimage. They were three visits to St. Peters, St. John Lateran, St. Maria Maggiore and one to the Basilica of St. Paul.

Levi is shown here on the steps of Saint Peter's Basilica during one of his visits. The only one of the three to attend the closing ceremony for Jubilee 1925 was Vince. The news reached the *Green Bay Press-Gazette.*

An article titled, "Ergonites Hear Interesting Talk on Christian Symbols," reviewed a presentation given by Mrs. Martin, wife of a member of the local Knights of Columbus. She mentioned the Holy Year, and near the end of her speech, she produced a heavy blue piece of paper marked with the seal of the Catholic Church. It was the document Vince used to gain admittance to the *Porta Sancta* (Holy Door) celebration. Both Mr. Martin and the head of the Knights of Columbus in Rome had collaborated to obtain this invitation for Vince while he traveled abroad.

The closing of the Holy Year made the news in many places. Msgr. Enrico Pucci, Rome Correspondent from the National Catholic Welfare Council, described the festivities in detail for *The Catholic Telegraph:*

Rome, Dec. 26 – Although accurate figures are not yet available, unofficial estimates here are to the effect that at least 1,000,000 pilgrims were drawn to Rome from all parts of the world by the Holy Year of Jubilee,

which came to an end on Christmas Eve. Germany far outstripped other nations in the number of pilgrims, approximately 400,000 making the journey to Rome from that country. France and Spain came next, with about 120,000 each. The United States, probably, ranks next, with a number which cannot yet be approximated. Then follow Switzerland, Belgium, England, Austria, Hungary, Portugal, Czecho-Slovakia, and Lithuania.

Large pilgrimages from Russia and China, for which arrangements had been made, had to be cancelled because of disturbed political conditions in the land of the Soviets; and there was one Turkish pilgrimage, the members of which were given a most cordial welcome in recognition of their courage in undertaking such a trip.

Touching Stories

Many touching tales are circulating here about the hardships which individual pilgrims encountered and overcame in their efforts to reach Rome. One woman of seventy tramped to Rome from Genoa. A group of ten boy scouts walked 700 kilometers in twenty days to reach Rome; and a parish priest from the North of Italy started on foot with thirty lire in his pocket, and reached Rome with ten lire which he offered to the Holy Father.

Though Levi, Vince, and John believed they met the requirements of the pilgrimage for the Holy Year, one detail was lost in translation. They made ten trips to the basilicas, but the papal bull called for all four basilicas to be visited in one day, for ten days. That would have been four times the number of visits they attained. Had they hopped on a train the moment they reunited in Genoa, skipped Pisa, slipped past Florence to Rome, they might have been able to meet the full requirements of the pilgrimage.

CHAPTER 33
BUON ANNO

From my dream castle
Built by some
good fairy,
Before this day is over
I say to you:
"Happy New Year"!

Levi added a watercolor drawing and poetry to an otherwise plain card to wish Chloe a Happy New Year.

Rome, Italy
New Years Eve

Dear Chloe,

A year ago tonite a bunch of the boys back in a small city called Green Bay were "whooping it up" in direct defiance of Mr. Volstead. I was there among them helpin' in the fun and it was a grand time we had; but that was a year ago and tonite I wonder if that was only one year ago. That all that has happened could happen in a year seems impossible. I left home immediately after the holidays and began my search for a job which finally led me to Washington where I found it, the biggest job man ever tried, --- and failed. They tell us that being beaten at twenty five is not so bad. At twelve tonite a new year starts. We shall see.

I received your letter with all the exciting news today. Came near tumbling into the waters of the Trevi fountain when I read that you had left Mrs. Tucker. Don't know how you girls can possibly manage to think of turning off the lights by yourselves. I like the way you tell me about Gertrude's engagement. "Shocked" is exactly what you said and you only redeemed that by adding that you were excited to hear the news. As for me I just said, "I'll be ______." Being a misogynist now I'm not much interested in weddings but you may tell me all about the romance.

When I read about Virginia coming to Washington for Christmas I just wished I could be there. If you see Warren say hello for me. Have you seen my roommate, Van? Haven't heard a word from him since leaving and I'm wondering if he broke his hand.

Today we attended the Solemn Pontifical High Mass in St. Peters and saw the Pope, the College of Cardinals and all the pageant that attends a service like this. I do not exaggerate when I say that there is nothing in the world that can equal it for impressiveness. Take yourself back to the fifteenth century; imagine what the greatest court in the world looks like and you have the identical same show today. The Swiss guard with their armor, swords and pikes, the Vatican guards that look like drum-majors, the Cardinals, upon whom the actual policies of government really depend, the Bishops, another guard composed of men of Royal blood and more and more until after several blocks of procession have passed the bugles announce the entrance of St. Peter's successor. There is a solemn chant by the Sistine Choir and amid the acclamations of the people the Pope enters carried on a sedia. I happened to be within ten feet of him when he passed and I pitied him because he seemed to be the last man in the world that would deserve such a terrible position. Father Geniesse described the daily program of a pope to me and I realized why it is considered the hardest in the world. The mass itself was too impressive to really pray. One was awed by the splendor of everything and realized the reason why St. Peters was built as it is.

Yesterday we saw the missionary exposition at the Vatican garden. There were exhibits from every known land. They had everybody from the tropics to the artics represented but I was disappointed; Alabama and Georgia were there but Virginia was not.

An interesting collection was that from the leper island of Molokai with the personal belongings of Father Damien whom you remember Louis Stevenson called the bravest and most noble man of history. They had casts showing the ravages of the disease on a human body; pictures showing the sisters and priests taking care of the human wrecks in order that they might not die with a curse on their lips. When you realize that all this is going on today; that some-time during this coming year someone will say goodbye to all he holds dear and depart for a leper colony never to return, with the prospect of dying sooner or later of the loathsome disease you know that nobleness and charity are not forgotten virtues.

The sharp contrasts of the humble missionary laboring and dying, for there have been martyrs even in 1925, with the pomp and ceremony of the services in St. Peters is matter for thought. -At first I felt that a pope ought to enter St. Peters barefooted and without ceremony. Which would be more pleasing to God I do not know but I doubt if my ideas would work. – As you said of evolution, this is too deep for me.

Chloe, I don't know if all these descriptions please you but they are the most interesting things in Rome. We leave for Naples (on foot) in the morning. Will tell you how they fry eggs on Mt. Vesuvius.

Till then, Lee

P.S. – The clippings – I really don't think you need advice on divorce. Possibly you can save them for Gertrude.

CHAPTER 34
NAPOLI A GENNAIO

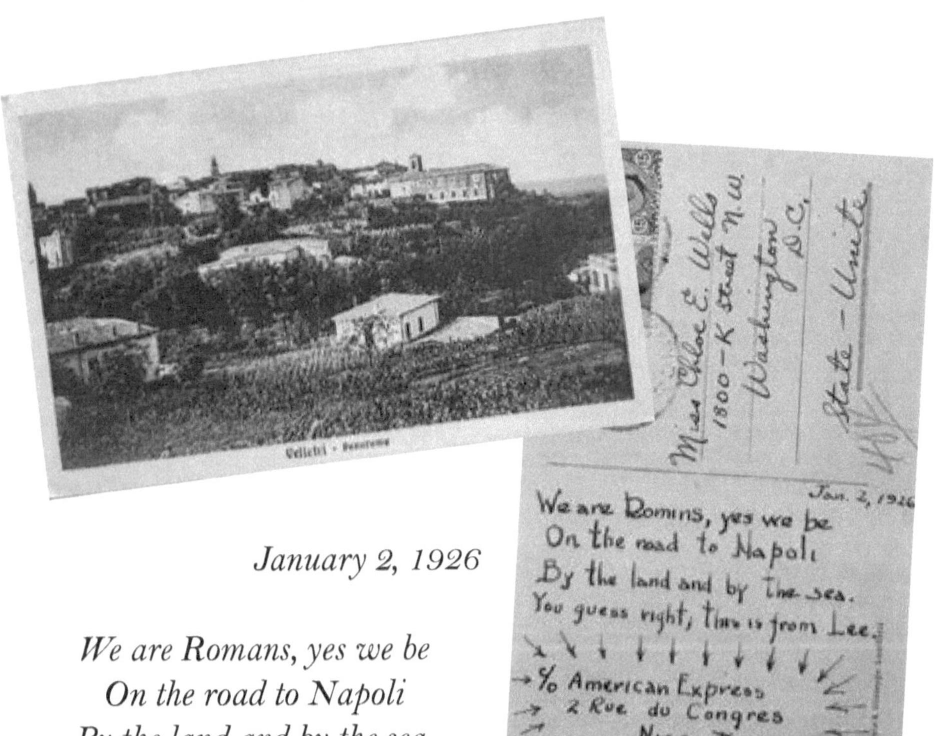

January 2, 1926

We are Romans, yes we be
On the road to Napoli
By the land and by the sea.
You guess right, this is from Lee

Naples, Italy
Jan. 3, 1926

Dear Father,

One days walking was enough to develop big blisters on my feet and the other is feeling the same way. We took the train in to Naples. We arrived here after riding most of the night in a crowded train. The third class coaches were filled with Italian soldiers some of them sleeping up above in baggage carriers. I sneaked into a first class compartment and after riding for two hours in comfort they came in and caught me and it costed four lire (16 cents) to keep from being put off the train. Some others had done the same as I were put off for getting "hardboiled" about it. It's lucky I couldn't "sass" the conductor if I wanted to but I figure that its like getting caught by a motorcycle cop; the best thing to do is grin.

By the way did I tell you before that Engels and another fellow were arrested for prowling around a Roman ruin after dark in Rome and it costed them 20 cents to bribe the two policemen into letting them go. Policemen are the same the world over but you can satisfy them with less here.

Monday Night

Walked around the city today and saw the most discouraging sights imaginable. This place is full of beggars and people who are deformed in some way. The side streets are filthy. You can imagine what our sidewalks would look like if everyone dumped their garbage on them, and that is just what they do here. You see children practically naked rolling around in dirt and it's a miracle that any of them live.

Sunday morning (yesterday) while we were waiting for a church to open we saw men driving flocks of goats thru the streets to be milked at the door of the house where the milk is ordered. Also we saw two goats come down the street by themselves and butt up against a door and enter into the hallway of a house where a woman came down and milked them; also saw a man milking a cow in a beer bottle with remarkable accuracy. This may all sound funny but it looks just as queer.

If you want to convert any Protestants don't send them to Southern Italy. Father Geniesse told us not to judge by outward appearances for they are sure against them. Yesterday Connell went into a church and put his hat and cane on the back of his chair. The sexton came along and told him to put them in front of him where he could watch them. --- Today I bought a bottle of wine called Lacrima Chrysti [Tears of Christ]. It is a famous wine made here in Naples. The wine shop in which I bought it had a shrine at one end where a candle burned before a crucifix. About every third shop here has a shrine either to the Virgin or some Saint. Some street stands selling newspapers have a crucifix and a votive light burning before it and --- they all rob you if they can. Practically everyone trys to short-change you and yesterday afternoon I almost had a fight with a cab driver because he tried to cheat me out of 12 cents.

Rex O'Malley, a Notre Dame student with whom we had some beers together in Rome with Don Gallagher came in our hotel this afternoon and we are going out to Pompeii tomorrow. He is taking the boat for New York the next day and will see Oswald in about a month at Notre Dame.

Mothers letter and New Years card came just before we left Rome. We're going back there in about a week then up to Florence, Venice, etc.

Your son, Levi

The *Green Bay Press-Gazette* published an article in December 1925. Several local businessmen gave a talk down at the old Moose Lodge, reflecting on their recent trip to Italy. After a lengthy piece covering multiple topics, they got to the point of milk. They were impressed, as Levi had been, with Italian forms of distribution.

> **"Milk delivery in Naples assured freshness and sanitation. Rival milk dealers would drive cows and goats up the narrow streets, while customers would let down a bucket, containing a coin, from the high balconies by means of a cord. The bucket would be filled direct from the source of supply and then would be hauled up again"**
> (Milk Delivery in Italy a Simple Matter 35).

It was fitting that men traveling from Wisconsin homed in on milk production during their stay in Italy. As recently as 1915, Wisconsin had become the leading state for dairy production, but life was different in Naples. The struggle to survive was evident around every corner, and in some ways, this Southern Italian city has not changed over the last century.

> *Napoli, Italia*
> *6 gennaio 1926*

Dear Chloe,

> *No longer can we sing "There ain't no flys on us." We've got them, - flees. The famous Italian flees have decided that now that the debt settlement is a fact there is no reason from withholding their attention from Americans. Engels claims that he caught one but that is preposterous. Connell and I have tried everything but just can't catch up with them so we'll have to take the advice of another American who told us not to try to get rid of them but rather to get use to them.*

Levi's remark about the debt settlement referred directly to the funding agreement between the U.S. and Italy that was signed in November 1925. The Editorial Research Report showed that Italy was in debt to the United States for $2,042,000,000. The agreement with France for almost twice that amount would be finalized in April 1926. Great Britain owed the most, $4,600,000,000 (Riefler and Boeckel 1059).

Levi's letter to Chloe continued the next day.

> *Jan. 7 -Naples*

> *This is written in sections as you notice. We've been so busy seeing things that I'm afraid to even attempt a description of the Neapolitan. Put this down: - he's a thief by nature and I do not believe he is morally responsible. Churches are kept locked in the day time because of thieves. Last Sunday during mass the sexton came up to John and warned him to put his hat where he could watch it. That was one of our first impressions of Naples and since then have seen that it was not foolish advice.*

> *We have seen more signs of poverty, misery and disease here than in any other city. Our first two days were spent without seeing the sunshine and two days of wandering*

thru narrow filthy streets seeing and hearing beggars in every doorway was enough to make us sick. When I saw some naked children playing in a heap of garbage (and I use the word rightly) that had been dumped in the center of a paved street about twelve feet between buildings I was ready to check out and go back to Rome.

This is probably disagreeable reading but you said my letters were educational so I'll wade right on. Naples seems to have a terrible reputation and ranks with the seaport town of Marseilles. There is poverty here such as you cannot picture and it makes me wonder about the "superior" Nordics of the United States deciding that the wealth, peace and happiness of America was to be distributed among the first 100,000,000 people that arrived. — We have had to apologize over here and try to explain many times that the Racial Discrimination Act is not the real sentiment of the American people. It's like trying to tell someone that you do not mean what you say.

Another picture — A fairly warm evening, a band of traveling musicians singing along the streets and accepting whatever coins you throw them with a "Gratias Signore." But can you imagine the bad taste of playing "Yes, We Have No Bananas" along with "Santa Lucia." - The scenery around the city is beautiful; the kind of sailboats you see in pictures swarm in the harbor and in the distance yet seemingly threatening the city smokes the mouth of Vesuvius. Perched about the modern city is several old monasteries and the fort of the King of Naples. I do not know enough Italian history to tell you of the history of this place. It seems to be so difficult to understand that no attempt is made to teach it in the U.S.A. — Something I must mention is the shrines every where.

Shops, stores and houses all have their pictures of

Madonnas, or statues and crucifixes with candles and electric lights or flowers before them. Overlooking one of these dirty streets I've described you will see a beautiful shrine with several vases of flowers before it. In America we associate cleanliness with Godliness but here 'tis good that it is not so or there would be no lowly Neapolitans at St. Peter's gate.

The three of us toiled, walked, climbed and crawled up Mt. Vesuvius not condescending to ride up the special contrivances that Thos. Cook & Son have built to the very top. When we reached the top after three hours of work in making four thousand feet we met five Germans that had done as we had but with the added load of a full pack on their backs. You can't help but admire Germans. They give us the impression of a man that says "I'm licked now but just you wait." We laugh at French fears but over here it is different. People seem to expect that Germany will repeat and win.

Vesuvius was worth the climb. We were lucky and tons of red hot liquid were hurled many feet into the air. It is best described by comparing it to a giant blacksmith's forge which spouts red continually with an occasional explosion.

Levi descended Mount Vesuvius with John Connell and Father O'Malley. Levi's two companions are shown here as they began their descent.

In the letter to Chloe, Levi mentioned the Racial Discrimination Act, which was officially known as the Immigration Act of 1924. Quotas for immigration were set by nationality, allowing each group represented in America to increase by two percent based on the population recorded in the 1890 census. The overall number of immigrants was capped at 150,000 per year.

Utilizing the 1890 census was an interesting choice. Since a population tally was completed every ten years, there were three more recent counts available. Reverting to the nationality distribution of 1890 gave preference to Northern and Western Europeans and specifically excluded a recent wave of Slavic and Italian immigrants. Asian immigrants were excluded entirely. The goal was to build an America that looked like it had in the "good ol' days," hence the commonly utilized title, the Racial Discrimination Act.

Levi's description of the state of Naples in 1925 did not conjure up material worthy of a visitor's guide. Few pictures were taken in Naples, and none depicted milk delivery, but this grain cart caught his attention.

Levi did not write in his travel journal during his time away from Rome. Instead, on January 12, 1926, he reflected back on their trip.

Back again in Rome after spending ten days on a trip South to Naples. We arrived in this seaport city at five o'clock in the morning and received the worst first impression of a place that is possible. We shall always remember those hours of waiting for a mass, so that we could get to a hotel and sleep. It was raining and the sight of the human wrecks coming into the shelter of the car station was enough to make us want to get away from the scene at once. Such poverty and misery I had never thought existed and as the days went on we saw that our first impression was a right one.

Naples itself is not a beautiful place but its background is all that could be wished for. The narrow filthy streets, the lack of all sanitation, the half naked children playing in the dirt were hardly things to impress us favorably but the shrines and lights or candles burning before them in every house and shop made me think. I can see where the Protestant has grounds for thinking that Catholicity tends towards idolatry but whether this thinking is justified even here among the Neapolitans is a matter for study.

CHAPTER 35
BLUE GROTTO BATHS

Rome, Italy
January 12, 1926
[travel journal]

The town of Capri and the visit to the Blue Grotto provided a day of keen pleasure. The excitement of entering the cave and the beauty within were enough to amaze us. On the way back from this cave, which was once the swimming pool of Tiberius Caesar, we met Thomas Luckenbill of New York. Connell and I came near joining him on a trip to Greece, Palestine and Egypt. I'll always remember him as a boy with a lot of nerve.

Within the pages of Levi's January 6 letter to Chloe, he offered additional details from this portion of their journey.

Today we took a three hours ride down the coast in a small steamer and then were taken thru the subterranean caves at Capri called the "Blue Grotto." This place was used by Tiberius Caesar as a bathing pool and is very beautiful. The steamer on which we traveled carried all tourists. Many were Americans and most of them enjoyable company. We three attracted much attention and met quite a few people but a laughable incident was that one successful American business man sneaked away from his wife and was enjoying himself in our party when his better half found him and her look said as plain as words, "Come, this is no company for you. You disgrace me where ever we go." Chloe, don't ever henpeck your husband like that. We disliked her as heartily as we pitied him.

We may have a priest join us on a part of our trip. He is about thirty years old and hails from Chicago; wants to rough it a bit and we're willing to show him the "ropes". Met a Baptist minister from Florida and his wife two days ago. You'll be surprised to hear this, - we got along without fighting.

As the growing group of travelers took a steamer to the island of Capri, Levi turned his camera towards the mainland. The smoke of Mount Vesuvius is visible in the photograph below.

As the steamer approached the island of Capri, Levi captured the moment. Villa Lysis is visible along the crest, where the rounded high point changes to a gentle slope. The villa was built in 1904, home to the industrialist and poet Jacques d'Adelswärd-Fersen. He passed away there almost three years before Levi and crew visited the island. It was a sad story, ending with a cocaine overdose.

Just over the highest point, not visible in the above photo, are the ruins of Villa Jovis, a palatial complex constructed by Tiberius Caesar. He governed the Roman Empire from here during his last ten years of reign in the first century. Legend says that Tiberius had anyone he found disagreeable thrown from the cliff into the sea.

Levi visited the island to see the Blue Grotto and not the preserved ruins of Roman rule. The color gave Capri its name, meaning a deep shade of sky blue. Those who have seen the Capri blue of the grotto, illuminated from a source below the water's surface, agree that it glimmers richer than the most beautiful blue sky. Bubbles form around anything submerged in the pool of water. The sub-aquatic light turns the bubbles silver, and they shimmer below the surface. Visitors to Tiberius Caesar's pool can validate Levi's amazement at the beauty of the grotto.

With the views of Capri under their belt, the steamer headed back to the mainland. Explorations of other areas surrounding Naples awaited their arrival.

CHAPTER 36
REI PUBLICAE
POMPEIANORUM

January 8, 1926
[From Levi's Letter to Chloe]

Just returned from Pompeii where we spent the day wandering around the ruins. Wasn't impressed by what remains there. Everything has been so completely cleaned of signs of the deluge of cinders that fell on the surprised Romans that it resembles an Indian village in New Mexico more than the civilization you would expect. Most of the valuable mosaics have been brought to the museum in Naples and the work far surpasses anything we do today. As someone said today after looking at the piping system of a Roman bath, "These Romans are far from dumb."

January 12, 1926
⌈travel journal⌉

Pompeii was another interesting day but for me it was marred by a very bad cold and headache. Father O'Malley of Chicago was along with us and he is a real man. Pompeii was about as I had expected with most of the valuables removed to the museum at Naples. The museum was interesting especially for several Roman mosaics and a great number of pieces of Roman sculpture.

Mount Vesuvius erupted in 79 A.D., and hot ash stopped many of the inhabitants in their tracks. Though it was discovered in the mid-1700s, the Encyclopedia Britannica notes that excavations did not begin until 1748. Fifteen years later, an inscription was found which identified the town as Pompeii – "Rei publicae Pompeianorum"(Jashemski). The lives of the inhabitants were preserved in ash. Painted political signs and messages of love can be read today, given that you speak Latin, Oscan, Greek, or Hebrew.

This photograph from Pompeii is of Vince Engels, John Connell, Father Charles O'Malley, and Vincent "Rex" O'Malley. The two O'Malley brothers were traveling through Italy with their father, Michael.

Rex and his father headed back to the States the day after this picture was taken. They boarded the Conte Biancamano and spent ten days at sea with New York City as their port of destination.

Father Charles O'Malley was pictured earlier as he and John Connell descended Mount Vesuvius. Father O'Malley was on vacation from Sacred Heart church in Manning, Iowa. Father O'Malley is pictured below as he purchased fruit from a street vendor in Naples.

CHAPTER 37
DEATH OF THE
QUEEN OF PEARLS

Rome, Italy
January 11, 1926

Dear Mother,

Back again in Rome and it seems almost as good as getting home. We are at our same "pensione" near Father and shall be here three or four days. – Today they buried the "Queen-Mother," or the king's mother as we would call it. This is the first time we have really seen the Italian people turn out for something. On Sundays and Holidays only half of them stop work or close their stores but today everything was closed until two o'clock. We saw the funeral procession and here I'll try to describe it.

There were about 100,000 soldiers lined along the streets to keep order. There were the Facisti all dressed in their black shirts, many different kinds of police and royal guards in their flashy uniforms, a couple hundred men in dress suits all covered with medals, about four hundred monks carrying lighted candles, a few Bishops and three cardinals, the open hearse, the King of Italy, the ambassadors of the different countries and the man who really rules Italy, Mussolini.

An interesting thing about the Queen they buried is that she opposed her husband, the king, when he took the Papal States from the Pope. She has always refused to live in the Quirinal Palace which used to belong to the Pope and even the present King and Queen do not live in the palace but only come there for the functions of the State. It seems that they believe they will be cursed if they live where the Pope used to.

For almost twenty-five years, Margherita of Savoy had been the Dowager Queen of Italy. Her husband, Umberto I, was Italy's second king after the unification. His assassination in 1900 placed their thirty-year-old son, Victor Emmanuel III, on the throne and made Margherita the dowager queen. Regardless of her title change, Margherita was powerful.

The *Green Bay Press-Gazette* ran the news of her death on page one the day she died, January 4, 1926. "Margherita, Queen Mother of Italy, Dies," the heading exclaimed. A photo of the elegant queen topped the column with her crown perfectly sized and placed. Seven strands of pearls encircled her neck; another strand hung lower, suspending a pendant just out of view. Five additional strands of pearls of unknown length appeared from behind her neck and completed the layered arrangement. Two large pearls hung like teardrops, one from each ear. No wonder she was known as the "Queen of Pearls."

They wrote of her illness, pleurisy, and that she died at age 75. Her charity made her loved by her subjects, and becoming a widow in 1900 filled the hearts of the world with sympathy for her.

The final paragraph was an unexpected addition to her legacy. "It was Queen Margherita's veto that prevented the marriage of the duke of Abruzzi to Miss Katherine Elkins, now Mrs. William F. R. Hill of Washington" (1). While the article ended there, the story certainly did not.

The Duke of Abruzzi was the Dowager Queen's nephew. He once was Infante of Spain; when that monarchy ended, a Republic was formed. The Duke was adventurous. He climbed Mont Blanc, Monte Rosa, the Matterhorn, and Mount Saint Elias. In 1909, he reached the highest altitude on record when he climbed K2 and even attempted to reach the poles.

In 1907, an American Senator's daughter, a commoner, stole his heart. The pope offered to make the girl's father a duke, giving him status. That was when the dowager's true reason for dismissal shone through; Katherine Hallie "Kitty" Elkins was Protestant, and the Italian duke and prince was Catholic. Queen Margherita never swayed, and the Duke never married. Levi would have found interest in the article if he had only been back home to read it.

CHAPTER 38
FASCIST STATE OF THE MONARCHY

Rome, Italy
January 15, 1926

Rome buried the King's mother last Monday. Again a wonderful procession with the army, royal guard, diplomatic corps, the Italian nobility, the clergy, with bishops and several cardinals, about five hundred monks carrying lighted candles, the King of Italy and the man who really rules Italy, Benito Mussolini. And I almost forgot the black shirted Facisti who saved Italy from chaos. We Americans hardly realize what has happened and is happening today in Italy. There has been a revolution, hardly any bloodshed but a very thorough change in government, nevertheless.

The Masonic order that ruled the country has been abolished by decrees of the Facisti. Mussolini has many enemies and many friends but he in time will go the way all men have gone who ruled Rome. The Italians have always rebelled against their rulers whether they were good or bad and Mussolini will be no exception. – Tell your pupils this,

Miss Wells, - Mussolini's name will go down in history.

Levi's prediction held. When the trio entered Italy, Victor Emmanuel III was King, and Mussolini was Prime Minister. Victor Emmanuel was the third king of only four to rule a unified Italy. The last king, his son, only held the crown for a month.

Victor Emmanuel was the son of the Dowager Queen, whose funeral Levi had just witnessed. He suffered from disabilities during childhood and, as a result, stood no more than five feet tall. One could wonder if he cowered to or was in awe of the charismatic Mussolini. Mussolini was well known for stating, "It is better to live one day as a lion than 100 years as a sheep."

Mussolini marched on Rome only three years before Levi recorded these reflections. The march was purely ceremonial; the power of the black shirted Fascists was already strong. The King requested that orders be drawn up to proclaim martial law, but he never signed the papers. Many within the government resigned, including Prime Minister Luigi Facta, to show their disapproval of the King's lack of action. Mussolini was then appointed prime minister.

Mussolini did go down in history as Levi imagined. On April 28, 1945, Mussolini found himself at the receiving end of a firing squad, a mere ten days before V-E Day and one day before Hitler committed suicide. Mussolini and his mistress's lifeless bodies were hung upside down for all to behold and desecrate at will. Il Duce, as he was known, was dead. Italy freed itself of Fascism and the Monarchy. The Italian Republic was born two decades after Levi made his apt observation in Rome.

CHAPTER 39
ADDIO ROMA

Levi would leave Rome on January 15th, 1926. A few days before his departure, Levi wrote to his father and then to Chloe on his final day in the Eternal City.

Yesterday we saw the Pope and here's what we saw. We had to pass about six sentinels inside the Vatican before we arrived at the chamber where we awaited Pius XI arrival. These guards (the Swiss Guard) were gorgeously uniformed and carried swords, spears and guns. They placed two big men that looked like drum majors to keep the fifty of us quiet. These guards each had a monstrous sword and every time any one coughed too much both of them would turn and frown as if they ran by clock works. After waiting an hour and a quarter the Pope entered with about ten men who were dressed up like "a horse and wagon." The Pope was dressed in a simple white cassock and he passed rapidly around the circle while we kissed the Papal ring (all kneeling). After that he gave us his blessing and departed as rapidly as he had entered. – The ceremony was not much but now I can say I held the hand of Pope Pius XI which is no exaggeration because he had to jerk away from me. Guess he thought I was trying to pick the stone out of his ring.

The desired audience with the pope had come to fruition. After almost three months of traveling together, the band of three was preparing to separate. Levi's travel journal gave the first rendition, but by the time he wrote to his father, the plan had changed. Originally, Vince was to see Northern Italy and parts of Germany with Father O'Malley, John was going through Italy to Switzerland, and Levi desperately sought the warmth of Spain. In his letter to his father, he spelled out their latest plans.

> *We shall probably leave Rome in two days for Florence, Venice, Milan, Genoa, Torino and then back to France to Nice. Father O'Malley is accompanying us on part of our trip. He wants to rough it but will soon tire of that.*

The distaste Levi had for traveling alone overcame his desire for warmer weather. He had these words for Chloe, just before departing Rome.

> *Today I saw a snowball fight in the streets of Rome and now nothing can surprise me. How Romans walked around in sandaled feet is beyond me. We can hardly accuse them of "cold feet." Naturally I went out and bought a coat and some "heavies" and now am set for the weather we shall find in Florence tomorrow. Here's hoping they have their art gallerys heated because it's hard to appreciate a picture when the air is befogged with ones breath. I am sorry to leave Rome. I like the old and the new Rome. As Paris differs so much from the rest of France so with Rome. Three weeks spent here has served to make me want to come back and if it pleases God, some day I shall.*

> *Without bragging, I think that Father Geniesse will be sorry to see me go. Tonite he was trying to arrive at the probable length of his life so that he could plan his work accordingly. I joked with him about it but underneath it all was the sad realization that he is preparing for the inevitable. It's now that I see the sacrifice of a priests life. Being all*

alone in the world in old age is no little thing.

Said goodbye to Don Gallagher tonite. We expect to see each other in four years at Notre Dame Homecoming. Things will be changed then and it will be hard to call him Father Gallagher.

Since coming back to Rome I have been eating with a German officer who studied at Oxford and at Cambridge and speaks six languages fluently. The same story again. He could not understand my not knowing more than one language. I told him however that I could understand Southern dialect as well as English.

It's interesting to get the other side of the story. When I asked about the comparative ability of the soldiers of the allies and insisted on finding out his opinion of the American doughboy he said, "Some of those that were well trained were not so bad". That may mean anything but possibly the bayonet scar he carrys was received from the American who would not fight.

The enclosed picture is very true in expressing us as we are. John the shiek; Vinc, the starving poet; and just another "bum" by the name of

Lee

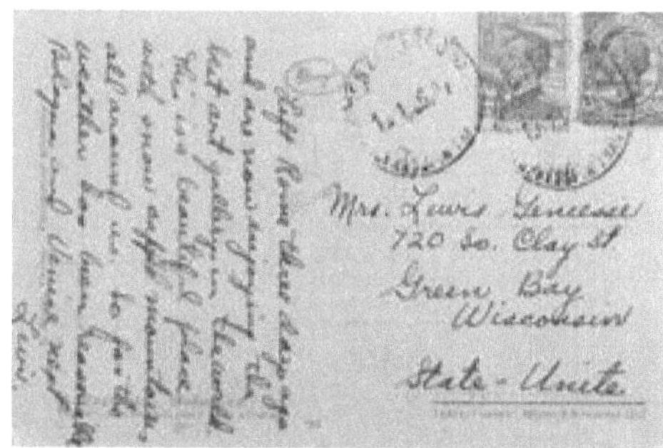

*Left Rome three days ago
and are now enjoying the best
art galleries in the world.
This is a beautiful place with
snow capped mountains all
around us. So far the weather
has been reasonable. Bologna
and Venice next. Levi*

The postmark is illegible – dated 19 Jan. 1926

The *Madonnina,* shown here on the front of Levi's postcard to his mom, is often referred to as "Madonna of the Streets." It was painted by Roberto Ferruzzi in 1897. It is not a Madonna, but rather a girl who captured the painter's eye as she took care of her little brother.

After appearing in the Venice Biennale in 1897, the Madonnina was purchased by Vittorio Alinari. John George Alexander Leishman, a former executive at Carnegie Steel and diplomat who served as U.S. Ambassador to Switzerland, the Ottoman Empire, Italy, and finally Germany in 1911, purchased the painting from Alinari.

When this postcard was mailed, Leishman had been eternally resting in the *Cimetière de Monaco* (Monaco Cemetery) on the French Riviera for nearly two years. The location of the painting remains unknown.

CHAPTER 40
REDIRECTED MAIL

Chloe's next letter did not make it to Rome in time. It would wait in Nice, France, for Levi's arrival in mid-February.

1800 K Street N.W.
Washington, D.C.
January 10, 1926

Dear Lee,

Your letters are very interesting and I find it necessary to study the geography of France, again, and also to review my mediaveal history in order to understand the accounts of your travels. — then maybe I can't appreciate them fully — nevertheless I enjoy reading about them.

You find France and Italy much colder than you expected — What would you do in England and Germany?

The description of Marseilles was very vivid. You are having some of your longed for experiences, aren't you? What is the quotation in regard to loyalty among thieves? It was applicable in the case you mentioned. It must have been a great experience to have seen this side of Marseilles.

Yes, I think you had a lot of courage to send the clipping denouncing the people down south — there isn't any more ignorance there, generally speaking, than in any other section of the U.S. – I think the article described the 'exception and not the rule.' Of course there are a few extremists in every section. You expected me to resent this, didn't you? Well, you aren't disappointed.

The little Christmas card is very pretty. Emma Ruth, with the aid of her French dictionary, translated the greeting for me.

I'm glad you found your friend and cousin in Rome so easily. When you are in a strange place and find someone you know it just does your heart good. From your letter I feel you like your cousin very much. You must find it very interesting to talk to him. Aren't you proud of him? Maybe there will be another one of the same family, famous, some day – for instance the builder of a magnificent cathedral on a little mountain near Green Bay, Wisconsin.

The Countess must be interesting. Does she look the part? I, too, would like to hear of her experiences in Bolshevik Russia.

I suppose by this time you've read that we've moved and that Virginia has come back from Florida. – She didn't go back after the holidays – but is living with us. She hopes to be reinstated in the public schools in February – now she's on the regular substitute list. I'm glad she's with us. It seems like old times – only some things are different.

Gertrude hasn't returned from her vacation – at least we haven't heard from her. I haven't seen Clayton yet. Ruth met him on the street one day last week – both were in a hurry – so simply said, "hello!" and went on.

I went home for the holidays – there was nothing exciting – Emma Ruth was relating some of her experiences – how much she had to study, etc. The "kids" were well and as full of mischief as ever. Mother was much better than she was last fall when I left. I am so thankful of that.

School is about the same – as for college I'm having to cram for exams at the end of the month – I have lots of reference reading to do yet. I don't have much time left after school, college and housekeeping. I hardly ever read the newspaper and feel quite ignorant of current events. If I didn't have to talk about them at school I probably wouldn't read at all.

We had a very exciting time last night – Grace had one of her heart attacks and gave us all a good scare – Purdy included.

Lee, I'm afraid you have me 'upon a pedestal.' I don't deserve what you said about me in your last letter. There are many, many girls who will be are much better than I and who would make you far happier. I could never believe in all the ceremonies and customs in which you believe and I'd be doing you a great injustice, as well as myself, to pretend I believed what I really do not - also I'd be guilty of that greatest of all sins, - hyprocrisy. I appreciate all the kind thoughts you have about me – As I've said many times before there'll always be a warm place in my heart for you. I, too, can wish you the words written on the fly leaf of the little book you gave me when you left.

– Chloe

This letter sat in the American Express Office in Nice, France, while the trio ventured through Northern Italy. The clipping Chloe mentioned came from Levi's Beaucaire letter, mailed a month earlier.

The clipping you will notice I carried a long time before summoning enough courage to send it along. If I could only be there to hear your "well!" when you finish reading it.

The gang is impatient with the last straggler leaving the place. One can't warm his feet by a fire all night on two glasses of wine.

Good night, Lee

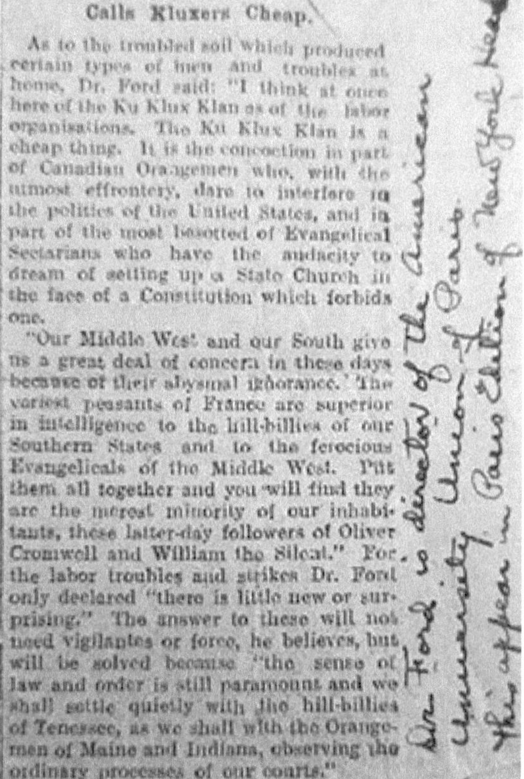

Levi wrote in the margin that Dr. Ford was the director of the American University Union of Paris. The source he gave was the *Paris Edition* of the *New York Herald*, but there is no date or page to reference.

CALLS KLUXERS CHEAP

As to the troubled soil which produced certain types of men and troubles at home, Dr. Ford said: "I think at once here of the Ku Klux Klan as of the labor organisations. The Ku Klux Klan is a cheap thing. It is the concoction in part of Canadian Orangemen who, with the utmost effrontery, dare to interfere in the politics of the United States, and in part of the most besotted of Evangelical Sectarians who have the audacity to dream of setting up a State Church in the face of a Constitution which forbids one.

"Our Middle West and our South give us a great deal of concern in these days because of their abysmal ignorance." The verist peasants of France are superior in intelligence to the hillbillies of our Southern States and to the ferocious Evangelicals of the Middle West. Put them all together and you will find they are the merest minority of our inhabitants, these latter-day followers of Oliver Cromwell and William the Silent." For the labor troubles and strikes Dr. Ford only declared "there is little new or surprising." The answer to these will not need vigilantes or force, he believes, but will be solved because "the sense of law and order is still paramount and we shall settle quietly with the hillbillies of Tennessee, as we shall with the Orangemen of Maine and Indiana, observing the ordinary processes of our courts."

CHAPTER 41
THE CRADLE OF THE RENAISSANCE

Florence – January 20, 1926
[travel journal]

*Five days since I left Rome and it has been five days
filled with visits to many art treasures. The Bargello with
its beautiful court and stairs, its Davids and John the
Baptists by Donatello and Verrochio and its Leda by
Michaelangelo; - and the wax scene called "The Pestilence"
impressed me very much.*

*The Uffitzi and its adjoining gallery the Pitti hold what
is Probably the best collection of painting in the world. This
last statement is just a guess which someday I hope to verify.
The paintings I especially remember here are Botticelli's
Birth of Venus, Several of Giotto's works, Raphaels and
Murrillos Madonnas.*

Two postcards were saved from the *Museo Nazionale del Bargello*
(Bargello National Museum) and a third from the loggia that overlooks the Piazza della Signoria. Postcards were inexpensive keep-
sakes of the artwork seen along the way.

Firenze - Museo Nazionale - Mercurio; Gian Bologna (Florence - National Museum - Mercury; Gian Bologna) A figure of Mercury, supported on a breeze provided by the god Zephyrus. A well-known work from 1580 by the mannerist Jean Boulogne, known as Giambologna. Ferdinando de' Medici commissioned this piece to be placed atop a fountain near the entrance to their villa in Rome. Mercury is one of Giambologna's most famous works. The elongated limbs of Mercury identify this as a mannerist piece, dating to the High Renaissance, just before the Baroque period.

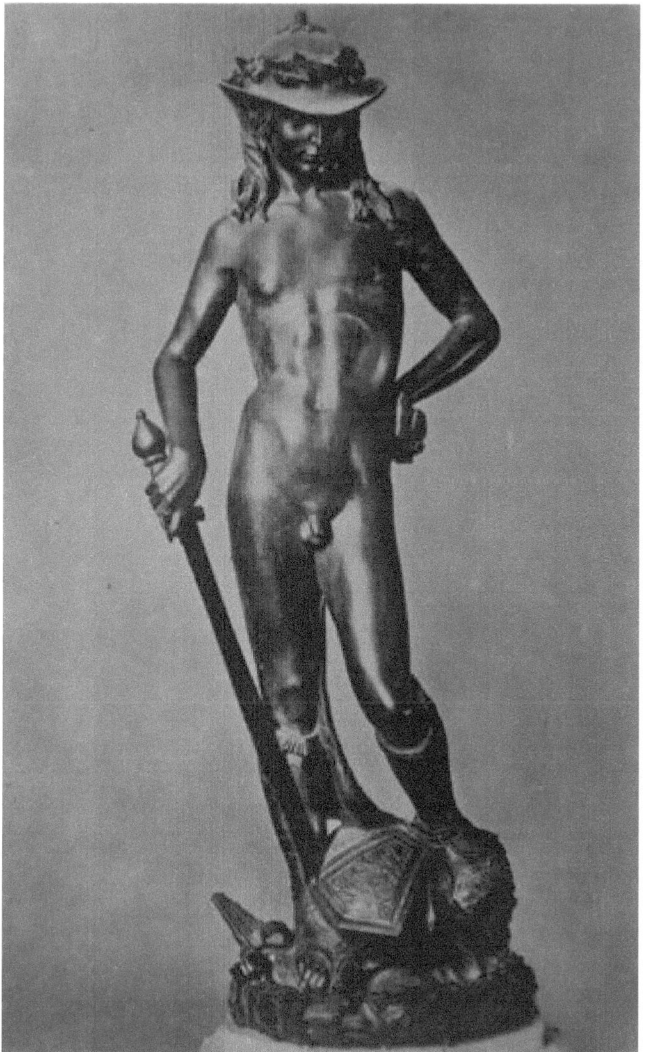

Firenze - Museo Nazionale - David; Donatello (Florence – National Museum – David; Donatello) A bronze statue of David (1446) resting his foot upon the severed head of Goliath. It was commissioned by Cosimo de' Medici and placed in the Medici Palace. In 1495, the statue was moved to Palazzo della Signoria, known today as Palazzo Vecchio. David symbolized Florentine liberty back in the late fifteenth century. In the sixteenth century, it was struck by lightning and later placed into storage. In 1777, the statue joined others at the Uffizi Gallery. The final move was to its present home at the Museo Nazionale del Bargello in 1865.

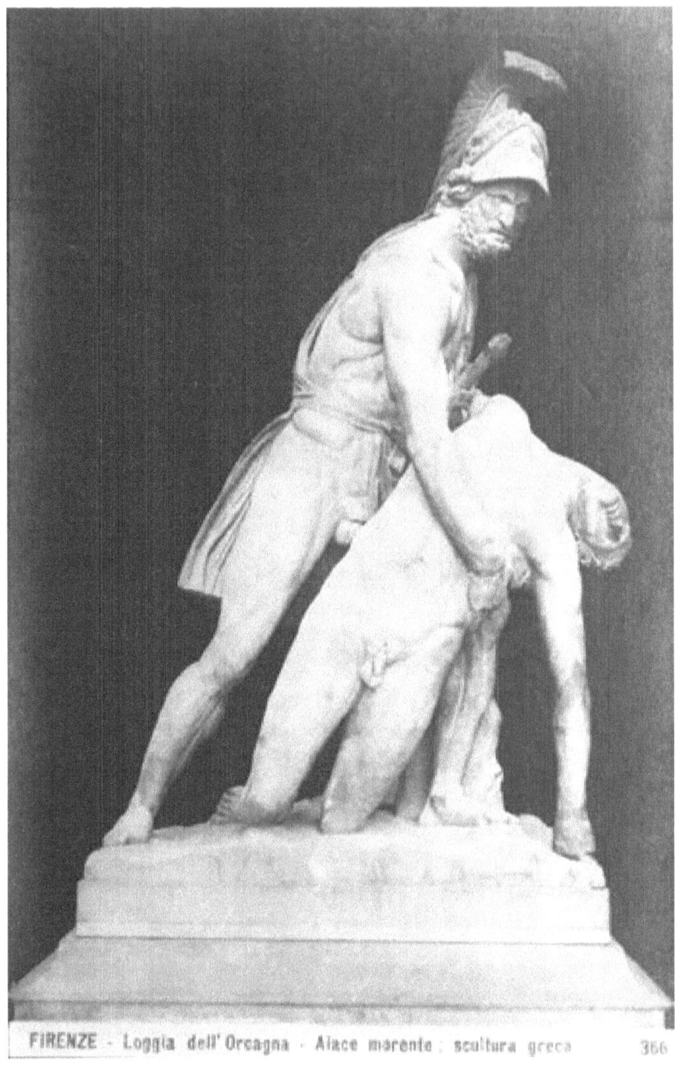

Firenze – Loggia dell' Orcagna – Alace morente; scultura greca. (Florence – Orcagna's Loggia – Dying Hazel – Greek sculpture) This Greek sculpture is in the Loggia dell'Orcagna, an open-air gallery, visible from the Piazza della Signoria. This is the same plaza where Michelangelo's David, or rather a reproduction of the masterpiece, is located. Today, this open porch lined with columns is called Loggia dei Lanzi. Whether this is Ajax holding the body of Achilles or it is Menelaus supporting the corpse of Patroclus is unknown. This is a first-century marble sculpture that is a Roman copy of a Hellenistic original from the third century B.C.

Levi was incorrect in his writing concerning *Leda at the Bargello*. *Leda e il Cigno* (Leda and the Swan) was created by Bartolomeo Ammannati, not Michelangelo, though it was inspired by one of his paintings. Michelangelo's 1530 tempera painting with the same name is assumed to have been destroyed in the seventeenth century at the request of Anne of Austria, Queen of France.

The sculpture of Leda and the swan is best viewed without knowledge of Greek mythology. According to the myth, Zeus lusted for the mortal Leda and charmed her by taking on the form of a swan. Anne of Austria certainly knew the story when she requested the destruction of Michelangelo's painting of bestiality.

The wax scene that left an impression on Levi is Gaetano Giulio Zumbo's *La Peste* (The Plague). It can be found in La Specola, a natural history museum located in the shadows of the Pitti Palace. This seventeenth-century diorama was constructed inside of an elaborate box of wood and glass. Zumbo used various colors of wax to depict the stages of death and decomposition experienced during the plague.

Beginning with the pink healthy skin of the poor soul tasked with delivering the dead, the wax transforms in color to varying shades of green and yellow, signifying bodies recently delivered. The length of time since death was expressed among the corpses by color. The dark, greenish-black bodies had been there the longest. These figures decomposed past the point of looking human and wax provided the perfect medium for this scene. The diorama is an intricately carved moment in time, a mangled panorama where none were spared.

Depending on the source, the plague was estimated to have taken 60,000 to 100,000 souls from Florence alone. That was roughly three-fifths of the city's population.

Florence, Italy
January 21, 1926

Dear Chloe,

Tonite I feasted royally in my little attic room. Dates, walnuts, bread, butter, oranges and for dessert a can of American baked beans. It is not often that we find them and luckily so because they cost just three times what they would in the States. That Italian storekeeper, sharp as a knife, guessed my weakness and I payed well for patriotism. — How to open the can was the next problem but that could not balk me and now my knife looks worst than father's razor after sister has been sharpening pencils.

Florence is what the name implies, the flower of Italian culture. Here is gathered the best of painting and sculpture and the best is like grand opera; it must be studied to be appreciated. I take great pride in saying this; I've reached the stage where I no longer have to force myself to look at Fra Angelico's and Giotto's works. When Giotto abandoned the Byzantine idea of painting objects according to set forms and attempted to paint them as they were he established his school of painting and if you follow his attempts as a boy, when he covered up what he could not draw, thru to his success as a man you can't help but appreciate the pioneer of modern painting. I just read that over and it sounds like a "long haired lecture." I'm sorry.

Savonarola's cell was interesting and I have promised myself to read all about him. The monastery of San Marco of which he was prior exists as it was and here also is the cell of St. Anthony who accomplished by prayer and good example what Savonarola tried to do by sword. Near by is the church in which Luther preached, on his way to Rome. Every where in Florence you find the present linked with the past and that past is the history of the Medici family, a family which bowed not to kings. Yes, I've also sworn that someday I shall know all about them.

Girolamo Savonarola joined the convent of San Domenico in Bologna and was ordained a priest in 1476 by the Order of Friars Preachers, the Dominicans. He had a Master of Arts from the University of Ferrara. Savonarola was assigned to bring the scriptures to Florence at the convent of San Marco, where Levi discovered his

"cell" or living quarters and acquired this postcard.

Savonarola spoke out against corrupt leaders within the church, including the pope at that time, Alexander VI. He preached against common sins within the community. Savonarola was an important figure in the reformation, which should appeal to those supporters of reform, such as protestants like Chloe. These men did not desire to break away from the Catholic church, but wished to reform it into what the church was meant to be, a place to turn towards God and away from the sinful ways of man.

Savonarola is remembered today for the burning of "vanities," items that infiltrated everyday living and led man towards sin. The items themselves were not inherently evil; they could have been mirrors, masks, or costumes from pre-Lenten celebrations. Some were more obvious, such as obscene images and lewd poetry. Lent was a time of repentance in preparation for Easter, and bonfires were the way Savonarola offered the visual learner a lesson on removing sin and temptation from this world. On Shrove Tuesday, commonly called Fat Tuesday today, the collected items were burned in celebration of reform. Savonarola was quoted from a Lenten sermon as saying, "Seek Christ in heaven; seek him not in the things of this life, neither in the things of this world" (Grubb).

The last place Savonarola walked was the Piazza della Signoria. Today, in front of Ammannati's Fountain of Neptune, a granite plaque marks the place where Savonarola breathed his last. It reads:

QVI DOVE CON I SVOI CONFRATELLI FRA DOMENICO BVONVICINI E FRA SILVESTRO MARVFFI IL XXIII MAGGIO DEL MCCCCXCVIII PER INIQVA SENTENZA FV IMPICCATO ED ARSO FRA GIROLAMO SAVONAROLA DOPO QVATTRO SECOLI FV COLLOCATA QVESTA MEMORIA

This translates to, "Here is where, with his brother Fra Domenico Buonvicini and Fra Silvestro Maruffi on 23 May 1498, for an unjust sentence, Fra Girolamo Savonarola was hanged and burned. After four centuries, this memorial was placed."

While visiting the Convent of San Marco, where Savonarola served as prior, Levi passed several frescos and other pieces of religious artwork. Another postcard was found among his souvenirs. This time it was *La Crocifissione* (The Crucifixion) by Blessed Fra Angelico, painted on the wall across from the entry to the Chapter House between 1441 and 1443 . The grand masterpiece measures

5.5 meters (18 feet) by 9.5 meters (31.2 feet). Skin tones consume the three crucified figures, including the bit of cloth that covers them. A dark sky fills the arch behind those nailed to the crosses. The many people standing or kneeling in reverence are draped in soft hues of pink, green, or blue. Mary, the mother of Christ, wears the deepest colors of red and blue, which separate her from the crowd. The black-and-white postcard shows the details of the piece and the friar's abilities, but much is lost with the lack of color.

Levi's January 21 letter to Chloe from Florence continued.

> *This afternoon I was impressed by finding a beautiful Hebrew synagogue here in the midst of the shrines of Catholicity. A little boy took me thru it and when I removed my hat on entering he motioned for me to replace it. The interior was dimly lighted and is just the kind of place one would seek to think and pray. There were many hanging (sanctuary) lamps and the seven branched candle stick but no sign of any image except the tablet of stone representing the Ten Commandments. The whole building was carried out in Moorish architecture and I suddenly realized that here was the oldest race without any remains of a former art and civilization. Why do you suppose they chose to build following the Moors rather than the Christians?*

The synagogue Levi visited, Tempio Maggiore, was built in the Moorish Revival style, a popular design among synagogues from the mid-nineteenth century. Traditionally, these holy places had a reading table, or "bimah," placed at its center, but this temple has the table placed at one end, much like an altar. The shape of the building and the stained-glass windows are similar to those of Christian churches, but this temple embraces the Moorish style.

Architecture made a cameo appearance in Levi's letter to his mom that he wrote the next day, January 22, 1926.

> *There is a great cathedral with a dome as high as St. Peters. Yesterday I went up the bell tower and took a picture of it from about 350 feet up. Don't worry however, there*

was a fence around and I'm not given to sitting on railings at that height.

Levi's travel journal offered more information on the Duomo.

Florence, Italy
January 26, 1926
[travel journal]

These have been delightful days in Florence. Everywhere one goes he sees signs of good architecture. St. Croce is a very interesting edifice and is a good example of the transition period with Gothic windows appearing with beautiful stained glass. Their churches, as most Italian churches, are disappointing. The best word that could describe them is gaudy. They seldom inspire one to devotion although the Cathedral here in Florence comes close to doing that. Father O'Malley and Vinc think that the dome on the Duomo is the best yet but I disappoint them in my disagreement.

Brunelleschi's mastery is unmistakable and impressive. The predominantly brick dome was completed in 1436. For Levi to say that the Duomo was not the best they had seen is a disappointment, but chances are that he was still awestruck by Michelangelo's dome at Saint Peter's Basilica.

The view of Brunelleschi's dome from the easier-to-ascend bell tower is unforgettable. The roof's white ribbing rises to a circle at the top. After a close inspection, a fence is visible at that level, protecting visitors who have climbed the dome to take in the beauty of Florence. Climbing between the inner and outer domes and reaching the base of Brunelleschi's Lantern, the cupola, is an unforgettable experience.

An airship flew over Florence and was captured in Levi's photo as he stood on the Lungarno Torrigiani. He was positioned just upstream from the Ponte Vecchio, the oldest bridge in Florence. The Uffizi Museum is visible in the foreground, just over the Arno River, and the tower of Palazzo Vecchio appears in the distance. That palazzo, or palace, faces the Piazza della Signoria, where the imitation David and the Loggia dei Lanzi are located.

The close-up taken of the airship shows the markings 'P.M.' This is not the Norge, which flew over the North Pole in May 1926. The gondola of this airship is suspended, where the one on the Norge is attached. Some dirigibles left over from the Great War were utilized

after the war, though this airship's exact purpose was unknown.

Escaping the present day and returning to the Renaissance is simple to do in Florence. Following the lives of the masters – Raphael, Michelangelo, Leonardo Da Vinci, Petrarch, and Dante – only scratches the Carrara marble surface this city has to offer.

After spending five days in the Capital of Artists, the quartet broke up. Vince and Father O'Malley stayed one extra day. Levi and John Connell left on January 26; Levi headed to Bologna and John to Venice.

CHAPTER 42
A FEW LINES FROM K STREET

1800 K Street N.W.
Washington, D.C.
January 24, 1925

Dear Lee,

Ruth's trying to do the 'Charleston' so my attention is divided – if you could see her you'd appreciate what I'm saying. The rest of the gang is trying to sleep. – Now someone is coming in to look at the apartment – (we are moving down to the third floor in a larger apartment – and Va. Is using the furniture from her house).

The accounts of your experiences in Rome are so interesting – The folks who drop by and ask about you – want to hear of your experiences and sometimes I read snatches from your letters because I can't express them like you can. I want to show Gertrude your description of the service in St. Peter's – Do you object?

Gertrude called this morning and wanted us to come over Thursday evening – I told her that you were curious to know the whole romance – but I'd have to hear about it first

– because I wanted to write you. The next time I write I'll have the information.

I too can hardly realize that it has been only one year since last Feb. – It seems more like two – I wonder if the events of this year will be any more impressive or leave greater effects.

I had to use the dictionary in order to find out what kind of an animal you had become – How many more words do you know like 'misogynist'? If I thought you were serious I'd lecture, but I don't think its necessary in this case.

There's nothing of special interest going on here – That is in and around this apartment – Gracee and Va. Have quarrels with Purdy and Warren once in awhile – they make up of course and then forget them. Ruth and Johnny don't fuss much – they keep rather quiet.

Of course you don't want to hear that I have two exams this week – and have to 'cram' for them – Probably I'll fail as I haven't studied – I can't concentrate anymore – I'm getting 'flighty' – eh? At least I've decided I don't want to teach in a Junior High School. If I decide to keep on teaching I'm going to quit the public schools – – go to college myself and then teach in a girls' 'Prep" school. Oh, I'm going to stick it out here another session – Maybe all of these are "air castles" – but I dread becoming like the people who have taught here for forty years.

I'm anxious to know how you like the boiled eggs – 'a la Vesuvius' style. Do you like them better than broiled ham with cloves? Are you going from Nice to Spain? (I haven't forgotten how to ask questions)

The 'gang' laughed when they saw your post card – "Just like Lee" – they said – Is this a sample of your poetry? Don't forget you promised to let me see the poem you wrote.

This whole gang is trying to learn the "Charleston", I'll have to too or be left out. If you haven't seen this new dance, you have something in store.

Sincerely, Chloe

Chloe's letter began and ended with the Charleston. It was January of 1926. America was introduced to the dance in October 1923, when the musical comedy, "Running Wild," debuted in New York City's Colonial Theater on Broadway and 62nd Street. The dance did not originate there; many theories attest to its beginnings.

Regardless of the direct path, these dance moves originated among the Gullah or Geechee people, descendants of West Africa, living in South Carolina. In Charleston, the Jenkins Orphanage Band took a group of children and their music on the road to help support the orphanage. They danced "geechie" while conducting the band. Flappers have been photographed imitating the children's moves as they played on the streets of New York.

As far as the tune is concerned, it was Harlem jazz pianist James P. Johnson who composed the famous melody.

Josephine Baker introduced Paris to these West African-inspired moves as part of *La Revue Negré* in October 1925. It was then that the "Charleston" began to travel the world and bend the knees of a generation in a uniquely Geechie style.

Chloe added a note in the margin of her letter, "I promised to send a snapshot sometime – this was taken at Christmas." The photograph was immediately separated from the envelope, and no further description was included. At least now Levi had more than just a few letters to carry around and reread.

CHAPTER 43
TRAINS TO VENICE

Ferrara, Italy
January 28, 1926

Dear Chloe,

I'll start this now but my fingers will probably be frost bitten soon. There is snow and ice here and it made me homesick to see it. Bologna is cleaning up the remains of about 18 inches of snow. Yesterday at Bologna there were some boys cleaning off a patch of ice and architecture was forgotten for the rest of the day. I watched them longingly. Had a room without any heat in this place. You can imagine as well as I how these people live, it's beyond me with snow on the ground how they can sit around a little jar of charcoal and imagine they are warm.

Bologna is a fine modern city of about a hundred thousand. It is easy to see the influence of German blood here and to what else could you attribute the large public bath. Yes I tried it. For twelve cents they give you a piece of soap, a towel, a room, a bath tub and —— some water. Most Italians do not feel the need of taking baths. They scratch themselves instead. Was disappointed in Bologna however because the sausage is not better here than elsewhere.

[Interruption while I rub my fingers with snow].

Someone told me to stop in Ferrara and that's why I'm here. Ferrara was a place that I could just as well have omitted. Haven't been able to find any other reason for lingering and I shall be on my way to St. Anthony's home town, Padua in an hour. This is the headquarters of the Fifth Army Corps and most of the churches and monasterys taken by Garibaldi back in 1870 are being used for barracks. Here I found a big church, the floor of which has been divided by wooden partitions into rooms where many poor families live. There was no ceiling on their small rooms except that of the church dome which towered 200 feet in the air.

The government has given back more than enough churches to serve the people and the people, as always, are building more instead of trying to perfect the ones they have. It's a good thing that the merit before God comes from the sacrifice rather than the result produced in Italian church buildings because they are sure jarring on American eyes.

Ferrara had 102 churches in the mid-1700s, but after the Napoleonic suppression of religion at the turn of the eighteenth century and Garibaldi's conquest of the area in the mid-1800s, the number declined. There are only 54 today. Garibaldi was a key figure in Italy's reunification. Any land that his volunteer army conquered was turned over to the first King of Italy, Victor Emmanuel.

A 1927 map of Ferrara by P. Corbellini showed several churches that were present during Levi's visit, which are no longer on the map. The losses could be due to the bombings of World War II, damaging earthquakes, age, or lack of upkeep. Some church buildings have been deconsecrated and have found other uses.

Levi mentioned *San Pietro* (St. Peter's), which has been turned into a house for the poor. It was once a gym, ballroom, and even a warehouse over time. Today, those once hallowed halls are now a porn theater called the *Cinema Mignon Per Adulti* (Mignon Cinema for Adults). Talk about a twist of faith (Cotton).

The letter to Chloe continued.

Chloe, before I forget it I wish you would look me up a recipe on how to cook goldfish. The Italians foolishly leave their brightly colored fish in the fountains at night and Engels and I are planning a fish-fry. Just think, – goldfish and German beer but then I'll bet that doesn't even sound inviting to you.

Saw another fight today and I understand why most of the Irish pugilists in the States are Italians. Am getting to feel the same way and came near mixing with a big but soft looking man who was highbrowing me in a 2nd class compartment yesterday. We usually ride third class where we are welcome but yesterday I entered a 2nd class car and when I notice the look of disdain that one "pill" gave to my muddy outfit I was delighted to walk over and ask him to move a bit. While he slowly considered the matter I sat on his hat and he was illbred enough to object.

Had just missed one train and just felt right for argument so he didn't. Vinc usually gives them a dirty look back, so he says, but John and I go around itching for trouble. As somebody said, "I don't care how big they are; -the smaller the better".

It's train time and I still must run the gauntlet of all the servants of the hotel who will be out to get their tips.

Padua, Italy

In Padua, St. Anthony's home town, there are four great churches. The Basilica of St. Anthony is probably the largest of these or at least the most impressive because it has been partly decorated in the brightest of colors.

Saint Anthony was Portuguese by birth, but he died in Italy. He grew up in Lisbon. His request was to be buried in the small church he founded in Padua, *Santa Maria Mater Domini* (Holy Mary Mother of God). They honored his wishes when he died from ergotism, an illness caused by consuming contaminated food. It was a parasitic fungus called ergot that grows on rye. Saint Anthony was only 35. The basilica was built, incorporating the small church, which became a chapel, *Capella della Madonna Mora* (Chapel of the Black Madonna). Relics of the saint can be found there today.

Levi continued his letter to Chloe after arriving in Venice.

Upon my word 'tis Venice
January 29, 1926

Ach! What a place for cats and drunken drivers and ducks. If you want to go fishing just throw a line out of your window. It was raining when the train pulled in and I rushed out of the station to take a cab downtown and almost took a bath instead. I wish they would put railings around their streets. They probably take their babies while real young and throw them into the water, those that swim they keep. The man that planned this place ought to be made to live here. Why they have built the sea right up to the houses and haven't left any room for cartracks. But you ought to see the subway system of sharp nosed motor boats darting every-where. If I only had my canoe I'd be all set. This is where that saying originated "Paddle your own canoe, save the difference and buy lots on the seashore at rock bottom prices".

Have been feeling exceptionally well today and now I'm worrying that something is going to happen. Possibly it's because I've been away from all American tourists for three days and that means more than you realize. In Florence we were all fed up on hearing and seeing Americans and English in the museums and art galleries. These cultured women [for most of them are — women] read a guide book criticism of a picture the night before, then standing in front of the painting with one of these "do-hicky" eye glasses they "spout forth" not to their companions alone but generously they let all of us [who are unlucky enough to be around] know what is good about it. — As Father O'Malley remarked, "They'll have to give us credit; we Americans are doing our best to become cultured anyway."

Here's another "pet peeve" — You are kneeling at Divine service in a church of the twelfth century. In this place are many frescoes, mosaics and paintings of the thirteenth and fourteenth centuries, for all the works of art have not yet been removed to art galleries where they are displayed to the mob like animals in a circus tent. Just when the noises of the busy street have died away and for a moment you forget all of, "the finer things of life," in crashes our American tourist, two, three or four of them with their canes, Baedeckers and their flashy knickers [knickers are so appropriate for roughing it in museums]. They stop a moment consulting guidebooks while one of them says something that provokes a smothered laugh from the party, then boldly marching down the isle they leisurely exam what ever works of art the idolaters and superstitious placed there centuries before. All this, mind you, while "ignorant" Italians are trying to pray believing that Christ is upon their altar.

They are safe, no Italian would put them out of a church and besides who are Italians that they should resent this. — I will not ask you in what Protestant church an interruption or distraction like this would be tolerated, because these Americans are no more Protestant than Catholic. To me they but prove the saying, "Scum as well as cream rises to the top."

I think incidents like this partly explain why French universities used as subject matter for their debates last autumn, "Shall American tourists be excluded from France."

Enough of that (I hear you say) just had to get it off my chest and now, do you know that there must be something fine about the German race. [Yes sir, he mused to himself they are a fine race all right, all right] Ever since I got my hair cut they've been taking me for Deutch and every where I go I am confidently addressed in German. I usually answer in French because the fewer people that know we are Americans the better off we are. Engels usually is taken for a Swiss or Russian or something while Connell should really be called Connelburg.

Tomorrow night I start studying Spanish and am going to try to learn a little of that language. Of Italian I know no more than when I arrived. I've been trying to pass as a native of France mostly by tucking a napkin in my collar and eating with both hands and feet a' la mode.

I shall probably meet Connell here tomorrow and we shall decide whether we are going to try Switzerland without "ear laps". Milan is our next stop then Torino and back to Genoa, if we omit Switzerland. Across France by train stopping at Nice and Marseilles then into the land which I have always longed to see, Spain.

At Barcelona I hope you will have many letters waiting for,

Lee

P.S. — If my grammar and spelling are terrible blame it on the wiskey cake they fed me tonite. Even I think that soaking sponge cake in alcohol is soaking things too far.

On that same day, January 29, Levi's first day in Venice, he updated his father, Lewis, on the latest information from Italy. The vast majority of the letter mirrored the words he said to Chloe. He apparently used the letter he had written, but had not yet mailed, to make it easier.

You are probably wondering how my finances are. Well I'm about ready to squeal. Italy ran about our expectations; we could live on $1.25 a day easily but the little extras like museum fees, tips, railroad fare (we ride for one cent a mile) have boosted the average above two dollars. When we get back to Spain and France we can cut it down again but all I have left now is $140.00 which ought to see me thru Spain. I intend to stay in Spain until the weather is suitable for bicycling in Northern France. Most of the great cathedrals are in the north and of course we haven't seen them yet. We plan about a month in England and about two weeks for Belgium and Germany. We don't intend to go far into Germany but just enter to Cologne where their great cathedral is and where we can taste beer where beer making is an art. – The way things look I would not be starting back before June possibly a little later. When I told Father Geniesse that I would probably run short of "jacks" he said I would be foolish to cut short a trip now that I would probably never have a chance to repeat besides he says, "you can save the money you spend now in a few months work at home". – This sounds like a regular college man's letter but anyway if you will send me an American Express Money Order for one hundred dollars to Barcelona I will figure out how much more I need later. [Tell them it is to be cashed at their branch office in Barcelona so that there will be no hitch about it].

Your son, Levi

P.S. Will repeat the last paragraph in my next letter in case this one should get lost.

CHAPTER 44
THE POWER OF STREGA IN VENICE

The quartet, the original crew, and Father O'Malley spent six rainy days in Venice and discovered some of the finer things to do indoors.

After settling in at the Universo Hotel for the first three days, the traveling crew spent their last three nights in style at the Hotel Savoia & Principessa Jolanda, facing the large Canale della Giudecca, drinking 80-proof Strega. Levi wrote to his mom, Louise, but he left out any description of the seventy-herb liqueur.

Venice, Italy
February 4, 1925

Dear Mother,

We are leaving tomorrow for Milan where we shall probably stay a couple days to examine the enormous cathedral and hear what is supposed to be the third best grand opera company in the world. Several nights ago we went to hear one called "Aida" which was wonderful. It was about the best music I have ever heard and I know if Pa would have hear it he would have appreciated it more than we. I have heard several masses here that Pa would have enjoyed also. As Father O'Malley remarked, "I know just enough about music to know that they are darn good."

Have I told you that he is still traveling with us; the last two days he and I went out to examine churches and museums together and tonite the three of us played "rummy." Connell is gone on ahead and we shall probably meet in Nice, France in a few days.

This is my third night in a classy hotel. The weather is so damp, rainy and generally miserable here that we felt that we had to have heat so we moved to a place which rates something like the Beaumont at home. – The summer rates are pretty high but we "Jewed" them down because they had only about ten guests in the place. My steam heated room with a big thick rug on the floor etc. costs including three darn good meals 41.60 lire which is $1.66 a day. When we struck the bargain the boss of the hotel asked us not to tell anyone else what we are paying.

The weather has been terrible here and we are getting out without seeing more than half the place. Six days is long enough for anyone to wait for the fog to lift and the sun come out. I never had the opportunity to take a picture of all the pigeons in front of St. Marks.

From Milan I shall probably omit my proposed step into Switzerland and go directly to Torino to see Tony Chiuminatto then back to Genoa and into France. At Genoa I hope to find some mail waiting. It's been more than a month since I've had a letter so you know how we long for news from home.

With love, Levi

Milan, Italy
February 5, 1926

Dear Chloe,

What do you think of this "doggy" stationery. The owner of this place was taken to an insane asylum the third day we were there. It was like this. He contracted to feed us all we would eat at a fixed price. The poor fellow. — but then you can hardly blame us for seizing the opportunity for which we had searched the 2400 miles since leaving Cherbourg.

It rained all the while we were in Venice. Those six days of mist and dampness got on our nerves and Engels, the Padre and I left (without pleasure).

Connell did not stay in Venice but left for Southern France as soon as he had given it the 'once over'. It is certainly a fine place to visit in Spring or Fall but never in Winter or Summer. The gondolas are as picturesque as I had expected and the architecture, all touched with Eastern ideas, is both interesting and good.

The history of Venice is almost as that of Florence and Rome. The present city is built around the Cathedral of St. Mark and the church itself was erected as a sepulcher for the body of the Evangelist, St. Mark. St. Mark's body was stolen from Alexandria by the venetians and today reposes under the center altar. Almost everything that made Venice was brought as plunder from somewhere and much of it is still exhibited in the museums. The weapons of the crusaders, their battle flags, their booty bring to us the idea that the crusades were not fiction but we also realize that the wealth of the Turks was the main reason the Venetians provided ships and fighters. – Just now while I was writing this the boys got into an argument which might interest you: - In the church of St. Lorenzo in Genoa the body of St. John the Baptist is kept in a side chapel of the church and no women is allowed to enter the chapel. Many a visitor is turned away indignant because of this tradition of allowing no one of Salome's sex near the body of the first to lose his head, - all because of a woman.

Levi described the hotel's letterhead as "doggy," a slang term that was lost to history. In the 1920s, doggy referred to someone or something that was ritzy or stylish, which puts a new spin on the opener and the stationery. It seemed to have a negative connotation on the first read. Context clues were nonexistent helpers. The stationery was great, but the rainy weather left Saint Mark's birdless.

Venice had been known as the City of Water for centuries, with the canals and dependence on water to get about town. But for Levi, the nickname carried a whole new meaning. It was a wet winter in Venice. Naturally, Levi recommended visiting in spring or fall, but April, September, and October have higher rainfall averages than other months. The best advice when visiting Venice is to empty your gondola's bilge and carry an umbrella.

As far as the argument concerning Saint Lorenzo's in Genoa, what could have been taken as farce had merit. In Mark Twain's book, *The Innocents Abroad*, he wrote of his trip to Genoa in 1867 and their visit to Saint Lorenzo. "The main point of interest about the cathedral is the little Chapel of Saint John the Baptist. They only allow women to enter it on one day in the year, on account of the animosity they still cherish against the sex because of the murder of the Saint to gratify a caprice of Herodias. In this Chapel is a marble chest, in which, they told us, were the ashes of Saint John" (Clemens 165).

Torino, Italy
February 7, 1926
[travel journal]

*Strega is powerful stuff and it was here I learned all
about shoes from Vinc. Also must mention Mrs. Smith's
Pensione and the Indian lady that wanted to go to the
museum with me. The art galleries here were disappointing
with the exception of several Bellinis, Titian and the
Tintorettos. St. Marks is the only church worthy of mention
in Venice. It is a perfect treasure of early Christian detail
and someday I shall try to visit it again.*

Locating Levi's favored masters – Bellini, Titian, and Tintoretto – is a useful endeavor, rain or shine. These Renaissance painters were important to the Venetian School, but the Bellini that Levi favored is unknown. There were three Bellinis: Jacopo, Gentile, and Giovanni. The latter seems to be considered the most important during modern times, but his older brother Gentile was the best known during the Renaissance. Their artistry adorns the churches of Venice, while several other examples can be found in the Gallerie dell'Accademia.

The basilica was a five-minute walk from their ritzy stay at the Hotel Savoia & Principessa Jolanda. The gilded ceiling mosaics and intricate, patterned floors are a myriad of colors. The winged lion, symbol of Saint Mark and Venice, stands tall above the entrance. On a sunny day, the pigeons make great subjects for photographing, but the centuries-old practice of feeding them was stopped in 2008, so the numbers today do not compare to those of the past.

CHAPTER 45
LIFE AT THE BRADFORD ON K

Chloe and her three roommates – Ruth, Grace, and Virginia – moved to the third floor of The Bradford at 1800 K Street N.W. in Washington, D.C. in early February 1926. It was a larger apartment than their previous one and her fourth place to call home over the last year. No longer was she in the Government Hotels; Mrs. Tucker's watchful eyes were a thing of the past as they settled into their second apartment at the Bradford.

1800 K Street N.W.
Washington, D.C.
February 7, 1926

Dear Lee,

Both of your letters came yesterday. One had been sent to another apartment and I suppose the people were careless in returning it to the desk. The picture was quite interesting – Why didn't you keep your cap on? The gang raved over John's picture – He'd be spoiled if he lived in Washington – Maybe he is – is he? You never did send the poetry your friend wrote – and how about yours?

Lee, your letters are so descriptive I think I'll have to

have them bound and add the volume to my library. What shall I name the book? I'll let you suggest the title. I have pictures for it too, haven't I?

We went to see Gertrude about ten days ago and learned some more about the romance — She met Warren through Helen? (a girl in Green Bay). Ever since he met her (in Aug.) he has given her a great rush — the engagement is the result. We invited them to our Valentine party for Friday night — I'll tell you my impression of him the next time I write.

Grace and Purdy are to be married in Sept. They have been talking about their house, furnishings, etc. and Grace seems quite thrilled. You'd never think she was engaged to another man last year this time — Time heals all aches - ?

Do you know what happened one year ago to-night? Little did I dream then what was before me — what experience I'd have before another year passed. Did you?

Last week I worked so hard I had to stay in bed over the week end. My two exams at college; plus four sets of intelligence tests I had to correct at school; plus reports and midterm promotions were almost too much for me. I've decided to take only one subject this term. I haven't heard from my exams so I'm hoping I passed. If I didn't that was all because I was too tired to study many evenings. My pupils are much nicer this term but my principal is getting harder on us.

We moved in a larger apartment last week. Now we have two bedrooms, kitchen, parlor, reception room and bath. Virginia brought the furniture from her house here, so we have much more room and I like so much better. We are still in the Bradford. You should have seen us moving and getting the furniture put up. We needed your assistance — Aren't you glad you weren't here?

We've had one unpleasant experience since we've been here. The night we came back from Gertrude's (about 12 o'clock) and Johnny had just gone, there was a tap on our door and thinking he had returned for something, Virginia opened the door and saw four tousled headed drunken men at our door. She shut the door quickly and yelled. We were so scared we couldn't sleep that night and the next morning when the postman knocked with your package I didn't know whether to answer the door or not. These men go to Georgetown. We reported them to the manager and she said others complained about them and as we saw an old man and woman enter their apartment we think and hope they've moved. No, my opinion of drunken men has not improved. This is a discourse on prohibition? I hope you'll find Spain interesting.

Write to, Chloe

The past year brought change to many of the girls in her flat. Gertrude no longer lived with the group. A year ago, she was on a "blind" date with Van and canoed with him last summer. Van's experiments with the romance of moonlight did not turn out well. Gertrude's heart now belonged to another, her betrothed, the mysterious Warren Atchinson.

Ruth seemed to embrace the 1920s – living in the city, working for the U.S. Government, and practicing the Charleston. Levi kept this photo in his album. Chloe is on the left, Ruth is on the right, and the fellow in the middle is a friend named Everet.

Virginia was set to marry Warren Poole in November. She had been preparing for their start together over the past months.

Grace and Purdy were getting married even sooner, in September. Purdy came in and swept the broken-hearted girl off her feet. Previously engaged, as recently as a year ago, Grace was now planning her future home and furnishings.

With all the wedding plans encircling their lives, it must have been hard for Chloe to see the anniversary of her blind date with Levi come and go, leaving only plans of friendship in its wake. At least she seemed content and did not regret the experiences from the past year. Chloe's thoughts of the past year left her wondering about the future.

CHAPTER 46
ART AND ARCHITECTURE IN MILAN

Levi's letter from February 5, 1925, written on the *doggy* letterhead from the Venice hotel, continued.

We spent three days of miserable weather at Milan but the cathedral and the opera were worth it. The cathedral of Milan is wonderful as advertised. I spent most of today prowling around the place but of course we took time out to go over to see Leonardo da Vinci's "The Last Supper." One can see that at one time it was a great painting but seven restorations [It still needs an eighth] have done it no good.

We are going to an opera tonite called Aida. We heard the same one four days ago in Venice and considered it so good we were going again tonite but with true Italian efficiency they postponed it about an hour before the curtain. Tomorrow night they play "Twilight of the Gods" and we go to hear it — by the Scala Company of Milan. The name meant little to me but they say it is the best in Italy which means about the best anywhere for we'll admit that Italians know music. Everyone seems to attend grand opera and the audience stands up in their seats and cheers, as we do prize

*fighters in America. We entered into the spirit of the per-
formance several nights ago and Vinc and I would see if
we couldn't drown out the rest with our "Bravo." One thing
I couldn't help noticing. Just try to talk during the singing
and there will be plenty of hands (willing hands) to throw
you out.*

If a visit to Milan were restricted to a review of the cathedral, Da Vinci's mural, and the Scala Opera House, it would be a trip worth taking. The continued rain was not enough to dampen his enjoyment of the capital of Lombardy.

The Duomo of Milan stands alone when compared to other Gothic beauties in Europe. One hundred thirty-five spires reach toward the heavens, each is capped with a figure, though not all of them are saints. The highest spire is topped with a gilded statue of Mary, called the Madonnina. She has looked over Milan from this high perch since 1774. The Madonnina is one of 3,400 figures at the Duomo.

High above the main altar of the church is a cross. In the center, a glass chamber holds a horse's bridle. Saint Borromeo processed through the city streets with this relic during the plague of 1577. According to legend, the horse's bridle was made from a nail taken from Christ's crucifixion. It was meant to protect Emperor Constantine. On the closest Saturday to September 14, the Archbishop of Milan ascends in a basket, retrieves the relic, and presents it to the people. This tradition dates back to the sixteenth century and is still performed today. Since Levi visited in February, he was not aware of the relic or the tradition that takes place here.

*Torino, Italy
February 7, 1926
[travel journal]*

*We spent three days of miserable weather at Milan but
the cathedral and the opera were worth it. Leonardo da
Vinci's Last Supper is but the faintest suggestion of its past*

*greatness We were disappointed in finding the vaulting
painted to represent tracery in the cathedral. The exterior
is wonderful, the interior impressive, the statues and other
sculpture a perfect example of true architecture which means
sacrifice. The opera at the Scala theatre was called "The
Twilight of the Gods". – It was the greatest thing I have
ever heard – also I shall never forget the thrill we had when
we thought the scenery was afire.*

Levi was disappointed, architecturally, in finding the ceilings above the aisles of the nave painted to represent intricate tracery. John Ruskin agreed with Levi in *The Seven Lamps of Architecture*, published in 1849. Under the section titled "Surface Deceits," Ruskin used the Milan Cathedral as an example. It is "seemingly covered with elaborate fan tracery, forcibly enough painted to enable it, in its dark and removed position, to deceive a careless observer. This is, of course, gross degradation; it destroys much of the dignity even of the rest of the building and is in the very strongest terms to be reprehended" (37). The intricate patterns appear to be carved from stone, but they are trompe-l'oeil.

Milan could not be visited without seeing *The Last Supper*, no matter how faint it had become. It was a truly unforgettable piece if viewed just after it was completed in 1498. In the centuries since, the materials that da Vinci used and the wall itself have deteriorated. As early as 1532, Renaissance polymath Gerolamo Cardano wrote that the painting was "blurred and colorless" in comparison to what he had seen as a boy (Wykes 26). Recent estimates of the amount of surviving original paintwork run between 20 and 50 percent, after many restoration layers were removed in a twenty-year project that ended in the late 1990s (Bonsanti).

Last on Levi's list was the Scala Opera House. The thrill of believing the scenery was on fire was quite an experience for the time of silent movies and newsreels! The opera house opened in 1778, named in tribute to Santa Maria della Scala, an old church that was demolished to provide this central location.

During World War II, Allied bombs wreaked havoc on the splendidly crafted opera house. The ceiling collapsed into the area where countless thousands took in fabulous artistic performances. The destruction is no longer visible. What could have been seen by many as a complete loss and teardown has been authentically reproduced.

The group split apart in Milan. Levi reported the plans at the end of his February 5 letter to Chloe.

> *Sunday we separated, probably for several months. Father O'Malley (Padre) is going on to Nice with Vinc and then he shall probably sail for home. Vinc is going back to Paris where he shall study a bit at the U. of Paris and do some work on the Paris Edition of the New York Herald. John Connell intends to get back home soon and has gone on ahead into France. I am stopping several days in Torino with an acquaintance of old Green Bay [there ain't another place like it] then I'll get my bike in Genoa and start for Spain. I shall be alone there and am making a desperate effort to learn a little Spanish because it is a country that the ordinary tourist does not see and therefore few people will be able to give any information in English. In Genoa there will be mail and then I shall write — and spell better.*
>
> *Sincerely, Lee*

CHAPTER 47
TONY IN TORINO

Torino, Italy
February 7, 1926
[travel journal]

Arrived here today and am camped in Tony Chiumi-
natto's bed. This is a fine city and with Tony to show me
around I can't help but have a good time.

The adventures from *Torino* (Turin) were captured in two letters sent back to the states from Nice, France, a February 12 letter to Chloe and a February 13 letter to his father, Lewis. Levi's main reason for separating from his traveling companions was to visit an old friend from home, Antonio "Tony" Chiuminatto. To Chloe, Levi wrote the following.

I spent three very busy days trying to see Turin [Italy]
under the guidance of a friend from the old home town. He
is studying music over here and has two more years before
returning home. I was the first one he had seen in fourteen
months and he took his desire to speak English out on me.

About the same time, Tony's classmate, Guiscardo Tirotti, introduced him to two other students, Cesare Pavese and Massimo Mila. The two wanted to practice speaking English. Letters between

Tony and Cesare are preserved in Mark Pietralunga's book, *Cesare Pavese and Anthony Chiuminatto: Their Correspondence*. They met often and discussed English and American slang.

Tony's two classmates were born and bred in Italy. Tony left Italy in his youth but returned to expand his studies in music.

A look over Pavese and Mila's lives uncovered that both were arrested and imprisoned at some point for anti-fascist activity. Chiuminatto recalled that they often met at the *Café Mugna* or Mila's home "when he was under house

arrest for something having to do with the black shirts" (Pietralunga 321).

In 1926, Tony, Cesare, and Massimo became 22, 18, and 16, respectively. All were embarking on a journey that would earn them the attention of millions. Pavese is often referred to as one of the most influential Italian writers of his time, an Americanist, and a pre-eminent translator of his generation. Mila was a highly respected musicologist and critic. Chiuminatto earned his professorship in Turin and then his master's degree before returning to the States, where he earned a Ph.D. at Northwestern University.

During his time in Italy, Tony stayed out of politics. His friendships, as reflected in Levi's letters, crossed political boundaries.

Turin was the location of a massacre barely three years before Levi's visit. In October 1922, the National Fascist Party took control of the Kingdom of Italy, and Mussolini became Prime Minister. Two months later, between December 18 and December 20, the Fascists killed somewhere between eleven and twenty-four members of a local labor movement in Turin. The numbers vary by source. The goal was to break the resistance to fascism found among the laborers and the working class in general. Turin was a center of political conflict for years. Levi's letter to Chloe continued.

> *Learned that Mussolini came from Turin and that the place is full of Communists who hate him for wrecking their plans. Met a Marshall of the Italian Army and went to hear Il Trovatore [The Troubadour, an opera] with a Lieutenant of the Facisti.*

In Levi's letter to his father, he described Turin.

> *Spent three days with Tony Chiuminatto in Torino. The grandmother could talk a little French and we got along fine. I learned to eat a lot of Italian dishes and drank many new wines while there. Met a Marshall of the Italian army and drank some of his wine too. The last night I was there Tony, I and the lieutenant of the Facisti went to hear a grand opera together.*

The same moments in time were reflected on from a slightly different point of view when Levi wrote to Chloe.

> *Made a wonderful discovery that beautiful complexions come from drinking wine. – The last was the answer I received from the beautiful cousin [Tony's] in response to my, 'whence the pretty complexion?'. How many bottles shall I bring back to 1800 K Street N.W.?*

PARIS
Italy
Nice
Marseille
Aboard the
Sidi Brahim

FRANCE II & MONACO
February 1926

CHAPTER 48
LA BELLE PAYS

Nice, France
February 12, 1926

Dear Chloe,

The sun came out today. Actually the sun appeared two days ago when your letters were handed to me. I have tried to write for the last two days but a letter from my brother has put me in such a state of mind that even now this will hardly be a cheerful reading to you.

Just a few lines it was, telling me that my mother was much better and that I need not worry. An attack of heart trouble which it seems was explained to me before. There has been a gap of about a month in all my mail which I haven't been able to locate. You can imagine how I feel with the uncertainty of how serious it really is. Am going on to Spain now where I shall be practically lost for the next five weeks. It is either that or home now because Northern France and the cathedral country of England are too disagreeable for architectural study.

Am writing this out along the Mediterranean about two miles across the bay from Nice. It is a beautiful day, about the best we've had in Europe and coming after fifteen days of snow and rain it is appreciated. Had just taken my "bike" from the railroad station with the intention of s elling it but I didn't have the heart to part with it so here I am dodging the French "bugs" and the American Limousines, that fly by on what is probably the most beautiful drive in the world. [I still let my enthusiasm carry me to exaggeration but you would too in this instance.]

The weather was still terrible in Genoa so I came thru to the border and after a lot of red tape and standing by while the French searched my bag I came to Nice. I hope they don't search that thorough when I get back to the U.S.A. or I'll spend my declining years behind the bars.

Nice is in the midst of their big carnival. From the looks of things they intend to beat the K.K.K. parade from last year in Washington. "The Battle of the Flowers " takes place tomorrow but I'll not attempt to describe it. The Pathé News pictures show the festivities every year and they can give you a better idea than I. The city is crowded, hotel prices are up 400% and that hurts. Everyone of importance in the Social World seems to be either here or at Monte Carlo which is only 16 miles away. There are probably thirty thousand Americans here and they along with the English seem to monopolize everything. Of course the other nations are all well represented to what they tell us will be one grand orgy before Lent begins. The irony of the thing is that in all the crowd gathered here there are hardly any that observe Lent or any other season of penance. A big proportion of the Americans here are Jews and it's almost laughable to see a newspaper refer to the affair as a little relaxation before the rigorous observance of Lent.

I spent yesterday afternoon with Vinc Engels at the Casino of Monte Carlo. Just couldn't resist and after the smoke cleared away I was a weeks expenses behind. Used to

*think that I was immune when it came to gambling but it
was worth the cost to know what it is like to forget everything but the whirr of the roulette wheel. The movies do not
exaggerate gambling scenes. They do not even approach them
in their awfulness.*

*I told you of my impression of Marseilles and its
derelicts. They were a sad lot to look upon but the faces
around the tables in the casino were too pitiful for one to
even pity. Those in the place may be roughly divided into
tourist spectators who play a little just to say ——, those
who are there to try to beat the game and earn a living that
way, the usual "hangers-on" both men and women who are
picking their prey and finally the extremely wealthy who are
trying to find a thrill in life.*

*I suppose you could also add the several clergymen
including an Anglican minister and our own "Padre" who
are getting material for hell and brimstone sermons.*

*A pretty girl sat across from me at one table, evidently
a drug addict! She played her chips with glassy eyes and*

twitching lips while along side was a woman in "widows weeds" who played 10,000 francs at a shot with seemingly no concern as to whether she won or lost. As Vinc said, "My widow will never get the chance to do that." —— Then there was the man and wife, haggard and desperate who played only after consulting some system they had. All nations seemed to be represented and I especially noticed a group of turbaned Indians who played their rupees as recklessly as the jaded American, his dollars. – Women seemed to be the greatest gamblers and such women as you have probably never seen. Their circled eyes, puffed with years of the dissipation of "Society", their sagging chins and bulging bodies make one realize that there is little to chose between the two extremes of the social ladder. These same women avoided children, – it was incompatible with a fine figure and today – well I guess I've said too much already. – "The world, the flesh and the devil", as Padre commented, "are all before you at Monte Carlo".

However that is only one side. It is an extremely beautiful place. The music is grand and there is a certain tense air about the place that could not be reproduced elsewhere. – Padre took Vinc and I to supper last night [In order I guess to eradicate the gloom memory of our loses]. It was a "swell" restaurant so much so that I felt out of place until the cocktails started working.

The two things I'll always remember about it was the fact that we had four waiters hovering around our table and that they brought big bottles of champagne, [a la movies] the bottles reposing in cracked ice in large silver pails. The stuff is all they say about it and I have been worrying ever since as to how I'm going to get some home with me.

Like Cinderella, today I drank beer and ate cheese sandwiches.

When you tell me the gang is learning the "Charleston" I feel that I'm thru. Never could learn this new fangled stuff so now is a good time for me to quit dancing — what's that Virginia said, "He never started".

Chloe, I resolved to leave all talk of religion out of my letters but I can't help but say this. You mention "ceremonies and customs" as the stone wall. It is not so. I care no more for them than you do. The real difficulty is the Holy Eucharist and reason alone can never make one believe in the True Presence. The Grace of God alone can do that. If you pray to Him for guidance and your opinion does not change it is His will and I am silent.

You shall not be bothered with any more of this. Three weeks spent with my cousin in Rome were not wasted. He taught me much if you had met him he could have helped you in your faith.

Lee

CHAPTER 49
CARNIVAL, SINCE 1294

Nice, France
February 18, 1926

Dear Chloe,

 The celebration of the Carnival here is over and they are burying the dead. It was the grandest thing I have ever seen where a whole city joined in the spirit of the thing. Something like armistice day at home.

They threw flowers, confetti and finally small balls of plaster. Has anyone described the great game they have here during the carnival. About five thousand men, women, boys and girls get themselves wire masks and big bags of balls made of hard plaster. The idea, as we see it, is to put out each others eyes. We poor Americans softened by living in Western luxury happened to find ourselves in front of the reviewing stand where they put all those injured out of their misery. Some one turned their thumbs down, — and down came about a ton of these little rocks. After it was all over I counted myself and still have the required number of arms and legs but I've been exhaling confetti and plaster ever since.

I full expected they would throw bottles next but it seems that the French use their bottles again. We spent most of the night [and that wasn't all] in the Café di Paris and it was what the name implies. Champagne and confetti were the two outstanding things I remember. Also we learned that it's perfectly all right to kiss someone else's wife during Mardi Gras. As someone described the scene, "There wasn't a single Puritan there."

Did I tell you that I tried a dip in the Mediterranean and enjoyed it but that when evening came around I went to bed with all the symptoms of typhoid fever, pneumonia, rheumatism and the "flu". If Pussyfoot Johnson had his way over here I'd be wearing a "stiff overcoat" now but the French, however poor they may be, still have medicine for the "chill."

Also saw a dolphin swimming along the beach. Thought it was a shark but some bystander dampened my thrill.

We are leaving for Marseilles this afternoon and while our itinerary is not decided for Spain we are not going to try bicycles there because of bad roads.

Lee

Lent began with Ash Wednesday, February 17, 1926. Levi, Vince, and Father O'Malley found themselves in one of the largest celebrations in Nice, the annual Carnival. The theme in 1926 was *La marmite aux Enfers* (The cauldron in Hell). Floats, *grosses têtes* (big heads), and other decorations centered around the Greek myth of Orpheus and his descent to Hell to rescue Eurydice, his wife (Maurandi). The forty days of Lent started the day this letter was penned. It was time for reflection, preparation, and fasting.

CHAPTER 50
HOORAY!
BACK TO MARSEILLE

Marseilles, France
February 19, 1926
[travel journal]

Back in La Belle France; already eight days although I don't know what we've done during that time. Arriving at Nice I found the hotels crowded and could not find a suitable room. The next morning I met "Padre" and Vinc and we went out to Monte Carlo where I lost 160 francs as did Vinc. The Prince of Monaco is the richer but "Padre" made up our losses and we dined well that night . We wanted to know what prayers he said but he wouldn't tell us.

Went in swimming at the "Le Grand Bleu" beach where I met Turbilinsky who came over on the Leviathan with us. The same day he took us on a bus ride to La Turbie and the monastery of Notre Dame de Laghet. Pilgrimages are made here every year and it is a great spot of devotion to the Blessed Virgin. The walls of the church are covered with cheap water colors and drawings showing how the miracles happened. Some of these prints certainly justify skepticism of the actuality of the miracle. The same night I was taken with a severe fever and chill but several glasses of cognac seemed to help.

The carnival was worth noting here. The people, the joyful spirit of everyone, the confetti, costumes, masks (wire) the balls of plaster are all beyond my power of description. – The last night supper at the Café de Paris. The champagne made us feel like kings and act like fools. Vinc and I had quite a walk that night, half way to Antibes.

We said good bye to Padre yesterday and came here last night. Padre plans to go back to Rome and then sail for New York. Vinc and I are all set to sail for Algiers, Sunday noon.

I sold my bicycle today for 200 francs. It hurt to get rid of it but I was cold and hard and my faithful servant of steel and rubber stands tonite in the shop of a second hand dealer.

February's beach time on the *Côte d'Azur* (French Riviera) was captured on film. The photo on the left is of Father Charles O'Malley, "Padre," and Levi. Levi stood with his back against the railing as he faced *La Promenade des Anglais* (Walkway of the English).

Levi mentioned their visit to *Notre Dame de Laghet* (Our Lady of Laghet). Often called the "Little Lourdes of Nice," this is not a Marian apparition site. Pilgrimages are made to this church because of the many miracles that have occurred here, dating back to 1652, the earliest recording. There are over 4,000 ex-votos here, artistic pieces the faithful have left behind in thanksgiving for the intercession of the Blessed Mother Mary.

Notre Dame de Laghet is located in the Maritime Alps, not far from Monaco or Nice. This photo shows Father O'Malley in the foreground and Vince Engels further up the trail near this pilgrimage site.

Saturday, February 20, was the last day Vince and Levi spent in and around Marseille. These lines from Levi's travel journal are all that exist from that day.

We met our new American friends again, Mr. and Mrs. Thomas L. Fanoler. – They were in the same launch the first time we tried to reach the island and turned back because of rough weather. They were very interesting and I may accept their invitation "to tea" next summer in London.

Last night Vinc and I again watched the sun set from Notre Dame de la Gard. Scenes like that are too glorious to describe.

Levi left no details of his visit to the Island of If. The only reason to travel there would be to see the sixteenth-century fort, Château d'If, which protected the port of Marseille. By the 1800s, it was determined that the fort could serve the public better as a prison. Swift currents deterred any escape attempts. In 1890, the fort was decommissioned and turned into a tourist attraction only thirty-six years before their visit.

The Château d'If appeared several times in classic literature.

Alexandre Dumas wrote *The Count of Monte Cristo* in 1844. The main character, Edmond Dantès, spent fourteen years within the stone walls of this prison, unjustly convicted of treason. Dumas never visited the Île d'If, but he aptly envisioned being imprisoned there. Edmond was the only person in history to successfully escape the Château d'If, a feat more suited for a fictional character.

Dumas was not the only author to write about this island prison. In 1867, Mark Twain (Samuel Clemens) hired a sailboat and a guide while he and his traveling companions visited Marseille. Their goal was to tour the compound, though it was not yet open to the public. In *The Innocents Abroad*, Twain wrote of dungeon walls being covered with many names from prisoners who watched their lives slowly pass. "We loitered through dungeon after dungeon, away down into the living rock below the level of the sea, it seemed. Names everywhere! - some plebeian, some noble, some even princely. Plebeian, prince, and noble had one solicitude in common – they would not be forgotten!" (102).

Vince and Levi said farewell to France once more. Their plans had drastically changed; they would travel to Spain via Africa. Levi's most recent letters to Chloe were answered, but her responses were mailed to Barcelona and forwarded to Madrid.

Monday Night
February 22, 1926

Dear Lee,

So you are not going to Switzerland now – but to Spain. Lee, I wish you weren't going alone. Please be careful and not lose your temper over some hot headed Spaniard. Maybe they aren't any more high-tempered than the Italian but I just have a feeling they are.

I could just tell from your letter of Jan. 28, that you did not like Venice. I was disappointed, because I had always pictured it as being beautiful. I hadn't thought that the seasons might affect it.

I can imagine how some American tourists conduct themselves. Last Friday afternoon I heard Fritz Kreisler, and there were two women in front of me criticizing him, the theater, etc. – Their conversation was for the benefit of all who wanted to hear and those who did not. At least I have an idea of what it is to try and appreciate art under trying conditions – at the last minute of course there were no seats left and I was so determined to hear him I bought standing room. Maybe I could have appreciated his music more if I hadn't had to shift from one foot to the other every five minutes. The concert lasted two hours but I'm so glad I heard him. I've wanted to, ever since I learned anything at all about him. He has the right description – the master violinist.

I know it hurts when you see people who are so irreverent. Don't criticize them too harshly – probably they don't know any better – just feel sorry for them – you don't have to go to Europe to find Americans with this characteristic.

Clayton called up and asked for your last address. He said that he had written to you and didn't understand why you didn't get his letters.

Since you'll be in Spain when you receive this letter I'm afraid the recipe for cooking goldfish would not do you any good. – (Suggestion – Cook them Indian fashion – boil them over coals). I'm glad you've had enough to eat at last – from your letters. I was afraid you'd be very "skinny" by the time you reached America at least now you won't feel like eating everything we keep in our ice box – (you'd starve if you depended on that, wouldn't you?)

You are becoming very 'cultured' – you even like grand opera, etc. – Did you read the story of Aida before you heard it? (In true all-American tourist style) – I even read the story of Carmen before I saw it last year. Don't you think I'm mean? – The very idea of your comparing grand opera with prize fighting – Which do you like better? This is an unnecessary question — You wanted to be a prize fighter your-self at one time, didn't you?

Forgive me for teasing you — I've been in that mood all day — I'll get paid back soon, I'm expecting it.

I hope you'll like Spain as much as you've anticipated. Don't forget to be careful and please,

Chloe

Nothing quelled the pleasure of experiencing the mastery of Fritz Kreisler. Jessie MacBride with The Washington Times attended the same event at the Polis Theater that Friday. His article, "Kreisler's Art at Best Here," appeared in Saturday's paper. MacBride compared Kreisler to a familiar subject, stating, "Kreisler's art is always as permanent, as sure, as a great piece of architecture. But yesterday, to carry the parallel further, his flawless beauty of detail was like the flowering tracery of a Corinthian capital, and he, as artist, stood as lofty as this pillar, crowning the world of violin music with a peerless nobility " (7).

Fritz Kreisler appeared on the cover of *Time Magazine* a year earlier, on February 2, 1925. The article recognized Kreisler as the "World's Greatest Violinist." He served in the Great War, but his Austrian birth and service to his native country left him unaccepted by many Americans, despite his talents (15).

Sunday Evening
February 28, 1926

Dear Lee,

When your letter came saying that your Mother had had a heart attack — many thoughts passed through my mind — what she said about your going to Europe and also what your Father wrote just before you left. — My responsibility flashed before me. Lee, I hope nothing serious happens. I'll always feel blamed if anything does. Again, I didn't know whether to write or not and I remembered what you said about needing my letters more than ever at a time like this. I'm surely in a predicament! I try not to worry but be patient and remember that "all things work together for good to those who love

God." Has your Mother been subject to heart attacks? I'm anxious to hear how she is and I have to wait until the news goes to Europe and then comes back again.

Your description of the Casino is the best you've written yet. I read a novel last year that pictured scenes at Monte Carlo — your description is similar but seems more real — (because I know the person who is seeing and experiencing actual life there?)

You certainly have been fortunate in meeting friends of yours in Europe. How many have you met? I'm afraid you'd not get through the customs house if you attempted to bring some wine for our complexions. My Mother would say drink buttermilk! Wouldn't you exchange your glass of wine for one of buttermilk?

I haven't been doing anything thrilling of late. Went to a bridge party Friday night and the bunch of us went to the A.B. dance Sat. night at the Gov't Hotels. Ruth met a man from Wisconsin — the northern part I believe — He said that he graduated from the University of Wisconsin and had spent one year at Harvard. John James Klak is his name. He said he was a Swede — but we can't decide whether he is a Pollock or German. Help us settle the question.

Lee, I've learned a lot from you — My ideas of Catholics are entirely different. I firmly believe that a good Catholic is one of the best people in the world. The real religion is one of the heart I believe and not of theology. The two should be combined. I'm not absolutely sure of what I believe in regard to the Holy Eucharist. I believe what your faith teaches is possible (because all things are possible with God) but I can't help from feeling that Christ was speaking symbolically when he explained this to his disciples. I could tell you this much better than I can write it. I'm glad to hear you say that religion is not based on reason (as you once wrote me).

*Please be careful – will you? Don't worry about your
Mother. Just take your troubles to a Higher Power and trust
in Him.*

Your friend, Chloe

Chloe used the word "Pollock." The correct spelling is Polak, or
Polack in English, referring to a person of Polish ancestry. The term
dates back to the fifteenth century, but it was not considered deroga-
tory until the early to mid-1900s.

In 1926, most immigrants in Wisconsin were German, with Poles
being the next largest group. The largest wave of German immigrants was the poorest. They arrived between 1875 and 1890 from
Prussia and Pomerania and were displaced agricultural laborers.

John Klak, the Wisconsin native Chloe met through Ruth, claimed
to be Swedish. In 1926, the Swedish population in Wisconsin was
small and isolated to the northwestern quarter of the state, closer to
Minnesota. Klak was from Thorp, Wisconsin, a small town in central
Wisconsin. The population there was less than 800 according to the
1920 census. Most of the population in Thorp was Polish.

There was no significant negative sentiment towards the Swedes
as there was towards other nationalities in the 1920s. Anti-German
sentiment rose in America after the U.S. declared war on Germany in
1917. The Immigration Act of 1924 favored Northern and Western
European countries, a shift from the recent influx from Southern and
Eastern Europe.

Klak attended Harvard. He enlisted in the U.S. Navy right out of
high school and was one of twelve chosen to attend Harvard Radio
School. During World War I, John was a gunner and radio operator.
In 1923, James completed his electrical engineering requirements
at the University of Wisconsin. In 1927, James joined the reserves
and became a pilot in 1928. While working for the Commerce Commission, John took night classes at George Washington University's
Law School. In 1938, he passed the bar and joined the Court of Appeals in D.C. Reactivated for World War II, James was a Commander
at Pearl Harbor. He retired from the Navy in 1946.

John Klak was neither a Swede nor a German. Arguably, he was
not Polish either; he was an American.

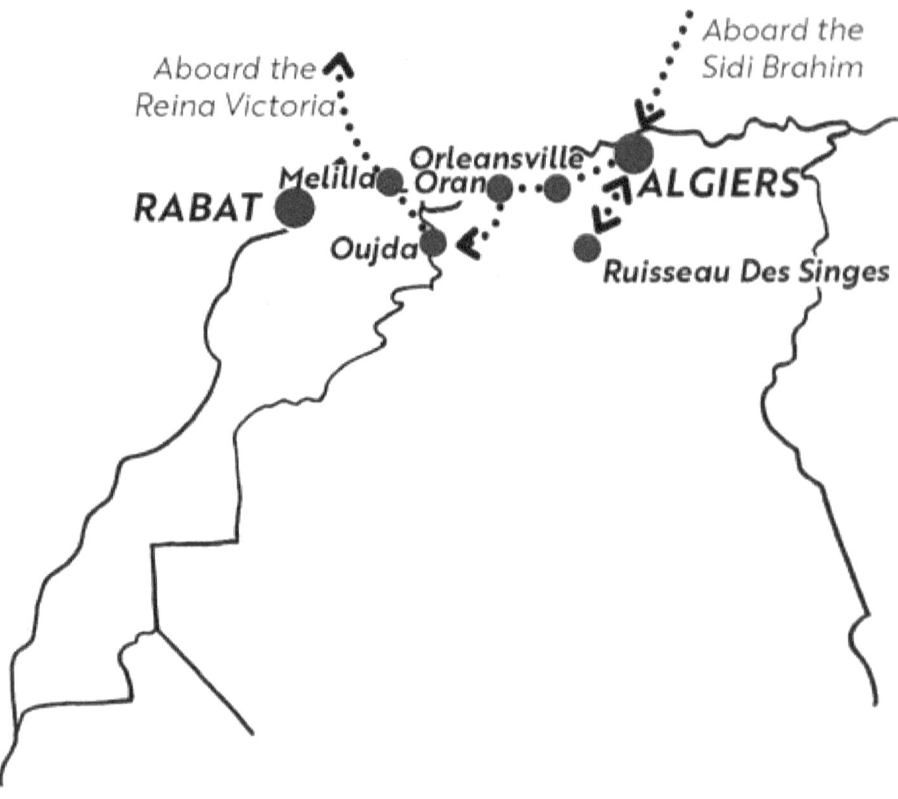
Aboard the
Reina Victoria
Aboard the
Sidi Brahim
RABAT
Melilla
Oran
Orleansville
ALGIERS
Oujda
Ruisseau Des Singes

ALGERIA & MOROCCO
February 1926 – March 1926

CHAPTER 51
CONTINENTAL DRIFTING

Levi traveled to Africa on a large French steam ship, the Sidi Brahim. While this journey took him 29 hours to complete, modern-day travel times have been cut down to just 18 hours. Engineering marvels like the Badji Mokhtar III can carry 1,800 passengers and 600 vehicles.

While on board, Levi pulled out his Handy Notes pad. A tattered page lingers between the fabric-covered flaps, a page that is no longer attached to the spine.

Gulls
[From the Sidi-Brahim]

Holy gee whiz! What a beautiful sight
Look at those birds, they've followed all night.
They took up the chase as we left yesterday
Right with us they'll be when we enter the bay.

Behind us, behind us they wing and they glide,
A few swift strokes and they're up along side
To wait for their dinner as we mortals do
Who order oeufs au plat or plain Irish stew.

Staying true to tradition, Levi's first letter from a new country was written to his mother, Louise.

Alger, Algeria, Africa
February 22, 1926

Dear Mother,

We've been in Africa four hours and it's simply great. I have not seen any cocoanut trees yet but have just finished some mighty big oranges. This is the land of figs and dates and we ought to be fed up on them before leaving. I don't know what you think Africa is like but this place is about the size of Milwaukee and they have street cars and everything. The scenery is wonderful with white and pink buildings setting against the blue and green hills. Below is the Mediterranean and you never saw a more pretty and smooth body of water. We crossed it in 29 hours in a big French steamer [called Sidi-Brahim]. I did not get sick and enjoyed everything except the famous French cooking. Theoretically I ought to like French foods but the meal we had here tonite tasted better to me. They brought in a dish of fish covered with cinnamon sauce and it was very good but I wouldn't advise you to experiment with it. – Living seems to be cheaper here than in France. We have a large well furnished room, overlooking a park of bamboo trees, with two large beds, tapestries, mirrors etc. all over the walls. This is in a large hotel called the Hotel Royal and costs us each 60 cents a day. In several days if we stay here long we shall move to a still cheaper place.

You are probably wondering how we happened to come here when we started for Spain. Well we argued about the best way to enter Spain and finally decided to cross to Africa, spend a week here. Then take the train along the coast till we reached a place where we could cross back to Spain and work our way north [i.e. that doesn't mean work for passage as we still have enough money to carry us back to France].

It is costing us no more to make our trip this way and we are getting an idea of what Africa is like. Of course, all we will see here is the civilized part where everyone speaks French. This city is full of Mohamedans and their mosques are everywhere. This afternoon on the boat one of them spread his overcoat on deck and facing Mecca he prayed for half an hour on his knees. Sometimes he would bow until his face touched the floor and all the while we stood around him. As Vinc remarked, "If that fellow doesn't go to heaven I don't know who will."

Christian "dogs" are not allowed to enter their temples here but I'm going to see all I can from the outside anyway.

We took about a two hour walk after we landed and all the while a bunch of Arab children followed begging us for money. Their mothers who go around the streets veiled did not seem to care. What joy it must be to be a boy without having to worry about manners.

We went to the post office and tried to buy stamps with French money and found out that while this is a French colony, they have Algerian currency which we must use. It costs us nothing to change our francs so we don't care if they use sea shells for exchange.

If the next couple of days are nice as I hope they will be we are going to take hikes out of here and climb some hills overlooking the desert. They have a train that runs out to a place called the oasis of the monkeys. We shall probably go there and each get a pet monkey. When we got off the boat today a sailor tried to give us a water Spaniel to take along with us but my cold blooded calculations won over Vinc's sympathy for the poor homeless waif and we are still without a dog.

When I think that today on Washington's birthday, Green Bay must be freezing and it is just comfortably warm here it makes me blue because I know how you would enjoy it here. I bet that I sure will feel the winter in Green Bay next year after all this soft time. Vinc was just saying that I've been hollering about finding a warm place ever since we hit Europe and now we've got it.

Pa needn't worry about that money he will have sent to Barcelona because I have already written to the American Express there to take care of my mail. From now on please write everything to Paris and I shall have it forwarded to where ever I am.

Will write again soon and tell you all about this place.

With love, Levi

Algers, Africa
Feb. 22, 1926
[travel journal]

A new continent and I just can't get used to it. We landed this afternoon and have a very nice room here in the Hotel Royal. Our little Arab guide was a nuisance all day but we were glad to have him take us home at dark. Here's to my first night in Africa. They can't possibly be worse than Italian flees.

CHAPTER 52
ALGIERS, ALGERIA

Orleansville, Algeria
March 1, 1926

Dear Chloe,

Vinc Engels and I sailed from Marseilles to Algers,
found the most delightful spot in the world [even better than
Green Bay] and spent a week in its hills.

Algers is a great commercial city with all the interest of
a large seaport. To prove its modernity I counted some thirty
cinemas in the town. The architecture with its beautiful
Catholic cathedral and dazzling white Moslem mosque
side by side was enough to endear me to the place but the
hills with their masses of color, wild flowers of every kind,
scrub pines and palm trees, mandarins, oranges and – no
not breadfruit, but lemons have made it hard for us to leave.
This is not the tropics but it is Spring in a land that would
be beautiful in any season.

Levi was consistent in his misspelling of Algiers, always writing
"Algers." Algiers is the capital of Algeria, its largest city, located in the
center of the Algerian coastline on the Mediterranean Sea. In 1926,
Algeria was under French rule as it had been since the conquest
of 1830. Though the original terms of surrender guaranteed that

Muslims would retain their places of worship, many were seized. None affected the populace as much as the conversion of the Ketchaoua Mosque into Saint Phillip Cathedral, the Catholic cathedral Levi described.

Built in 1612, the Ketchaoua Mosque was considered the most beautiful in the area, which made it the focus of the Minister of Police, Duc de Rovigo, back in 1832. On December 18 of 1832, 4,000 Muslims barricaded themselves within the mosque. The French army took possession of the holy structure by force and immediately began the transformation into a cathedral. Six days later, on Christmas Eve, 1832, the first mass was celebrated there. This transition marked the permanence of the French presence in Algeria.

By the time Levi and Vince landed at the port of Algiers in February of 1926, Saint Philip Cathedral had been a Roman Catholic place of prayer for just over 93 years.

What Levi thought was a dazzling white mosque was the Dar Hassan Pacha palace. It was not until 1962 that this cathedral was converted back into a mosque.

Algers

February 25, 1926

Today we heard a requiem mass at the cathedral. Either the French are more devout in the colonies or they came to hear the music because the church was crowded [about half men].

The March 1 letter to Chloe continued.

Just had a long interruption while I listened to Engels tale of woe. He is consoling himself with a bottle of "vin blanc" while he scratches his flee bites. Why from a discussion on obnoxious insects he should diverge to love and marriage I don't know except that they both drive a man "nuts".

Our yesterdays hike was one that you would have enjoyed if you like the pictures in the National Geographic magazine. We passed a camp of about fifty Arabs who live by the roadside where they break stones to serve the footsteps of their fellows. They have tents of patched burlap about four feet high into which they crawl amid pots and pans to curl themselves up and sleep the sleep of those whose only enjoyment in this world is unconsciousness of the gnawing desire for something else if it be but a soft piece of sod and a full stomach.

I snapped a roll of film among them yesterday and here's hoping it's the best ever.

Levi turned his camera over to Vince and posed with those native to Algeria. Memories from his travel journal continued.

Visited the Basilique of Notre Dame d'Afrique this afternoon and was surprised to find some veiled Moslem women in church. They seemed to enter as though it was a usual occurrence with them and this seemed strange because Christians are not allowed in their Mosques.

The Basilique Notre Dame d'Afrique is located at the top of a hill facing the Mediterranean. Though hard to discern in the following photo, the basilica appears on the hilltop, which seems to be a remote location rather than a scenic viewpoint, overlooking a port city.

The basilica is a Neo-Byzantine design that was popular in the mid-1800s. Several comparisons can be made between the basilica and the Ketchaoua Mosque: the use of domes, the shape of the arches, and the balance and symmetry in the façade. The Virgin Mary stands above the main entrance, only surpassed in height by the cross atop the magnificent dome. Inside the church is a 1993 mosaic, a partial reproduction of work completed in 1937. The mosaic is washed in light as rays from the sun enter through well-positioned openings, illuminating the image of Mary as she holds the infant Jesus. Many important figures appear there, for example, Saints Cyprian and Augustine, who were originally from the region.

Levi's recorded memories in his travel journal continued.

Another hike in the hills with beautiful views at every turn in the road. This is one place that I'll admit equals if not surpasses old Green Bay as a place to live. After watching the goats grazing today Vinc decides that we ought to start raising sheep in Northern Wisconsin's cut timber land. How they would talk if an architect were to decide on sheep herding as his lifes work. It's decisions like that that require courage.

I took a roll of film today that if it comes out well will probably be the best I have ever taken. They are snaps of Arab stone breakers along the road. Will probably have to wait until we get to Spain before I can see the results of the four francs I spent to induce them not to hide their faces. These natives realize that their appearance is worth something to them and they make you pay a few cents or they turn their backs to you.

On the next page, Vince is pictured along with an Algerian native.

Levi and Vince visited the Hamma Botanical Garden. No written description exists. The last photo was taken from a high vantage point that offered a glimpse of the 1800s French-English gardens.

CHAPTER 53
OUED CHIFFA

Alger, Algeria
Sunday Night
February 28, 1926

Dear Father,

Tonite marks the seventh night we've spent in Africa and both Vinc and I are agreed that it is the most beautiful place we've been in. There is nothing I know that can describe it as well as a flower seed catalog. All we've done all week is take hikes, look longingly at the mandarins over the fences and enjoy the scenery and the odor of many flowers. It would not take much to make me believe that the Garden of Eden was in Africa and not in Arabia. -Yesterday we wandered up a hill overlooking the city and the sea. We could see miles in every direction and near by was a small shepherd's hu t with goats being milked at the door. Possibly we drink some of the milk back at the hotel in our chocolat but if we do I can tell the difference. Tonite they had snails on the bill of fare but lost my nerve at the critical moment and can't tell you what they taste like.

Our food here has been the best yet and coupled with the cleanest room imaginable we can help but like the place. The famed French cooking is at its best not in France but in its colonies. The prices are more reasonable than France and Italy. We get a meal for 24 cents (6 francs). Here is what we had tonight. – Soup, bread, crabs boiled, artichokes, fresh green peas and roasted chicken, endives, a strip of cake, one mandarin and half a liter of "vin rouge". – Don't ask me how they can give you all that for 24 cents but they do. By the way you had better start storing away barrels of wine for when I get home – to drink with my meals. Either that or Ma will have to make beer soup often.

In an attempt to see the great Sahara Desert, Vince and Levi headed south into the interior of Algeria. Levi defined the distance traveled as being about a 60 kilometer train ride to the Sidi Al Madani station. Instead of desert, they encountered Mount Tamezguida, part of the Atlas Mountain range which separated the Mediterranean coastline of Algeria from the desert. This is the place Levi mentioned to his mother on the day they arrived, the oasis of the monkeys. The letter to his father continued.

It was this day that we did our greatest piece of bargaining. When we got off at the station we hired a back driver to take us out about 15 kilometers wait a while and then take us back again to the station. A total distance of 18½ miles with a team of horses for 80 cents. Things like that we just can't help bragging about though I suppose he would still have come down lower for a native. When I get home Ma had better send me to do the family shopping from the education I'm getting over here.

Located just south of the Sidi Al Madani train station is a nineteenth century French restaurant and hotel built in the middle of the gorges of Oued Chiffa. This is one of the oldest tourist attractions in the Blida Province of Algeria. Notables such as Emperor Napoleon III, Prince Philip Duke of Edinburgh, Alfred Hitchcock, and Paul Newman have visited the inn and restaurant.

Levi's photos show that the visiting duo hiked up the hill above the inn to capture the image of *Ruisseau des Singes* (Monkey's Stream). They traveled and hiked in a full suit, tie, hat, and walking cane. In a picturesque fisherman's pose, Vince explored the water at the bottom of the ravine.

The restaurant, established in 1850, retains the charm of the past. The walls hold images of the many notable figures who visited the macaques here.

CHAPTER 54
THE TRACKS TO ORAN

Levi's letter to his father from February 28 in Algiers drew to a close.

> *We are taking the train West tomorrow to a small place*
> *called Orleansville which is five hours (203 km) from here.*
> *After breaking our journey there we start the next day and*
> *ride 220 kilometers [a kilometer is .62 of a mile] to Oran*
> *from which we shall cross over to Spain. When you get this*
> *we ought to be in Seville or Cordova.*
> > *With love from your son, Levi*

Orleansville was renamed al-Asnam in 1962, then Chlef in 1980.
Its most modern name references the Chelif River, the longest river
in Algeria.

> *Orleansville, Algeria*
> *March 1, 1926*

Dear Chloe,

> *Don't look for this place on the map. It isn't. We arrived*
> *here this afternoon on our way to Oran from Algers. A week*
> *in Africa and I haven't seen any camels or cannibals yet.*
> *As we rode thru our dinner hour today with the French*
> *couple at our side who had every conceivable thing along*
> *to eat and drink there arose in both Engels and I a desire*

to take, to eat at all costs. You have probably never felt that hunger, that unreasoning passion which calls for satisfaction at any cost. This very air breeds cannibals and my teeth are becoming long and pointed already. Is it possible that such is to be the end — but no, such colorful themes are for scientists and explorers; architects attempt poetry and end their days in — [yes, doctor the cell is padded, he'll not hurt himself again].

From Oran we are going to Spain, if I should weaken and agree to Vinc's wild plan we go to the mouth of the Congo. He says, "If we "burn" up the river we shall be the first that has ever tried it." It's the word "try" that I don't like. Sometimes I remember that I came to study architecture so the next will be from Spain.

A page from Levi's "Handy Notes" pad, dated the second of March, says:

Written in answer to Engel's request for a poem on caterpillars — the request following our watching a train of caterpillars at Orleansville, Algeria.

The amorous caterpillar glides
Thru rustling paths of deadened leaves;
The while a tender note he slides,
Betwixt the sighs of her who grieves
The one that's gone as caterpillars do
Beneath the sole of man's cruel shoe.

Soothing words he pours into her ear
That she may bear the ghastly sight
That once was him, now but a smear
To feed the flys far in the night.
Hesitating she sighs for him just killed
And lo! The careless wanderers shoes are filled.

Oran, Algeria
March 4, 1926

Dear Mother,

I don't know whether you'll get these seeds I'm sending in time for this years planting. I bought them in Orleansville where we saw so many beautiful flowers. I did not recognize the names or pictures on these packages so I hope they are some of the strange varietys they have over here.

We stayed over night at Orleansville on our way here. It is a small walled town for defense against the Arabs in case of uprising but there is little danger of that in this part of Africa. It was so quiet and peaceful there with the hills in many colors caused by thousands of wild flowers. If you ever want to see something beautiful just plant several acres of mustard and poppies together.

Oran is quite a seaport and commercial city and is not as picturesque as Algers with its natives in their own style clothing. We shall probably leave here tomorrow for Spain and right here I'll say that there will probably be a gap of some time in my letters because there are few boats from Spain to America.

They are having a war over in Morocco and it seems they are expecting more trouble from the Germans. There are some big fortifications here so they are always on the lookout for spys.

They tell us that a big religious festival starts in Seville in two weeks so we ought to be there about the time you get this. Here's hoping I find the Spanish men not afraid to enter a church. – Had a sample of some chili today and I'll sure have to get an asbestos lining in my mouth to eat that stuff in Spain.

With love, Levi

The uprising Levi referenced was an ongoing conflict known as the Rif War. The Berber people whose various tribes occupied the areas of the Rif Mountains were fighting for independence from Spain.

Germany had recently been defeated along with the other Central Powers in World War I, and they lost any stronghold previously held in Morocco. Spain, having remained neutral, retained colonial possession of the area. With the Rif Wars raging, Spain had to be mindful of not only the natives in the Rif Mountain range, but also of any country from either side of the Great War.

A few years before the duo's jaunt through North Africa, France had joined forces with Spain. The Rif Wars ended in 1927 and the Republic of the Rif was dissolved after the Spain-France victory.

Today, Melilla and Ceuta are autonomous cities of Spain located on the North African coast and surrounded by Morocco. These are the only two places today where a European country controls land on the African mainland.

CHAPTER 55
THREE MERCENARIES AND WINE

Oran, Algeria
March 4, 1926
[travel journal]

Monday we took a miserable train ride in a crowded
coach to Orleansville. Arrived there about as hungry as I
have ever been. The meals were good, the hotel fine and the
scenery as wonderful as ever. Here I learned that one should
never smile at a Moslem girl unless he wishes to go thru
with it.

From Orleansville to Oran went faster than we expected
and getting off the train we secured a room in the Grand
Hotel de la Gare. – A ground floor room opening on a court
and smelling as if it had been used as a poultry house.

Levi described this next section better in a March 12 letter to
Chloe, written on a Spanish train to Seville.

We arrived at Oran seeking a sailboat to Spain and met
a very interesting group of men at a wine shop. The first

*was a "Max" the Swiss a deserter from the American army
and now a member of the French Foreign Legion and is the
typical mercenary soldier. He was on duty as an M.P. along
with "Blackie" an American negro who had also served in
our army and was now in the Legion. The third member
of the "gang" we bought drinks for was a Swiss who had
been recently discharged from the Legion. He carrys a scar
received from a Sengalese knife in a fight "over women."
All of them had been fighting Riffs in Morocco and the last
campaign had been hard enough that they were back for a
rest. These men thinking we were completely down and out
decided to help us and took us to see a smuggler named
Pedro. Pedro agreed to take us to Spain and we started to
wait for his boat.*

The recording of events continued in his travel journal from
Oran, March 4.

*Max took us over and introduced us to a smuggler
named "Pedro" who promised to help us get a boat to
Melilla and from there give us a letter to the captain of his
boat who would take us to Spain. We planned to accept his
offer and meanwhile did the best we could to avoid "lend-
ing" money to our new acquaintances. — About eleven o'clock
at night we had a quarrel with the hotel keeper because he
insisted on being paid in advance; Vinc thought he should
be paid, I quarreled with Vinc and started out to find another bed. — Max and the Swiss, George, followed me and
tried to get me to stay with them when I refused George took
me down to a hotel where I could get a room for six francs.
They thought I was broke and being caught in my own lie I
spent a night of misery at the Hotel Dahan. Morning came
at last and going to find Vinc I was told that he had been
arrested by the French Secret Service. — After a shave,
haircut and a lot of questioning Max and Pedro I started*

out with Blackie to find the American Consul. He was not very encouraging but promised to enquire into the case.

Here I must note a line concerning a little French girl, Lucienne Perrin, with whom I went walking, who told me all about her fiancee who is in the penitentiary for man-slaughter. — She knew every beggar in town and insisted on my being generous to them all. She took me in to "see" a Catholic church and was surprised and delighted when I showed her a rosary. — Another example of a lily in the mire. Here's hoping she stays a lily.

Levi walked with Luzianna near the penitentiary, while officials at the American consul started to investigate Vince's arrest. On the first page of Levi's small sketchbook, Luzianna signed her name below her drawing of "Alphonsse," a misspelling of his middle name, Alphonse; the name Levi used when he wanted to appear French. *Souvenir d'un petit alsacien abitan Oran le 3 mars 1926* (Memory of a little Alsatian living in Oran 3 March 1926) identified the artist as Luzianna.

Along their walk, Levi and Luzianna stopped for a moment. Levi

captured a photo of the *lily in the mire* he encountered. This idiom comes from Christian teachings used to describe someone who remains pure and righteous while surrounded by evil and temptation.

Vince's experience with the Secret Service in Oran was best told in the *Green Bay Press-Gazette*.

Green Bay Man Arrested in Africa as French Deserter

Traveling in Africa has its compensations, but there are always drawbacks, as a recent experience of Vincent D. Engels illustrates. Engels, a former Press-Gazette man, who has traveled through Europe for the past five months, is spending some time in northern Africa.

With his companion, Levi Geniesse, he sought a hotel upon arrival at Algiers. The hotel keeper demanded payment in advance and Geniesse protested and refused to stay at the hostelry. Engels, however, preferred his sleep to his American dignity and paid the price. He went to bed and Geniesse to another hotel.

Early the following morning a loud knock disturbed Vincent's slumber and partially clad he opened the door wide to admit Geniesse. But in place of his pal there stood two frock coated gentlemen who bowed themselves into the room, "Secret service men inquiring into the business of the stranger." After scrutinizing the passport they tumbled all the baggage on the bed and finding nothing incriminating, tumbled it back again, closed the cases and told the astonished young man to complete his dressing and accompany them.

Conversing in French between themselves, the secret service men decided that the traveler was a deserter from the army and that the young man who had been with him the previous day must be a German. "He has traveled all over Europe" they said "but his passport looks like new."

After three hours detention during which Engels made frequent demands for the American consul and an attorney, he was liberated. The officials told him that it was unusual for a tourist to go unaccompanied and a person traveling for study was always old and scholarly, and that there had been a mistake. Whereupon Engels relates, he left, with the smile adorning his countenance but the blackest of American curses under his breath.

Following a short sojourn in Spain, Engels expects to return to Paris and enter the university. He is a son of Mr. and Mrs. W. P. Engels. Geniesse is the son of Mr. and Mrs. Lewis Geniesse, 720 S. Clay St. (7).

An excerpt from Levi's letter to his mother dated March 4 offered additional information from Oran.

They are having a war over in Morocco and it seems they are expecting more trouble from the Germans. There are some big fortifications here so they are always on the lookout for spys.

After a few hours Vinc returned telling how he had been searched and quizzed on the supposition that he was either a spy or a deserter. That being over we suddenly became suspicious of the smuggler who for some reason seemed very eager to have us aboard his boatload of smuggled tobacco. We found out that he had run arms to the revolutionists before and deciding to keep out of the "mess" we took an automobile ride along with three other passengers to a place called Oujda about two hundred miles inland.

CHAPTER 56
THE PATHS LESS TAKEN

Malaga, Spain
March 8, 1926
[travel journal]

We left the smuggler and his friends wondering why we did not return. Oujda was reached by car with a maniac driver from Oran. Oujda was a crowded place and Vinc and I slept in a bed in a building that was being remodeled as a hotel. That I slept at all after that ride along the edge of precipices and canyons is a wonder.

Vinc just reminded me not to forget that the lemon drops saved us from being nervous wrecks on our wild ride to Oujda. The ride was a nightmare. As darkness came on the driver became more reckless until we were rounding curves on two wheels with canyons four hundred feet below. I had a bag of lemon drops for the ride but every time we came to a dangerous place I wasted a whole piece. Anyway we arrived thanks to St. Christopher and the hosts of Saints whom we asked to pray for us. We thought bicycle riding was bad enough in the mountains of Italy but car riding with a crazy man in Africa has that beat.

They had car trouble on the way to Oujda, Algeria. A French Colonial officer and Vince faced the camera while the driver focused on fixing the flat. Their adventure was not over in Oujda. Levi's travel journal entry continued.

Another car took us to Morocco from Oujda and we crossed into Spanish territory on horseback. Honestly, I'd rather walk.

We spent two days at Melilla, the headquarters of the Spanish army, before getting permission to leave the city. It was little inconveniences like that that made us realize we were in a country with a battle line only a short distance away.

We had no trouble entering Spanish Morocco but to leave required the commanding Generals permission and that took two days to get. Our friend "Garcon d'Hotel" whom we called "Beaucoup Travael Firpo" served us faithful, very obligingly changed Vinc's twenty dollar bill. It was Sunday we had to have the money in pesetas and Firpo having connections with the financial world heard that the value of the American paper dollar had dropped alarmingly.

We were stuck then but poor Firpo couldn't extract a tip from us even with the three policemen to help him at the dock.

Vince submitted an article to the *Green Bay Press-Gazette* while they played the waiting game in Melilla, a city of Spain, located on North African coast.

SPANISH COLONIES IN AFRICA ENJOY
A LITTLE GAME OF WAR
By Vincent D. Engels

Melilla, (On the Riff) – Melilla, as has been said of every city in every land on earth, is a stage. And the play that is being enacted here is a pretty little comedy of war and business. Pretty, because the actors themselves deserve no better adjective than that. And if one is being forced to wait here for an hour – a few hours – a day – a few days, for a cunning rubber-stamp on his pass-port so that he may thus formally announce to the authorities his intention of leaving Spanish colonial territory for Spain itself, he must either find some amusement in this spectacle, or go to bed, and there await the appointing of the august hour.

If he chooses the first alternative, he finds a city that has made a business of war, and a war out of business – not unusual, surely, in a military center. Originally a fishing village numbering a few thousand inhabitants, in recent years Melilla has been made the headquarters for the Spanish army in Morocco, and since soldiers need such things as food and clothing, it has attracted a civilian population of about 20,000. A civilian army feeding, and feeding on, the soldiers. Or rather, if one looks closely enough, on the officers. For where the soldiers are, no English speaking inhabitant of Melilla has been able to tell. Some are in the mountains, and with the assistance of France's Foreign Legion, that strange outfit of American negroes, Chinese, Japanese, Danes and Swiss, are keeping the Moors there, too; others are idling or training in the desert; but certainly for all the thousands of uniforms one sees in the streets of Melilla, there are very few privates here.

An Officer's Army

It may be that the Spanish army is composed almost entirely of officers; from a superficial observance of things, at least, that would seem to be the case. And, again superficially, it would also seem that the officers are ranked according to their beauty. For, whatever be the basis of promotion, it is certain that the high officers in the Spanish army – the officers whom the people point to, admiringly, who ride limousines, who enter a room and make all the lieutenants stand while they chat amiably with civilians, are remarkably well-featured men. Those few who are baldheaded manage to make a fine showing with beards of proportion and design, but those whose scalps are still heavy with hair are clean shaven. This, apparently, is a rule, but whether it is enforced by the power of the King of Spain and Primo di Rivera cannot, at the moment, be ascertained.

Whatever may be said of the physical splendor of many of the Spanish officers, the few soldiers one sees in Melilla are far from imposing specimens. Averaging, in height, within fractions of five feet, five inches, and in weight about 120 pounds, they compare poorly with the tall and robust Moors. One realizes that without the advantages of modern warfaring equipment, the Spaniards might be hard-pressed to withstand the attacks of the kinsmen of these same Riffian tribesmen; indeed, it is generally admitted here that, given proper artillery and a decent air force, Abl-el-Krim would long ago have driven every white man from Morocco, and might even now, omitting the intervention of other powers, be engaged in the re-conquest of the Andalusian homes of his ancestors.

Smugglers Are Fearless

Rifles and rifle ammunition the Riffs have been able to get through the aid of those gentlemen of the sea who ply the age-old trade of smuggling, Spanish and French among them. So openly is the business carried on that, while in Oran, I was actually approached and offered passage on a smuggler's boat into Spanish territory. The smugglers evidence no fear whatever of the Spanish patrol boats; as a matter of fact, the ships assigned to the patrol work are lying, for the larger part of the time, at anchor in the harbor of Melilla.

So the little comedy goes on. In Melilla, the officers sit about the cafes, in highly ornamental poses, planning excuses, no doubt, to obtain leave for a trip to Malaga; inland, and not very far away, Abd-el-Krim makes a sudden sally from his mountain fastnesses, and retreats in safety; smugglers sail the open Mediterranean, and the patrol boats rest in the harbor.

Meanwhile, Melilla decided that war isn't such bad business after all (13).

Irun
Train to Lourdes
Burgos
Valladolid
El Escorial
MADRID
Toledo
Cordoba
Seville
Granada
Malaga
Aboard the
Reina Victoria

SPAIN
March 1926

CHAPTER 57
ANDALUSÍA,
LAND OF THE MOORS

On board the Reina Victoria bound from
Melilla to Malaga
March 7, 1926
[travel journal]

Boat's pitching like hell. Am going on deck. Here I go.

Malaga, Spain
March 8, 1926
[travel journal]

Talk about meals — we stowed away enough in two meals today to last us a week. Didn't eat last night and it was better so. However about ten oclock Vinc induced me to try to buy a pesetas worth of bread from the cook. He refused and Vinc went to bed after having consigned the whole Spanish Merchant Marine to a warmer place than Africa. — We arrived this morning on the Reina Victoria. It was a beautiful night but below decks it was miserable with the

*Spaniards closing the window and our Spanish of
insufficient quality to produce any results with the officer
whom they called in to arbitrate the case.*

The SS Reina Victoria Eugenia supported Britain during World War I. She became the flagship of the Spanish Navy, deployed to support their forces during the Rif War in Morocco. Levi and Vince traveled aboard the light cruiser from Melilla to Málaga, both of which were considered Spanish land despite being on different continents. Málaga was a wonderful seaside municipality with the mountains to the north insulating the inhabitants from winter's chill. The city prided itself on being one of the oldest in the world, dating back to the Phoenicians in 600 BC (Bierling 4).

At the time of Levi and Vince's visit to and through Spain, the number of foreign passengers entering Spanish seaports annually was just over 5,000 (Cirer-Costa 12). Half of those visitors were British, fewer were from Germany, and an even smaller number visited from France. Levi was correct in reporting that Americans did not visit Spain. As late as 1986, Americans still represented less than two percent of foreign visitors to Spain (Solsten and Meditz).

*Granada, Spain
March 10, 1926
[travel journal]*

*Arrived here last night after a pleasant although long
train ride from Malaga. Spanish trains are in no hurry
but the scenery all along makes one enjoy its lazy progress.
T'was on the train that Vinc introduced me to "his friend"
Dolores Diaz. She was friendly and we kissed our bottle of
wine good bye.*

*Vinc is busy with his flea bites and they're keeping me
busy too. He has a theory that since dogs bite their flee bites
that he ought to rub his with saliva.*

*This morning we saw the Alhambra and tomorrow will
find us back. When I see a building like that it makes me*

resolve to study the history of the Moors. The walk at sunset was like a church sermon. Why should the Spanish worry about civilization and progress. They have all that matters now.

Granada, Spain
March 11, 1926

Dear Father,

This place would be a regular heaven but for one thing. They are as vicious as wasps and somehow always manage to jump just before your hand lands on the spot where they were. At night we count our bites and estimate how many we'll have in the morning.

So far the eats in Spain have been better than in Italy or France. The Spanish come closer to our American style of cooking than do other nationalities. We stayed at a pretty good hotel our first day in Malaga and they fed us royally. Here's what they put before us just for one meal — soup, radishes, sausage, olives, fish, artichokes, two courses of meat, cheese, bread, oranges, apples, bananas, raisins, walnuts, mandarins and to wash it all down a bottle of wine. We ate so much there that all we could do was lie down and groan for hours afterward.

Landing at Malaga we stayed two days enjoying the scenery, looking at the large cathedral and getting sunburned.

In the next photo, Levi was in Málaga, Spain, perched atop the Alcazaba. This palatial fortification dates to the eleventh century, with modifications and additions made through the fourteenth century. Málaga Cathedral is visible in the distance. Nicknamed *La Manquita* (Little Arm or Hand) by the locals, the original plans called for two towers, but the second was never built due to a lack of funds. The unfinished look of the cathedral, with only one tower completed, leaves an appearance of being incomplete or still under construction.

Levi's March 11 letter to his father continued.

A seven hour train ride brought us to Granada which was the city captured by Ferdinand and Isabella the year Columbus discovered America. — The Alhambra which was the palace of the Moorish king still is in a good state of preservation. Everywhere are fountains, flowers and orange trees. If Ma could see the flowers here she would want to move right away even if she had to cross an ocean.

Yesterday afternoon I climbed a very high hill to where the gypsies have the caves in which they live. There a mob of children started following me all the while asking for money. Finally a crowd of children, girls and women stopped me; they formed a circle and one little girl started to dance while the others chanted something. I took a few pictures but had to pay each subject before I could get them to stay still for a moment. These people would be miserable elsewhere but here in the spot where the weather is always nice they live like lizards toasting themselves in the sun the whole day long.

The place we are staying at here is a "pension" where a bunch of Spanish students are living. The price for two meals and bed is 84 cents and the meals are O.K. I killed one bed bug the first night here but haven't felt any yet. Old travelers in Spain tell us that they're like measles, everyone has to have them.

Tomorrow we leave for Seville which is a hop of 288 kilometers or 179 miles. The railroad schedule calls for nine hours riding so we shall consider ourselves lucky if we get off after eleven hours. They sell peanuts, oranges, etc. at every station and stations are about five miles apart so we manage to pass the time somehow. Coming here I started to play my mouth organ and soon had a crowd collected around.

We came thru a stretch of mountains with peaks and caverns that were the best yet. These are the Sierra Nevada mountains after which those in the United States have been named.

By the way, we're no longer Americanos here. They reserve that name for the people from South America and call us yanquis which is their version of Yankee.

From Seville we go to Cordova, then Toledo and Madrid. From Madrid to Valladolid, Burgos and out of Spain at the Irun pass. We shall probably just be leaving Madrid when you get this letter. I am having all my mail that was sent to Barcelona forwarded to Madrid and if my present plans hold I shall not see Barcelona.

We get up at six tomorrow morning so I'll close and roll in.

With love, Levi

The gypsies of Granada still dance amid the caves in the mountains facing the Alhambra. Productions of their version of the Flamenco, Zambra Gitana, may not have been available in 1926, but today, those traditional dances are performed inside the caves, an intimate setting for travelers to enjoy. Music and dancing fill the space with the sounds and movements of past generations.

At the Alhambra, Levi reviewed the *Puerta del Vino* (Wine Gate) in detail. He sketched and watercolored in situ. This gate is one of the oldest structures at the Alhambra. It was carved from sandstone in the 1300s, and is the last gate that visitors passed through before entering the fortress of the sultan.

The photo was taken within the *Patio del Cuarto Dorado* (Patio of the Gold Room). Changes have been made to this facade over the past hundred years. The sixteenth-century exterior wall, the outermost archway in the image, has been removed since Levi's visit. Today, with the ornately carved arches revealed, the Alhambra appears as it had at the time of the Moors. This change both enlarged and beautified the patio.

Shown here is the well-known *Palacio de los Leones* (Court of the Lions), which has changed little over the past hundred years. The lions stand strong beneath the bottom basin as they have since the mid-1300s. The tiered centerpiece shown in the center of the fountain in Levi's photo has been removed and placed in the gardens. This change returned the fountain to its original pre-sixteenth-century design.

The final photo, seen below, is of the *Patio de los Arrayanes* (Court of the Myrtles). Vince sat in a sunlit chair just to the left of the center doorway. His blurry reflection appeared in the still waters of the basin before him as he wrote. The small dome over the center archway has been removed, keeping with the Moorish design.

After they reflected on the designs and life at the Alhambra, Vince and Levi headed west to Seville. The Moorish influence would follow them there.

CHAPTER 58
THE RAILS TO MADRID

On a Spanish Train
March 12, 1926

Dear Chloe,

I'll try to keep to the lines but somehow this train seems to have gotten off the rails, the engineers asleep in the cab and generally this is no ride for a man with a monocle. When the idea of building a railroad first entered the Spaniards head, or wherever he thinks, it was suggested that the roadbed be made smooth. They answered that they would not attempt the impossible, and they have not.

We're on our way to Seville from Granada where we spent three days admiring the Alhambra and enjoying the sunsets.

The travelers spent five hours in Seville before Levi continued the letter to Chloe.

Here we are camped in the Hotel Argentine. The meal was fine although I have a suspicion that the beef came from the flock of goats we passed on entering the city. So far we are casting all our votes for Spanish cooks; they have the French backed off the map.

Seville is famed for its beautiful women and we had planned to spend the evening in a "characteristic" café but Engels has spent several hours battling the flees and now utterly tired and defeated he has gone to bed. I suggested that he write an 'Ode to a Flee' but he said the only thing he'd do to a flee would be to torture him.

Seville, Spain
March 13, 1926
[travel journal]

We're in "fine" humor with this place. Spent the whole morning finding the cathedral and then finding our way back again. We arrived last night and are camped at the Hotel Argentina. The flees are terrible and we are doing our Lenten penance by enduring them.

Coming from Granada we had two interesting passengers in our coach. A German student who had been traveling for about two years and a fine old gentleman who said he was superintendent of schools in Trieste. We had an example of "dutch" treat and I'll always remember the German taking out a bottle of perfume to scent his hands after eating cheese.

Went to Mass in the Cathedral at Seville this morning before leaving for Cordoba. It was a relief to find Latins who are devout as those hearing mass this morning were. Yesterday we heard a High Mass in another church and the choir who were talking and laughing throughout the service drove me to a desire to horsewhip out of the place. The cathedral itself would be a fine building if they had sense enough to leave it alone instead of using all their baroque decoration. They were erecting a monstrous monstrosity of wood and gilt in the classic style behind the choir. I suppose it will play a part in the Easter religious celebrations. Celebrations is the right word for that is what a Latin makes of an act of worship to God.

The Cathedral in Seville offers much to the historically intrigued individual. Originally, it was a mosque ordered to be built in 1172 by Caliph Abu Ya'qub Yusuf. The mosque's minaret, the tower from which a muezzin calls Muslims to prayer, was completed in 1198. Today, the mosque has been converted into the largest Gothic cathedral in the world, officially known as *Catedral de Santa María de la Sede* (Cathedral of Saint Mary of the See), or Seville Cathedral. The minaret, known as La Giralda, has been converted into the cathedral's bell tower.

With King Ferdinand's conquest of the Moors in the late fifteenth century came a change in religion. Catholicism replaced Islam. Many mosques were turned into churches, but Caliph Yusuf's mosque was enormous and would have been a financial burden to convert at that time. Interior changes were made and partitions utilized until an earthquake in 1356 proved disastrous. Only parts of the original mosque are still visible, such as the sahn or courtyard in Islamic architecture. Ritual preparations such as washing took place here before entering to pray. This sahn is known as *El Patio de los Naranjos* (Courtyard of the Orange Trees).

By 1433, plans were made to dismantle the Islamic building

being used as a church and build a cathedral. Construction was not completed until 1506.

The previous photograph was taken near Seville Cathedral. This entryway once led to the *Colegio de San Miguel*, the cathedral's choir-boy school. While the arch has survived to this day, the remainder has been transformed. The doors are always closed.

Inside Seville Cathedral is the impressive tomb of Christopher Columbus. Four tall figures representing the kingdoms of Spain, Castile, Leon, Aragon, and Navarre carry his casket. Levi made no mention of this grand tribute to the explorer. Even the inscription around the base leaves out integral parts of Columbus's travels. The epitaph tells the story of Columbus's trip from Cuba to Spain but makes no mention of how he came to be on that island in the first place.

Columbus died in Valladolid on May 20, 1506, and was buried nearby. He requested to be buried on the island of Hispañola, present-day Dominican Republic and Haiti. A cathedral worthy of his remains had been planned but not constructed.

Three years later, at the request of his son Diego, Columbus's remains were reinterred at the monastery of *Santa María de las Cuevas* (Saint Mary of the Caves) in Seville. Diego found this to be a more appropriate burial site. When Diego died, he was buried at the same monastery in Seville, less than three kilometers away from Columbus's current resting place.

Once a cathedral worthy of Columbus's remains was built in Hispaniola, Diego's widow moved her father-in-law and her husband to the new cathedral in Santo Domingo, the capital of the present-day Dominican Republic. *Santa María la Menor* (Saint Mary the Lesser) was the first cathedral in the Americas, and it became Columbus's third resting place.

Columbus's remains stayed within the cathedral for the next 200-plus years. In 1795, Spain ceded Hispaniola to France, and Columbus's remains were relocated to Havana, Cuba, until the beginning of the Spanish-American War in 1898.

Columbus's final voyage across the Atlantic occurred almost four hundred years after his death. In 1899, the tomb visited today was completed, and Columbus's remains were placed into his fifth and final resting place at Seville Cathedral.

After Levi and Vince attended mass on Sunday at the cathedral in Seville, the March 12 letter Levi wrote to Chloe was mailed. It concluded with an update of their plans.

> *We shall be in Madrid in a week where I shall expect to*
> *have mail. Vinc is then going straight to Paris and I shall*
> *get there in about three weeks from now. St. Patrick's is but*
> *five days away. This year will be different for,*
>
> > *Lee*

> *Cordoba*
> *March 14, 1926*
> [travel journal]

> *Just arrived in Cordoba and settled at the Hotel Andulu-*
> *sia. A typical Spaniard runs this place.*

Cordoba was a stopping point on the way to Toledo. A bit of poetry scribbled in Levi's notepad was all that marked the time they spent there. On March 14, 1926, Levi prefaced with, *After an experience in Spain.*

> *Bedbugs*
> *Last night a Yanquis slept alone*
> *A mild and peaceful thing.*
> *Tonite others with him lie*
> *The air with curses ring.*
> *Sticks and spars and iron bars*
> *But beat at them in vain.*
> *It frights them not from some soft spot*
> *When hands upon them rain.*
> *They've come to stay from dusk till day*
> *Along our back they'll crawl.*
> *Gone are your chills your other ills;*
> *With bedbugs you have all.*

March 16, 1926
Toledo, Spain
[travel journal]

Slept last night at Castellejo and were awakened by the
barnyard quartet. Vinc insists that I told him that the
turkeys gobble was made by a pig. The ride to Castellejo was
tiresome and uneventful except that we saw two nuns eat a
ten course meal alongside of us and top it off with what
looked very much like wine.

Met a German this morning who was very friendly. We
had an argument about the Great War but parted friends.
When we arrived at Toledo we spent an hour trying to get
information on how to get to Toledo. – This place is great
for sketching and I expect to do quite a few tomorrow.
Tonight I entered a church and attended church services.
There was Rosary, Litany and Elevation of a crucifix and
the Stations of the Cross. The church was filled with men
and women who were very devout. A pleasing change from
what we have seen in Italy and France.

In a letter dated March 18 from Madrid, Levi's description of
Toledo was more detailed for his mother.

Toledo was a beautiful old town with gates and walls
still standing from the Middle Ages. It has a beautiful
cathedral and of course many smaller churches. I stepped
into one of them for stations one evening and heard some
beautiful singing by the whole congregation. It was a
Dominican church and like most churches run by that
order it was very neat and orderly with pews etc. instead of
chairs. So far I like the Spanish people and their cooking.
Haven't been able to get any hot tamales yet.

We had a funny incident when we arrived at Toledo. –
We understood we had a change of trains a few miles out-

side of the city so when the train stopped we look out and saw a very large sign on the station "Cantina". I asked one man with our usual motions if we stayed until a railroad man motioned to us to get off. We got out of the station just in time to see a big bus filled with passengers drive out of sight.

We hollered Toledo again and someone pointed after the bus so we concluded that it was transferring the passengers from one station to another. – Taking our luggage we started to follow but soon lost our way and every where we enquired where to get a train for Toledo we were given a queer look. Finally I stopped and asked a red headed police-man how to get to Toledo. – He looked at me searchingly then said something shrugging his shoulders. I got sore and started to call him names in English but it didn't help one bit. Finally Vinc came along with the same luck I had had but wandering around another half an hour we tried to get to a hotel and discovered that we had been in Toledo all the while. – This morning we learned that "Cantina" means lunch room. – As Vinc says "It will be hard to convince the people that we were not drinking".

Toledo inspired poetry, architectural drawings, and photography, which left no time for letter writing. The Romans were the first to wall the city, and the Visigoths expanded and improved these secure structures. Every conquering group enlarged the city and refurbished the walls. The Moors followed the Visigoths, and the Christians arrived in 1085 when Alfonso VI of Castile took the city. This was the first major city of the Islamic Al-Andalus region to be conquered by Christian forces.

The architectural element that Levi drew on March 16, 1926, shown on the following page, seems to only exist now on paper. The old town was on the front lines at the beginning of the Spanish Civil War, a few years after Levi and Vince's visit. Franco's Nationalists took over the Alcázar, a stone fortification overlooking Toledo.

The siege ended on September 27, 1936, and two days later, Franco was named Generalissimo, the highest military rank in Spain. By October, he was the head of state. In that time, this architectural detail was lost to history.

Levi's belltower sketch, shown above, is part of the *Iglesia de San Sebastián* (Saint Sebastian Church). As is common in this part of Spain, a mosque was built here between the tenth and eleventh centuries to replace a Visigoth church, which itself was built over the ruins of an earlier pagan temple.

Saint Sebastian church is shown on the following page. It faces south, a requirement of the mosques in Spain, and overlooks the Tagus River. Levi photographed the front of the church. The dirt in the foreground is now covered in stone, and the raised wall that surrounded the front entrance no longer exists.

An eleven-minute walk north of the church leads to the Plaza del Padre Juan de Mariana. Toledo's cathedral is visible from this square, as shown in the photo on the following page. In a 2009 blog titled *Toledo Olvidado* (Forgotten Toledo), Eduardo Sánchez Butragueño wrote about this fountain. It was placed there in 1863 as an access

point for the public to gather water from the Pozuela springs. The fountain is now located in the Plaza de San Justo.

The above image was a small mosque known as the Mezquita Bab-al-Mardum . The name originated from the nearby city gate. It is one of the few remaining structures from the Islamic period within the Al-Andalus region.

Across the face of the mosque, just below the corbels, is a Kufic inscription, the oldest style of Arabic. Carved here are the names of the patron and builder as well as the completion date; Muharram 390 in the Hijri calendar, or December 999AD.

The Christians conquered the Muslims here in 1085. Sometime after 1186, a transept and apse were added to the small square mosque, completing the conversion to a Catholic church.

Levi walked from the mosque-converted church and exited the old city walls through the *Puerta Bab al-Mardum* (Walled Gateway) and turned right. Another city gate, *La Puerta del Sol* (Sun Gate), is shown on the next page.

While a majority of the structure was built in the thirteenth and fourteenth centuries, parts of it date back to the eleventh century. Above the archway is a depiction of the ordination of Saint Ildephonus, the patron saint of Toledo.

The last photograph from Toledo was of Santiago del Arrabal church, located in the northwest corner of old Toledo. The bell tower was like the one Levi sketched. This church was another example of a converted mosque, evident through the horseshoe archways and openings. The bell tower is thought to have been the minaret of the mosque.

In the above photograph, right, Levi faced the south transept, the crossing part of the church that separates the apse from the nave. The main entrance was around the corner at the west end, as was customary.

In 1958, the two gate-covered archways belonging to the *portico* (porch) of the south transept were removed, along with the covered portico. The roofline covering the space between this south transept and the tower has also been removed. The tower, barely visible on the right side of the photo, is now a free-standing structure. The wall where the gentleman rests with his basket has been shifted to the right and now attaches to the right corner of the bell tower.

Before departing old Toledo, Levi penned a few words in his notepad.

The molten ball of day sinks low
Beneath the purple hill,
A solemn silence fills the land
The birds and all are still.

The shadows lengthen on the plain
Fireflys flash throughout the wood
Our petty pains and wrongs forgot
We feel that all is good.

The Angelus chimes out o'er the fields
The points of light appear;
All the world is hushed in prayer
Almighty God is near.

March 16, 1926 - At Toledo

CHAPTER 59
MAIL CALL

Madrid, Spain
March 18, 1926

Dear Mother,

We arrived here this morning from Toledo and it was a great day for me. There were thirteen letters waiting and four of them were from you and Pa. – The money orders arrived safe and they have been converted into 703 Spanish pesetas. Interruption [Vinc and I just went downstairs to eat supper. They told us it was served from 8:30 P.M. to 9:30. It's 8:40 now and no signs of eating yet. It is a Spanish custom to eat very late. Their movie shows start at 10:00 o'clock in the evening.] - I had no trouble cashing them where I had my mail forwarded to but could not get dollars so I took pesetas seeing they gave me a very good rate. I can change whatever I have left into French francs as easy as I could dollars. – [Thanks and warning to Pa that I shall probably "hit" him up again before getting home.]

Am glad to hear that the packages I mailed at Rome arrived safe. I did not expect that you would read the book on death by Father Geniesse. I told him I would try some-time but I suppose it's too "spooky" to read before going to bed. The postcards I am sending back are mostly all examples of architecture that I want to remember. I would be buying a lot of pictures if it were not so hard to send them home.

So Harry has another addition to his family. He is getting what you'd call a head start on me. I can't imagine myself with that much responsibility but I know before Harry married he felt as I do now. Nothing was ever more true than, "Getting married makes a man settle down."

Madrid is a city about as large as Milwaukee but very beautiful with wonderful parks, art gallerys, churches etc. We have barely started to see it but at a glance one can see that it is very modern and not at all like other Spanish cities.

In Old Madrid
March 19, 1926

Dear Chloe,

"A bit of pleasure came today, A note of joy from far away". 'Darned' if I could finish it but, if I had, it would tell you how glad I was to receive your three letters. Our plans were changed so often that I hardly expected the American Express to have followed instructions in forwarding my mail. Yes'm I'm for 'em.

Madrid is a very modern and beautiful city. Probably better than anything we boast of in America.

Have just been interrupted by a visit from William Luckenbill of New York City. He's the fellow we met in Naples and with whom I almost started for Palestine. While I was looking at a picture in the Prado gallery this after-noon someone greeted me with, "What do you suppose was the matter with him when he painted that." We said good bye in Naples never expecting to meet again on this side of the Atlantic and he pops up with a story of adventure in

Tunis, of an eight day hike thru the desert with another fellow from Princeton and a pack burro. They were treated royally by Arab chiefs, given a body guard for two days, slept in Bedouin tents, drank sour goats milk and many other things that just make Vinc and I green with envy. I've had "sweet" goats milk but have never had the patience to wait for it to sour, besides "sweet" is good enough for me.

Luckenbill was saying he met people in Tunis who thought that the United States was a French province. He says it took a reef out of his sails and that passing as an Englishman was the only way that natives would respect them.

The Prado Gallery here, which probably neither you nor I ever heard the name of before, holds today for us the greatest there is in painting. I suppose we'll say the same of the Louvre when we get back to it again but just now Velasquez, Titian, Rubens, Rembrandt, Van Dyck, Jordaens, Murillo and Ribera hold the stage. Raphael also has a room but his best pictures have stayed in Italy. The thing that surprises us is that these pictures were painted in Spain for Spaniards which is more than can be said of the art that finds its way into America, England and a large part of France. – They also have two painters with something different. El Greco, called the mad painter, and Goya who was mad. Goya who it is said scorned the Church and would not use religious subjects has painted many trifling things well when he suddenly seems to become possessed by the Devil [should I say Beelzebub] and mad men eating babies, ghosts, insane people gibbering together and many other blood curdling pictures are the result. – Enough or I'll not sleep tonite thinking of them.

You spoke of pictures for the book you are going to have bound. Am sending this so you'll have something to identify me when I arrive to raid the ice box. [Am bringing a loaf of bread along].

Tomorrow there is a Corrida de Toros which in old English means bull fight. The three of us expect to see it. I shall probably be sick before it's over but that's part of our education.

After that Vinc and "Lucky" are going on to Paris and I stay in Spain for about two more weeks. Vinc is going to Paris to see if his job is awaiting him. When you get this I shall probably be in Lourdes and from there Bordeaux, Toulouse and Paris. Shall have mail more regular from now on because Paris will be headquarters for side trips into the chateau country and cathedral towns. That's a gentle hint.

When does school close and when do you leave Washington for Champ? [Just asking that one question before answering all yours].

You are probably wondering about my mother. Letters from home removed most of my worry. She is much better and my brother says there is no immediate danger or less remote which should call me home now. Was planning on September but I know now that I'll be homesick long before that.

I shall not forget your letter concerning my mother. Thanks can hardly express the gratitude I feel.

Sincerely, Lee

Levi was drawn to architecture, religion, and the wonderful depictions of all things God. Still, he could not escape the intrigue and emotion that clenched his soul when he encountered the macabre, whether it was Zumbo and his wax plague-infested models in Florence or Goya's Black Paintings in the Prado; our traveler was transfixed, practically spellbound.

Goya's fourteen paintings, known as the Black Paintings, were not created for royalty or any other patron of the arts. They were simply an artist's expression of his inner thoughts while caught in a world without sound. Goya previously depended unknowingly on his hearing; he found himself to be deeply expressive once that sense was lost. These artworks once bedecked the walls of Goya's home on the outskirts of Madrid. They were painted directly on the wallpaper. Goya's brush spread oil paint into dark, profound figures. The images were later removed from the walls, along with their paper backing, and attached to canvas. In the Prado, they continue to grasp the attention of those who enter unprepared.

El Escorial, Spain
March 22, 1926
[travel journal]

Left Madrid this morning after spending most of our time there in the Prado gallery. The Coronation by Velazquez is as beautiful as I have seen. Madrid is a very modern city and we were surprised to find a very efficient subway system in operation.

Levi's favorite at the Louvre in Paris was Murillo's *Immaculate Conception of Los Venerables* by Bartolomé Esteban Murillo. The artist's use of light, angels, and clouds, with Mary as a focal point, appealed to the architect. That painting was created for Seville. Today, it hangs in the Prado with the painting that became Levi's new favorite, Velázquez's *Coronation of the Virgin.*

In Velázquez's painting, Mary was once again center stage, but this time the Holy Trinity joined her. Both Christ and God the Father were draped in royal robes, with Mary's robes being painted in blue and white as was customary. This time, Mary was in the heavens, supported by angels and clouds, with her eyes cast downwards towards the Earth.

Both paintings are beautiful, mid-seventeenth-century pieces, proudly painted in Spain for Spaniards.

CHAPTER 60
CORRIDA DE TOROS

El Escorial, Spain
March 22, 1926
[travel journal]

Yesterday we saw our first Corrida de Toros. It was an exhibition of great nerve and disgusting cruelty. – The bull charging into the arena is a thrilling sight as is the first men who venture in the ring to tease him with their colored cloaks. – The leading in of blind folded horses to be gored

by the bull is just a disgusting form of unsportsmanship and cruelty. The picadors advancing against the bull with nothing but sheer nerve to protect them is probably the best of the performance. The matador who finally kills the bull gets most of the ovation his act being gaily finished by the galloping teams who enter the ring to drag out the dead horses and the bull. Six bulls and thirteen horses were killed yesterday. One grand thrill when a bull jumped the fence. As one American we met said, "We would soon put a crimp on that kind of a show in America."

On March 28, 1926, Chloe wrote from Washington, D.C.

I hope you'll see a bull fight in Madrid and will write me about it. Don't forget.

Just by chance, Levi responded to her request that same day, in his letter from Lordes.

The Corrida de Toros was about what we had been told to expect. Parts were disgustingly cruel, parts of the performance gave you thrills and an exhibition of courage that we dislike to admit of Spaniards. And now I under-stand why they tied the bull for Rudolph Valentino — and I don't blame him a bit. There were twenty thousand people watching the exhibition in which six bulls, thirteen horses were killed and two men slightly injured.

Their shouting for blood was much like what I have imagined of old Roman crowds at a gladiatorial contest. It was not 'nice' but I've been at an American prize fight where the same cry was raised and it was human blood they thirst for.

Levi, Vince, and William Luckinbill of New York took in the local attraction on March 20. Vince's impression of the bullfight appeared in the *Green Bay Press-Gazette*, page four, on April 22, 1926

IT'S THE BLOOD THAT COUNTS NOT THE BULL, AVERS ENGELS
By Vince Engels

MADRID, Spain – Seville, that proud metropolis of Andalusia, may rightly claim to be the scene of the greatest of bull-fights, the home of the world's series in that sport, where the champions of the Matadore's League meet the strongest and fiercest of the bulls of the Beef Association. But Madrid, while it cannot aspire to the glory of Seville, is nevertheless the stage for performances which are certainly in the major league manner, and which are quite good enough for an uninformed spectator, at least. A Spaniard wishing to see a football game, would no doubt find as much entertainment in a match between the Green Bay Business College and the Elks' club as in the annual Packer-Bear riot. And an American attending his first round of bull-fights is sure to obtain as much pleasure in a contest between a consumptive matadore and a decrepit bull as in the greatest of the programs held in the famous arena at Seville.

One afternoon recently just such an American was watching the third bull of the day, a very frisky specimen, demolish seven horses, leap over the first, or interior railing of the arena, leap back again, and continue to fight every spot of red in sight until three long swords had been thrust into his neck. It was all very impressive.

Might Have Said "Dear Me"

The American was surprised, and showed it. He might have said "Dear Me" or something equally expressive. But his Spanish companion, taking note of this, smiled and said, "A fair bull. Yes, a fair bull. But only last week" – and then with all the ardor which in other countries accompanies the story of a successful round of golf, or the capture of an incredible muskellunge, the expert described how a certain bull had cut short the lives of ten horses in the five minutes allowed for the horse-butting round, had routed the bandilleros so thoroughly that they were able to attach to his hide only one of the six darts prescribed by Hoyle, or the Marquis of Queensbury, or whoever it is that dictates the rules of this game, and then, bloody but still fighting, took five swords before he would kneel, and even after that rose again to his feet, and made a lunge for the matadors, only to topple in the midst of his charge. "Now that," the Spaniard concluded, "was a good bull."

But even the least of the animals sent into the arena is sufficiently ferocious to satisfy the untutored patron of the sport. Be it understood that the bulls which are used to test the art of the matadors are not the common garden variety of bull. They are the very special product of centuries of development, speedier, stronger, and more temperamental than the pampered lords of the dairy herds. And their anger is quite easily aroused. As one of these bulls is sent into the ring, a tiny pin, to which is attached a ribbon tied in the form of a bow, is thrust into his back.

And this inconsiderable scratch is yet sufficient to send him galloping at an amazing speed toward the fighters grouped about the far side of the arena, whereupon these candidates for a place in the Spanish sun judiciously hop the fence. No man is so imprudent, so lacking in natural caution, as to attempt to sidestep that first wild charge. Before the bull can be played with, he must first be slowed up. After he has been made to run two or three times across the huge ring, the game begins in earnest. The arena is suddenly full of men waving red cloaks. Time and again the bull charges those flashing colors, his anger increasing as, on each attempt, his horns meet only with the air or at best a flimsy yard of cloth. Then, when his wrath is at the fever point, picadors, on horseback, enter the ring. What happens had better be guessed at than described.

Uses Barbed Darts

The horse business lasts only a few minutes, and is followed by an exhibition of skill and bravery, or of plain foolhardiness, whichever you will, the like of which can be seen, perhaps, in another sport. Without the red cloak by which he might hope to attract the attention of the bull away from his person, armed only with two barbed darts about the size and shape of roman candles, "bandillero" enters the arena, waves his arms once or twice to arouse the notice of the bull, and then runs at full speed toward the animal. The bull, head down, comes to meet him. And just as a collision seemed inevitable, the "bandillero," by some magic or foot-work, swerves aside, at the same instant throwing out his arms so as to thrust both his darts into the neck of the bull. This performance is repeated by two other "bandilleros," after which a trumpet sounds, and they withdraw; it is the beginning of the end for the bull, that is; it is the inning of the matadore. He comes on in a business-like manner, and prepares to do the carving. Sometimes kneeling directly in front of the bull, sometimes standing, he plays with the animal at will, leading him about, by means of the red cloak, to the left, to the right, in circles and semi-circles and triangles, and then, having fully exhibited his skill, ends the act by killing the bull with one sword, or two, or as many as may be needed.

Horse Butching Brutal

But whether a man enjoys his first bull fight or not, he must admit that a great deal of nonsense has been preached and published in condemnation of this favorite Spanish pastime. It is true that the horse butchering is a brutal and a bloody business, but it is only a preliminary to the real fight; it is quite an incidental and minor part of the program. Could this be eliminated, bull fighting could not reasonably be called more brutal than many another game which is accepted in other lands as sport.

It would only be more dangerous than the others. Nor can the Spanish audience, which shouts for the blood of the bull, be called a more cruel gathering than an American audience which shouts for the blood of an umpire, or a prize fighter. Who that has attended a boxing bout, watching Battling So-and-So pommel Kid Somebody-or-Other has not heard the crowd scream: "Kill him. Kill Him. Knock his head off." And in the next round, when Kid Somebody-or-Other rallies, and takes the advantage, is he not likewise advised to dismember the Battler? As W. O. McGeehan, an expert sports writer, recently asserted: "Customers of the boxing game want to see the 'claret' and they want one or both of the contestants horizontal." It matters not, apparently, who is damaged, or whose blood flows.

But to the Spanish audience, it does matter. The man must kill the bull, and if he does, applause will follow; the bull dare not kill the man, and if that accident should happen, there will be no wild, rockety cheers for the bull. There will be only mourning. The Spaniard may deride a matadore for failing to kill a bull with neatness and grace, but in his sane and simple fashion he sees that it would never do for the bull to kill the man, no matter how neatly and gracefully the task were performed.

What Do Methods Matter

Of course no one argues that, all applesauce aside, prize-fighting is more brutal than bull-fighting. But men may very rightly argue that bull-fighting is at least as humane as prize-fighting, or for that matter, many another sport. The Frenchman, on a day of recreation, goes to his gun club, where a number of fat, tame, slow-flying pigeons are released, at a distance of fifteen yards, before his twelve gauge gun. The Englishman hunts a single fox with a pack of forty hounds, and each of the forty is faster and stronger than the lone fox. Yet no one questions his sportsmanship. Again, he will hunt a deer with hounds, of course, and run the animal to utter exhaustion. And then he will draw blood.

Quite obviously, it is all a matter of taste, - of taste in bloods. The Spaniard wants the blood of a bull, the Frenchman, of a dove, the Englishman, of a fox or a deer, and we, of America, will be content with nothing less than the blood of a pugilist, an umpire or a negro.

What do the methods matter? It is the blood that counts! (4)

In this classic comparison-contrast piece, Vince wrote of the Americans' call for blood, but not the blood of an animal. Instead, Americans cried for the *blood of a pugilist, an umpire, or a negro.*

As far as pugilists were concerned, Jack Dempsey reigned in the 1920s. He held the world heavyweight championship title from 1919 to 1926. The "Manassa Mauler" won sixty-nine of the eighty-four fights he entered ("Jack Dempsey: Inducted 1965 – Boxing").

Umpires were second on Vince's list. "Kill the Umpire" was a favorite phrase in the ballparks of the 1920s. One of the first recorded uses appeared in San Francisco's *Daily Examiner* on the third of June 1888, in the middle of Ernest L. Thayer's poem, "Casey at the Bat."

"From the benches, black with people,
there went up a muffled roar,
Like the beating of the storm-wave
on a stern and distant shore,
"Kill him! Kill the umpire!"
shouted some one on the stand;
And it's likely they'd have killed him
had not Casey raised his hand" (4).

The call for the blood of the Negro hit the hardest, which is why Vince included that group last. Lynchings continued into the 1920s. According to statistics provided by the Archives at Tuskegee Institute, Douglas Linder reported that just over one hundred Blacks were lynched at the turn of the century. Throughout the twenties, the numbers were still in double digits each year. The lynching of Black Americans did not reduce to single digits until the mid-to-late thirties.

As the bullfight came to a close, the blood thirsty Spaniards, appalled Americans, and others left the ring. Levi's desire to witness this "attraction" was satisfied. He gladly returned to American boxing matches. At least nobody died in those, as long as you exclude: Andy Bowen, Walter Croot, Tommy McCarthy, Luther McCarthy, Andy Thomas, Jean-Baptiste Rampignon, and Frankie Jerome. Those were the boxers who had lost their lives in a bout before the day that Levi, Vince, and Lucky witnessed the loss of blood in a ring. One month later, it would be Clever Sencio who died, on April 19, 1926, just hours after the bout at the Auditorium in Milwaukee, Wisconsin ("Sencio's Body Will Be Shipped Home to Philippine Islands" 17).

CHAPTER 61
LIFE AT THE BRADFORD

Sunday Night
March 28, 1926

Dear Lee,

Lots of things have happened since I last wrote – I hardly know where to begin. First, we're moving again! but just up to the fourth floor again – Disappointed? You thought we'd been mixed up with some scandal again, didn't you? It's like this – Velma is going out of town to teach school and Ruth is expecting to move into an apartment with Gertrude. She had "spats" with Virginia and Grace – There are too many in the apartment for her, Johnny didn't like such a crowd, etc. So she and Gertrude are going to live to-gether for awhile. She's gotten angry with all the girls except me – She wanted to know when I was to lecture her. Poor child! Johnny rushed in one evening and announced that he was going with Captain Byrd on his polar expedition. We haven't seen or heard of Johnny since. The expedition is to leave New York April 1.

I went to the station to meet Ruth to-night, but she didn't come, so now its my turn to lecture. Shall I? Ruth's resigned her position in the Gov't and begins work with a corporation here in town Apr. 1. She decided to take her few days annual leave and go home. She asked me to meet her to-night. I spent the afternoon out in Cherrydale, (where I used to teach) and some friends brought me in town and to the station. If I had come in on the street car and had stood shivering in my spring regalia, for a half an hour at Rosslyn junction I'd probably been in an ill humor.

Emma Ruth spent last week end with me. She had two days for spring vacation – (no holiday Easter). I believe she's as crazy about Washington as I am. She didn't want to leave – her work is so hard she says. This is good for her?

About ten days ago we had a fire in the basement of our apartment house. We were very scared when we awoke choking with coal gas and smoke. My first fire experience, and standing in the cold for 3 hrs. partially dressed gave us colds. Gertrude came around to see us the next night and brought Warren. He seems very pleasant but not as cute as I expected him to be – (Don't tell Gertrude).

I saw Clayton at the drug store across from G. W. not many days ago. He said that he'd been working so hard that he didn't have time for anything else. He 'flunked' two of his classes last semester and is trying to make them up. Did I tell you I made B (90-95) on History and C (80-90) on Education? These professors are easy graders because I certainly didn't study.

When your letter from Africa came I wondered, where the next one would be post marked. You are having 'wild and wooly' experiences – Thrilling? I'll say!

Saturday, (yesterday) Va. And I had several girls for luncheon. All of us were school teachers so you can imagine the conversation. Poor children! Aren't you glad you don't have to listen to similar conversations?

I didn't do anything unusual on St. Patrick's Day. Many

of my pupils wore green and asked me to wear a shamrock leaf and pipe. I said that I wasn't Irish, but I'd compromise and wear them on my yellow dress.

I seem to be doomed to religious discussions. One day last week while most of my class were at shop and cooking, I heard several of my girls talking very loudly in the class-room, so teacher-like I reprimanded them. Then one asked me if I'd settle a question for them — "Should you be afraid of God?" was the topic of discussion — (you know we aren't allowed to discuss religion in school so I hesitated to answer) I thought that saying God was a God of love as well as fear wouldn't hurt no one's belief — and stopped my part of the discussion there, tried to quiet them but one asked this question — Why should there be so many religions? — I simply said I'd like to know the answer to that question, myself. The question of Catholicism vs. Protestantism arose. You can imagine the nature of it — Mixed marriages were discussed and even these children knew that they were un-happy and one little Italian girl said that a mixed marriage was a sin. The bell rang and the discussion continued until I had to send them home. They were informing me as if I didn't know of these things. What would you have done?

Easter holidays begin Friday and I'm going home Thursday night.

I don't think I've left any gossip out of this letter — Do you? Isn't this a "Literary Digest"? Ruth has come — She missed her train, so I'll postpone my lecture and await your permission.

From, Chloe

Chloe recorded memories of March in her autobiography, written in the Spring of 1977.

*One night I looked out of our apt. window and saw
flames coming out of the basement window 8 stories below!
Alarms rang – We had to take the smoke filled stairs to the
lobby – We took the things we thought important! I grabbed
Lee's letters from Europe, and my shoes! Soon the fire was
out and we went to sleep!*

Ruth's fella, Johnny, was the second from the group to head out on a grand adventure. He accompanied Captain Byrd and Floyd Bennett, the first to fly above the North Pole. To this day, there is speculation as to whether they completed their goal or not. *Pathé News* reported on the historic event, as did every paper in town.

CHAPTER 62
FAREWELL TO SPAIN

Levi's anticipated departure from Spain began in Madrid. He ventured alone through Ávila to Salamanca. A bend in the trail turned Levi northeast towards Valladolid, Burgos, and the Irun Pass at the westernmost border between Spain and France. He wrote about these days in a letter to Chloe dated March 28, 1926.

Lourdes, France
Palm Sunday

Getting back into France was a joy because since Vinc
went up to Paris and I found no one with whom I could say
a word things got on my nerves. Six days of cold dreary
rain ended what had been a very fine trip thru Spain. The
El Escorial outside of Madrid was a "fizzle". It is a giant
building, a monastery built by a certain King Philip II in
atonement for destroying another during one of his battles.
Like Seville it has been made by the tourist companies.

The unimpressed architect stood at a UNESCO World Heritage site from the late sixteenth century, a massive complex that influenced Spanish architecture for half a century. King Philip II oversaw the construction of this grand monument, which needed to be worthy of holding the remains of his father, King Charles V, the

Holy Roman Emperor. Phillip vowed to build a monastery dedicated to Saint Laurence after the Battle of Saint-Quentin in 1557, since Spain's victory over France occurred on the saint's feast day, August 10.

The buildings followed a grill pattern, mimicking the torture of choice used to kill Saint Lawrence in 258 A.D. The saint was placed on an iron grill above a slowly burning fire as ordered by the Prefect of Rome. Legend says he smiled while being tortured and said, 'Turn me over, I think I'm done on this side.' What was Saint Lawrence's offence against Rome? When he was asked to bring forth the church's treasures, Saint Lawrence led his arresting officers to the slums of Rome, pointed towards those who lived there, and said, "There is the treasure of the church!" ("Portraits of the Early Church: St. Lawrence of Rome" 1:06:00).

Levi's travels alone through Spain continued, as did his March 28 letter to Chloe.

> *Avila is a beautiful walled town, as beautiful as Toledo*
> *but the cold, rain and poor hotel spoiled my enjoyment of it.*
> *The cathedral and the church of St. Thomas where the tomb*
> *of Cardinal Torquemada is, were of special interest. The*
> *town was filled with small examples of Romanesque detail.*

Cardinal Juan de Torquemada, an educated theologian and supporter of the papacy, was involved in the councils of his time. He was part of four conclaves to elect a pope. It was Cardinal Torquemada who cast the deciding vote, placing a white zucchetto upon the head of Tommaso Parentucelli, making him Pope Nicholas V. This well-known cardinal was painted at the feet of the crucified Christ in 1453 by Fra Angelico. But it was not Cardinal Juan de Torquemada who rested in the tomb at the Real Monasterio de Santo Tomás in Ávila. As a matter of fact, Cardinal Torquemada and Fra Angelico are both resting in peace in the church of *Santa Maria Sopra Minerva* (Saint Mary Above Minerva) in Rome.

The Torquemada buried in Ávila is the Cardinal's nephew, Tomás de Torquemada. After joining the same order as his uncle, Tomás attained a bachelor's degree in theology. He longed to live the life of a simple monk, but his focus was on ridding Spain of heresy. Tomás

was the confessor of Princess and later Queen Isabella. He supported her union with Ferdinand II of Aragon and begged the princess
to rid Spain of all heretics should she ever become queen. Tomás de
Torquemada was the Grand Inquisitor. He started what we know
today as the Spanish Inquisition, a torturous history where strong
forces united to rid Spain of all non-Catholics. The killings continued for approximately three centuries after Tomás' death.

The tomb Levi witnessed at the monastery did not hold Tomás's
or his uncle Juan's remains in 1926. Tomás de Torquemada's tomb
was ransacked in 1832, only a few years before the end of the Spanish Inquisition. His bones were burned much in the same manner
as the 2,000 souls whom he burned at the stake during his time as
Grand Inquisitor. It is unknown whether supporters or adversaries
of the famed friar were responsible for removing his remains after
334 years, but all that is left of Tomás de Torquemada is his name on
an empty tomb.

Valladolid, Spain
March 24, 1926
[travel journal]

*Arrived here last night from Avila after having a real
3rd class ride. Awoke up at Medina del Campo and found
myself all alone, the lights out and the car left in the middle
of the freight yards. Finally got another train and arrived
in Valladolid at 12:30 P.M. Valladolid is a larger and more
modern city. Its cathedral, while spoiled by plaster work as
usual is a good example of what could have been done with
the Renaissance design in church building. The church of
San Pablo is interesting with its ornate façade but would
hardly be called good design by anyone. Another church
called San Benito has a curiously designed porch and tower
barely commenced. Am leaving for Burgos in the morning.
It snowed coming in Avila and the weather is far from what
we had in the South.*

The three religious structures Levi mentioned in Valladolid - the Cathedral, San Pablo, and San Benito - were built from the Gothic to the Renaissance periods.

The Cathedral was the newest of the three, shown above, left. The congregation broke ground here in 1589. The original plans would have made this the largest cathedral in Europe, but in the 1560s, the capital moved from Valladolid to Madrid, and there were no longer sufficient funds or a need to complete the structure. The cathedral was only built as far as the transept, the crossing portion of a cathedral. Today, this cathedral is known as *La Inconclusa* (The Unfinished). The tower added in the early 1700s collapsed in 1841. The existing tower was completed in 1890 and topped with the Sacred Heart of Jesus in 1923.

San Pablo was the oldest, visible in the photograph to the right. Commissioned by Cardinal Juan de Torquemada, the two side towers were not part of the original design.

Levi did not photograph San Benito church. The curiously designed porch and tower, which appeared to Levi as *barely commenced*, had been shortened in the 1800s due to structural instability. An online image attributed to Mmoyaq is provided to show the original design. By 1926, the two upper stories of the porch and towers had been removed, and a small structure holding two suspended bells was erected. That structure does not exist today. Only the lowest two sections with single arches remain, leaving a façade that appears incomplete.

Returning to Levi's March 28 letter to Chloe, he had this to say about Valladolid.

Valladolid had several fine churches and is interesting historically because it was there that Columbus died. The most appropriate monument ever built has been erected in his memory. Here too in the Plaza Major the first and last acts of the Inquisition took place. As our friend "Lucky" said last Sunday after seeing a bull fight, "Now I can understand the Inquisition."

Burgos, Spain
March 25, 1926
[travel journal]

On leaving Valladolid I had the usual argument with the hotel keeper. Expected to have the police stop me but my 'hunch' was right that he didn't have the nerve to carry it to a police court. Spain, Italy, France they're all the same.

Took a second look at the monument to Cristobal Colon on leaving Valladolid. It was here he died and near by is the square where most of the tortures of the Inquisition were carried out.

Levi has reason to be impressed by the 1905 monument commemorating Christopher Columbus. It was commissioned by the Spanish Government for placement in Havana, Cuba, to commemorate the four hundredth anniversary of Columbus's arrival in the Americas. The Spanish-American War thwarted those plans, and the masterpiece never left Spain. Valladolid, being the deathplace of Columbus, won out over other Spanish cities, and the monument was unveiled there in 1905. At the pinnacle of the monument behind the genuflecting explorer stands Faith, who guided Columbus through his explorations. Both are perched in a barge being battered by wind and waves while Faith holds firm to the cross that rises above all, extending 16.4 meters (53.8 feet) into the air.

This monument, as captured by Levi in the above photograph, is located on the extension of an otherwise large triangular park in the heart of the city, *Parque Campo Grande* (Large Field Park). The tall memorial is bordered on three sides by city streets. A fifteen-minute walk separates the tribute to Columbus from the site of the Spanish Inquisition at *Plaza Mayor* (Main Square).

Valladolid not only hails as the deathplace of Christopher Columbus, but it was here that the adventures of Don Quixote poured from the pen of Miguel de Cervantes. The history and architecture of Valladolid are certain to hold the interest of any visitor to the Castile-León region of Northwestern Spain.

Burgos, Spain
March 25, 1926
[travel journal]

Another rainy day and I had to force myself to make
preparations to stay here tomorrow in hopes that I can see the
cathedral in sunshine as well as spend a last pleasant day in
Spain. Burgos has the finest cathedral in Spain but two days
of rain drove me away, all the way to the French border.

It was almost April, the second wettest month traditionally for this area of Spain. The train route from Valladolid to the Irun Pass went through Burgos. For five centuries, this was the capital of the Kingdom of Castile until the unification of Spain in the mid-fifteenth century. Queen Isabella hailed from this part of Spain.

Burgos was a stopping point for pilgrims on the Camino Francés, the most popular route to Santiago de Compostela. During the medieval times, pilgrims who followed the Camino passed in front of the entrance at the north transept and entered the cathedral. Just

inside, a double-flight staircase called the *Escalera Dorada* (Gilded Staircase) descended to the floor level. The double staircase extends in mirror image to the left and right. As the stairs bend and return to the center, stone carvings of scallop shells mark this as a point on the road to Compostella. When Levi visited, the entrance had been sealed for about one hundred years.

Levi did not mention the Camino in any of his writing, though he visited several important stops on this pilgrimage route. According to a writer identified only as Maria, a quarter of a million devout travelers followed the Camino each year during the twelfth and thirteenth centuries. Popularity faded due to war, plagues, and the Reformation. It was not until the 1980s that a resurgence occurred, with present numbers surpassing those of the Middle Ages.

After Burgos, Levi crossed the border from Spain into France at the Irun Pass.

Hendaye [Franco-Spanish Border]
March 26, 1926
[travel journal]

Have just passed the customs without a bit of trouble. Met a German on the train with whom I had an interesting conversation. Believe me, these Germans are diplomats. Left Burgos this morning in the disagreeable rain. The ride was pleasant with agreeable people all the way. Met a Spaniard that had been in New York for six months. Was eager to return but as he said, "Spaniards are not allowed in America anymore." Everywhere they throw that into our faces and our weak explanations only make matters worse.

At Irun I saw a group of boys leaving to serve their term in the army. Each one had a pan and a blanket.

France again and its like getting home (almost). Here I can understand a part of what they tell me and can also tell them what I think of them in my best Belgian.

Levi's May 28 letter to Chloe, written in Lourdes, continued with his thoughts of Spain.

Spain was different; it has not been spoiled, as Italy has, by the tourist but it's safe to predict that when they improve their railroad service and modernize their hotels, Cooks (Thomas Cook & Son, a travel company out of London) *and the American Express will start boosting it. In mine and our opinions Spanish cooking is the best yet but we just couldn't get used to eating the evening meal and then rushing immediately to bed in order to get to sleep before daybreak.*

This trip has shattered our ideas of things. For instance I've always thought Americans were the "night hawks" of the world and here we find them starting their shows at 10:30 P.M. – For a good reason I cannot tell you what time they arise in the morning.

The two things we pride ourselves of, Liberty and Democracy we have the least of when compared to countries like Italy, France and Spain. But here's one thing we excel in and that's common courtesy. Possibly the French are polite but I've always disliked politeness for about the same reason as perfume. Why polite people usually will bear watching I don't know but it is a rule that seems to hold.

Shall probably be in Paris for Easter and the Easter parade but if I find a quiet town I shall stay there for Good Friday and Holy Saturday because freethinking, broadminded, anticlerical Paris would probably jar on my nerves, just a wee bit.

When you get this I, or possibly we, shall be starting to see the great Cathedrals of Amiens, Rhiems, Chartres and Bourges.

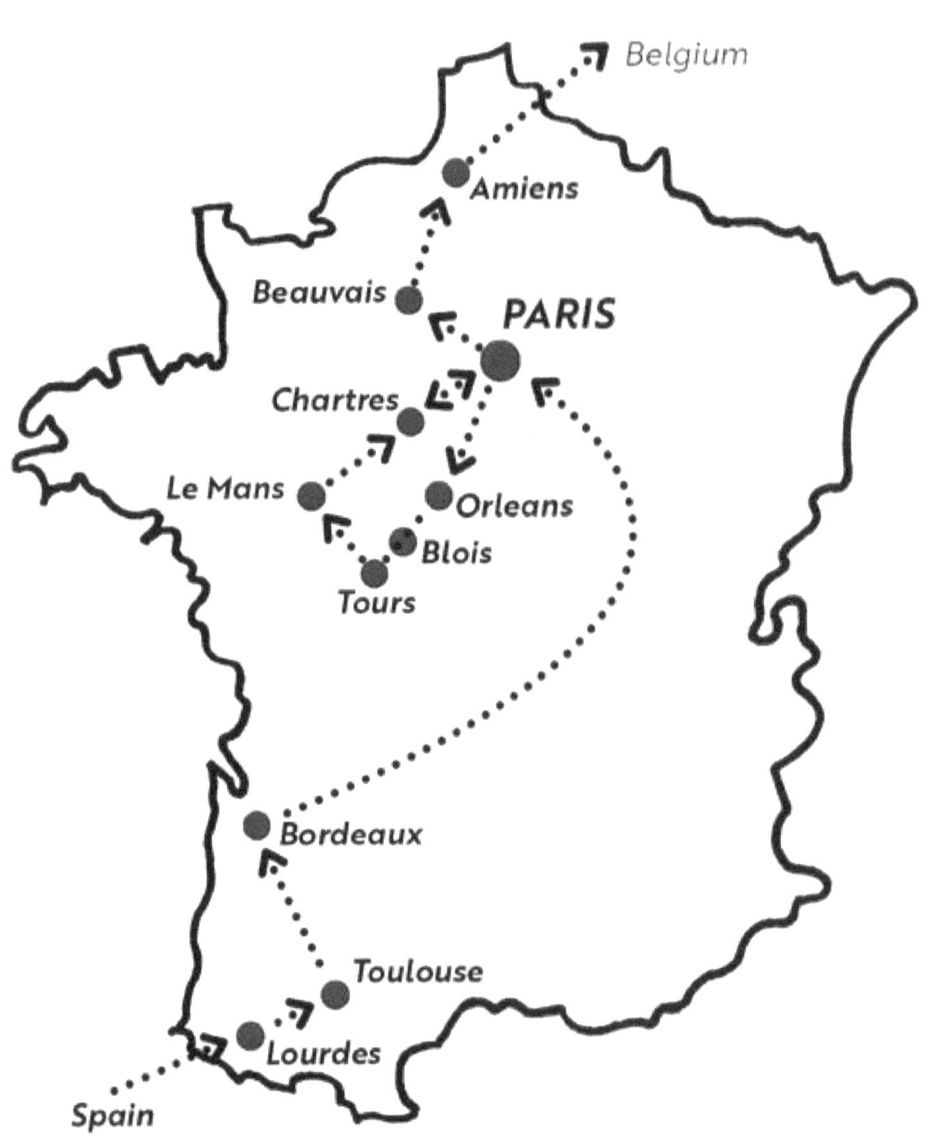

Belgium
Amiens
Beauvais
PARIS
Chartres
Le Mans
Orleans
Blois
Tours
Bordeaux
Toulouse
Lourdes
Spain

FRANCE III
March 1926 – April 1926

CHAPTER 63
HEALING WATERS

Lourdes, France
Palm Sunday

Dear Chloe,

*   You would like this place. There is no cinemas on Sunday and when I asked why the hotel keeper's wife told me that the people here were very religious. This morning the manager of the hotel took it upon himself personally to see that I got up for mass and when it seemed like I was to be late he almost had a fit. He rushed me out of the breakfast room much as a man gets his wife off on her vacation. — The church was filled with men and verily that proves it's a strange place.*

*   I shall not try to give my impression of this shrine because I do not know what I think. That miracles happen here, that people come and are cured of incurable diseases is not a matter for doubt. Science records that but gives no explanation. Whether the Mother of God actually appeared here in 1858 is not an article of faith and that means we are free to doubt any part or all of the story. If I stayed here long I probably would believe because the atmosphere of devotion is such as I have never seen before. Several hundreds*

of pilgrims have prayed before me since I arrived yesterday and it seemed almost a sacrilege to watch them. I believe the tourist has sensed something of this because for once he has made himself inconspicuous.

Imagine a mother with a crippled child, a sister or a wife leading a blind man, men and women praying for health and happiness, a mother asking God to pardon a wayward son, a son praying for the health of a mother or father; if you can imagine that you have a picture of the Grotto at Lourdes.

Last fall an American answered my question as to what he thought of Lourdes by saying it was quite evidently a fraud. If he thought that he should have said it was the most damnable thing he had ever seen; but somehow neither he nor anyone can watch suffering humanity praying and feel that they pray to nothing but a statue and a candle smoke cave.

Bordeaux, France
Tuesday Night
March 30, 1926

Dear Mother,

I am lugging three bottles of Lourdes water in my pack with the hopes of arriving home with one without breaking it. When the chambermaid tried to pick up my pack (as they all insist on doing in European hotels) to carry it to my room it didn't raise off the floor. Guess she thought it was nailed to the floor until I picked it up. Anyway I hope to be in Paris soon where I can unload a bit. If I get a chance I shall mail a couple books on Lourdes home.

I was very pleased with Lourdes because I had expected almost anything but a well regulated place of worship. A church has been built above the cave but the cave where the eighteen appearances took place is still intact except of course for the cement floor, the candles and kneeling benches.

The spring flows on as ever and people come usually with a candle, they kiss the floor or a rock of the cave and when finished praying they take a drink of water. The water is run in reservoirs and baths have been built in a building adjoining the cave. For once I found a place that was not spoiled by tourists. The whole city of Lourdes makes its living either from hotels or religious article stores. I stayed at a little hotel in a very picturesque spot. Above the place about a thousand feet high they have erected a cross which is lighted at night. While I was there the moon was full and the light reflecting on the icy mountain peaks about twenty miles away gave the place an 'air of heaven'.

There were not so many at the shrine at this time of the year. The pilgrimages come later and if you can imagine about fifty thousand people crowded into a place with a population of 6000 you can realize why I'd rather come when there is only about two hundred people around. — Lourdes is a strange place because they haven't a movie

theatre. I asked the hotel keeper why not and he said the people were very religious there. That's true because I found the church crowded with men Sunday which would be quite an event anywhere else in France. I will not try to describe the history of Lourdes but will let you read the little book I am going to send.

Arrived in Bordeaux this afternoon from Toulouse where I slept last night on arriving from Lourdes. Had about an hour of daylight tonite and in that time I decided that tomorrow will probably see me in Poitiers which is another jump towards Paris. This is a big seaport but outside of that there seems to be little of interest. Becoming so used to entering new towns that I feel like a traveling salesman.

This morning I went to see Prof. Soula, one of Dr. Senn's friends at Toulouse. Received a hearty reception and when he found that I intended leaving right away he spent two hours of "rapid fire" French at me, part of which I understood. Vinc and I have found if you say "oui oui" ever so often that's all that is necessary. When I get home I won't be able to make myself understood with my mixture of English, French, Belgian, Italian and Spanish.

Today I had a narrow escape. A woman came to get on the train with a lot of bundles and a two month old baby. After taking her bundles into the compartment she handed me the baby to hold while she went to get something she forgot. I was panic stricken at the thought of being like 'Uncle Walt with Sheezix' in the Funny Pictures but luckily she came back and since the baby had on oilcloth clothes all was O.K.

Guess I'll go to bed because tomorrow I must see a town as big as Milwaukee in half a day. I'll be in Paris when you get this and will always have my mail there from now on.

With Love, Levi

Millions of the faithful visit Lourdes each year, seeking healing in the spring at the *Grotto of Massabielle* (Grotto of the Apparitions). In 1858, it was recorded that the Virgin Mary appeared eighteen times to a fourteen-year-old girl named Bernadette Soubirous. At the time of Levi's visit, Bernadette was on her way to sainthood. She was declared blessed in 1921 and canonized in 1933. Her body was exhumed on several occasions. In 1925, her incorrupt remains were transferred to a glass coffin, which resides in a chapel at her former convent in Nevers, France.

Levi's took this photo while standing in front of the Basilica of Our Lady of the Rosary, the third church built on the site. Beside this church is the Basilica of Our Lady of the Immaculate Conception, commonly known as the Upper Basilica. Its crypt is part of the first church built directly above the grotto.

CHAPTER 64
LITTLE TO SAY ABOUT VERSAILLES

Paris, France
Good Friday
April 2, 1926
[travel journal]

Arrived here last night and had trouble finding a room. Am here in the Hotel Ponthieu in a fair room but last night I had to be satisfied to sleep up in the attic because they had nothing else. This noon I started to find some church where I could spend three hours in meditation and finally after visiting four of them I gave up. A Frenchman thinks Good Friday is a great day to have concerts and raise money by charging admission to the seating space. I was so disgusted with the whole thing that I spent several hours along the Seine wishing I were anywhere else but here.

From Toulouse I went to Poitiers to see Notre Dame la Grande. It was hardly worth the pain and inconvenience it caused me. I made up my mind there to come straight to Paris because I can neither study nor enjoy travel feeling as

I do. My stomach had been upset since leaving Madrid and after drinking a bottle of milk of magnesia I felt better last night but today it has been the same old story. I am going out now to see if I can eat something after which I shall go down to meet Vinc, John and "Lucky".

Tours, France
April 10, 1926
[travel journal]

Paris over the Easter weekend was very disappointing. I found it impossible to realize that it was Easter. – On Easter Sunday afternoon Harl, Vinc, Lucky, John and I went out to Versailles after missing the boat on which we had planned a trip to St. Germain.

Nothing more was said of Versailles. The name "Harl" never appeared again.

Among Levi's belongings was a 10-inch by 13-inch monograph. Black ink accented with light blue watercolor decorated the aged cardstock. On the cover, *A Monograph of Versailles: History of Architecture, L. Geniesse* was written. The report appeared as follows:

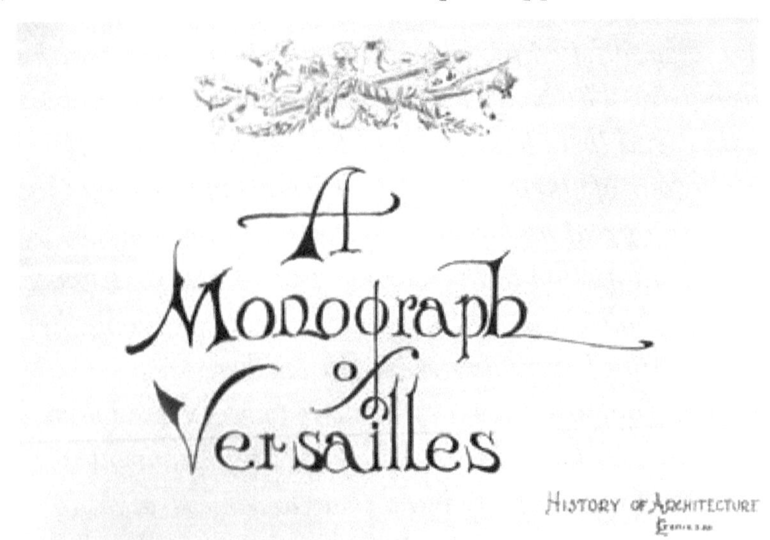

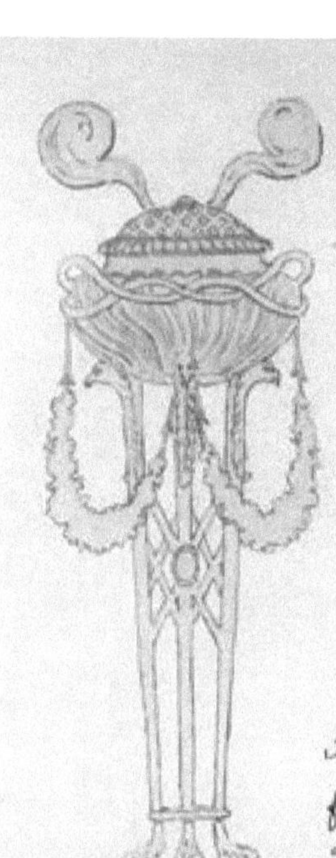

The Palace of Versailles had its beginning in a hunting lodge which Louis XIII built for himself about eleven miles from Paris, buying the land for the lodge from Francois de Gondi, the first bishop of Paris. After his father's death Louis XIV took up his residence at Versailles and Le Vau was given the commission to design a palace. Later Jules Hardouin Mansard extended the North and South wings of the Palace. Other portions were added by Gabriel during the reign of Louis XV.

The three avenues of St. Cloud, Paris and Sceaux converge in the Place d'Armes which is the center of the Palace façade. The façade is more than a quarter mile in length and facing it between the avenues stand the former stables of the Palace now occupied by the artillery and the engineers.

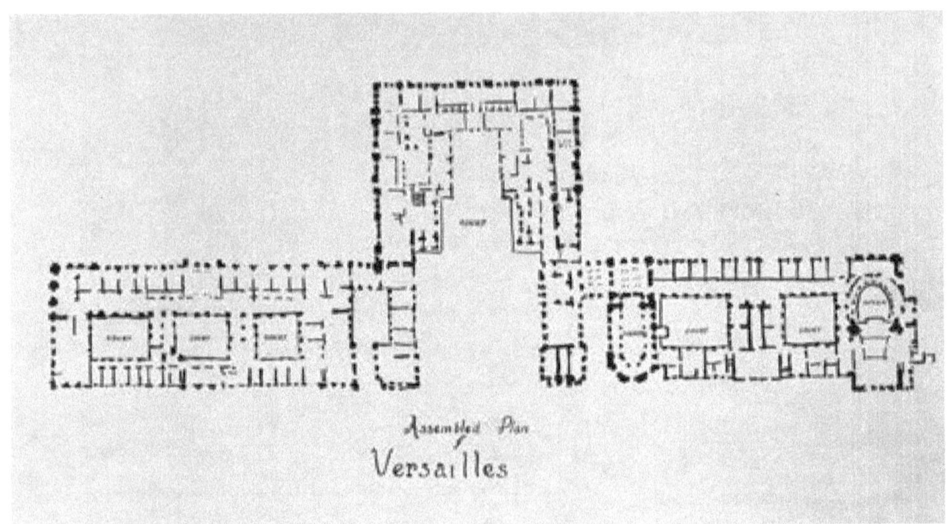

Assembled Plan
Versailles

Westward from the Palace extends a broad avenue, planted with large trees, and having along its centre the grass of the "Tapis Vert". It is continued by the Grand canal 200 feet wide and one mile long. On the south two staircases lead past the Orangery to Swiss Lake. On the north an avenue with twenty two groups of three children each group holding a marble basin from which a jet of water rises, slopes gently down to the Basin of Neptune which is remarkable for its fine sculpture and abundant water. The Orangery designed by Mansard is probably the finest piece of architecture at Versailles.

The Palace of Versailles with its sumptuous apartments forms a museum of the decorative art of the period. Its magnitude and ostentatious ornament are the expression of the extravagance which characterized the period before the French revolution.

Westward from the Palace extends a broad avenue, planted with large trees, and having along its centre the grass of the "Tapis Vert". It is continued by the Grand canal 200 feet wide and one mile long. On the north an avenue with twenty two groups of three children each group holding a marble basin from which a jet of water rises, slopes gently down to the Basin of Neptune, which is remarkable for its fine sculpture and abundant water. The Orangery designed by Mansard is probably the finest piece of architecture at Versailles.

The Palace of Versailles with its sumptuous apartments forms a museum of the decorative art of the period. Its magnitude and ostentatious ornament are the expression of the extravagance which characterized the period before the French revolution.

At the highest point of the court is an equestrian statue in bronze of Louis XIV and behind it stands the central buildings one behind the other as far as the Marble Court. To the north the Chapel Court and to the south the Princes Court, with vaulted passages, leading to the gardens, separating the side from the central building. The main features of the Palace are the Chapel (by Mansard), the Opera (by Gabriel) the Gallery of Glass (by Mansard) and decorated by Le Brun, the eleven halls of historical pictures, the rooms of Louis XIV and the queen's room occupied successively by Marie Therése, Marie Leczinska and Marie Antoinette.

The magnificent formal gardens laid out by Le Nôtre, on axial lines cleverly manipulated to give vistas of avenues and water canals was only completed after great difficulty because of the lack of water.

Without any additional ephemera from Versailles, the monograph from Levi's days at the University of Notre Dame was all that he retained. The depth of this work signifies Versailles's importance to this architect. For his efforts, Levi scored an 80 on this project.

CHAPTER 65
MONTH-AND-A-HALF ARGUMENT

Snail mail took at least one week to cross the Atlantic in the 1920s. Transportation to and from the ports required additional time. Loved ones were often left without news for two weeks or more. As Levi traveled, his incoming mail awaited his arrival, extending the time between letters even more.

This delay in conversation turned what would be short disagreements into long-winded debates. After one of the two writers posted their grievance, they had weeks to cool off before a response could arrive. Instead of festering over time, ill feelings dissipated, only to be promptly resurrected upon receiving a rebuttal. With the next mailing, the cycle repeated.

Tours, France
April 9, 1926

Dear Chloe,

Am perched up on top of a suspension bridge over the Loire so if these few lines seem disconnected remember that my attention needs must remain on this railing and the water below. After this length of time over here we have come to fear water, in fact we abhor the sight of it and gazing down at many basins and bathtubs full makes me __

I almost said dizzy but you know that water has nothing to do with that.

Was to talk about "probition" [It never did prohibit so they've changed the spelling] but every American paper we see tells us it will not be long before we exiles can all go home. If you could meet all the Americans who are over here driven out of the States by the so many fanatical laws you would immediately vote to get us home --- maybe.

Connell and I are down here together "doing" the chateaus. Tomorrow we are going to Angers and then I go back to Paris and he goes to Nantes. A friend of his sisters is there and he has been trying to persuade me to go along but I'm afraid of French girls besides I'm eager to start out for Cologne where it is said there is good beer. There will be a great demand for brewerys soon (I hope) so I had better study the design of them now.

Back in our suite, a couple hours later.
A neatly dressed policeman with a nice shiny sword politely informed us that we had better get off our balustrade so here we are. We respect European policemen especially when they carry swords. The French gendarmes are the most courteous police we have met. They seem to be chosen for their intelligence, – a system which might be tried in choosing our "rednecks".

Connell, "Lucky" and I were out in the Montparnasse Café district Easter Sunday night watching the 'Bohemians' sip their drinks and watch their fellow eccentrics. All you need is a dazed look or a vacant stare and people (foreigners like ourselves) think that surely there is a starving artist. I looked the "starving" part but didn't tell a soul there that I was a poet. Please don't tell anyone either. Leave them find it out for themselves.

Paris was flooded on Easter with our brothers across the way, the English. Every clerk in England that can save six or seven pounds crosses the channel for Easter and sees the gay Parisians, mostly foreigners because the natives flock out of the city about the time the invasion starts. Don't know how I'll stand England because after seeing and hearing the English for several days I was glad to get away from Paris until their vacations will be over.

As one in our crowd commented, "They sure do murder the English language." Connell says that he things it's possible to pick up enough of the language in several weeks to get by in England. If I get stuck I'll fall back on my jumbled French which has taken me thru Italy and Spain.

My mother tells me that Gertrude is to join the "empty ice box gang" [just another hint] on April 1st. The reunion reminds me of the time Van and I were, by some miracle, saved from the effects of deadly coffee. Should I for any reason ever have occasion to visit apartment 305 I'll surely be on my guard for coffee or any other drink served me especially if Virginia does the serving.

Connell plans to sail from Ireland June 4th. He is going to spend most of his time until then in England and Ireland while about the time you get this I shall be in Brussels, Belgium or possibly Amsterdam. Right here I'll say that my mail will follow me so let me know how many of your pupils you are going to fail.

Vinc Engels is staying in Paris for the summer and may even stay over another year. Connell seems to have someone calling him while I'm eager to get back to work.

My sailing is not fixed, in fact I'll be in a fix if a certain letter should happen to be lost. [I hope I mailed it] – Hope to read yours in Paris in a couple days.

Till then, Lee

Sunday Afternoon
May 2, 1926

Dear Lee,

It's a good thing that your last letter contained no sarcasm; there was enough in the one you wrote April 9. What possessed you when you wrote that one? When I read it I almost declared I'd not write again. You said so much about prohibition that extracts from your letter would be suitable for "wet" propaganda. The more I see and hear of drunkenness the less I like it. You should have heard Va's and Grace's description of the sorority dance they attended last night. I'm glad I escaped going (by a hair's breadth). Everyone was about drunk except Va. and Grace and they had to refuse drinks time after time. I like to go to a dance but I can't see any fun in a dance with everyone half drunk. I can have a good time at a party and I don't have to drink in order to have a pleasant time. Other people can too if they want to. There's no use my saying anymore about drinking to you. You know how I feel on the subject and I'm hard headed you know.

Do you feel any better after criticizing the English? Isn't there any good in them to see? I suppose you were trying to make me angry in that letter. You succeeded. Are you satisfied? I feel better; I've had the satisfaction of letting you know how I felt when I read your letter of April 9.

Chloe mailed her response on May 3, in care of the American Express office in Paris. The letter was redirected to London, but Levi would not arrive there until May 20.

Paris, France
May 24, 1926

Dear Chloe,

I received your last letter in London about a week ago

and it took until now for me to "cool off" sufficiently to write. Possibly you will think I did not wait long enough — however.

It may seem strange to you that people that drink intoxicating beverages should resent being classed as drunkards. Most of them do and none resent it more than I.

The day is too beautiful for me to say more of what I thought of your letter or answer your question in regard to the English.

This one argument took almost two months to hash out, something that may have taken only minutes if discussed face-to-face. The topics were not overly important. None compared to the religious difficulties they were experiencing.

Even after this length of time, there was no true resolution. The feelings they expressed were stronger in written form. Any thoughts that were meant as humorous sarcasm did not travel well preserved on paper.

CHAPTER 66
CHARTRES'S MEDIEVAL GLASS

Tours, France
April 10, 1926
[travel journal]

We have been out of Paris six days, first going to Chartres and enjoying that cathedral very much. The stained glass is especially wonderful and makes one feel as if he were listening to some grand symphony when he gazes on the rose window.

The windows at Chartres Cathedral depict a variety of religious scenes; 167 stained glass windows date from 1190-1220. "The Blue Virgin" window, *Notre Dame de la Belle-Verrière* (Our Lady of the Beautiful Window), has been referred to as the most famous window in the world. It is located on the south side of the cathedral near the entrance to the choir. The four central panels of the window, where the Virgin Mary and Christ are located, survived the fire of 1194. They originally hung elsewhere in the cathedral. In the thirteenth century, the panels were encircled with additional glasswork, increasing the overall dimensions of the window (Connick 179).

The scenes at Chartres were created using a combination of five different colors of stained glass: red, blue, green, purple, and yellow. Various oxides were added to the glass to alter the color when heated. Red came from oxidized copper, blue from cobalt, green from iron, and purple from manganese. The yellow was formed by using sulfur or soot.

Forty-two windows were donated by local merchants and tradesmen, which incorporate their images near the bottom of the window: wine merchants, carpenters, wheelwrights, coopers, and others.

Levi mentioned only one rose window, but Chartres has three. He most likely meant the largest, located above the Royal Portal at the main entrance on the west side. Jesus is seated above the center doorway.

The easiest way to identify a cathedral as being Chartres is to inspect the spires. The oldest spire is Romanesque, dating from the 1140s, located to the right of the main entrance. The matching spire was lost during the fire of 1194 and rebuilt in the early sixteenth century. It is an example of the late Gothic style known as Flamboyant. The name fits the intricate design, which does attract attention.

These images are from a souvenir booklet Levi purchased. Printed on a military green cover is *Cathédrale de Chartres: Textes Français et Anglais*, attributed to a Parisian publishing house, Neurdin Freres, founded about 1885.

Incorporated in stone on the floor of the cathedral is a labyrinth from the thirteenth century. If the western façade were reflected onto

the floor, the center of the rose window would match up with the center of the labyrinth.

Dark and light stones were used in constructing the floor, forming a pathway for pilgrims to follow while meditating. According to Charles Chaliline's manuscript, circa 1640, a metal plaque was once located at the center, depicting Theseus and the Minotaur in combat (143-144).

Today, the chairs are moved and the labyrinth is revealed, offering the faithful a place for meditation every Friday from Lent until All Saints' Day, excluding Good Friday.

CHAPTER 67
SAINT MARTIN
PROTECTOR OF FRANCE

Tours, France
April 10, 1926
[travel journal]

In the Basilica of St. Martin here in Tours there is a
marble-Reconnaissance slab given to thanksgiving by
Marshal Foch and dated November 11, 1918. The basilica
is of Romanesque design and the interior is rather good.

This Romanesque and Byzantine structure, sometimes referred to as Neo-Byzantine, pales in comparison to its predecessor. The original medieval basilica burned several times and was always rebuilt, since it was a significant pilgrimage stop in the Middle Ages. This was the burial place of Saint Martin of Tours and Charlemagne's fourth wife, Luitgard. It was considered one of the largest places of worship in the Christian world.

Roman historian Sulpicius Severus recorded the life of Saint Martin in 397 AD in *Vita Sancti Martini.* Martin was a Roman soldier in the cavalry under Emperor Constantine. As the son of a veteran officer, Martin was required to serve Rome. He grew up in Northern Italy, where he was exposed to Christianity, the official religion of the Roman Empire as of 323 AD.

Severus knew Martin and told of his encounter with a poor man who was poorly clothed. Taking hold of his red Roman cape, Martin split the garment in two and gave half to the man in need. In a dream that night, the beggar turned into Christ, and it was He whom Martin had clothed. Shortly afterward, Martin embraced Christianity, was baptized, and left the cavalry.

Saint Martin's cloak had long been venerated and even carried into battle by armies that sought the intercession of the peace-loving saint. During the medieval period, the cloth and the miracles attributed to Saint Martin made Tours an important stop for pilgrims.

In 1562, the Huguenots ransacked Saint Martin's Basilica and destroyed his tomb. It was the French Revolution that brought about the complete demise of the enormous structure. To ensure that a new basilica would never be built on this site, two streets, Rue des Halles and Rue Descartes, were laid over the original location.

Today, the once-grand basilica is remembered through light-colored pavers along Rue de Halles, where the nave's columns once stood. Two towers survived and stand today: the *Tour de l'Horloge* (Clock Tower) and the *Tour Charlemagne* (Charlemagne's Tower). Originally, the *Tour de l'Horloge* stood to the right of the main western entrance, with the *Tour Charlemagne* at the end of the north transept. It is believed that Charlemagne's fourth and final wife, Luitgard, is buried beneath this tower.

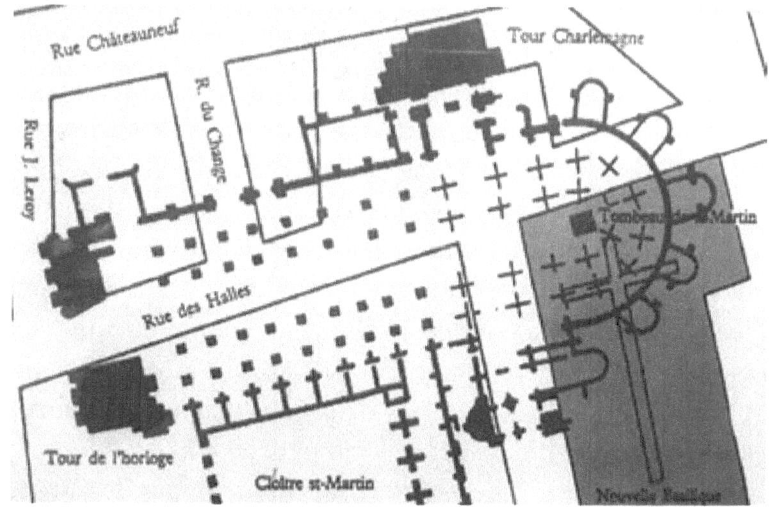

Levi's granddaughter, Barbara, provided images of items found in the basilica. The map on display there shows the location of the surviving towers, Saint Martin's tomb, and the new basilica. In 1860, the burial site of Saint Martin of Tours was found beneath a house on Rue des Halles. The church purchased the home and surrounding properties to build the new basilica on top of where the original altar once stood.

The crypt of the new basilica is lined with ex-votos, or offerings to the saint in thanksgiving for various answered prayers. The cream-colored stone panels are engraved in red to match the color of Saint Martin's cloak. Of the many ex-votos in the crypt, one caught Levi's attention.

This panel was presented by Marshal Ferdinand Foch, the French general who was Commander-in-Chief of the Allied Armies during the Great War. It is marked with the date of the signing of the armistice. The eleventh day of the eleventh month at eleven minutes past the eleventh hour was chosen in remembrance of Saint Martin, the patron saint of soldiers, whose feast day is November 11.

The flag shown here was not the official symbol for France. The Sacred Heart of Jesus was added to the white panel of the tricolored flag during World War I. Many French soldiers attached this flag to their uniforms, whether as a pin or patch, marking themselves as followers of Christ. These soldiers turned to Christ and called for the intercession of the soldier saint, Martin of Tours, for protection.

CHAPTER 68
REFLECTIONS FROM TOURS

Tours, France
April 10, 1926
[travel journal]

[We traveled] *from Chartres to Orleans and then to Blois where we "made" the chateau there, the one at Chambord and another at _______ . This trip out of Blois was made on bicycles which we rented. I'm still sore from the ride.*

From Blois to the Chateau of Ambois and then to Langeais and Azay le Rideau out of Tours. The chapel at Ambois is a little gem of a Gothic and Azay le Rideau is the best chateau I've seen. Am going out now to look the cathedral of Tours over again.

Connell is gone to see the Chateau of Chenonceau and I am waiting until he returns. We are then going to Angers.

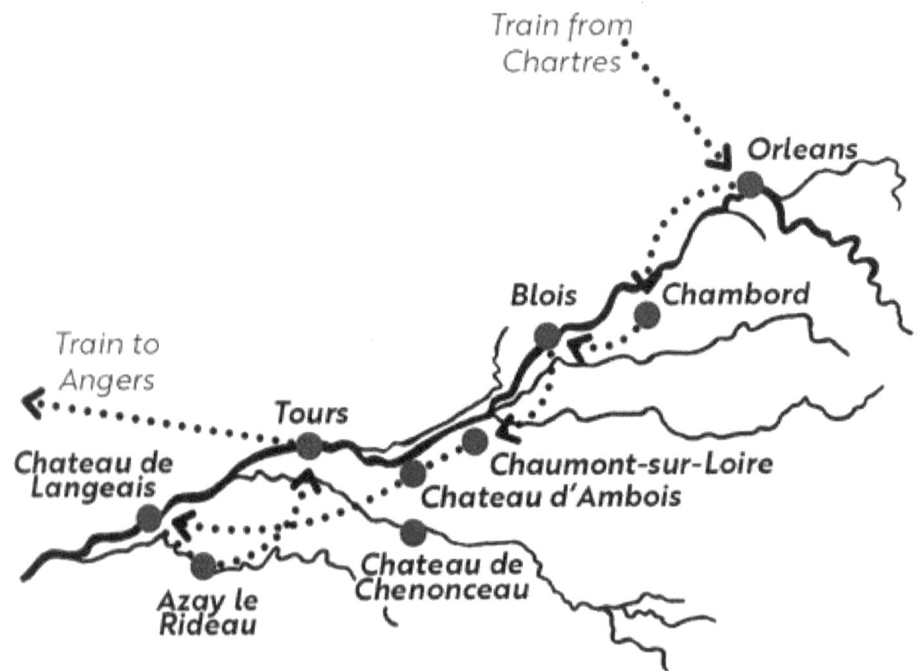

Quite a bit of travel took place in the days after Easter. The whole crew had been together in Paris, and now it was Levi and John in the Loire Valley. Lucky went off on his own adventures, and Vince stayed in Paris for work. There was no other mention of Harl, the one who tagged along to Versailles.

The chateaus the two visited, along with others in the area, witnessed many historical events over the years. Within these walls, a Catholic duke was assassinated as well as his brother, a cardinal, at the order of a Protestant king, Henry III. Frère Jacques, no relation to the children's nursery rhyme, guaranteed that the king followed them into the afterlife.

The blank line Levi wrote in his travel journal was a placeholder for the name of a chateau that evaded him. It could have been one of several found along a bike route from Blois to Tours. Originally, the Chateau de la Vicomte and the Chateau de Fourchette were considered. Thankfully, John Connell's daughter Cathy solved the mini mystery.

Among the sketches that John made during those April days biking through the Loire Valley, a door handle appeared which he identified as being from Chaumont-sur-Loire. Fitting perfectly in the route between Blois and Tours, it was the Château de Chaumont that did not come to mind when Levi wrote in his journal. Jacques-Donatien Le Ray de Chaumont lost this chateau along with his fortune after financially supporting America in her fight for freedom from imperial rule.

The *little gem of a Gothic chapel* is on the grounds of the Chateau d'Amboise. Levi's photograph of the entry to the Chapel of Saint Hubert is shown here. Charles VIII had this chapel built atop the protective wall for his wife, Anne of Brittany. The royal family abandoned the beautiful Chateau d'Amboise in 1560 due to the stench of rotting Huguenot corpses that littered the grounds after they tried

to overtake the French monarchy.

A familiar notable is buried here. Leonardo da Vinci lived out his final years as the guest of King Francois I. After he died in 1519, Da Vinci was interred at the Chapel Saint-Florentin on the grounds of the royal Château d'Amboise. That structure and many others on the grounds were later destroyed. The tomb of Da Vinci was located, and his remains were reinterred in the Chapel of Saint Hubert.

In Levi's sketchpad, a corner of Château de Langeais was drawn on April 9, 1926, from the viewpoint at Rue Foulques Nerra, shown below. This is the most medieval of the chateaus in the Loire Valley and one of the oldest, built in the 1460s. Langeais hosted Charles VIII in 1491, as he wed Anne of Britany.

By remaining in Tours while John ventured out alone, Levi missed the beauty of Chenonceau. It was there in July of 1559 that King Henry II's widow, Catherine de Medici, Queen of France, cast out Diane de Poitiers. Diane had been the king's mistress who received Chenonceau as a gift from the king. Diane was not left destitute; the chateau that Levi left unnamed, Chaumont-sur-Loire, became her home in exchange.

Chenonceau rivaled Levi's favorite, Azay-le-Rideau, reflecting into the Cher River Azay-le-Rideau does into the Indre.

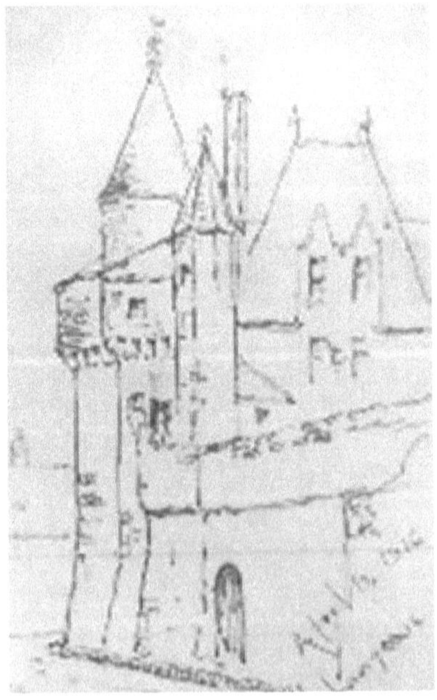

CHAPTER 69
LOVE AND RELIGION

Wednesday Afternoon
April 14, 1926

Dear Lee,

Very little of importance has happened since I last wrote — there was enough gossip last time, do I hear you say?

I went home for the Easter holidays and acquired a cold — a very bad one, so bad that I'm in bed to-day. All because I wore my spring coat and didn't take my winter one. I'm paying for it now. I hope to be able to go to school tomorrow — it's too lonely to stay here when the others are gone. My father once said that he'd never been lonely but he had a habit of talking to himself, when alone, so this accounts for his statement, I suppose. Maybe I'll try his stunt before the day is o'er.

We like our new apartment very much — of course I miss the rest of the gang — Ruth wrote me last Sunday (a week) that she and Gertrude liked their abode very much and that she wanted me to come to see her when I came back. Va. says that she doesn't want Ruth to come here when she's home —

Grace hasn't expressed herself on the subject but I suppose she feels the same way. So if I see Ruth I'll have to meet her out. Does this sound ridiculous to you? You "predicted this" didn't you? That used to be a favorite expression of my father's when something he foretold came true.

Va. says that you must have been crazy when you wrote the caterpillar poem. As for the other, it is pretty, but you shouldn't have written it. You know this just as well as I do. I'm afraid you have forgotten what we agreed to before you left.

The poem that Levi wrote, which Chloe said he should not have written, appeared as part of Levi's March 19 letter from Madrid. Without the addition of a title, he began with:

Here is an example of what red wine will do to a man:

Long years I searched the indifferent skies,
And then my star shown clear.
I would have grasped it heeding not
The danger I should fear.

Its holy radiance blinding me,
Bewildered I wandered till
Times' soothing hand upon my brow,
Subdued the unruly will.

Tenderly scarred I look again
My quest an unconscious prayer;
Wondering what shall guide me now,
And lo! My star is there.

Levi wrote of his lengthy search for his one true love, using the skies as a metaphor. The skies had been indifferent, neither good nor bad. No person held his interest until his star shone clear when he found Chloe. Levi would have grasped that love and paid no attention to potential danger, but the "holy radiance" was certainly hard to ignore.

Any relationship where you sense you have found your one true love comes with a sense of danger that brings fear. It may be the sense of wanting to protect the heart, but when you find your one true star, losing your heart is the goal. Overwhelming concern arises from feeling unworthy, sensing you do not match the other person in a way that would assure permanence. If this was Levi's fear, it was not the main source.

In this case, the danger to fear was their religious differences. Chloe had a holy radiance that left Levi bewildered and aimlessly wandering, both figuratively and literally. He saw her as a devout believer.

He found the passing of time soothing, as shown by his unruly will to pursue the one he loved, having been subdued. Levi was not harmed during his pursuit of perfect companionship. He was tenderly scarred, and he subconsciously prayed for a companion. Levi's search was for that one who would guide him and put him on track for the future.

Similarly, the Three Kings searched the skies for a star. Matthew 2:9 says, "and lo, the star, which they saw in the east, went before them" (The Holy Bible 882). This was taken from Chloe's Bible. Levi's Bible used the synonym, "behold," while "Lo" was uniquely Protestant.

Chloe's letter continued and ended on a happy note.

> *If you look like the man in the comic picture you sent I suppose you'll expect me to look like the woman. Horrors! Let's hope for the best.*
>
> *Sincerely, Chloe*

CHAPTER 70
CROSSING CENTURIES

Le Mans, France
April 10, 1926
[travel journal]

Just can't make myself realize that it is the month of April already. We spent this afternoon in Angers a la American Express style. The interior of St. Laud and the cathedral were fair. Of St. Laud one can say more. It was very good modern Romanesque. There is some very good Romanesque detail in an old arcade the remains of which are in the Prefecture of the city.

A quick train ride took John and Levi from Tours to Angers, France. Given their short stay in Angers, they might have missed Saint Laud church, but it is located in proximity to the train station. Saint Laud church, the Cathedral of Saint Maurice, and the Maine-et-Loire prefecture can all be seen within a twenty-minute walk of town. Even the Chateau d'Angers could be added with no additional effort, but the Cathedral of Saint Maurice made Angers a required stop.

Eglise Saint Laud was a six-minute walk up Rue Marceau. Levi described it as modern Romanesque, which can also be termed neo-Romanesque or Romanesque Revival. It was not constructed in the eleventh century like most Romanesque architecture, but instead during the resurgence of the Roman style used in the mid-nineteenth century.

At Saint Laud, there is a large stained-glass window in the transept. It is filled with images from the life of Foulques V, the Count of Anjou, who came from this area. He became the king of Jerusalem alongside his second wife, Queen Melisende.

Two bombs severely damaged this church during World War II, had the 1876 window was left in pieces. Five thousand shards of glass were recovered, and master glassmaker Éric Boucher reassembled the window. The resulting beauty returned to the church in 2008, sixty-four years after the bombing.

A quick comparison of Saint Laud church with the Cathedral of Saint Maurice makes the former seem older. The cathedral transitions from Romanesque to Gothic and Baroque. The Gothic additions to the cathedral are specifically Angevin Gothic, which flourished in this area during the twelfth and thirteenth centuries. Visible characteristics of this style are found in the single dominant nave and the use of thick walls to support the vaults instead of buttresses. Many of the ribs in the ceiling are elaborate, and the vaults are high, giving almost a dome-like appearance.

The Baroque takes center stage at the baldachin, or canopy, that draws the eye to the main altar. Baroque carvings also support the organ's pipes that rise to the ceiling above the main entrance. The cathedral embraces the centuries of construction that created the structure seen today.

Saint Maurice Cathedral also endured the destruction of its medieval stained-glass windows during the bombings of 1944. While some of the windows were removed for protection, others were destroyed. Some retain very few fragments of medieval glass.

Levi mentioned the prefecture or government office building. This was originally Saint-Aubin Abbey, which dates back to the eleventh century. The arcades, or grouping of continuous arches, were part of the cloister. These arches and supporting columns, a door from the old chapter house, and a twelfth-century tower are all that remain of the old abbey.

The two travelers continued onward that same day to Le Mans.

Le Mans Cathedral, also known as the Cathedral of Saint Julien of Le Mans, is less than a thirty-minute walk from the train station. Levi's description of the cathedral was part of the same journal entry from April 10.

Le Mans Cathedral was very interesting with its Romanesque Nave and its Gothic transept and Apse.

The Romanesque nave dates to the eleventh and twelfth centuries. Rounded arches surround the faithful and reflect this architectural style. The original wooden roof burned in 1134 and was replaced by stone vaults. There are many similarities between this cathedral and the one in Angers.

The transept and apse are Gothic due to a mid-1200s expansion. They removed the Romanesque chancel and broke through the protective Roman walls to enlarge the church. Gothic features common in the thirteenth century became part of the overall design. Chapels radiate out from the new apse in much the same way they had in the earlier version. The north transept is shorter, missing the Romanesque tower that once stood there. A rose window from the fifteenth century adorns that end of the transept.

One of France's oldest stained-glass windows is in the south aisle. The 1120 Ascension Window hangs in its original location. The background of the panels mimics a hopscotch court with alternating rectangles of red and blue.

Reading from bottom to top, the lowest level has two blue panels, one to either side of a center red rectangle. The pattern alternates at the next level, moving blue to the center, flanked by red panels. Shown within these panels are six of the twelve apostles. On the third level, the backgrounds return to two blue panels astride one red. Three apostles are in each of the blue panels, and the crowned Virgin Mary takes the center red space. She wears a blue garment with a white veil, contrasting with the deep red background. All thirteen individuals have their faces either turned upwards, observing, or downwards in prayer, as they witness the Ascension of Christ. The fourth and final level repeats the anticipated blue center and red sides. It is curved at the top in Romanesque fashion, fitting the opening. The brighter blue panel depicts Christ's ascension, while the deeper red panels to either side add the darkness needed to define His route.

As was the case in Angers, the prefecture for Sarthe is located within the ruins of an old abbey, Saint-Pierre de la Couture. Notre Dame de la Couture, which was once the abbey church, sits next door. This photo was taken as Levi faced east toward the altar, surrounded by Romanesque arches. The ambulatory is located just out of sight in the darkness. Early Gothic plate tracery allowed light to enter through the lancet windows, trefoils, and quatrefoils.

Le Mans not only linked the Notre Dame University alumni to the town through architecture, but a founding father who was important to Levi and John got his start here. Blessed Basil Moreau was a Le Mans priest. He was born in a nearby town at the turn of the nineteenth century. In 1837, Blessed Basil formed the *Congregatio a Sancta Cruce* (Congregation of the Holy Cross or C.S.C.).

Father Edward Sorin was among the first to become part of Moreau's new Congregation. The young priest and six Holy Cross brothers were sent out from the chapel in Le Mans to spread the mission of their Congregation to America. They departed in August of 1841. By 1844, the Indiana General Assembly issued the required college charter, and the University of Notre Dame was formed. This founding father became the first president, a position he held until 1865.

In Levi's college scrapbook, the photo shown on the next page was titled, "Our Lady's own Notre Dame." The building closest to the lower wing of the biplane is Old College. It is a small, light brick building with a dark roof that faces Saint Mary's Lake. This was the first building Father Sorin and the others in his group built on

campus.

Father Sorin is buried in Holy Cross Cemetery on the strip of land between the two lakes. The Old College building is almost visible from his final resting place. In 2016, Levi's eldest son, Father Joseph Geniesse, C.S.C., was buried here among many other Holy Cross priests and brothers.

CHAPTER 71
NOTRE-DAME d'AMIENS

April 15, 1926
Beauvais, France
[travel journal]

Left Paris this morning on our way to Belgium. After leaving Chartres I went to Paris and did little there but plan to leave the city. John intends to sail from Ireland and I intend to come back to France. Was out to see C. McCabe and his wife last night. Two bottles of port and one of Mousseau (Mousseux) were used to initiate the Barretts, brother and sister, into the fraternity of "wets." Their adversion to liquor is slowly disappearing in "La Belle France."

Beauvais is north and slightly west of Paris. It is located a similar distance from the City of Love as Chartres is to the southwest. There is no mention or a single photograph of the magnificent Gothic cathedral in Beauvais, La Cathédrale Saint-Pierre. The vaulted ceiling of the choir is the highest of all Gothic cathedrals. The rose window is topped with the rose of creation in the stone tracery. The vines, leaves, and several figures are carved in stone or created from plaster. Several of the sculptures lost their heads during the Revolution, but much of the beautiful work has survived. Levi reflected on Amiens from Amsterdam.

April 21, 1926
Amsterdam
⌈travel journal⌉

> *From Beauvais we went to Amiens where we saw a*
> *beautifully proportioned church but without its stained glass.*
> *From Amiens we rode straight into Belgium.*

Levi wrote no more in his journal about the thirteenth-century Gothic beauty, but the place is worthy of further description. Inside the cathedral at Amiens, a vaulted ceiling towers above a two-toned floor of blue-black and aged white tiles. There are many cathedrals attributed to *Notre-Dame* (Our Lady) in France: Paris, Chartres, Amiens, Reims, Laon, etc.

Notre Dame de Amiens is the largest Gothic cathedral in all of France. The western façade compares in design to the other cathedrals, but Notre Dame de Amiens extends 23 feet past the cathedral in Reims and is 49 feet longer than Chartres. The structure at Amiens is three times taller than it is wide. The entirety of Notre-Dame de Paris could fit inside Amiens' cathedral twice with room to spare.

In an April 19 letter to Chloe sent from Amsterdam, Levi offered a bit more detail.

> *We were just a bit disappointed in our last cathedral*
> *in France. Amiens with the best part of its stained glass*
> *destroyed lacks something that can be found only at Notre*
> *Dame of Paris and that of Chartres. Haven't seen Rheims*
> *yet but John and Vic tell me that the greater part is de-*
> *stroyed. That would be a black mark against the Germans*
> *if there were not something to their story that the French*
> *were using the towers of Rheims for an artillery observation*
> *post. After comparing French and German attitudes toward*
> *churches I'm inclined to believe the Germans, - but that's*
> *hardly news or history.*

It turns out that the stained glass was not destroyed during World

War I. Amiens Cathedral was only slightly damaged thanks to the intervention of Pope Benedict XV, who persuaded the Germans to turn their guns away from the cathedral. An article appeared in the *Green Bay Press-Gazette* on June 19, 1918. News had come out of the Washington headquarters of the National Geographical Society.

> **In some respects the reported destruction of the Cathedral of Amiens at the hands of the Germans, whose big guns have been bombarding the ancient capital of Picardy for several weeks, is almost as great a loss to the art world as the demolition of the more historic Cathedral of Rheims.**
>
> **That scene is gone forever for Amiens. Her noble and ancient place of worship is a shattered, smoldering ruin; her devout multitude is scattered – homeless and helpless. The spirit of Amiens alone survives (Cathedral at Amiens 6).**

The report could not have been more wrong. The stained glass was gone, but not at the hands of the Germans.

In preparation for war, all of the stained glass was removed for safekeeping. In 1920, a fire broke out while the stained glass was in storage, destroying these medieval masterpieces. What could be salvaged was returned to the church or used to construct new panels. Clear glass was used to replace the missing panels. Bright white light fills the nave now, where dim, colorful light once shone.

The *Green Bay Press-Gazette* article redeemed itself by including a visitor's first-hand impression of Amiens Cathedral in 1838. Due to the fire, Levi was not able to see Amien in this colorful light.

> **If you [have] never heard of [or] seen it, you cannot imagine the sublimity of a procession in such a church as that of Amiens. I can almost fancy that I see it now, as I saw it for the first time. The stupendous height of the vaulted roof, the rich foliage of the piers, -- the tall lancet arches throwing themselves upward, -- the richness of the stained-glass, the glow of the sunlight on**

the southern chapels, -- the knotted intricacies of the vaulting ribs, -- the flowers, and wreaths, the holy symbols that hang self-poised over the head, -- the graceful shafts of the triforium, -- the carved angels that with outstretched wings keep guard over the sacred building, -- the delicately carved choir stalls, -- the gorgeous altar seen faintly beyond, -- the sublime apse, with its inimitable slim lancets, carrying the eye up, higher and higher, through the dark triforium gallery, through the blaze of the crimson clerestory, to the solemn grandeur of the vaulted roof, lights and carving, and jewels and gold, and the sunny brightness of the nave, and the solemn greyness of the choir, -- these all are but accessories to the scene (Cathedral at Amiens 6).

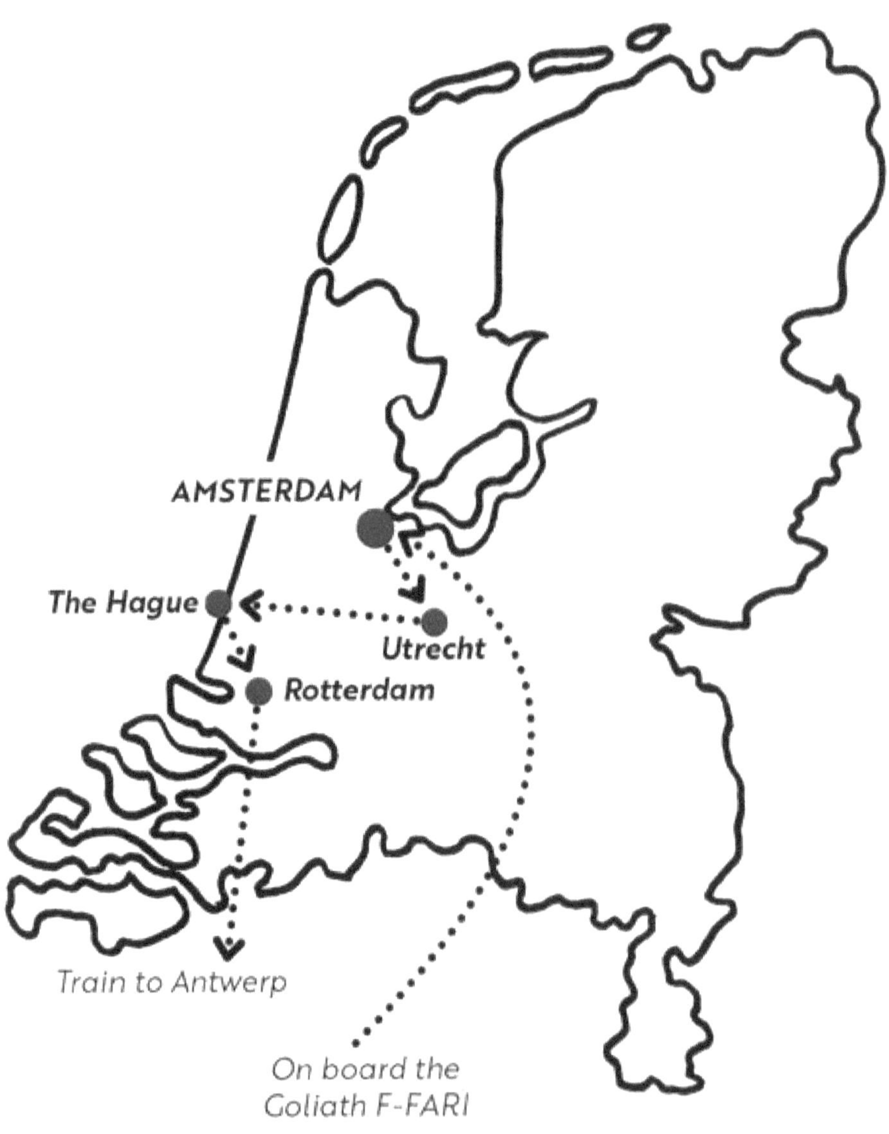
AMSTERDAM
The Hague
Utrecht
Rotterdam
Train to Antwerp
On board the
Goliath F-FARI

THE NETHERLANDS
April 1926

CHAPTER 72
IN AND OUT OF BELGIUM

Amsterdamn, Holland
April 19, 1926

Dear Father,

Arrived here this afternoon from Brussels. Connell wanted to come thru to here now so that we 'make' Holland together. We shall spend about four days in the "Pays-Bays" [Netherlands] then back to Brussels. From what we saw of Brussels we decided it was a fine place but let me say here that the natives don't know how to talk Belgian. Some of them talk French and the rest talk Dutch. All signs are printed in these two languages and in some places they also print them in English. There seems to be a great number of English in Belgium and in Holland. Arriving here today the first four people we met could speak a few words of English so that when we meet a word like "Reisgoedbewaarplaats" which is the Belgian word for luggage room we call on them and usually find that they can help us out.

Coming into Belgium from France we had a lot of fun with the customs officials. They went thru John's bag and made him carry half of his property to the appraisal office. After examining it carefully they let him off without paying any duty. They paid no attention to me whatever and treated me as if I had been a native but it's my guess that they were looking for "dope" in John's queer souvenirs.

The weather ------- in Paris it was great but ever since we got up into this section it reminds me of our record on the victrola which goes "Take me away from Belgium where it's rain, rain, rain".

From Amiens all the way to the Belgian border we saw signs of the fight that ended eight years ago. New villages alongside of the foundations of their old towns, fields which are still pot-marked with shellfire and here and there signs of some partly filled trench, and of course the neat little cemeterys (but many of them) with their "crosses row on row".

The French have made a great effort to erase the signs of war. Brick and tile factorys have sprung up to fill the great demand for building and all new houses etc. are of salmon brick and red tile roofs much like that on St. John's church .

In Belgium we see less signs of damage as it seems that the Belgian is much better off financially than the French.

In Holland from what we've seen in a couple hours here prices seem to be about the same as America which means that we shall be getting out as soon as possible. We shall probably see The Hague, Rotterdam, Utrecht then back to Antwerp, Belgium, then Malines where Cardinal Mercier had his cathedral, Louvain, Naur, Liege, Bruges and Ghent. Then over to England from Ostend.

From what we've seen the Belgians seem to be good Catholics, in fact the best yet. Today is the first time we've been in a Protestant country since leaving the United States and that means I'll have to stop genuflecting without looking on entering a church.

The beer is good and my chest expansion is increasing rapidly. It costs from 3 to 5 cents a large glass and one of the best known brands in Brussels carrys the name of Vandenheuvel. Sometimes the place reminds me of Green Bay with so many names and faces that resemble those at home.

When you get this both John and I will be in England. From there he intends to go to Ireland and then sail home. I have a question mark behind Ireland but intend to go back to France again and probably sail from Cherbourg – If present plans hold out I shall be home for Oswalds graduation. I would land in New York, stop a couple days in Washington then come straight to South Bend. If you want me to come all the way home first I can make that just as well. If you can't decide now you can write later in care of Clay at Washington.

With love, Levi

This letter requires a few corrections; the word for luggage room is Reisgoed Bewaarplaats, and it is Dutch, not Belgian.

On occasion, Levi will write two letters at one sitting, though only one letter is included in his story. Often, only one letter will be included to avoid repeating information. This is one time when two letters were written back-to-back, but they were completely different. Levi even recorded the town differently; Amsterdamn, Holland, to his father, and Amsterdam, Europe, to Chloe. While his letter home began plainly, Levi's letter to Chloe painted a completely different approach.

Amsterdam, Europe
April 19, 1926

Dear Chloe,

We came down out of the clouds into Holland and after searching a while the pilot found a small plot of grass to jolt us to a stop. The end of a miserable hour and three quarters (I counted every minute of it) in which I had reminiscences of the time I learned to chew tobacco. At first I was afraid we would fall on the roof of some Dutch gabled house and then I feared that we wouldn't. So much for the Imperial Airways. I would say more but my eyes fill with tears and I sniff, sniff, sniff --- all because it was much colder up there than the place we fully expected to find ourselves.

We left Brussels this noon after enjoying the Belgian lace factories — and the brewerys. It is a healthful city and my chest expansion is increasing steadily. As John says, "If this keeps up I'll be able to run for alderman when I get home." Amsterdam also seems to be a fine place to train politicians.

But of Amsterdam let it be said that the waitress did not faint when I asked for a glass of milk — not to drink of course but after this length of time one gets curious. — Brussels is a beautiful place and we shall be back there again. Can you imagine two able bodied men (except that I have a hole in one shoe) spending two nights and some francs listening to Belgian grand opera where we should have been out where 'men are men' in the beer gardens.

They were "Gwendolyne" and "Taviata" and Connell admits they were all right so I have to grant him something when we get to Ireland. Not sure yet whether I'll cross the Irish Sea. That will depend on how I enjoy the channel trip.

I sure take off my hat to Johnny but if he really wanted to go to some cold climate he should have picked out Italy in the winter time. Here in Holland its not cold but an umbrella and rubbers are not out of place at any hour. The symbol of this country "the duck" or maybe it's a swan is very appropriate.

The day before leaving Paris John and I met an honest, genuine, aged in the wood American artist who took us up to his studio and showed us his works. There were no models around but we met his sister who is over here chaperoning him. Judging from the pictures we saw it was a wise thing to have her here. If I could meet a "cubist" painter now to explain what their work is all about I'd be satisfied that I have a start on studying modern "art". A few days ago we saw a painting in cubist style and after standing on our heads and shutting our eyes we decided it was a tree. If we had had more time possibly we would have arrived at which way was up but as one lady explained, possibly for our benefit, that to really appreciate modern work one must make an intelligent effort.

When you get this we'll be "doing" merry England and here's hoping we don't get the roast beef rare. The ales all right, we sampled that before deciding to cross the channel. Can't go up into Scotland because I'm afraid I'd get sick of oatmeal but we're taking a crate of oranges along to Ireland just to see what happens. Don't be hard on your seventh grade and write to,

Lee

P.S. Will be back to Paris in a month.

This was trans-Atlantic flirting at its best! Levi's letter was filled with tales of stunt flying, dangerous landings, and harsh winter survival. Chloe must have swooned as she read his letter. How could Chloe's roommate's beau, Johnny, have any comparative experiences?

Johnny was part of the base crew who supported Admiral Bird and his copilot, Bennett, in the first flight over the North Pole. Could winter in Italy be compared to summer at the North Pole? Hopefully, for Levi's sake, Chloe would be amazed by Levi's sense of adventure.

Levi kept this double-exposed photo for posterity. This plane belonged to the Lignes Farman fleet. Levi seemed confused about the name of the company that ran the flight. Imperial Airways offered several international flights beginning in 1924, but they flew out of Croydon Airport, south of London. John and Levi flew out of Brussels. Lignes Farman had the first regularly scheduled commercial international airline service, and they were the only company to

fly from Brussels to Amsterdam at that time.

The registration markings on the plane in the photo were F-FARI, a Farman F.60 Goliath, which was upgraded to an F.60bis in February 1926. The Goliath aircraft was a heavy bomber, designed for service in the Great War, but it was just completing the testing phase when the war ended. Retrofit to carry passengers instead of bombs, this aircraft single-handedly created regularly scheduled commercial passenger airline service internationally.

A fabric-covered wooden frame formed the cabin. Four passengers sat in wicker chairs in the nose of the plane, ahead of the open cockpit, and eight additional passengers were seated in the larger rear compartment. The pilot perched in an elevated seat, visible from the walkway that separated the two passenger areas. The open cockpit placed the pilot between the parallel wings of the biplane, with one motor-driven propeller to either side. Landmarks on the ground were used as a guide.

On October 23, 1929, this Goliath, F-FARI, made an emergency landing in a field shortly after takeoff from Brussels Airport. The pilot, mechanic, and three passengers onboard evacuated without injury. The aircraft was damaged beyond repair (Hubert).

CHAPTER 73
PICTURES WORTH
143 WORDS

Levi's impressions of Utrecht, The Hague, and Rotterdam, as well as plans for Antwerp, Belgium, filled less than two pages of his small, black, leather-bound travel journal. Levi's trusty travel companion measured seven inches by four inches, and by the end of his journey, it contained 104 pages of Levi's innermost thoughts and reflections. The terms smidgen, scintilla, iota, and morsel are too large to describe what Levi wrote of the Netherlands. He turned, instead, to his Kodak camera.

In his letters and travel journal, Levi referred to these lowlands as Holland instead of the Netherlands. The two names have been used interchangeably over time, and some decades have used one term over the other, but they are not synonymous.

The Netherlands consists of twelve provinces, two of which include the word Holland: North Holland and South Holland. Since the three largest cities are in either North or South Holland, it is understandable why Holland prevailed as the term to describe these Dutch lands. In 2020, the Kingdom of the Netherlands formally removed the term Holland from its branding to spread tourism around to all twelve provinces.

Rotterdam is the second-largest city in the Netherlands, following Amsterdam. The Hague is the third largest, yet all there is to accompany this town in Levi's journal is the date they visited, April 22,

1926. Thankfully, when the pen failed, the camera assisted with the story.

Captured here is cart #4029 belonging to G.J. Voged, bloemist. The location is unknown but the term "bloemist" is Dutch for florist which links this photo to the Netherlands.

Levi often suffered from ulcer-like symptoms while he traveled. A longing for comfort appeared on his face as he posed beside a Melk cart, which is Dutch for milk. The Milwaukee front he wrote of gaining was missing from the photo. He had a long way to go before he would reach alderman status.

A furry sidekick seemed to be the norm among street vendors. This one hid stealthily beneath the carriage. In a 2017 Smithsonian Magazine article, Andrew Amelinckx wrote that dogs were often used to help farmers pull small carts from the country to the city to sell their wares in the streets. Amelinckx added that this was especially true in Belgium, France, Germany, and the Netherlands. The practice continued until the end of the nineteenth century, but was banned in England in the mid-1800s on the grounds of animal cruelty. Based on these photos, dogs were utilized well into the twentieth century, at least in the Netherlands.

In April 1926, Levi stood with his Kodak folding camera and captured the corner where Haarlemmerstraat crossed the Korte Prinsengracht canal.

After two days in Amsterdam, the traveling duo stopped off first at Utrecht, the fourth largest city in the Netherlands, and the capital of the province that shared the same name.

Utrecht
April 21, 1926
[travel journal]

Spent about four hours here and in that time saw several works of modern architecture which merit attention. The post office with its elliptical vaulting in black and yellow was especially noticeable.

The old post office's elliptical vaulting is not anticipated when viewed from the exterior. Converted into the Neude Library in 2020, the original beauty of the 1924 post office has been retained. Built in the Amsterdam School style, this space merges the beauty of nature and light with the strength of brick, softened by the curved ellipses of the vaulted ceiling. Contrasting black art deco figures accentuate the verticality of the room. The eye is drawn from one geometric shape to another. In his sketchbook, Levi captured the end of the elliptical studded space, where the clock continues to keep time.

On April 22, Levi noted nothing other than the date and their present location, *Den Haag* (The Hague). It is the capital of South Holland and home to the Peace Palace,

shown in the photograph below. Completed in 1913, the building had been functioning as a center for international law for 13 years when Levi stopped to take this photo.

Rotterdam
April 23, 1926
[travel journal]

*At The Hague we saw the Peace Palace, an art gallery
with Rembrants "School of Anatomy" and a few "true to
live pictures". – Also a large church that has been
Protestantized by removing the altar and facing all the pews
towards the pulpit.*

The gallery Levi mentioned is the Mauritshuis. The seventeenth-century residence of Count Johan Maurits of Nassau-Siegen was purchased by the state in 1820 to house the Royal Picture Gallery. Vermeer's famed *Girl with a Pearl Earring* hangs there. She is one of twelve paintings donated by art collector A. A. des Tombe upon his death. That single pearl has been a source of fixation since it joined the collection in 1902.

Levi made note of Rembrandt's *The Anatomy Lesson of Dr. Nicolaes Tulp* (1632). Seven surgeons were mesmerized by the teachings of Dr. Tulp during the dissection of a recently hanged thief, Adriaan Adriaanszoon, also known as Aris Kindt. Many have discussed the accuracy of the dissected left arm. One group noticed an error in the origin of a muscle, while others agreed that Rembrandt's representation of the scene was flawless.

The last place in The Hague was a church that was once Catholic, dedicated to Saint James the Greater, an apostle and cousin of Christ. Known as *Grote Kerk* (Great Church), this church became Protestant after the Reformation. The Grote Kerk is no longer used for weekly services, but the Dutch royal family continues to use this church for christenings and weddings. Dating back to the fifteenth century, this Gothic structure is an iconic landmark and a strong symbol of Dutch history in the center of The Hague.

Though Catholics were stripped of their churches, they were not completely deprived of being Catholic. Many converted for various reasons, but others created hidden churches to continue their pursuit of heaven according to their own teachings and traditions. Several of these clandestine churches have survived, such as Our Lord in the Attic and the Beguinage Chapel in Amsterdam.

Rotterdam
April 23, 1926
[travel journal]

We are leaving this place in half an hour for Antwerp
Belgium. Spent the morning along the waterfront watching
the boats loading and unloading for all parts of the world.
— A few minutes ago we had an argument over the price
of flounders and found that the "Dutch" are not to be left
behind in the grand scramble to cheat Americans.

Levi showed some fascination with the waterfront. Though these two waterfront photographs were not labeled, they appear to come from the port of Rotterdam. It was the top port of the Netherlands in 1926, a position formerly held by Amsterdam.

Netherlands
Ferry to
England
Ostend
Bruges
Ghent
Antwerp
Mechelen
Leuven
BRUSSELS
Liernu
Liège
St. Denis -Bovesse
Namur

BELGIUM
April 1926 - May 1926

CHAPTER 74
BELGIUM WITH JOHN

St. Denis – Bovesse, Belgium
April 28, 1926

After leaving Rotterdam we spent the next two nights in Antwerp where we "did" about all the dance halls in town. The cathedral was a bit disappointing but the art gallery is the best since leaving Paris. – A picture I shall especially remember is Pope (Julius?) and Luther by a modern painter. The seaport was interesting and watching the boats leave their sheltered places for the rushing tide and open sea provide examples of seamanship that I had never seen before.

No other ephemeral evidence of the dance halls that were "done" in Antwerp exists. There was no account written about the girls, their looks, movements, or language, both verbal and not. Were the fellas dressed to the nines, or did they spruce up their afternoon attire? Did they have a chance to hear a Mortier dance hall organ, or did live bands keep up with the latest hits? This information has unfortunately been lost to history

What has not been lost to history is Levi's surprising disappointment in the Cathedral of Our Lady in Antwerp. This is another soaring Gothic beauty built between the fourteenth and sixteenth centuries. It is the largest Gothic church in the Low Countries.

The structure was gutted by fire only twelve years after most of the initial construction was completed. The south tower was incomplete at the time of the fire, and progress was delayed and ultimately postponed while funds were put into rebuilding. In 1559, the church became a cathedral, housing the seat of the bishop after the establishment of the Diocese of Antwerp.

The Iconoclastic Fury of 1566 witnessed the destruction of the cathedral's interior once more. By 1581, Antwerp was under Protestant rule, and churches were to be "purified." Many art treasures were destroyed. Spanish rule returned in 1585, and the faithful embraced the Baroque. Peter Paul Rubens graced this space with his mastery in the early 1600s. Antwerp Cathedral is one of only a few churches to have originals painted by this Flemish Master hanging just where they did six hundred years ago. Though plundered by Napoleon and taken to Paris, each stolen painting had been returned by 1815.

Stepping through the western doors of the Cathedral of Our Lady in Antwerp transports visitors through time. Signs of Medieval life can be found. Previously hidden wall paintings have recently been discovered. The south tower was never completed but the original plan was for it to match the north tower in its majesty.

The final item mentioned from Levi's 1926 visit to Antwerp was a "modern painter's" portrait of Martin Luther and a pope, possibly Pope Julius. Though there are many museums in Antwerp and some were established prior to 1926, the one that became an obvious contender was the Royal Museum of Fine Art, known as the KMS-KA, *Koninklijk Museum van de Schone Kunsten. Pope Paul III in front of Luther's portrait* by Albrecht de Vriendt (1883) was acquired in 1885 and aligns with Levi's description.

Since Pope Julius was the Bishop of Rome in the fourth century, Levi undoubtedly meant Pope Julius II, who was pope for nine years just prior to the beginning of the Protestant Reformation. A comparison of portraits of both Pope Julius II and Pope Paul III exposed the potential confusion. Both popes dressed in red, had lengthy white beards, and held their position in the early sixteenth century. Though there were three popes between them, Julius II's papacy only predates Paul III by 21 years.

Pope Paul III, seated in the painting facing a portrait of Martin

Luther, was the first pope of the Counter-Reformation. He inaugurated the Council of Trent, excommunicated Henry VIII because of his divorce from Catherine of Aragon, commissioned Michelangelo to paint the Last Judgement on the wall of the Sistine Chapel, and supervised architectural work on the recently begun Saint Peter's Basilica in Rome. The placement of Pope Paul III with a portrait of Martin Luther exemplified the pope's dedication to reform within the Catholic church.

The visit to Antwerp ended with a trip to the seaport. This photo was either taken at the seaport of Antwerp or Rotterdam. Levi's journal entry from April 28 continued.

> *John and I stepped off at Maline to see the cathedral and the Hotel de Ville. From what we heard of the chimes they must provide wonderful music when played at their Monday night concerts. At Brussels we heard another opera called "Hansel and Gretel". John left for England where I shall meet him in about four days.*

Levi mentioned a few times his plan to stop in Malines to see Saint Rumbold, Cardinal Mercier's cathedral. Malines was a historical French name for the Belgian town of Mechelen.

The cardinal's cathedral was yet another Gothic beauty. This one is specifically Brabant Gothic, meaning that it features architectural influences from the Low Countries. An easy way to define Brabant Gothic is to note the type of stone used; in this part of Belgium and the Netherlands, limestone or sandstone was common. These softer stones allowed the carvings to be more intricate, but the crispness of the designs faded quickly due to erosion. Another interesting aspect of Brabant Gothic is that the style was often used in nonsecular buildings, such as town halls, the building Levi referred to as the Hotel de Ville.

Like all churches of this age, Saint Rumbold Cathedral is a survivor. Whether revolutions, religious wars, or world wars, this cathedral survived with many renovations made along the way. The tower was never completed due to financial constraints.

This was Cardinal Mercier's church. He was well known throughout Wisconsin as a Belgian Cardinal and only the second in Levi's lifetime. Cardinal Mercier was laid to rest in a crypt beneath the altar of the medieval church on January 28, 1926.

Cardinal Mercier earned his doctorate in philosophy from the University of Louvain in 1877. He traveled to America in the Fall of 1919 and made a plea for the $500,000 needed to rebuild and replace the university's library that the Germans destroyed. Levi mentioned the University of Louvain in his travel journal.

Ghent, Belgium
May 1, 1926
[travel journal]

> *Must mention here that I visited Louvain before going to Liege and had the superintendent of the Foundation company take me around the new library they are building for the University of Louvain with American donations.*

Louvain University is in Louvain-la-Neuve, Belgium, located southeast of Brussels. Cardinal Mercier did not live to see the fruits of his labor, but he was certainly aware that Americans had come through to replace the treasured structure. Many individuals and universities around the world helped restore the irreplaceable treasures that were lost. Unfortunately, the Germans set their sights on Louvain University's library again in World War II and destroyed the library once more.

CHAPTER 75
DIGGING UP BELGIAN ROOTS

Levi may have been a second-generation American, but his lineage was 100% Belgian. His parents were born in Door County, Wisconsin, to parents who were both Belgian immigrants. The cousin that Levi visited in Rome, Father J. B. Geniesse, was Levi's first cousin once removed. More roots of this family tree were found in Grandpa Geniesse's old hometown.

Liege, Belgium
April 27, 1926

Dear Father,

Am stopping here tonite and going on in the morning to Namur out of which I shall hunt up Louis Geniesse at a little village called Liernu which in turn is near another called St. Denis. He is an old man (about 65 years) living all alone and the last one of the relatives over here. You would laugh to hear me talk my "Walloon" never was good but after mixing it with French, Italian, Spanish and Arab it's a wonder that they can understand anything I say. For myself I understand practically everything and today in Liege I had no trouble getting by with my Belgian.

After about three more days in Belgium I'll join Connell in London. He left for England yesterday because he's eager to get to a place where he can talk too.

Walloon is a language, similar to French, which originated in the Wallonia region of Belgium. The language has four dialects depending on where in Wallonia it is spoken. Belgium is divided into three regions: Brussels, Wallonia, and Flanders.

St. Denis – Bouvesse, Belgium
April 29, 1926
[travel journal]

Am waiting here for the "Tooneville Trolley" to get to Liernu where I expect to find Louis Geniesse who is a very distant relative. Spent last night in Liege and this morning in Namur. – They are both picturesque spots and I felt much at home hearing the "Walloon" spoken which I am accustomed to in the settlements around Green Bay.

The "Tooneville Trolley" referred to a comic strip by Fontaine Talbot Fox Jr., which debuted in 1913. Fans followed the antics of locals from Toonerville, centered around their local trolley. It was one of the most popular comics during World War I. Many papers mistakenly labeled it the Tooneville Trolley, as Levi had in his journal. This sample appeared in the *Casper Daily Tribune* (6).

Pictured here, above, are two more of Levi's first cousins, once removed. Louis Geniesse is on the left, and John Baptiste is on the right. Both men are first cousins to Levi's father, Lewis, just as Father Geniesse in Rome. None of the three are brothers; they all come from separate lines, leading back to Levi's great-grandparents.

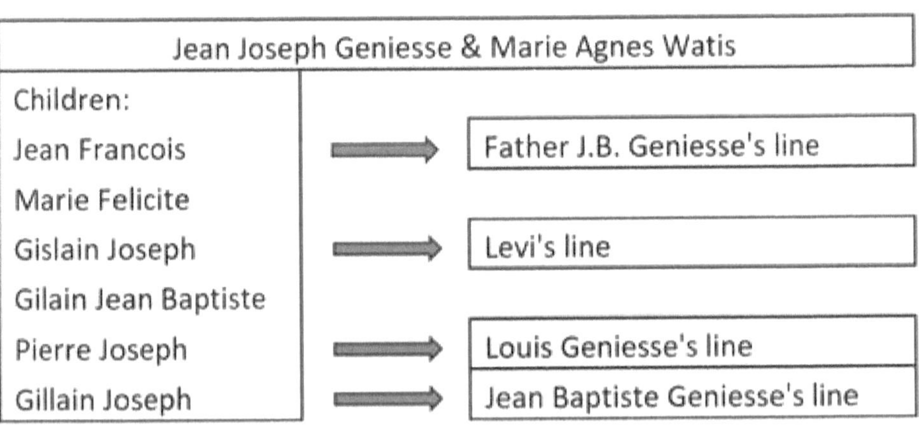

Jean Joseph Geniesse & Marie Agnes Watis	
Children:	
Jean Francois	→ Father J.B. Geniesse's line
Marie Felicite	
Gislain Joseph	→ Levi's line
Gilain Jean Baptiste	
Pierre Joseph	→ Louis Geniesse's line
Gillain Joseph	→ Jean Baptiste Geniesse's line

Oxford, England
May 6, 1926
[travel journal]

Of my trip to Namur I will now say a few words. I left Namur for St. Denis-Bouvesse and there I caught the "Tooneville Trolley" for Liernu. While waiting at St. Denis-Bouvesse I talk with the café owner there and was surprised when he asked me if I was from Green Bay, Wisconsin. His explanation was that seeing I was an American he thought I must be from the same section where so many Belgians from around that village had settled. — Getting off the tram at Liernu I started enquiring the way to the house of Louis Geniesse. Everyone would give me a different estimate of the distance but after about three-quarters of an hour of delightful walking where I enjoyed trying my "Walloon" on everyone I met I arrived at his home but was afraid to enter because of the dog he had guarding his gate. A neighbor showed me to his garden where when I had introduced myself he gave me the French salutation of three mouthfuls of whiskers then we had some fried ham together and I talked until dark with him another meal then some more family history until I saw he could hardly keep his eyes open. He is sixty nine years old and accustomed to go to bed early. The next morning he got up hours before I was awake and worked in his garden. The neighbors roosters awakened me and breakfast followed by more talk while waiting for another cousin to arrive from a neighboring village called Rhisnes. Louis and I finally set out to see the giant oak and the little church in which my grandfather was baptized. John Batiste arrived on his bicycle and I never saw a man more excited and delighted to see someone other than he to see even so distant a relative as

I. – After another meal together Louis took me to the steam-train station while John Batiste returned on his bicycle after making me promise to see his daughter in Namur if only for a few minutes. – I shall not forget the farewell with Louis whom I probably shall never see again. – Arriving at Namur I waited almost until train time before going to see Cousin Louise Geniesse. – She proved to be a wonderful girl and all the people in that store can vouch for me that I did not neglect my opportunities as a cousin.

She left work and I forgot my express train in the pleasure of her company. We took a long promenade together in which she talked to me as if we had known each other all our lives. I came near falling violently in love with her and it is just as well I had to leave that evening or -----. When I passed thru Rhisnes [the first station out of Namur] on my way to Brussels, John Batiste Geniesse and his family were lined up alongside the depot to wave me a farewell. It was almost dark when I sped by and the sight of them waiving me a goodby to carry across the ocean was something I shall never forget. – I had come to Namur wondering what to expect and I left pleased and full of kind thoughts for those who had remained to carry on in the old world.

Louis Geniesse took Levi through town to see the famous tree, the "Gros Chêne de Liernu." It is not the oldest nor the tallest tree in Belgium, but it is the thickest! The largest girth recorded to date is listed on the "Monumental Trees" website as 11.21 meters, by Jeroen Pater (Pedunculate Oak 'Gros Chêne de Liernu' on the Place de Liernu, Namur, Belgium).

During their walk about town, Levi was introduced to a man who remembered his paternal grandfather. Ghislain and his wife, Amelia, left Liernu in early 1856, seventy years before Levi's visit. In the photo on the next page, the only man old enough to match this description is the one on the left of the group, between the child and the cart-pulling oxen. The gentleman to the far right is 69-year-old

Louis Geniesse, born too late to have ever seen his uncle Ghislain.

A few lines in Levi's letter to his mother dated May 2, 1926, stood apart from the memory he recorded in his journal. He had this to say of his visit to see Louise Geniesse, Jean Baptiste's daughter, in Brussels.

> *John Batiste had insisted that I go back to Namur and take an Express train from there to Brussels meanwhile stopping to see his daughter (age 25) who worked there. He called her to tell her I was coming and when I arrived at the store rather reluctantly and found myself the center of curiosity of nine girls who were all waiting to see what Louise's cousin from America looked like. — Well Louise was a "knockout" and I made up for having to kiss so many whiskers before.*
>
> *My train left without me and we went for a four hours walk in which we talked "Walloon" together. She was very pleasant, attractive and intelligent and I don't know when*

I've enjoyed myself so much. If I had lingered longer there I might find myself coming home with a Belgian girl despite your warning. When I passed the little station where John Batiste lives he and several of his family were standing to watch for me as the train flashed by. Those people standing there waving to me as they receded into the dusk and I sped on towards Brussels made me realize how strong a blood tie is even though ever so remote.

Jean Baptiste's daughter and Levi's second cousin, Louise Geniesse, was special to Levi from the start. The two exchanged letters. Louise's letter in October was mailed from Rhisnes to South Clay Street in Green Bay. She started with *Cher cousin* (Dear cousin) and ended simply *Votre cousine Louise* (Your cousin Louise).

CHAPTER 76
FINAL BELGIAN DAYS

May 1, 1926
Ghent, Belgium
[travel journal]

Arrived here this afternoon and have a pair of sore feet from walking around the city. This place has some beautiful examples of architecture including three churches and a chateau which is about the best piece of military architecture I have seen.

Figuring out which churches and chateau Levi visited is an impossibility. The likely candidates are Saint Bavo, Saint Nicholas, and Saint Michael, with Gravensteen for the chateau. These structures are located along a 17-minute walk through the parts of Ghent most often visited. One can peer out over the walls of Gravensteen in one direction and see the architectural pieces that characterize these three churches.

Saint Bavo is the seat of the Diocese of Ghent, which makes it a safe choice. A mighty king was baptized here, Holy Roman Emperor Charles V. Suspended above the high altar is *The Conversion of Saint Bavo* by Peter Paul Rubens from 1623. This classic baroque painting captured the moment in time when Allowin, a Roman soldier living in Ghent, gave his money to the poor and his life to God. Though impressive, the Ghent Altarpiece draws the most attention.

Known as the *Adoration of the Mystic Lamb*, this masterpiece by the van Eyck brothers, Hubert and Jan, was unveiled on May 6, 1432. Eight exterior panels open from the center to reveal twelve interior pieces. The complete masterpiece was saved from destruction in 1566, threatened by a purifying Calvinist flame. The altarpiece was seized as the spoils of war and returned to the church through various means. Today, the original altarpiece is housed in a separate visitor's center and kept behind glass. If Levi visited this piece in 1926, it would have been one of the last times the complete altarpiece could have been viewed in situ.

From Saint Bavo, an architectural wonder is located just across the Sint-Baafsplein town square. Belfry Tower is a medieval structure that was used as a watchtower, storage for municipal archives, and a post from which to proclaim new laws to the populace. This is the tallest belfry in Belgium.

Continuing west of the tower is the church of Saint Nicholas. Built in the thirteenth century, this Late Gothic structure replaced a previous Romanesque house of worship. The tower located above the crossing is too massive to have gone unnoticed. The influence of the merchants who worshiped here is evident, but much has been taken from this church or destroyed over time.

It is hard to say what the church looked like in May of 1926. Many buildings once surrounded the structure and obstructed the view of the exterior walls of the church. Restoration began in 1912 with a plan to return Saint Nicholas to its thirteenth-century roots. Firmin De Smidt reported that reconstruction was not completed until after World War II. It is very likely that Saint Michael was the third cathedral. It is also possible that Levi reviewed the architecture of Saint Jacob or Saint Peter, but it would have been impossible to get to Gravensteen without noting Saint Michael.

This stroll through Ghent follows an "L" shape with Saint Michael located at the vertex. The Gothic structure dates to 1440, though it was not completed until 1825. One set of plans called for a tower surpassing that of Saint Bavo. The truncated tower fell prey to a lack of funds a few times over the years.

Many pieces of artwork adorn these hallowed walls, but two

from the seventeenth century are not to be missed. *Golgotha* by Anthony Van Dyck (1630) depicts Christ on the cross surrounded by the typical three who were present at the crucifixion: Mary, John, and Mary Magdalene. A statue of Mary, seated with the child Jesus standing before her, was inspired by Michelangelo but completed by Rombaut Pauwels. It is a beautiful rendition of a piece known as the Bruges Madonna.

Stepping away from the spiritual side of Ghent and crossing the river Lys (Leie in Dutch), a turn north leads to a grand medieval palace. Several buildings once butted up to the existing walls, much as they had at Saint Nicholas church. A resurgence in preserving Belgium's history began with the destruction of these buildings. By 1893, all signs of their existence had been removed, and the castle's need for restoration was exposed. Gravensteen was the face of Ghent during the World's Fair of 1913, and all restoration was completed in time for the international debut of the "Castle of the Counts."

Bruges, Belgium
May 2, 1926

Dear Mother,

I am writing this letter under difficulties. There is a grind organ under my window and from every part of the city you can hear noise that poses for music. Arrived here today from Ghent and found myself in the midst of a "fête". I had intended to leave here tonight for Ostend but they are going to have a big religious procession here tomorrow morning. It is an annual feast in honor of the Precious Blood of Christ. A vial of the Blood of Christ brought from the Holy Land in the tenth century is to be carried in procession. There is a special chapel built at Bruges to hold this relic and I went there this afternoon to venerate it. Bruges is a beautiful city with much fine old architecture. It reminds me of Venice with all its canals and waterways. Ghent was also very interesting and I wished I could have spent more time there but I promised Connell that I'd arrive in London May 3rd so I'm crossing the Channel tomorrow afternoon.

The Procession of the Holy Blood through the streets of Bruges dates back to 1303. On Ascension Thursday, forty days after Easter, various Christian communities celebrate the ascension of Christ into Heaven. On that day, a grand parade takes place in Bruges, and the reliquary of the Holy Blood is processed through the streets for all to see.

In the center of the above photograph is the shrine from 1617 that houses the Holy Blood. A vial was brought back from Jerusalem during the Second Crusade, and a piece of cloth reputed to have been soaked with the Holy Blood of Christ is visible through the glass. Joseph of Arimathea prepared Christ's body for burial after the crucifixion, and this piece of cloth is said to have been saved during the preparation.

On other days throughout the year, the relic resides in an upper chapel of the Basilica of the Holy Blood. This basilica is divided into two parts: the upper Gothic level and the lower, older, Romanesque chapel dedicated to Saint Basil. Various items from the Basilica are carried along with the Holy Blood. Shown in the inset on the following page is a carving of Mary holding the tortured Christ, known as the *Pieta*. Sculpted in 1900, this piece resides in the Chapel of Saint Basil.

Other reliquaries made their way through the streets of Bruges, alongside reenactments of important events related to the Holy Blood and the life of Christ.

BOCK GRUBER
RUBER

BOCK GRUBER

There were times when the city's government was Calvinist, and the vial was stored away for safety. Two hundred years later, the French occupied Bruges, and they put a stop to the procession of the Holy Blood as well.

In 1926, Easter fell on April 4, and Ascension Thursday would have fallen on May 13 that year. From 1303 until 1969, the procession took place on the first Monday after May 1. In 1926, that was the third of May, Levi's last day in Belgium. The procession began early enough to give Levi time to attend and still cross the channel to London.

If the parade route in 1926 followed the same path as it does today, the celebration would have begun in a well-known area of Bruges called the Rosary Quay or Rozenhoedkaai. Levi stood there and faced the Dijver Canal when he captured the iconic image of the Belfry of Bruges, shown on the left.

A six-minute walk southwest along the Dijver Canal leads to the Church of Our Lady, shown at the top of the next page. It is the second-tallest brick building in the world.

This church houses Michelangelo's Bruges Madonna, the only Michelangelo statue to leave Italy during his lifetime. The Bruges Madonna was later taken by French Revolutionaries and returned after Napoleon's defeat at the Battle of Waterloo. It was stolen again by retreating German forces during World War II, and the Monuments Men are credited with her safe return.

The present parade route turns at the Church of Our Lady and heads up Steenstraat. The street view at the bottom of the next page was taken from about 38 Steenstraat, roughly halfway between

Sint-Salvatorskathedraal (Saint Salvator Cathedral) and the Belfry of Bruges. Saint Salvator appears above in the distance.

Though the angle of earlier photograph makes the Belfry of Bruges appear to be at the end of a canal, it is not. The base of the tower faces *Grote Markt* (Market Square), the largest square in Bruges. This is the present-day end of the parade route.

The photo on the next page was taken from the southeast corner of the Market Square. The façade on the left belongs to the Belfry of Bruges. Less than a quarter of the square is visible in the photo.

After the celebration, Levi headed west to Ostend to catch a boat and cross the channel. John awaited his arrival in London.

Manchester
Retford
Lincoln
Liverpool
Peterborough
Ely
Worcester
Oxford
Cambridge
LONDON
Ferry from Belgium
Gloucester
Tewkesbury
Bristol
Dover
Bath
Winchester
Wells
South Hampton
Salisbury
Ferry to France

ENGLAND
May 1926

CHAPTER 77
A CONSTITUTIONAL MONARCHY

May 3, 1926, from the *Green Bay Press-Gazette*, page two.

GREAT BRITAIN FEELS GRIP OF LABOR'S MIGHT
Trades Union Makes Good Its Threat to Halt Industry

LONDON – (AP) – Great Britain today felt the grip of labor's might. At midnight the millions of workers under orders of the Trades Union congress quit their labors in a struggle to enforce the coal miners' stand against lower wages and increased hours.

By noon the streets of the capital were a maelstrom of milling pedestrians and crawling motor vehicles, with the unaffected workers striving to get to their places of business, while in some places radical strike sympathizers sought to turn them back.

Had Dramatic Setting

The beginning of the strike had a dramatic setting in London. Large crowds had gathered about the parliament houses and in Whitehall where they whiled away

their time singing the "Red Flag." Big Ben boomed out twelve (2).

"The Red Flag" was written in 1899 by Jim Connell. In 1926, baritone Rufus John, aka John Goss, recorded these lyrics to the tune of "O Tannenbaum." It started off like this:

> The people's flag is deepest red,
> It shrouded oft our martyred dead,
> And ere their limbs grew stiff and cold,
> Their hearts' blood dyed its every fold.
>
> So raise the scarlet standard high,
> Where in its shade we'll live or die,
> Though cowards flinch and traitors sneer,
> We'll keep the red flag flying here.

The red flags that waved in this crowd represented solidarity with the Trades Union Congress (TUC), a federation that represented most of the unionized workers in England.

On May 4, London locals received an update through the *Daily Mirror* on the status of life in London.

HYDE PARK CLOSED:
A GREAT MILK POOL FOR LONDON
FLEET OF OVER 200,000 CARS

In preparation for its use to-day as a great milk pool for London, Hyde Park was closed yesterday. Over 200,000 vehicles will be available for dispatch to milk producing centres, to collect milk and bring it back to London.

The Postmaster-General request that no telegrams should be sent or telephone calls made that are not absolutely necessary. No foreign or Colonial parcels will be accepted.

As in 1919, the milk will be rationed to the various districts should it not be found possible to maintain a full

supply. London Provision Exchange has stabilized last Friday's prices for cheese, butter, bacon, lard, etc., as the maximum until further notice (2).

Oxford, England
May 6, 1926
[travel journal]

Am writing this in a railroad lunch room here while waiting for a train to Worcester. Left London yesterday morning on foot because the general strike had stopped most transportation. Things look very serious for England and the people are talking of the possibility of a revolution. Arrived in London May 3rd, crossing from Ostend to Dover without being seasick.

Gloucester, England
May 7, 1926

Dear Chloe,

You would like England if it would only stop raining. I've been here five days and if my mother would know that my feet have been wet all that time she would probably send me a pair of rubbers.

Connell has stepped across the street to hear a labor union leader give a speech on the strike. By the time you get this letter the general strike here may be over or the British engaged in quelling a revolution. Things look very serious with practically all factories, railroads and steamship lines idle. I arrived in London just three hours before the Union men were called out and found Connell waiting for me and worrying how he would leave the country.

All buses, taxies, trams and subways have stopped in London so that we have found it hard to see the city and decided to take a hike through southern England carrying the usual toothbrush and a pair of socks somewhat in need of repair. Am trying to get used to wearing holy hosiery so that I'll not be forced into matrimony for that reason.

Traveling has been by foot, truck, bus, railroad and steam truck. We traveled from Oxford to Worcester in the first train over the road since the strike began. The whole system is run by volunteers as all unions have stopped work.

We have been to St. Albans, Oxford, Worcester and Tewkesbury before coming here. A church or abbey in each place has been of great interest. The different college buildings at Oxford are the best collection I have ever seen. The city is beautiful and I would enjoy nothing better than going to school there. The students wear the baggest of baggy clothes and I suppose they set the style for the rest of the college world but the average Englishman is little influenced by what the Prince of Wales or the boys at Oxford wear.

We have met some "decent" Englishmen and find, what we really expected, that the touring English are not typical of their country. The difference of language is more than we realized and every section of England has its own peculiar dialect sometimes unintelligible to natives from another corner of the country. You might be interested to know that our 'beautiful' Southern pronunciation resembles the middle cockney of the English. ----- John has come back all-het-up and says that the crowd in the hall are as intelligent as in a K.K.K. meeting. The speaker after the usual "down with the capitalist" speech started waving a red table cloth and red flags appeared all over the hall. The leader then said that Russia stood ready to help them and everyone cheered. – That incident is typical of the attitude of the laboring class in England. – In France there is great agitation for the restoration of the monarchy and Belgium is also on the edge of a civil war. Russia has just concluded a treaty with Germany and her munitions factories are working overtime. Everywhere people seem to be uneasy and the surprising thing is that the Europeans expect that we will be at war with Japan before long. What's more they predict the defeat of our country. All this is probably wild fancy but it certainly is interesting to us.

The government has taken over the distribution of the food supply and in London they have converted one of the parks into a giant milk depot. So far everything has been all right with us and we haven't noticed anybody profiteering with the excuse that there may be a food shortage later on.

The hotel man just told us that the lights will be turned off early because of lack of power. News has just come thru that a big section of London is in darkness so things are getting more exciting every minute.

In London you realized fully why the English flock to Paris. London is a big city, the biggest in the world, yet Chicago seems much larger to me. For me, their museums and galleries do not rank with those of the continent and at least Americans do not have to bow to England in that re-spect. The churches here [those of the Church of England] are kept in fine order and are not cluttered with all the brick-brack that mars the catholic edifices of the Continent. If good taste were the only argument I would surely become an Episcopalian.

This is all very dry I suppose but after arguing Socialism all day to keep ones mind off the blistered feet while bum-ming the road and can't force myself to talk of prohibition,

Expect to get home for my brother's graduation but with this strike I do not know just when you'll see,

Lee

P.S. Will not receive any more mail after June 28 (He meant to write May 28) *as I shall probably be back and leave Paris then. Save all the news until I drop in for my "feed".*

The first stop was Saint Albans, twenty miles from London's city center. Saint Alban was Britain's first Christian martyr and saint. Both he and the priest he sheltered were buried here. Their place of rest has been destroyed and restored over the years. Today, medieval shrines to Saint Alban and the priest he protected, Saint Amphibalus, are housed in the cathedral.

Saint Albans Cathedral influenced Levi's architectural style throughout his life's work. He embraced the simple, clean lines of the churches in England and used them throughout the years on the many municipal buildings he designed. The style of Saint Albans, Saint Sebastian church in Toledo, Spain, and a little mosque from the same Spanish town were major influences in Levi's design for Saint Hubert Catholic Church in Wisconsin, shown below. Though he longed to build a cathedral, this church in the Belgian area of Wisconsin's peninsula was the only one to come to fruition.

From Saint Albans, Levi and John headed to Oxford. Levi mentioned the Prince of Wales, Edward Albert Christian George

Andrew Patrick David. The future King Edward VIII also held the titles of Duke of Cornwall and Duke of Rothesay in 1926. Earlier, in October 1912, he became an Oxford man and was known throughout the 1920s for his sense of fashion. The effect that Oxford students had on fashion was an interesting observation, but Levi missed the bigger story from Oxford in the 1920s.

When Levi visited in 1926, women had recently earned the right to graduate from Oxford. For decades, they had been allowed to study but not graduate. Annie Rogers took her last finals in 1879 without fanfare, celebration, or credit. It was not until October 14, 1920, that Annie received the BA and MA she had earned at Oxford.

Setting fashion and education aside, it is not hard to understand why Levi was impressed by the buildings at Oxford University. Every century was represented, from the thirteenth-century University Church of Saint Mary the Virgin to the Outpatient Department for the Radcliffe Infirmary, the most recent twentieth-century addition in 1926. One of Europe's oldest libraries opened to students there in 1602. The world's oldest surviving museum building was completed in 1683.

Gloucester, England
May 8, 1927
[travel journal]

Arrived here last night from Worcester and stopping off
at Tewkesbury – Each of these places has a cathedral of
interest and Worcester has some fine modern stained glass.

Worcester Cathedral is a wonderful structure for architectural study. Almost every influence over centuries can be found there. Starting with the Romanesque, additions were made in the early and late Gothic periods. Levi focused on the stained glass there. The original medieval stained glass was lost during the English Civil War in the seventeenth century. The "modern" stained glass that Levi described was added during the Victorian Era, specifically in the 1860s and 1870s.

Levi wrote little to nothing of Tewkesbury, possibly because he was not aware of the story. Construction began at the turn of the twelfth century. This Romanesque architecture can be further defined as Norman, one of the finest examples in all of Britain. The tower rises above the cruciform building at the crossing, much like the tower at Saint Albans, though this tower climbs higher.

At the Battle of Tewkesbury, the heir apparent to the English throne died in battle. He was from the house of Lancaster and was buried at the abbey. His forces took refuge at Tewkesbury Abbey, but soldiers from the House of York forced their way in. The resulting bloodshed caused the abbey to be closed for a month to be cleaned, purified, and re-consecrated to God.

Another main event here was the selling of the abbey to the townspeople. All abbeys and monasteries were dissolved by the crown in the sixteenth century, which left this building's metal roof and church bells in line to be sold for scrap. The parishioners paid the value of the metal to the crown and saved the abbey.

Bristol, England
May 8, 1926
[travel journal]

Came by bus from Gloucester thru a delightful stretch of country. The cathedral and several other churches are of note and especially the tower of Bristol College.

Willis Memorial Tower at Bristol College stands as a memorial to the first chancellor, Henry Overton Wills III. Designed in 1915, the tower did not open to the public until June 1925, after delays caused by World War I. The vertical lines identify this structure as perpendicular Gothic, meaning that several parallel lines intersect the ground at a 90-degree angle.

Bath, England
May 9, 1926
[travel journal]

John and I are hiking on our way to Wells. We bummed a ride from Bristol to Bath on a gasoline truck. There was not much to see in this city. There are hot spring baths on the site of the old Roman Bath but we did not enter them.

The Roman baths in Bath were still used for bathing in 1926. While they are no longer open for use, visitors today can still enjoy the ancient Roman architecture.

A trip through Southwestern England would not be complete without seeing England's smallest city, Wells. When your heart belongs to a maiden with the last name of Wells, it would be a sacrilege to pass and not stop.

Wells, England
May 10, 1926
[travel journal]

Arrived here on the back of a steam truck, eyes filled
with cinders and looking like coal-heavers. The cathedral is
large but not especially good. There were several good pieces
of domestic architecture.

Those cinders must have clouded Levi's vision. The scissor arches of Wells Cathedral alone are magnificent. Added in the early to mid-1300s, the giant curved "X"-shaped supports function to support the weight of the center tower without impeding the view of the faithful. Wells Cathedral was the first Gothic cathedral in England and it is a real showstopper, especially the west façade where three hundred carved statues welcome the faithful.

Salisbury, England
May 11, 1926
[travel journal]

The spire of the cathedral here is one of the best I have
ever seen. Undoubtly it makes this cathedral one of the
leading churches architecturally in England.

It must be the height of the spire at Salisbury Cathedral that captured Levi's attention. The spire at Salisbury Cathedral is the tallest in England at 404 feet and predates Ulm Minster, the tallest church in the world at 530 feet, by over 500 years.

The Chapter House of Salisbury Cathedral contains the best of four existing copies of the first Magna Carta. Six different versions of the Magna Carta were issued from 1215 to 1300 under Kings John, Henry III, and Edward I. Levi's travel journal entry from Salisbury continued.

Had another quarrel with Connell, I lost my temper and I'm sorry for that. Our natures are as incompatible as could be. I had promised myself to keep my temper no matter what he said realizing that he never knows or realizes that he is insulting one. My resolution went up in a puff of flame and smoke. If I had not been so angry I would probably have said things I would regret. His last act on leaving the hotel was to hand me two pounds and leave his roll of tape behind.

For the moment, Levi was off to travel alone.

Stonehenge, England
May 11, 1926
[travel journal]

A ten mile bus ride and a two mile walk to see a pile of stones. Well I've been here now and no American Express tourist has anything on me.

Researchers debate the original purpose of this site. What is clear is that the stones were aligned with the solar system sometime between 3000 and 2000 BC. From Stonehenge, Levi trekked back to Salisbury.

Southampton, England
May 11, 1926
[travel journal]

Arrived here by rail from Salisbury about five o'clock this afternoon and after four hours along the dock watching the

Union pickets and the boats unloading I am ready to leave for Winchester. – The Agustania and the Homeric were in dock and are to leave on schedule despite of the strike. Two bus or "charabancs" arrived from London with passengers for the Homeric. The chimes in the Church of St. Mary which is near the cricket field were played this evening and sounded very well.

Unfortunately, Levi left his camera in London. Though Stonehenge has not changed over the last hundred years, and many of the places he visited remain mostly unchanged, a view of the docks, pickets, and ships during the strike of 1926 would have been a rare sight to behold.

On May 8, 1926, *The Brooklyn Daily Eagle* ran an Associated Press article in their New York paper. A few excerpts from that article gave impressions of Southampton during those tumultuous days.

AMERICANS, CURIOUS TO SEE STRIKE, QUIT LINERS FOR LONDON

Friends of arriving passengers on the Leviathan who went to meet the big liner at Southampton testified today to the absolute quietness of the countryside. The only sign of militancy, they said, consisted of a dozen armored cars, with tin-hatted crews, slowly moving toward London from the Aldershot military camp...All the big shipping companies report that they have been able to move their lorries to and from the ports without interference from the strikers, but they have prudently avoided passing through Eastleigh, a busy railway junction a few miles outside of Southampton...The Leviathan's wireless was kept busy receiving frantic messages from America directed to passengers by relatives and friends. These people, alarmed by the highly-colored dispatches in some American papers, picturing riot and bloodshed, begged the passengers to land at Cherbourg instead of Southampton. The messages were not without effect, and several persons changed their minds and

debarked at the French port...Altogether 300 passengers came to London in seven charabancs after spending last night aboard ship, while 60 came last evening in private motorcars...The pickets at the Southampton dock questioned the drivers of the lorries, but made no trouble... The White Star Line sent 62 passengers to Southampton to embark on the Pennland. The charabancs in which they were transported will serve to bring to London the passengers from the Homeric, due at Southampton at 3:00 p.m. (3).

The paper mentioned several ocean liners in and approaching Southampton. The Homeric, a liner from the White Star Line that both Levi and the Associated Press article mentioned, could transport 2,145 people, not including crew. In port that same day, May 11, was the Aquitania, a comparable vessel from the Cunard Line. Because of the strike, anyone disembarking from Southampton would have to travel in charabancs - large, covered carriages with bench seating, either horse-drawn or motor-driven. Given the 80-mile distance to London and each charabanc's ability to hold approximately 40 people, they were most likely motor-driven. What an amazing time for an American traveler to have four hours to sit, watch, and experience trying times in England.

Winchester, England
May 12, 1926
[travel journal]

The cathedral here is very good interiorly but the choir is disappointing because of the imitation stone vaulting. The reredos is very good and the traces of Norman work are also of value to the architect. Am now at the station trying to get a train to London.

Founded in 1079 and completed within 30 years, significant changes were made to the architecture of Winchester over the following 500 years. New architectural styles replaced the old throughout much of the cathedral.

The earliest sections are Norman architecture as seen in the transepts and crypt. These features are easily identified after a search for Romanesque curved arches and low, massive pillars. It was here that Levi found the traces of the Norman work he praised.

The architectural term *reredos* refers to an altarpiece or screen located behind the main altar, often referred to as the Great Screen. At the time of Levi's visit, the statues adorning this screen replaced the originals that were destroyed during the Reformation.

The vaulting of the choir is not stone, and Levi recorded his disappointment. The imitation stone vaulting he referred to is actually carved wood.

With the review of the longest medieval cathedral in the world completed, Levi's southwestern loop of England came to an end. A train ride stood between Levi, London, and hopefully John.

CHAPTER 78
STRIKE ENDS

On May 13, 1926, the front page of London's Daily Mirror featured the headline "Running Supplies Through the Strike Brigade," followed by two large photos.

The first photo showed people lining the streets, with four or five bicycles heading in one direction. On the opposite side of the road, a line of open-bed trucks marked "food only" in white paint stretched out as far as the eye could see down a straight London street. Two armed guards were seated on top of the supplies in each truck. The convoy left little space between the vehicles. The caption read, "A convoy of lorries with food on its way from the docks under military guard. – Armored cars acted as escort."

The second photo covered the remainder of the front page. A tugboat was shown, with two barges, captioned, "A tug, manned and guarded by sailors, towing barges laden with oil fuel up the Thames. The attempt to deprive London of its essential supplies has been promptly defeated by the authorities." These photos were misleading; the strike ended a little after 1:00 p.m. the day before.

Page two of the same edition began:

GENERAL STRIKE CALLED OFF

T.U.C. Decision after Downing St. Conference
PEACE AT LAST!
THE NATION HAS WON

We know that it will take weeks and months to repair the damage inflicted so rashly and wantonly upon the community. We can already see, in diminished employment, in the suffering of workers, in the waste of millions, the hideous results of the action of a group of fanatics who have posed as friends of the working men and women. The unconquerable spirit of our people has been aroused again in self-defence – as it was against the foreign foe in 1914.

The people of Britain have won this battle. But they have won more than a single battle.

They have won all battles of this kind – proved, once and for all, that they are stronger than those who try to stab them in the back...Once again they have secured, in Lincoln's famous words, that government of the people by the people shall not perish from the earth.

Any reader should have found this news confusing. Was the strike over, as reported on page two, or not, as the front page alluded? Levi also seemed a bit confused. If he secured a spot on the train from Winchester, then he arrived in London just as the strike ended. In a May 14 letter to his father, our man on the beat updated on the status of the strike.

> *With the strike still hanging on and all subways, street cars and auto buses stopped it makes it miserable for everyone trying to get to work or for us who are trying to get around to see the town. – The food supply for London come in on big trucks with two soldiers guarding each truck. Practically all train service is stopped and those running are made up of crews taken off of steam-rollers and threshing machines but somehow they get there slow but sure.*

The news from London's *Daily Mirror* on May 13 may have been confusing, but the International News Service made everything quite clear a day earlier on page one of *The Greensboro Record.*

HIGHLIGHTS OF STRIKE
by International News Service.

The general strike cost Britain approximately $8,500,000 every hour it was in effect. Total estimated cost, $1,700,000,000 or about $200,000,000 a day. Went into effect – Midnight, May 3; called off shortly after 1 o'clock on the afternoon of May 12. Worker affected – Coal miners, 1,200,000; other industries, about 4,000,000 workers. Cause of general strike – A virtual "lock out" of 1,200,000 coal miners who refused to submit either to a cut in wages or the lengthening of their hours of labor. This was followed by the general strike, declared in sympathy by the trades upon congress. Results of general strike – Mobilization of volunteer workers by government to keep transportation moving, food supplies adequate, navigation active, essential industries going.

Levi's latest letter to Chloe, dated May 7, would be the second to the last he would send from Europe. Her response, written May 23, was delivered to the American Express Office in Paris, but it arrived too late to reach him. Chloe's letter was forwarded to Levi's family home in Green Bay. Much time would pass before he had a chance to read the following:

Sunday Afternoon
May 23, 1926

Dear Lee,

When I first saw the card – "Johnnie Walker Scotch Whiskey", I was provoked I thought you were teasing me again (Maybe you were?). The scenes and the "name" redeemed the card, so I'm not peeved now. My ancestors probably came from this remote section of England, we have no record so I cannot boast of the fact. Without a doubt the name is English. Agree?

Your experiences in England were great. I believe the

people in America were getting alarmed over the general strike in England – at least my History Prof. said this. I'm glad its over now. Speaking of History reminds me that there is an exam Fri. and then it'll all be over. – until next session. I haven't decided what I'll take then.

Since you are spending a bit of time in England I wish I'd asked my mother the name of the town in which my grand-father Sturt lived. There is probably no one there by this name as he was the only boy and the last of the family. After his moth-er's death he lived with a bachelor uncle, who has been dead at least fifty years. Tracing relatives in this family would be about impossible. It's very interesting that you found some distant relatives in Belgium. I was telling Gertrude about this last night (She and Ruth invited me to dinner). There was no exciting news with them – Gertrude hasn't set the date for her wedding yet. She and Warren seem quite happy.

I'm enclosing a much wrinkled newspaper clipping telling of Johnny's letter and pictures of Purdy's fraternity making camp up the river. Both Grace and Purdy noticed the article about Johnny but didn't see Purdy's picture. As soon as I glanced at the page I recognized Purdy. How's this for close observation? I had a little training in this while in school so that's the reason – Ruth wanted to see Johnny's letter so I folded (rolled?) the clipping and tucked it in my pocket to show her last night. This accounts for the wrinkles.

Did I write you that Grace had asked Virginia and me to be bridesmaids in her wedding, Sept. 3? I felt conscience stricken when she asked me and remembered some unkind things I'd said about her – once upon a time. The wedding hasn't taken place yet – Last year this time she expected to marry Maurice in Sept.

We have four more weeks of school there have been

so many tests recently that I feel the end should be nearer. I'm tak-ing several classes on Sat. morning in preparation for my Bible School work this summer. Sometimes I wish I hadn't agreed to do this as I'm usually exhausted at the end of school and this position has too much responsibility attached. When August comes I'll be relieved. Now say I'm lazy because I'm afraid of working in the summer. This is my first experience.

If you leave Paris June 28 (Levi incorrectly wrote June but meant May 28), *does this mean be here the first week in July? — about the seventh — I'm anxious to hear more of your experiences and I'll see that the ice box isn't empty if you give me a little warning as to when you'll arrive — if you don't you'll probably find it in its usual state.*

When you come we'll have to have the whole gang around one evening — Do you suppose Clayton would like to come and bring his girl? We'll ask him if you say so.

Sincerely, Chloe

P.S. Johnny wrote Ruth that he'd probably be back by July 1 so you two can exchange experiences.

The enclosed clipping did not remain with the letter.

CHAPTER 79
LONDON AFTER THE STRIKE

London, England
May 15, 1926
[travel journal]

Leaving here this morning for my northern tour before crossing back to France. Saw Westminster Abbey, St. Paul's, The Tower with its crown jewels, the Houses of Parliament and finished up the National Art Gallery all on this trip — Met John, paid him all I owed him and after a couple "bitters" we decided to go on to Cambridge together. Ordered a suit yesterday and I am wondering what the tailor's conception of an American style will be. — Had an amusing experience on returning to my hotel for my second night in London. I had not paid in advance in the morning for the next night so they took my baggage out of my room and when I asked about it the women started calling me names for hanging my socks on the bed. After telling the proprietor what I thought of his way of doing business I got another hotel.

At Saint Paul's Cathedral, Levi witnessed a familiar scene from the early twentieth century: pigeons, children, and a woman with a plan to make the children smile. It was right out of *Mary Poppins.* One child's inquisitive nature and the sheer joy of the other were captured in the square as a bird made a soft landing on her fur-collared coat.

The buildings in the background are gone, lost in the Blitz of World War II. Some of the granite bollards in this photo remain unchanged, miraculous given the surrounding destruction.

The National Gallery is west of Saint Paul Cathedral, a thirty-minute walk down a main street that bends with the Thames River. In 1926, newspapers reported on the continued controversy over thirty-nine paintings that once belonged to Sir Hugh Lane. He perished when a German U-boat sank the Lusitania, the act that brought the United States into World War I.

The paintings were on loan to the National Gallery in London and became their property when he died. Questions arose after papers recently signed by Sir Hugh were found in his office after his death. These documents would have transferred the paintings to a gallery in Dublin, but they had not been witnessed and therefore were not legally binding.

In 1926, all of the paintings hung in London's National Gallery, where they would remain together for another thirty years. The National Gallery owned them legally, but the Dublin gallery had moral rights to the collection. Finally, the two galleries agreed to share the paintings and exchange them regularly. Sir Hugh's collection includes masters such as Monet, Manet, Renoir, Pissarro, Corot, Degas, and others.

A seven-minute walk down Whitehall from the National Gallery, toward Parliament Square Garden, leads to the Royal Horse Guard. Officially known as the King's Life Guard, the Household Cavalry Mounted Regiment has been protecting the monarch since 1660. There are other armed guards on site, but this view has not changed over the last century.

Levi's final shot from London was taken from the north side of Great George Street, across from Parliament Square Garden. The square tower in this photo is Victoria Tower, the monarch's point of entry into Westminster Palace. Big Ben, the clock on Elizabeth Tower, is located to the left, at a corner of the palace that is just out of view.

London, England
May 14, 1926

Dear Father,

Your first two letters containing four $50.00 money orders arrived O.K. and I'll say in the nick of time. We just arrived from Winchester having finish (to our satisfaction) a tour of southern England.

Tomorrow we are leaving for about five days trip up toward Liverpool after which John goes to Ireland and I come back to London and then back to France.

(ten hours later)

Been out all day and have been measured up for a suit and bought a pair of shoes too. Clothes are a bit cheaper here and seeing that I'm going thru my last shoes and suit now and that I'll have to look respectable when I arrive at Notre Dame I decided to get something to keep the rain out.

Their ale is something like beer but very bitter. Haven't tasted any of their wiskey over here and from what we tasted of it in France and Italy I'd rather drink bay rum. Instead of the wine they give you to drink at meal times on the Continent they feed you tea. I've gotten so I can drink it but postum will not be half bad when I get home.

(Connell is talking to me as I write so I'm getting everything backwards.) He is busy packing all his souvenirs as he intends to ship one of his bags ahead to Ireland. He bought his boat ticket today and sails from Queenstown, Ireland on June 4. – I am not deciding what boat I'll get until I get back to Paris where I hope to save a few dollars on account of the big drop in the franc. I am planning on spending several days in Washington before coming thru to South Bend where I ought to arrive on June 12th. – If you want me to come home to drive down I could leave Washington immediately on arriving. (Probably get in Washington June 7th at night, and could leave the next morning and get in Green Bay on the 9th in time to start driving back.)

I thought maybe the Engels might want to drive down so you could have gone together but whatever you decide will be O.K. with me. I will enclose Clayton Van's address in Washington and you can write there telling me what's what so I know immediately.

As I said before we are leaving for Cambridge in the morning and when I get back in about four or five days your other letter ought to be here.

With love, Levi

c/o Clayton Van – 607 22nd Street N.W. Washington, D.C.

CHAPTER 80
NORTH BY NORTHWEST TO LIVERPOOL

Cambridge
May 15, 1926
[travel journal]

The college buildings here are very good especially the Chapel of King's College. The students are "college" and many of them are just returning in their "plus fours" after acting as volunteers on buses etc. in London during the strike. – While at Southampton I saw them unloading meat from ships while dressed in these same "knickers".

The tour of Northwestern England started on Saturday morning, May 15. Cambridge was first on their list via a short train ride from London's city center. King's College Chapel is another fine example of Perpendicular Gothic; thousands of vertical lines plunge into the earth, connecting it to the heavens. The windows' arches are pointed, not rounded as they would be in the Romanesque style. The change of stone in the edifice shows the stop-and-go of construction over time.

Henry VI had the building started in 1446. The crown of England passed through the hands of five additional kings before the chapel was completed by Henry VIII in 1515. These were tumultuous times for the monarchy. The War of the Roses began in 1455. Control of England fluctuated between the Houses of Lancaster and York until Henry VII of the newly formed House of Tudor defeated Richard III, ending a thirty-year exchange of power.

The infamous King Henry VIII oversaw the completion of the chapel. His father, Henry VII, left specific instructions to complete the project that his uncle, Henry VI, had begun.

Carvings on the rood screen, the large wooden structure that separates the nave from the chancel, celebrate the wedding of Henry VIII to his second wife, Anne Boleyn. Various roses carved from stone are scattered throughout the chapel in tribute to the House of Tudor that united the white rose of the House of York and the red rose of the House of Lancaster.

The chapel ceiling is covered with the largest span of fan vaulting in the world. Levi must have been thrilled with the actual use of stone instead of wood, but this carved vaulting is hollow. Solid stone would have been too heavy for such an artistic display.

Ely, England
May 16, 1926
[travel journal]

Waiting to get a bus to Peterborough and also to have an argument with our hotel keeper over the price of our meals. These English can show all other nations a lesson when it comes to cheating travelers. The cathedral of Ely is very good on the interior with its Norman work especially.

This cathedral dates to the reign of William the Conqueror, 1066 to 1087. The Norman design Levi spoke of is evident in the rounded arches. Often described as Romanesque, the term Norman is added for grand buildings in England built after the conquest. The ceilings of Norman structures are often made of wood instead of rounded stone vaulting. The painted timber ceiling above the nave dates back to the mid-1800s.

March, England
May 17, 1926
[travel journal]

*This place was named rightly. We walked about five
miles looking for a hotel and again we had to humiliate
ourselves by sleeping in a Temperance hotel. Nothing here
and we are going to try to get a train to Peterborough. The
city police force here will be greatly relieved to find that their
two suspect safe breakers have left the town.*

Peterborough, England
May 17, 1926
[travel journal]

*Arrived here; saw the cathedral and are on our way to
Lincoln. The Norman interior of the cathedral redeems the
poor west front. There is nothing else of interest in the city.*

This cathedral solidified Levi's Romanesque preference in architecture. He was gravitating away from the Gothic style he once
seemed to prefer. The *poor west front* Levi spoke of was a Gothic addition to an otherwise Romanesque beauty.

Henry VIII's first wife, Catherine of Aragon, once rested in peace
within the walls of Peterborough Cathedral. This well-educated
daughter of King Ferdinand and Queen Isabella of Spain had defended
her new country. As queen, she led soldiers into battle during her
husband's absence and even sent Henry the bloodied coat of the King
of Scotland to announce the victory.

Mary Queen of Scots was also buried here. Charged with treason
for her involvement in planning the assassination of Queen Elizabeth
I, Mary Queen of Scots was beheaded and later interred here across
from the woman who had killed her grandfather, King James IV of
Scotland. Despite this, when Queen Elizabeth I died unmarried and
childless, Mary Queen of Scots's son James VI of Scotland took the

English throne as King James I of England. He moved his mother's remains to Westminster Abbey in London, close to the crypt that Mary I and Elizabeth I came to share.

Catherine of Aragon's remains are no longer here. Oliver Cromwell's troops ransacked her tomb in 1643. A memorial plaque reminds all who visit of this grand woman who once lived and ruled over England.

Lincoln, England
May 18, 1926
⌈travel journal⌉

Just leaving this place for Liverpool. The cathedral is large, very large but is very poor in design. As Connell said, 'it looks like a plumber and decorator had charge of the building.' — John insisted on leaving early this morning but just missed his train so both of us came back for the breakfast we had passed up because we were awakened late. Am taking Connells bag to Liverpool while he is on his way north probably to Scotland. Expect to see him again in South Bend on June 13th if all goes well.

Levi made note of the immense size of the cathedral in Lincoln, England, and rightly so. Rising higher than the Great Pyramid, this cathedral was the largest building in the world for 200 years. Now, Lincoln Cathedral is the fourth largest in the United Kingdom, and Liverpool Cathedral is the largest.

Retford, England
⌈*2 hours later*⌉
⌈travel journal⌉

If I could only think up something bad enough to call these English. Am stalled here for I don't know how long because the train conductor told me to change farther down the line at Sheffield while the express for Liverpool left from

*here while they had my train sidetracked. No one seems to
know when a train leaves, where its destination is, or if it
will complete its whole trip.*

*Manchester, England
May 18, 1926
[travel journal]*

*Just leaving here after a two hours wait and another
experience with English railroad "efficiency". This place
reminds me of South Chicago and I am glad to leave. – It's
raining of course. Has been since I arrived in England.*

Levi and John separated in Lincoln, and Levi finally reached his
end target, Liverpool.

*Liverpool, England
May 19, 1926
[travel journal]*

*This is a great seaport but does not impress one as do
the ports where one can see most of the shipping at a glance.
– The new Episcopal Cathedral with the apse, choir and
transept completed is the best thing I've seen of modern
architecture in Europe. – I hope I shall live to see it
completed. The New Catholic Cathedral is still on paper as
no suitable site has been found on which to build it. – There
are some good watercolors in the art gallery and the large
room of the courthouse is worth seeing. I mistook it for a
Protestant church on seeing a pipe-organ at one end. It seems
that the room is also used for recitals, receptions and even
dances. Am leaving now for London and here hoping I find
that the tailor's version of an American suit is O.K.*

A significant feature of the Anglican cathedral in Liverpool is the tower, which did not exist in 1926. The cathedral was completed in Levi's lifetime, but not until 52 years after his visit. World War II halted construction, and repairs were required after damage endured during the Blitz. The cathedral is Gothic. Given the time of construction, this structure would be considered Gothic Revival, built too late to be considered truly Gothic. Levi mentioned the cathedral to Chloe in the last letter he sent her from Europe. He reflected on Liverpool from Paris on May 24, 1926.

> *I traveled all across England to Liverpool to see the new Episcopal Cathedral that is about one third finished. It was worth the trip and I considered it about the best piece of modern work in Europe.*

The Catholic cathedral did transfer from paper to reality, but not until 1933. The crypt was built first, and the proposed Byzantine design would have made this the second-largest church in the world, second only to Saint Peter's Basilica of Vatican City. The planned dome would have surpassed all others in size. World War II also halted construction at this site. The completed crypt was used as a bomb shelter. By 1959, all plans for the grand cathedral were abandoned, and competition for a smaller cathedral began. A modern design was chosen, circular with the altar at the center. Known locally as "Paddy's Wigwam" due to the association with Irish Catholics and the exterior favoring a concrete teepee, Liverpool Metropolitan Cathedral opened on the Feast of Pentecost in 1967.

With Liverpool checked off of Levi's travel list, the train headed back to London.

CHAPTER 81
LAST FULL DAY
IN LONDON

London
May 20, 1926
[travel journal]

My last hundred dollars arrived and now it's up to me to get home as best I can. My English version of an American suit is "not so good" and I am having the trousers with the accordion pleats altered. The tailor says it's all the rage but I can afford to have people rage when they see them.

Westminster Abbey, with all its "fine dust" did not impress me over much. It would be a good interior if they took all the tombs and monuments out. The strike is over and many lines of transportation are back to normal.

Walking through Westminster Abbey is akin to turning the pages of an extensive history book. From monarchs to writers, scientists to politicians, over 3,000 people are buried beneath the floors of the abbey. Even an impoverished poet's remains are placed upright in the crypt, since laying them flat at Westminster would have proven too expensive.

The ceiling of the Lady Chapel at Westminster looks like cascading three-dimensional lace. It spans from the arch supports around the edge of the room and into large circular patterns. These structures fan out from a central pendant and extend down from the ceiling, terminating in a gilded hexagon. It is a mastery of late medieval architecture.

Beneath the central aisle of the Lady Chapel lies King George II and his wife, Caroline. He was the last royal buried at Westminster, on November 11, 1760. Two simple white stones set into the black-and-white checkered floor mark their graves.

Notable queens, such as half-sisters Mary I and Elizabeth I, are buried here. After King James VI of Scotland became James I of England, he rearranged the crypt beneath the Lady Chapel. The remains of Queen Elizabeth I were stacked atop those of her predecessor and half-sister Queen Mary I. They often hated each other in life, being the daughters of Henry VIII's first and second wives, but the two queens were made inseparable in death. The body of Mary Queen of Scots, the new king's mother, was taken from Peterborough Cathedral and given an appropriate burial in the acquired space. Though Mary Queen of Scots had been beheaded and buried twenty-five years earlier, there was no place more respectful to hold her remains than the Lady Chapel at Westminster Abbey.

Paris, France
May 22, 1926
[travel journal]

Arrived here last night or rather this morning a little after midnight. We left London, two big trains of us, at four in the afternoon and had one grand rush to find room on the boat. — Went by way of Dover-Calais and was not seasick.

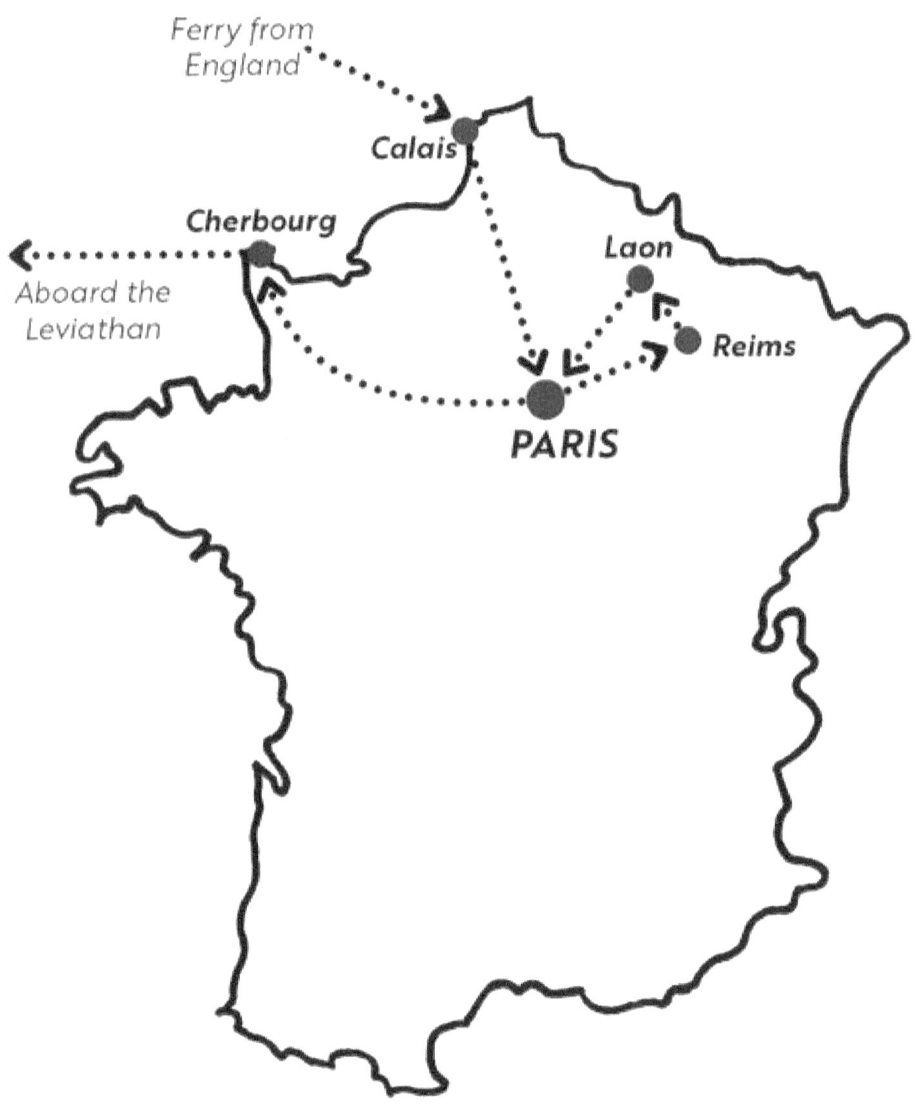

Ferry from
England
Calais
Cherbourg
Aboard the
Leviathan
Laon
Reims
PARIS

FRANCE IV
May 1926 - June 1926

CHAPTER 82
LAST DAYS IN PARIS

May 24, 1926
Paris, France

Dear Chloe,

I traveled all across England to Liverpool to see the new Episcopal cathedral that is about one third finished. It was worth the trip and I considered it about the best piece of modern work in Europe. Coming back to London I had an "experience" with an English tailor then joined the exodus to Paris for the Whit-Sunday week end.

Arrived in Paris three days ago and found Engels gone on a short tour of the chateau country. John Connell and I parted company in Lincoln and he took a train north into Scotland while I took his luggage to Liverpool I was in a rush to get back to France while Connell is crossing to Ireland and intends to sail from Queenstown on June 4th.

The day before yesterday I went back to the Louvre to see, if I could, why Mona Lisa is so famous. I can't, the mystery remains like her face to me.

The Luxembourg galleries and the Rodin museum were "done" yesterday then I loafed till dark in the Luxembourg gardens.

An article from the Associated Press offered a sense of how the Luxembourg gallery appeared when Levi visited. While the article was published in several U.S. papers, this copy was taken from the *Chattanooga Daily Times*, May 9, 1926.

MORE MODERN MEN IN FRENCH ART

Effort to Bring Luxembourg Gallery Up to Date.

New Custodian Eliminating Dead Ones – Impressionists Now Center of Exhibit

PARIS, May 8 (AP) – Charles Masson, new custodian of the Luxembourg gallery, has made a great effort to bring the gallery up to date. As a result visiting hosts of Americans who dutifully go the regulation round of sights of Paris this year will find Luxembourg which is really, or nearly, what its founders proposed it to be – a museum of modern French art with representative exhibits of the best contemporary artists.

Painters dead in every sense have been eliminated in favor of more modern men. The impressionists, formerly relegated to a small room on the right of the entrance, now form the center about which the whole exhibition revolves. There, Cesanne, whose talent is still much disputed, reigns with Manet, Monet, Pissaro, Sisley, Berthe Morisot, Miss Mary Cassatt, A. Guillaumin, Degas and Renoir.

The revolutionaries of another day look almost as old fashioned as the masters they replace, for close beside them M. Masson has hung such advanced men as Van Dongen, Van Gogh, Lautrac, Signac, Henri Matisse, Maurice Denis, Othon Friesz and Utrillo, in such a way as to show clearly the development of modern painting during the last half century (37).

Levi's visit to the Luxembourg Gallery coincided with the effort to eliminate the non-living artist's works from the collection. Those pieces would move to the Louvre, making room for contemporary artwork. As for the Rodin Museum, Levi did not offer any impression within the pages of his letter to Chloe.

> *On my way home*
> *June 1, 1926*
> [travel journal]

> *Visited Rodins special gallery and all I can say of his works is "It's a pity that he should have wasted his talents so".*
>
> *The Salon gave me a full afternoon and was more wonderful than I had expected. It tells why Paris is the art center of the world.*
>
> *Just watching people which has become my favorite sport. If I don't change by the time I get home I'm going to open a fruit stand on some busy corner and watch the world pass by.*

Auguste Rodin was often regarded as the greatest sculptor since Michelangelo. Though Rodin also carved images from blocks of marble, he is better known for his dark bronze figures cast through a lost wax process. These bodies showed motion and offered a sense of life, breaking from the posed bodies of the past.

Levi also mentioned visiting the Salon. Starting in 1667, King Louis XIV required all royal painters and sculptors to display their work in the Salon annually. Originally, the works hung in the Salon Carré and nearby rooms in the Louvre. The exhibition was limited to French artists until 1795. Americans joined this elite group in 1800.

It was the rejection of the Impressionists in 1863 that extended the use of the term Salon to other exhibits, starting with the *Salon de Refusés* (Exhibition of Rejects). This second "Salon" was held in the Palais de l'Industrie, an exhibition hall built for the Paris World Fair of 1855 and demolished in 1897 in preparation for the Grand Palais of the 1900 World Fair. The creation of additional salons in the late nineteenth and early twentieth centuries diminished the significance of the original Salon in Paris.

In a 1926 article, the *Kansas City Times* explained the evolution of the Paris Salon.

WE OUGHT TO KNOW: WHAT IS THE PARIS SALON?

The Paris salon is a world famous exhibition of the works of living artists, held every year at the two palaces of fine arts in Paris from May 1 to June 22. Oil and water color paintings, sculptured figures, engravings, pastels and etchings make up the exhibition, the prizes consisting of medals and the coveted Prix de Rome. The awards are by a jury selected by ballot by the exhibitors, who are organized under the name Society of French Artists. The same jury decided which works are worthy of exhibition. Dissatisfaction over the award in 1889 resulted in the formation of a new society, organized as the National Society of Fine Arts, which holds an independent salon from May 15 to July 15 in the Champ de Mars. It is known as the New salon, as distinguished from the original, or old, salon (8).

Levi's last letter to Chloe from Europe continued as he wrote from Paris on May 24.

Am writing this on the edge of the Bois Vincennes over looking the aviation field. Today is a holiday in France. Yesterday was Pentecost and here like in Italy the people take the proximity of a religious feast day as an excuse for a day of picnics and excursions. There is to be an exhibition of French army aviation in an hour. Yesterday 200,000 people visited the grounds and more are expected today so you can picture the constant procession that streams by. It's the typical holiday crowd; the same the world over. Balloons, tin horns, canes, candy, sandwiches and beer bottles are everywhere. Everything but pink popcorn. If these people only knew of our food of the gods — but they do not and are happy in their ignorance.

*The first airplanes are tuning up and I'll ask to be
excused for a while. Still am in favor of the development of
aviation although from now on I favor it from the ground.*

*Well that's that. A ham sandwich just saved my life. We
have Americanized France to that extent although they insist
on calling them the ridiculous name of "sanweech jambon".*

*The French aviators gave us plenty of thrills but I
believe the program at Washington last year was better.*

The air show Levi referred to in Washington, D.C., took place on
July 4, 1925. *The Washington Herald* summed up that day's events.

MIMIC AIR WARFARE BEST EVER STAGED:

Secret Flight Maneuvers Draw Brilliant Capital Crowd

With all the energy and daring for which they are respected the world over, the army's reserve flyers, in
Defense Day maneuvers at Bolling Field, yesterday
demonstrated their ability to defend the National Capital
from surprise attack by an enemy. From the moment
"contact" was given at 2 o'clock and until late in the afternoon, realistic mimic warfare raged over the entire
field. Aerial acrobacy, destruction of a miniature village
and the bringing down in flames of an "enemy" observation balloon, thrilled more than 5,000 spectators.

The "take-off" stilled the crowd that buzzed with
excitement and expectancy. The deafening shrieks of the
rising planes silenced the hum-drum noise of thousands
of spectators – "they're off" – the cry that riveted all eyes
on cloudland and held a crowd breathless. Thousands
had come to witness the Defense Day celebration at
Bolling Field. Thousands had come wondering, and were
thrilled at the flight of the reserve officers. An exhibition of aerial photography, an observation balloon shot
down by machine gun fire and "balloon sniping" were a
few of the stunts that awed the crowd.

Through the skies those champion flyers went – marched and counter-marched, pirouetted and turned and bowed and dipped and rose again toward the sun, as graceful and as lovely as moving statuary. At one moment, when five planes formed the fleur de lys, a wild shriek broke out from the crowd...That long low plane – which had journeyed here at Patrick's direction from McCook Field, in Ohio – now dashed forward and circled the field. A squadron of Martin bombers from Langley Field, Virginia, now will demolish the 'enemy village' in the center of the field...That rear plane, with Lieutenant William Wilson, of the Ninety-sixth squadron, at the stick, suddenly dipped. Leaving far out, one could see two bombs striking that village and tearing it off the face of the earth. Wilson had struck his objective twice out of four chances, and Pascale and Mofat had missed only by a hair's breadth (2).

Levi attended Washington, D.C.'s airshow with his roommate, Clayton Van Thullenar. Clayton posed with the Martin bombers that destroyed the makeshift village described in the article.

Levi's May 24 letter to Chloe continued.

After milling around in the biggest crowd I have ever seen assembled for about three hours I joined those who were trekking back to the city. A dusty tired mob flocks by who like myself have given up the idea of transportation home. It's a long way back and corns do not improve with age but I deserve all this for having you walk home so many times. John and I had plenty of time in England to study the formation of blisters. It was our week thru the Southwestern part and with the railroad strike on there was nothing to do but walk. Had always wondered where Corot and the other famous painters of woodland scenes ever conceived their ideas. In that part of England [Southwestern] the old forests remain as they always have been and the farms are really not farms at all but country dwellings of men who have some other income. It's the ideal life, a country gentleman, but Connell insists that only a successful man can become a squire or whatever you call them and that I haven't a ghost of a chance. – He's wrong I've the first requisite already, the vice of sleeping late. If I could only acquire that of "early to bed" I'd grow fat and dignified. As it is one of these days you will see a gaunt starving painter or poet or whoever it is that starves in novels burst in 1800 K Street N.W.

*hallowed eyed and delirious he will probably seize a pencil
and on your kitchen table show his art for bread (a whole
loaf). Column on column shall rise mingled with pediments,
scrolls and gargoyles until before you appear a magnificent
palace or cathedral. Then smudging the giant phantasie he'll
sketch a soul writhing in torment and collapse feebly calling
for a glass, a glass of buttermilk.*

*Engels intends to stay in Paris for a few months more
and I sail on the Leviathan June 1st. All tourist class is sold
and I am coming back with the emigrants. We are scheduled
to arrive in New York on June seventh at noon. If I pass the
intelligence test at Ellis Island I'll reach Washington sometime during the evening of the seventh. (I can hear Virginia
saying don't expect him then).*

*If I don't see any fires I may be over "bout eight", will
you be at home?*

Lee

Levi captured a few moments with Vince during their final days
in Paris.

CHAPTER 83
FINAL DAY TRIPS
FROM PARIS

While Levi was staying in Paris, he took several day trips out of the city to visit a few final points of interest before he returned home. The traveling architect reflected on these trips in his travel journal.

> *On my way home*
> *June 1, 1926*
> [travel journal]

Vinc and I visited Versailles again and spent a beautiful day around the grounds. I also took a trip to Rhiems [Reims] and after viewing what once was a wonderful cathedral I saw and wondered at the champagne cellars of Pomercy [Pommery]. On my way back to Paris I stopped at Leon [Laon] and climbed a long steep hill to the cathedral. It was worth the climb but does not rank as a major edifice architecturally.

Vince captured this moment when they visited Versailles. Levi stood in front of Marie Antoinette's estate, Petit Trianon, on the palace grounds. This was the place where the queen and her friends

would dress as peasants and act as if they were farm maidens, milking cows and churning butter. Her public was not amused.

Another day trip out of Paris landed Levi in Reims. Vince and John had visited previously, but Levi could not leave the continent without seeing this cathedral. Reims Cathedral was the poster child of Germany's insensitivity to culture. Much of the town suffered complete annihilation during World War I. A 2019 *Smithsonian Magazine* article stated that eighty-five percent of the buildings in the city were destroyed (Boissoneault).

Levi's photo of the west façade shows that a temporary roof incompletely covered the nave. The sky was still visible through the Gothic openings, once filled with glass. Reconstruction had begun in 1919, but the cathedral would not reopen until 1938.

German bombs hit Reims Cathedral on September 19, 1914, fifty-three days into the Great War. A *Daily Mail* dispatcher was sent out the next day. Within two days of the bombing, an article appeared in *The Times*, London.

DEVASTATED STREETS

There is the theatre, with holes in its scarred sides and not a window left...And then you turn into the cathedral square, and you are face to face with the greatest iniquity of all. There is not much to see as one expected from the outside, for the towers and walls still stand, and the scars on their beautiful Gothic decoration caused by the German shells are not easily distinguished by the stranger's eye from those worn by the weather of 600 years. But the great doors yawn nakedly, for the old oak portals are entirely consumed...In front of the cathedral lies a medley of half-burnt straw, dragged out while the fire was going on, and dozens of charred and blackened beams. I could not enter, for the deserted square was occupied by three French Territorial soldiers with orders to allow no one to go into the building, but through the open doors I could see a chaos of fallen rafters, over-turned confessionals, charred and ruined woodwork. One of the towers, I was told, was injured, but so far as one could see at so cursory a view there should be a possibility of restoring the cathedral in time and at great cost...There is the great rose window in the west end, for instance, that was filled with wonderful amber-coloured glass. Not all of this has gone, happily, but there are holes in it that are sad to see ("Reims Cathedral: A Masterpiece of the Middle Ages - The Church of Joan of Arc" 10, 26).

The theatre mentioned in the article was the Opéra de Reims, originally known as Le Grand Théâtre. The bombs destroyed the interior and left only the shell of the building. Levi found the theater just as the soldiers had left it, completely open to the elements, as seen in the photo on the following page.

Thousands of the inhabitants of Reims took refuge in the Pommery champagne caverns beneath the city. These Roman ruins may have been designed to store champagne, but they were quickly altered into a hub of subterranean life. Children attended school and played there. The wounded were nursed. At the time Levi walked

these halls, the soft chalk walls still carried the marks of those who lived there just over a decade earlier.

Levi's mention of Laon was brief and mainly focused on his climb to the cathedral there. Cathedrale Notre-Dame de Laon, attributed to Our Lady, compares directly with Chartres, Reims, and Paris, though it is the oldest of the three. It is a lesser-known place of worship, but no less noteworthy.

CHAPTER 84
WORLD'S LARGEST PASSENGER LINER

On my way home
June 1, 1926
[travel journal]

Much has happened since writing last the greatest event being leaving Paris this morning homeward bound. – We arrived in Cherbourg this afternoon and finally climbed on board the Leviathan and had a much delayed meal about 8:30 P.M. – We weighed anchor at eleven o'clock and are now headed for the open sea. – These last few days in France have been busy ones and enjoyable although the problem of making "ends" meet has been a hard one.

Came very close to missing my boat because I had not the fare to Cherbourg but McCabe stood by to the extent of five hundred francs and if luck holds I shall reach Washington with that.

Five hundred francs was the equivalent of about sixteen dollars in 1926. Levi's last two hundred dollars arrived in London on May 20, and that was supposed to last him until he reached Washington,

D.C. Thankfully, another Notre Dame alumnus and friend, Clarence McCabe, was able to save the day. Clarence graduated from Notre Dame in 1922, two years before Levi. He worked for an American paper in Paris, where Vince was also working. McCabe remained in Paris for three years before returning to the States and settling in Washington, D.C.

In the 1920s, the S.S. Leviathan sailed from New York City to Southampton, England, and stopped in Cherbourg, France. The Atlantic crossing took six days, and the boat arrived in the States just before Levi turned twenty-six.

These two photographs completed Levi's scrapbook. Levi wore his new suit from London. His shoes and socks were free of holes. Samuel Mercier Audibert with his cabinmate. Levi called him Sid.

Levi's final journal entry fell onto page 104 of his travel journal. Over seven months and two continents of memories filled the pages. It was June 4, 1926, and Levi was out on the Atlantic, without the other two musketeers

On board the Leviathan in mid-ocean
June 4, 1926
[travel journal]

*Came up for air this morning after two days in my bunk.
– Started reading a book on Christian Science the first day
but it didn't work. My cabin-mate, Sid Mercier Audibert,
has been keeping me company which I must confess made me
feel better.*

*It is Friday, a beautiful day and I'm keeping my fish and
potatoes well, thank you.*

EPILOGUE

Levi returned to the States, where he and Chloe remained friends for life. Things started right where they left off in October of 1925. Levi was convinced he should move on, but after seeing Chloe in person, the old feelings of hope came rushing back. Chloe stuck to her guns; she still felt he would be happier with a Catholic bride. She was right.

Over the next few months, they exchanged thoughts and pleasantries in their letters whenever one or the other was away visiting family. By the spring of 1927, something was different. No letters exist to offer a timeline, as both were in Washington.

Some decision was made before Chloe left for Champ in the summer of 1927. While traveling through Upstate New York with her mother, a letter from Levi arrived. He ended in a new and unfamiliar way, *Mit Liebe und Küsste* (With Love and Kisses).

Summer waned, and the mother-daughter duo departed New York and headed home by way of Washington, D.C. On the last day of July, Levi was invited to Chloe's flat. Chloe and her mother planned to spend only one night in D.C. The time had come for Emma and Levi to hash out their differences.

After departing from D.C. the next morning, a flurry of letters began. On August 2, 1927, Chloe expressed the following.

I expected a lecture from Mama when you kissed me
goodbye on the train — but she didn't say a word, just looked.

I didn't return her look – She hasn't expressed her opinion about you. I've made Emma Ruth promise to tell me what she says.

Levi's note, written the next day, crossed Chloe's in the mail. He also touched on the subject.

Has your mother given you a lecture for kissing every Tom, Dick or Harry you meet on the train yet? Besides she can't blame you because it was stolen, wasn't it? Or possibly she thinks that a person who is careless [shall I say invites theft] is as responsible as the thief?

The eighth letter sent between them in August had been written by Chloe on August 9.

When Mama saw the card telling her that the Columbia magazine was coming to her for one year she even chuckled in spite of her chagrin. She said she'd have to send you The Christian Herald. The fight is on.

To-night we had quite an argument. Mama said that if I married you she didn't think that I'd ever want to come down here again. I asked her if she'd come to see me. She said that she wouldn't express herself. She said that she wouldn't even come to Washington to see me married. If I couldn't be married down here she wouldn't be present. Emma Ruth said she would come. Lucinda said she wouldn't want to but Collier said, "Yes he could see me married by a priest as well as by anyone else". The arguments were flying thick and fast for awhile.

By August 14, Levi's concern had grown.

I just can't get you off my mind, so I might as well be writing to you. Last night even as we pulled into our little grimy station in Green Bay I wondered if you were being "talked out of it".

Levi's family remained relatively quiet when it came to Chloe.

My mother and father say nothing about you except to speak about Virginians in a general way. Today I told them that your mother would not ride a streetcar or bus on Sunday and they could not understand that but my father said, "Well, that is their way of honoring God so it's all right".

After two-and-a-half years of correspondence, dates, and the sharing of numerous articles, everything came to a head.

September 28, 1927

Dearest Emma Ruth,

You poor kid! I know you think you're the most neglected sister in all the world. Well, I do love you in spite of the bad treatment I've given you.

Last week was just a rush of luncheons, tennis, dates with Lee, etc. Saturday we went to see the boat races on the Potomac. It was quite thrilling to see the motorboats plunging through the water.

Sunday we went to church and then sat in the park for awhile before dinner. In the afternoon we went on a boat down the river. On our way back about sunset Lee gave me my diamond. It's a solitaire set in a combination of Tiffany and basket setting. This is about the size of the stone. Are you shocked? I feel a bit embarrassed and can't believe I'm not living in a dream.

In Chloe's next letter, mailed along with the last, Chloe's conversation with her sister continued.

So you think my ring is exciting! Well, I can hardly believe Chloe Wells is the heroine in this story. I've been engaged a week! It all seems so strange! As for Lee he is darling and I just love him! Can't you hear me rave?

They married on April 9, 1928, at Saint Patrick Catholic Church in Washington, D.C., a short distance from where they first met three years earlier. It was Easter Monday. The flowers throughout the church perfumed the air. With Emma Ruth as Chloe's maid of honor and Clayton Van Thullenar as Levi's best man, Father Hurney declared Levi and Chloe husband and wife. Chloe's sister Lucinda attended. Their mother, Emma Sophia, remained in Champ watching over Lucinda's three children.

Chloe had been right all along; she would always be Levi's friend, and he would be happier married to a Catholic girl.

The following letter had been sent to Levi after their Christmas visit to Champ.

Champ, VA
January 7, 1928

Dear, Lee,

I recieved your welcome letter am glad you enjoyed the visit. As to Chloe's being a catholic just as far as she follows Christ I am with her for anyone to preach any other doektrin even though it were a angel from heaven they are and aways will be another Maranatha to me. All thats any church is for is to should be to bring the followers of the great sheppard of the sheep. I don't accept any cloak too big to make one think that it is not your influence over Chloe her thinking she should be catholic nothing washed over will stand the test of lifes woes and the only important thing is to have the heart filled with the love Christ that He may be her guide and comforter and He alone will give her strength and wisdom to fight Sin in all his trickery. I do not know enough about the catholic church to condemn it - but I do know to do the right is no childs play and to get right in the eyes of God and to searve Him is all I want my children to do

Sincerely Emma Wells

Years later, while writing this book, I searched for a letter to explain why Chloe converted. I shared with one of Chloe's daughters that it seemed I would never know. "I know," she responded. "I asked her years ago myself."

Levi had searched the Library of Congress for assistance with his troubles. He discovered information on Swithun Wells, a Catholic martyr from Southern England. His homestead was not far from where Chloe's maternal ancestors originated. He provided a haven for priests and offered them a place to celebrate Mass in secret during the Reformation. For this, he was hanged outside his home.

Chloe realized, whether this man had been a long-lost ancestor or not, her family had once been Catholic. In some way, converting took her back to her ancestral roots. She was a reformist who embraced the reformation that occurred within the Catholic church over the centuries.

Thirteen months after their wedding, almost to the day, Levi and Chloe welcomed their first daughter. In all, they raised five children. Levi started an architectural firm and converted it into a partnership with John Connell for a few years in the 1930s, Geniesse & Connell.

In Green Bay, Chloe and Levi worked through the trials and tribulations of the Great Depression and the Second World War. They managed to see all five kids through college. The boys attended Notre Dame, and the girls attended either Rosary College, Saint Mary's of Notre Dame, or both.

Though most of Levi's designs were for hospitals and schools, his dream was to build a cathedral. The travels through Europe were to study church architecture, to appreciate the spirit which resulted in noble monuments to God, but he only built one church, Saint Hubert's in Door County.

On October 9, 1988, an article appeared in the *Appleton-Neenah-Menasha Post-Crescent* newspaper. Levi's youngest son, Peter, weekend editor at the time, reflected on his father's legacy shortly after his passing.

IN HIS OWN WAY, LEVI BUILT HIS CATHEDRAL

He had outlived most of his friends and relatives and there were few who came to the wake at the funeral home. A couple of younger architects paid tribute to his talents. They noted that all those schools and hospitals in Wisconsin and the Upper Peninsula would be lasting landmarks to his name. His family talked of his lifetime longing to build a cathedral.

A middle-aged woman knelt down before the coffin. Then she introduced herself. She said she met that man 20 years ago when her husband was injured and out of work and her baby was sick. They had no money, no friends.

She said he visited their dingy apartment almost every day for awhile. He brought groceries, paid the rent and arranged for medical care for her son.
"Your father believed in us when no one else would," she said. "I just had to come here to thank him."

A young architect overheard the conversation and said, "I think your father just built himself a cathedral" (16).

AUTHOR'S NOTE

I had the pleasure of meeting Chloe in 1992. By that time, Alzheimer's had taken hold. There were moments when her speech was clear and other times when her daughter let her know the words were garbled. Chloe would sigh, wait a few moments, and try again.

Chloe and I walked into the study with her grandson, Paul. This was the space where Levi spent his final days. This photo, shown on the right, sat in an Art Deco frame on his desk. Chloe picked it up, turned the picture towards me, and said, "That was the day we married."

Moments before, Paul revealed a secret he longed to share with her, "Gramma, this is the girl I want to marry." The small-framed woman, dependent on the support of her cane, looked me up and down twice. I stood still, held my breath, and minded my posture until our eyes met. She softly

replied, "Okay." With that, we had the blessing of the matriarch.

I have been introduced to Levi through the ephemeral memories found in these pages, since I never had the opportunity to meet him in person. I have come to know both of them better and have even surprised their children with a story or two. I appreciate these two wonderful individuals for the responsibilities they embraced and the nurturing they offered to those who brought life and love into my world.

LEGACIES

GENIESSE, LEVI A.

Born June 16, 1900, in Union, Wisconsin, Levi lived predominantly in Wisconsin, though he spent a few years in Washington, D.C. He graduated from Notre Dame University with a degree in architecture, Class of 1924. He was a self-employed architect and designed numerous schools and hospitals in Northeastern Wisconsin and Michigan's Upper Peninsula. Levi married Chloe Eliza Wells in 1928. They celebrated five children and sixty years together. Levi was involved in his church and community until his passing in 1988 at the age of 88.

(WELLS) GENIESSE, CHLOE E.

Born November 25, 1900, in Dinwiddie County, Virginia. Chloe lived in Virginia, Washington, D.C., and Wisconsin. Chloe graduated from the State Normal School in Harrisonburg, Virginia, now known as James Madison University, with a degree in education, Class of 1919. now known as James Madison University. She completed additional courses at George Washington University in Washington, D.C. Chloe taught grades four through seven during her career. She married Levi Alphonse Geniesse in 1928, and they had five children. Chloe was involved in her church and community until she died from complications related to Alzheimer's at the age of 93.

CONNELL, JOHN F.

Born August 4, 1899, in Delavan, Illinois, John lived predominantly in Illinois, Indiana, Wisconsin, and Colorado. He graduated from Notre Dame University with a degree in architecture, Class of 1923. John and Levi became friends in college. He was an architect and designed several hospitals, schools, and churches. John married Mary Jane Worden in 1932. The couple celebrated the birth of six children. John was involved in his church and community until he passed away unexpectedly in 1957 at the age of 58.

ENGELS, VINCENT D.

Born December 9, 1901, in Green Bay, Wisconsin, Vince lived in Wisconsin, Indiana, and Maryland. He graduated from Notre Dame University with a degree in journalism, Class of 1923. Vince and Levi were childhood friends. They attended the same schools through college. Vince married Mary Aloise Emery in 1930. They were blessed with two sons before Mary's untimely death in 1957. Vince reported for the Green Bay Press-Gazette, the Paris Times, and Commonweal Magazine; he published a book on fishing in the Adirondacks. Vince served in the U.S. Navy and reached the rank of Captain; he was an intelligence analyst and editor for the Navy before transferring to the Defense Intelligence Agency. Vince died after a lengthy illness in 1992 at the age of 90.

GENIESSE, LEWIS J.

Born November 1, 1873, in Union, Wisconsin. Lewis lived solely in Wisconsin, between the Door Peninsula and Green Bay. Lewis was a self-employed contractor. Lewis married Louise Mary Evrard in 1899. They welcomed the birth of two sons and celebrated fifty-three years together. Lewis was a tenor, and he sang at Assumption Day Services in Robinsonville for fifty-five years. He died from a heart attack in 1952 at the age of 78.

GENIESSE (EVRARD), LOUISE M.

Born July 13, 1875, in Tonet, Wisconsin. Louise never moved from Wisconsin and lived either in Door or Brown counties; she was a homemaker. Louise married Lewis Joseph Geniesse in 1899. They had two sons and celebrated their golden wedding anniversary in 1949. Levi was their eldest, and Oswald their youngest. Louise was an active member of Saint John Church in Green Bay. She died after a lengthy illness in 1962 at the age of 86.

GENIESSE, OSWALD G.

Born June 30, 1902, in Green Bay, Wisconsin. Oswald, called "Os" for short, lived in Wisconsin, except for his time away at college. Os graduated from Notre Dame University with a degree in commercial science, Class of 1926. He was a halfback for Notre Dame's Fighting Irish in 1924 when they won the First National Championship, a back-up for Green Bay native Jim Crowley. Os married Josephine Antoinette Garot in 1928. They welcomed a son seven months before Os suffered complications after abdominal surgery. Os died in 1930 before his twenty-eighth birthday.

VAN THULLENAR, CLAYTON F.

Born March 15, 1904, in Green Bay, Wisconsin. Clayton lived in Wisconsin, Ohio, Texas, Utah, New Mexico, Massachusetts, Germany, and the District of Columbia. Clayton studied at George Washington University. He spent his career in meteorology except for one year with Transcontinental Air Transport (now TWA) in the 1920s. He was Levi Geniesse's childhood friend in Green Bay, and later the two were roommates in Washington, D.C. Clayton married Iva J. "Pearl" Baxter in 1930; they had one son. Clayton became the Assistant Regional Director and later Director of the National Weather Service's Central Region in Kansas City. Clayton passed away in 1977 at the age of 73.

WELLS, DAVID F.

Born February 4, 1844, in Dinwiddie County, Virginia. David was always a Virginian. He was not well educated, he was illiterate, but he was a good farmer. David had three children with his first wife, Lucy A. Cabiness Belcher, before he was widowed. He married Emma Sophia Sturt in 1898. During his twenty-five years of marriage to Emma, they had four children. Chloe was the eldest of three girls and a boy. David served in Company H of the Hargrave Blues throughout all four years of the Civil War, captured at the Battle of Five Forks on April 1, 1865; General Lee surrendered eight days later. David died on Christmas Day in 1923, at the age of 79.

(WELLS) CHEADLE, EMMA RUTH

Born November 2, 1908, in Dinwiddie County, Virginia. Emma Ruth lived in Virginia her whole life. She graduated from State Normal School in Harrisonburg, Virginia, sometime around 1929, with a focus in home economics. Emma Ruth married Thomas Sutphin Cheadle in 1939, and over their approximately 18 years of marriage, they had one son. She died in 2003 at the age of 95.

(WELLS) OGBURN, LUCINDA D.

Born March 19, 1902, in Dinwiddie County, Virginia, Lucinda was a lifelong Virginian who made raising her children and managing their farm her life's work. She married James Collier Ogburn in 1922. They had three children in their thirty-five years together. Lucinda died in 1982, just shy of turning 80.

WELLS (STURT), EMMA S.

Born October 5, 1857, in Rosebush Township, New York. Emma's parents moved the majority of their family to the countryside of McKenney, Virginia, sometime around 1870. They settled near McKenney. Emma married David Frances Wells (widower) in 1898, in the parlor of her parents' home. They shared twenty-five years and welcomed four children, three girls and a boy. Chloe Wells was their eldest child. Their son died young from influenza. Lucinda (Wells) Ogburn was their middle daughter, and Emma Ruth (Wells) Cheadle was the youngest. Emma Sophia died in 1938 at the age of 72.

AKNOWLEDGEMENTS

This process began thirty years ago after discovering a stack of letters neatly tied together with a ribbon. Many pieces of paper, along with hours of research, revealed a story that was left behind. One hundred years ago, as of the launch date of this book, the Leviathan set sail with a few adventurers you have come to know.

I want to thank my husband for seeing this project through to the end with me, for his support, and for the needed push forward.

My three daughters pooled their talents, and their amazing work is greatly appreciated. From Martine's help with the physical therapy the writing process required, through Sydney's editing and artistic abilities, to Madeline's typesetting marathon and cover input, this book would not exist without these three.

Additional edits completed by Betsy Hughes and Cynthia Mayer fine-tuned this work. My appreciation cannot be put into words. The difference in the final copy is something every reader will appreciate.

Father McMorrow assisted with some of the hardest parts. Not only did I need help with today's religious world, but his knowledge was required over various centuries.

The beta readers were an appreciated resource. Their feedback demonstrated that this story appeals to a wider audience than expected. I enjoyed learning how these pages touched the personal lives of each reader. Karlee, the response to the non-existent letters prior to Levi's departure for Europe was priceless! Telling the main character to "pop off, I guess, follow those dreams," continues to make me smile daily!

Special thanks go out to my recently departed Aunt Annie, whose enthusiasm over the raw manuscript will not be forgotten. Aunt Joanne, I have relied on each reflection given, always so supportive and uplifting. Mark, filtering out the overabundance of rabbit holes was beneficial; I am indebted. To the family members of both John Connell and Vince Engels, it was fun taking this journey together. Cathy, I feel a spirit watching from heaven. Jim, I miss our communication and hope all is well.

With deep affection, I save two important people for last. Here's to Chloe and Levi for sharing their story. It was nice getting to know them through the many letters and photographs, and even better to see what life was like for them at twenty-five.

WORKS CITED

"A Protestant "Oecumenical Council"." Our Sunday Visitor, 2 Aug. 1925, p. 2.

Amelinckx, Andrew. "Four Weird Ways Dogs Have Earned Their Keep." Smithsonian
Magazine, 19 Sept. 2017, www.smithsonianmag.com/history/four-weird-ways-
dogs-have-earned-their-keep-180964948/#:~:text=Up%20until%20the%20
end%20of,bread%20carts%2C%20and%20other%20goods. Accessed 19 Jul. 2024.

"Americans, Curious to See Strike, Quit Liners for London." The Brooklyn Daily Eagle, 8
May 1926, p. 3.

"Big Hits on Columbia Grafonola at Benefield, Motley & Co.'s Music Dept., Corner Cran
head and Main Streets." The Bee, 11 Sept. 1925, p. 15.

Bierling, Marilyn R. The Phoenicians in Spain: An Archaeological Review of the Eighth-
Sixth Centuries B.C.E. -- A Collection of Articles Translated from Spanish. Ed
ited by Seymour Gitin, Penn State University Press, 2002. JSTOR, https://doi.
org/10.5325/j.ctv1bxh516. Accessed 11 Jun. 2023, p. 4.

Boissoneault, Lorraine. "The Debate Over Rebuilding That Ensued When a Beloved
French Cathedral Was Shelled During WWI: After the Notre-Dame De Reims
Sustained Heavy Damage, It Took Years for the Country to Decide How to Re
pair the Destruction." Smithsonian Magazine, 19 Apr. 2019. https://www.
smithsonianmag.com/history/debate-over-rebuilding-ensued-when-beloved-
french-cathedral-was-shelled-during-wwi-180971999/#:~:text=Around%20
300%20German%20shells%20smashed,incomprehensible%20brutality%20
of%20the%20conflict

Bonsanti, Giorgio. "The Director of One of Italy's Top Restoration Laboratories Re
sponds to Denunciations of Work Carried Out on Leonardo's Last Supper." The
Art Newspaper, 30 Apr. 1999, www.theartnewspaper.com/1999/05/01/the-di
rector-of-one-of-italys-top-restoration-laboratories-responds-to-denunciations-
of-work-carried-out-on-leonardos-last-supper. Accessed 4 Jun. 2025.

Bringe, Peter. "Presbyterians, Creation Days, and Evolution." For Christ's Kingdom, 9
Apr. 2024, www.forchristskingdom.com/2024/04/presbyterians-creation-days-
and.html. Accessed 10 Jun. 2025.

"Bryan Goes to His Rest." The Washington Daily News, 1 Aug. 1925, p. 3.

"Butler Act," 1925 March 21, RG 260: Acts of the General Assembly, Public and Private,
1790-present, 44122, Tennessee State Library and Archives, Tennessee Virtual
Archive, https://teva.contentdm.oclc.org/digital/collection/scopes/id/168,
accessed 2025-07-16.

Butragueño, Eduardo S. "La Plaza Del Padre Juan De Mariana." Toledo Olvidado, 19 Apr.

2009, toledoolvidado.blogspot.com/2009/04/la-plaza-del-padre-juan-de-mari ana.html?m=1. Accessed 29 Jun. 2023.

"Centuries-old Mystery of Christopher Columbus's True Origins Revealed in Study." CNN World, 13 Oct. 2024, edition.cnn.com/2024/10/13/world/columbus-ori gins-western-europe-study-intl/index.html. Accessed 20 Jun. 2025.

Chaliline, Charles. Recherches sur Chartres. Chartres, Société archéologique d'Eure-et-Loir, 1918, original manuscript written c.1640. pp. 143-144.

"Charter Airlines Push for Tours; Spokesman Says Scheduled Lines Block Fare Cuts." The New York Times, 13 Jun. 1968, p. 92.

Chathain, N. N. "Revelation." Catholic World, vol. CXXI, no. 721, 1925, p. 498, https:// babel.hathitrust.org/cgi/pt?id=uc1.$b623239&seq=512.

Chrystie, Jeanetta R. "The Pilgrim's Way." Christian History, no. 70, 2001, https://christianhistoryinstitute.org/magazine/article/dante-pilgrims-way. Accessed 18 Nov. 2022.

Clemens, S. L. (1869). The Innocents Abroad, or The New Pilgrims' Progress (1st ed., p. 165). American Publishing Company.

Connick, Charles J. "'LaBelleVerrière' of Infinite Variety." The American Magazine of Art, vol. 24, no. 3, 1932, pp. 179–81. JSTOR, http://www.jstor.org/sta ble/23935403. Accessed 16 Aug. 2025.

Cotton, Jeff. "San Pietro: Via Porta San Pietro/Via Spilimbecco." The Churches of Venice, 2007-2023, churchesofvenice.com/ferrara.htm#duomo. Accessed 16 Feb. 2023.

"Crosses Burned for Bryan." The Washington Daily News, 1 Aug. 1925, p. 3.

Delon, Dugene, and Marie-Joseph Delon. "Titre Inconnu; Nef De L'eglise Des Jacobins (Unknown Title; Nave of the Jacobins Church)." Wikimedia Commons, commons.wikimedia.org/wiki/File:Nef_de_l%27%C3%A9glise_des_Jaco bins._-_FRAC31555_26Fi55.jpg. Accessed 22 Aug. 2022.

DeSmidt, Firmin. "Dating Medieval Ghent (Belgium): Dendrochronological and Typolo gical Survey of the Roofs of Saint Nicholas' Church." International Journal of Wood Culture, vol. 3, no. 2023, pp. 26-46. Accessed 22 Aug. 2024.

"Editorial Page." The Washington Herald, 4 Sept. 1925, p. 18.

Engels, Vincent D. "Avignon." The Commonweal, vol. 6, no. 17, 1927, p. 396, https:// archive.org/details/sim_commonweal_1927-08-31_6_17/page/396/ mode/2up. Accessed 28 Sept. 2022.

Engels, Vincent D. "Former P.-G. Scribe Uses 'Bike' On Tour of France and Italy." Green Bay Press-Gazette, 22 Jan. 1926, p. 15.

Engels, Vincent D. "It's the Blood That Counts Not the Bull, Avers Engels." Green Bay Press-Gazette, 22 Apr. 1926, p. 4.

Engels, Vincent D. "Spanish Colonies in Africa Enjoy a Little Game of War." Green Bay Press-Gazette, 27 Mar. 1926, p. 13.

"Ephemera." Merriam-Webster.com Dictionary, Merriam-Webster, https://www.merriam-webster.com/dictionary/ephemera. Accessed 08 Oct. 2024.

"Ergonites Hear Interesting Talk On Christian Symbols." Green Bay Press-Gazette, 22 Jan. 1926, p. 8.

"Evolution Topic of Sermons in 3 Capital Pulpits." The Washington Post, 13 Jul. 1925, p. 2.

Fox, Fontaine T. Jr. "The Tooneville Trolley That Meets All the Trains." Casper Daily Tribune, 5 Dec. 1922, p. 6.

Franchi, Elena. Art in Wartime: Protection and Destruction of Pisa's Artistic Heritage During the Second World War. Edizione ETS, 2006.

Geniesse, Peter A. "In His Own Way, Levi Built His Cathedral." Appleton-Neenah-Menasha Post-Crescent, 9 Oct. 1988, p. 16.

Girard, Joseph. Évocation Du Vieil Avignon. Les Éditions De Minuit, 1957.

"Great Britain Feels Grip of Labor's Might." Green Bay Press-Gazette, 4 May 1926, p. 2.

"Green Bay Man Arrested in Africa As French Deserter." Green Bay Press-Gazette, 24 Mar. 1926, p. 7.

Grubb, Hyacinth. "Burning Our Vanities with Savonarola." Dominicana, vol. LIX, no. 1, 2016, https://www.dominicanajournal.org/burning-our-vanities-with-savonarola/. Accessed 4 Aug. 2025.

Hartt, Rollin L. "The Disruption of Protestantism." The Forum, vol. 74, no. 5, 1925, pp. 678-687, https://doi.org/sim_forum-and-century_1925-11_74_5. Accessed 23 Jul. 2025.

Hennes, Robert Graham. "David Van Wallace." The Notre Dame Scholastic, vol. 58, no. 22, 1925, p. 716, 725. https://archives.nd.edu/Scholastic/VOL_0058/VOL_0058_IISSUE_0022.pdf. Accessed 15 Jul. 2025.

Hicks, Hilarie M. "Montpelier: What's in a Name?" Digital Doorway, 30 May 2019, digitaldoorway.montpelier.org/2019/05/30/montpelier-whats-in-a-name/. Accessed 20 Oct. 2022.

Hoeniger, Cathleen. The Camposanto of Pisa in the Wake of World War Two: Loss and Discovery. Brepols, 2019.

Hubert, Ronan. "Crash of a Farman F.63bis Goliath in Brussels." Bureau of Aircraft Accidents Archives, 1990-2025, www.baaa-acro.com/aircraft/farman-f63bis-goliath. Accessed 24 Jun. 2024.

Huguenaud, Karine. "The Religious Marriage of Napoleon I and Marie-Louise in the Salon Carre at the Louvre, on 2 April 1810." Napoleon.Org, Mar. 2010, www.

napoleon.org/en/history-of-the-two-empires/paintings/the-religious-mar
riage-of-napo-leon-i-and-marie-louise-in-the-salon-carre-at-the-louvre-on-2-
april-1810/. Accessed 2 Mar. 2023.

"Hyde Park Closed: A Great Milk Pool for London." Daily Mirror, 4 May 1926, p. 2.

Irving, Washington. The Sketch Book of Geoffrey Crayton, Gent. New York, C. S. Van
Winkle, 1819. pp. 72, 75.

Isleib, Chris. "Centennial of the WWI Combat Death of American Poet Joyce Kilmer."
World War 1 Centennial, www.worldwar1centennial.org/index.php/commu-
nicate/press-media/wwi-centennial-news/4875-the-centennial-of-the-combat-
death-of-american-poet-joyce-kilmer.html. Accessed 23 Jun. 2022.

"Jack Dempsey: Inducted 1965 - Boxing." Colorado Sports Hall of Fame, www.colorado
sports.org/hall-of-fame/athletes/1965-inductees/jack-dempsey/. Accessed 15
Aug. 2025.

Jashemski, Wilhelmina F. "Pompeii." Britannica, 15 Jul. 2025, www.britannica.com/place/
Pompeii. Accessed 3 Aug. 2025.

Kilmer, Joyce. TREES & Other Poems. Garden City, Doubleday & Company, Inc., 1914.
pp. 13-16.

"Kreisler." Time, 2 Feb. 1925, p. 15. https://time.com/vault/issue/1925-02-02/page/17/

Linder, Douglas. "Lynchings: By Year and Race." UNKC School of Law, 2000, law2.umkc.
edu/faculty/projects/ftrials/shipp/lynchingyear.html. Accessed 23 Jun. 2025.

MacBride, Jessie. "Kreisler's Art at Best Here." The Washington Times, 20 Feb. 1926, p.
7.

"Mail Bag: Marjie's Peeved." The Washington Daily News, 4 Jul. 1925, p. 6.

"Margherita, Queen Mother of Italy Dies." Green Bay Press-Gazette, 4 Jan. 1926, p. 1.

Maria. "The History of the Camino De Santiago." Camino Ways, 3 May 2023, camino
ways.com/the-history-of-the-camino-de-santiago#:~:text=For%20Faith%20
or%20Money?,even%20to%20serve%20a%20sentence. Accessed 1 Dec. 2023.

Maurandi, Jean G. "Traditional Music from County of Nice (France)." MTCN, 1 Feb.
2001, mtcn.free.fr/lyrics/carnaval-nice-1926-fla-fla.php?lng=en. Accessed 17
Apr. 2023.

"Milk Delivery In Italy A Simple Matter, They Bring Cow To Door." Green Bay Press-
Gazette, 1 Dec. 1925, p. 35.

"Mimic Air Warfare Best Ever Staged: Secret Flight Maneuvers Draw Brilliant Capital
Crowd." The Washington Herald, 5 Jul. 1925, p. 2.

Mmoyaq. "Iglesia De San Benito El Real Con Anterioridad Al Derribo En El Siglo XIX
De Los Dos Pisos Superiores De La Torre (San Benito El Real Church Before the
Demolition of the Two Upper Floors of the Tower in the 19th Century)."

Wikimedia Commons, 24 Sept. 2013, commons.wikimedia.org/wiki/File:Esgl%
C3%A9sia_San_Benito_el_Real.png. Accessed 4 Sept. 2025. Licensed under
Creative Commons (https://en.wikipedia.org/wiki/Creative_Commons)
Attribution-Share Alike 3.0 Unported license (https://creativecommons.org/
licenses/by-sa/3.0/deed.en).

"More Modern Men in French Art: Effort to Bring Luxembourg Gallery Up to Date."
Chattanooga Daily Times, 9 May 1926, p. 37.

"Pedunculate Oak 'Gros ChêNe De Liernu' on the Place De Liernu, Namur, Belgium."
Monumental Trees, www.monumentaltrees.com/en/bel/namur/eghezee/922_
placedeliernu/#google_vignette. Accessed 15 Aug. 2024.

Pernin, F. P. (n.d.). The Fire. The National Shrine of Our Lady of Champion. Retrieved
July 21, 2025, from https://championshrine.org/our-story/

Photoglob Co., Publisher. Montpellier. Cathédrale et Faculté de Médecine. [Zürich, Switzerland: Photoglob Company, to 1906] Photograph. Retrieved from the Library
of Congress, <www.loc.gov/item/2017659795/>.

Pietralunga, Mark. Cesare Pavese and Anthony Chiuminatto: Their Correspondence.
University of Toronto Press, 1992. p. 321.

Pius XI, Infinite Mercy Infinita Dei Misericordia (29 May 1924), at The Holy See, https://
www.vatican.va/content/pius-xi/it/bulls/documents/hf_p-xi_
bulls_19240529_dei-misericordia.html

"Portraits of the Early Church: St. Lawrence of Rome." YouTube, uploaded by St. Paul
Center, 10 Aug. 2020, www.youtube.com/watch?v=tk1AeakCNjY.

Pucci, E. (1925, December 31). At Least 1,000,000 Jubilee Pilgrims. The Catholic
Telegraph, LXXXXIV(53), 1, 3. https://www.thecatholicnewsarchive.org/
?a=d&d=TCT19251231-01.2.17&e=-------en-20--1--txt-txIN--------

Rand McNally Washington Guide to the City and Environs with Maps and Illustrations.
1920 ed., Rand McNally & Company, 1920. p. 203.

Rice, Grantland. "Cadets Prove no Match for Speedy Backs." The South Bend Tribune, 19
Oct. 1924, p. 1.

Riefler, D. B., and R. M. Boeckel. "War Debts and Reparations." Editorial Research
Reports, vol. IV, 1928, p. 1059, https://babel.hathitrust.org/cgi/pt?id=rul.390300
39241882&seq=181. Accessed 3 Jan. 2023.

"Reims Cathedral: A Masterpiece of the Middle Ages - The Church of Joan of Arc." The
Times, 22 Sept. 1914, pp. 10, 26.

Rozett, Ella. "Our Lady of Miracles." Inter Faith Mary, www.interfaithmary.net/black-
madonna-index/orleans. Accessed 2 Aug. 2022.

"Running Supplies Through the Strike Brigade." Daily Mirror, 13 May 1926, p. 1-2.

Ruskin, John. The Seven Lamps of Architecture. New York, John Wiley, 1849. p. 37.

"Salon Carre of the Louvre." Fort Worth Record-Telegram, 16 Sept. 1923, p. 23. https://
     www.newspapers.com/article/fort-worth-record-telegram-salon-carr-o/
     166278712/

"Sencio's Body Will Be Shipped Home to Philippine Islands." Green Bay Press-Gazette,
     21 Apr. 1926, p. 17.

"70-Year Old Tenor Has Sung at Chapel Since '89." Green Bay Press-Gazette, 14 Aug.
     1944, p. 10.

Severus, Sulpicius. Vita Sancti Martini (Life of Martin). Translated by Alexander Rob
     erts, 397.

Shannon, Harold T. I. "Thousands Will Join 60th Pilgrimage to Robinsonville Shrine on
     Saturday." Green Bay Press-Gazette, 13 Aug. 1925, p. 12.

"Shrines Stand Intact Amid Lisieux Ruins." The Advocate, 18 Oct. 1944, p. 3.

Cirer-Costa, Joan Carles. "Spain's Tourism Models in the First Third of the Twentieth
     Century." Munich Personal RePEc Archive, 29 Jan. 2019, p. 12.

Solsten, Eric, and Sandra W. Meditz. "Spain: A Country Study." Country Studies US,
     1988,   countrystudies.us/spain/69.htm#:~:text=Although%20historical%20
     sites%20and%20unique,of%20the%20Mediterranean%20seashore%20areas.
     Accessed 20 Jun. 2023.

Thayer, Earnest L. "Casey at the Bat." The San Francisco Examiner, 3 Jun. 1888, p. 4.

The Aeroplane. Senior Class of East High School, 1921. p. 76.

"Cathedral at Amiens." Green Bay Press-Gazette, 19 Jun. 1918, p. 6.

The Holy Bible: International Series - Self-Pronouncing Edition. Philadelphia, John C.
     Winston Co. p. 196, 882.

"The Pont Du Gard Aqueduct." Avignon-et-Provence, www.avignon-et-provence.com/
     en/monuments/pont-gard-aqueduct. Accessed 24 Aug. 2022.

The World's Most Famous Court Trial: Tennessee Evolution Case. 3rd ed., National Book
     Company, 1925. pp. 13, 14, 45, 95.

"30 Days' Annual Leave." The Washington Daily News, 30 Jun. 1925, p. 7.

Trani, Elsa. "La Cathédrale De Montpellier. Présentation Historique, Artistique Et
     Littéraire .

Viollet-le-Duc, Eugène-Emmanuel, 1814–1879. La Cité De Carcassonne (Aude). Paris:
     Librairie des imprimeries réunies, 1888.

"We Ought to Know: What Is the Paris Salon?" The Kansas City Times, 8 Apr. 1926, p. 8.

"William Jennings Bryan Dies in His Sleep at Dayton on Eve of Crusade Against Mod
     ernism"." Washington Post, 27 Jul. 1925, p. 1.

Wykes, Alan. Doctor Cardano, Physician Extraordinary. Frederick Muller, 1969. p. 26.